Democracy and Nationalism in Southeast Asia

Jacques Bertrand offers a comparative-historical analysis of five nationalist conflicts over several decades in Southeast Asia. Using a theoretical framework to explain variance over time and across cases, he challenges and refines existing debates on democracy's impact and shows that, while democratization significantly reduces violent insurgency over time, it often introduces pernicious effects that fail to resolve conflict and contribute to maintaining deep nationalist grievances. Drawing on years of detailed fieldwork, Bertrand analyses the paths that led from secessionist mobilization to a range of outcomes. These include persistent state repression for Malay Muslims in Thailand, low-level violence under a top-down "special autonomy" for Papuans, reframing of mobilizing from nationalist to indigenous peoples in the Cordillera, a long and broken path to an untested broad autonomy for Moros and relatively successful broad autonomy for Acehnese.

JACQUES BERTRAND is Professor and Associate Chair of Political Science at the University of Toronto.

Democracy and Nationalism in Southeast Asia

From Secessionist Mobilization to Conflict Resolution

Jacques Bertrand

University of Toronto

CAMBRIDGE
UNIVERSITY PRESS

CAMBRIDGE
UNIVERSITY PRESS

University Printing House, Cambridge CB2 8BS, United Kingdom

One Liberty Plaza, 20th Floor, New York, NY 10006, USA

477 Williamstown Road, Port Melbourne, VIC 3207, Australia

314–321, 3rd Floor, Plot 3, Splendor Forum, Jasola District Centre,
New Delhi – 110025, India

79 Anson Road, #06–04/06, Singapore 079906

Cambridge University Press is part of the University of Cambridge.

It furthers the University's mission by disseminating knowledge in the pursuit of
education, learning, and research at the highest international levels of excellence.

www.cambridge.org
Information on this title: www.cambridge.org/9781108491280
DOI: 10.1017/9781108868082

© Jacques Bertrand 2021

First published 2021

A catalogue record for this publication is available from the British Library.

Library of Congress Cataloging-in-Publication Data
Names: Bertrand, Jacques, 1965– author.
Title: Democracy and nationalism in Ssoutheast Asia : from secessionist
mobilization to conflict resolution / Jacques Bertrand.
Description: Cambridge, United Kingdom ; New York, NY : Cambridge
University Press, 2021. | Includes bibliographical references and index.
Identifiers: LCCN 2021009382 (print) | LCCN 2021009383 (ebook) |
ISBN 9781108491280 (hardback) | ISBN 9781108868082 (ebook)
Subjects: LCSH: Democracy – Southeast Asia. | Nationalism – Southeast
Asia. | Conflict management – Southeast Asia. | Insurgency – Southeast Asia. |
Minorities – Political activity – Southeast Asia. | Southeast Asia – History –
Autonomy and independence movements. | BISAC: POLITICAL SCIENCE /
World / General | POLITICAL SCIENCE / World / General
Classification: LCC JQ750.A91 B47 2021 (print) | LCC JQ750.A91 (ebook) |
DDC 321.09/40959–dc23
LC record available at https://lccn.loc.gov/2021009382
LC ebook record available at https://lccn.loc.gov/2021009383

ISBN 978-1-108-49128-0 Hardback

À Ariane, Liam et Lisa

Contents

Figures and Tables

Figures

Tables

Preface and Acknowledgements

This book has its roots in a set of reservations that I had with debates about ethnic conflict, in particular from the vantage point of my long-standing engagement with Southeast Asia. Among others, I shared other scholars' concern about the conceptual vagueness of "ethnic conflict." At its origins, its study responded to expectations from modernization and Marxist theories that class interests and socio-economic grievances would largely supersede identity-based conflicts. But their persistence, of course, fed a whole multi-disciplinary field of study that retained the overarching conceptual focus on "ethnicity," without always refining its definition. Some scholars rejected its use and favoured instead "identity" based conflicts, yet the latter's scope became even broader and not analytically clearer. Others made strong cases that conflicts involving particular characteristics required different analyses; for instance, "race" or "religion" represented particular ways in which groups were identified (or self-identified) that required separate analysis.

In brief, there were challenges in the literature even at the level of defining the main attributes of groups to be analysed, and how best to call them. This was compounded by the near-consensus around constructivist approaches that viewed many forms of ethnic attributes as essentially malleable or, at the very least, politicized and manipulated.

I became uneasy, predominantly in large-N data, which to identify ethnic groups more broadly, particularly when using static and crude measurements such as the broadly used ethno-linguistic fractionalization measure, failed to capture some important distinctions in group characteristics with ramifications for our understanding of conflict. The rationale for the comparison between some groups was weak, at best, particularly when sacrificing some of the insights from debates on group formation for the sake of measurability.

Three developments in the literature further stimulated my reflection. First, there were promising areas of cross-fertilization between the literatures on nationalism and ethnic conflict. The parallel debate on the origins and causes of nationalism raised important questions regarding the ethnic basis of nation-alism, and many of its expressions that resembled what others analysed as ethnic mobilization and "secessionist" movements. Second, as a review by

Brubaker and Laitin emphasized, our analyses required greater distinction and refinement to disentangle the causes of violence from those of conflict more broadly. While much of the research, particularly large-N studies, pivoted toward explaining ethnic violence with more precision, other forms of conflict or long-standing ethnic tension with relatively low levels of violence fell off the radar of academic attention, even though they often disguised deep grievances that could potentially develop into larger scale, sometimes renewed, violent mobilization. Third, a growing debate about the impact of democratization largely sounded alarms regarding its violence-producing effects but prevailing explanations did not resonate with the Southeast Asian context. It certainly raised interesting propositions regarding the need for more dynamic analyses and to account for structural and institutional change to better understand their impact on ethnic groups and potential conflict. Moreover, I had found a long-standing debate comparing static institutional effects on ethnic "stability" or conflict to be somewhat problematic, as it became apparent to me, particularly in cases I observed, that any specific set of institutional solutions, such as autonomy or federalism, required a better analysis of the historical path and constraints leading up to their consideration, or adoption, in order to assess their impact on conflict and violence.

My experience working on these issues in Southeast Asia suggested that there were important differences between groups that sought some form of self-determination and other "ethnic" groups facing different types of grievances and related demands. While my own work on Indonesia had shown the importance of understanding the effects of a transition to democracy on a broad rise in ethnic violence in the country, involving different types of groups and conflicts, nevertheless I was left with the strong analytical sense that Papuans and Acehnese required separate analyses, as they held very unique sets of grievances and sources of mobilization as they confronted the state directly, and the latter was particularly defensive about their demands. The strong Indonesian nationalism that had partly inspired Benedict Anderson to argue that imagined communities created strong new bonds around a shared national consciousness clashed strongly and deeply with groups that challenged such national imaginaries and struck at their core. I started to think that we were missing some important aspects of understanding these conflicts by folding nationalist ones into broader analyses of ethnic conflict. While I agree with Brubaker and others that the fluidity of group boundaries can sometimes make such distinctions difficult, nevertheless the political project involved in claiming a territorial homeland and powers to govern are sufficiently different from other types to justify more explicit analytical attention. Within Indonesia, it was also striking to me that Papuan grievances, although in some ways much deeper than those of the Acehnese, nevertheless were much less noticed and would not appear in many of the larger data sets on ethnic civil wars or conflict, as levels of deaths or intensity of violent incidents remained low. It made clear to me that our measures of conflict based on intensity or frequency of violence (or deaths) not only skewed our understanding of such conflicts but also assumed that the absence of violence was somehow indicative of a resolved conflict, or one that would be counted as non-existent in large-N data sets.

These concerns guided my analysis and combined with my interest to address the question of democratization's impact on nationalist mobilization in the region. Southeast Asia has had a particularly large number of secessionist movements, which makes it an excellent source of comparative data that can inform broader debates. This book, therefore, is designed to address the question of how democratization has impacted secessionist conflict in Southeast Asia, with the aim to engage and add to larger comparative debates.

The study draws on years of cumulative fieldwork. For the Indonesian cases, I partially drew not only on fieldwork conducted in Aceh and Papua for a previous book but also on three subsequent trips to both regions. In the Philippines, some of my material from interviews conducted in the mid-1990s in Mindanao were also useful for parts of the chapter on the Moros, but I returned later to Cotabato city and surrounding areas a decade later for the most significant interviews for this book. I also conducted fieldwork in Baguio city (Cordillera) and surrounding areas, as well as in Pattani and Yala. I was fortunate to gain access to Pattani at a time when the region's militarization was on the rise and foreigners were not particularly welcomed by the authorities, but interviews were still possible. Other trips included interviews in Manila, Jakarta, and Bangkok.

In comparative work, and particularly when studying five different regions with varying accessibility to interview subjects, there is always a trade-off between the fine-grained, in-depth work that goes into knowing a particular region and spreading one's time and resources to cover more regions in a comparative effort. While I delved into the particularities of each region and immersed myself into each case to understand its unique aspects, ultimately my objective was to draw from in-depth inductive analysis some comparative points across regions and across time. Fieldwork constituted a core part of the data gathering but also allowed me to contextualize and understand local conditions. There is no replacement for the immense value that fieldwork provides to question one's assumptions when working on a case, and being open and ready to reframe, reinterpret, and abandon prior leads when face-to-face engagement challenges our expected findings. While there is a trade-off between inductive, detailed immersion into a case and more deductive hypothesis or theory-testing exercises, I strongly adhere to the view that engaging the on-the-ground empirical reality comes with a certain modesty of interpretation and a need to be sensitive to local understandings of their own problems. To build analysis from the ground up creates its own challenges for comparative analysis but strikes a balance between avoiding overly distorted rendering of empirical realities to fit preconceived hypotheses while attempting to seek patterns across cases and time, based on informed engagement with comparative theories. Furthermore, in building the empirical data for each case, drawing on local newspapers and oftentimes excellent locally based reports from civil society organizations can be not only a source of invaluable data but also an important way of triangulating information from interviews. I used a large number of such sources to complement interview data. Finally, I am very grateful to the large number of colleagues who are deeply knowledgeable of each case and whose work was necessary to gain another level of analytical understanding, and sometimes to supplement empirical information, particularly for more historical data.

There are a large number of people who contributed knowingly or not to this manuscript. Over the years, presentations and exchanges with a large number of colleagues helped me to refine and rethink several aspects of the analysis. I am most grateful to all of my interviewees who provided generous time to answer my questions. I have attempted as much as possible to retain some of their voices and convey some of their concerns, even though the data-gathering exercise and subsequent analysis often blurs the message they wanted to deliver. For many of my respondents, the issues discussed were profoundly emotional and several dedicated their professional lives, sometimes at great risk, to advance their cause and seek redress for many grievances that members of their group held. Others were dedicated to protecting the human rights of several who suffered at the hands of repressive regimes. Many interviewees hoped that contributing to the project would help the world better understand their perspective and their hopes. While I am grateful and sensitive to those requests, the need for analytical distance and interpretation often masked what might have been their expectations, but hopefully the book does help to better explain the sources of their mobilization and the conditions that have sometimes led to better outcomes.

I visited five regions in Indonesia, the Philippines, and Thailand, with varying interview conditions and help. There would be too many people to acknowledge but a few I would like to mention in particular. In Aceh, I was repeatedly impressed with the skill and initiative of several people I met after the region had been devastated by war and a deadly tsunami. Many thanks to the Aceh Institute for providing me with help on one of my trips, particularly Saiful Akmal who made every effort with great energy and dedication to ensure that I could meet as many respondents as possible. In Papua, I could only thank all of my respondents for opening their doors on short notice, and without reserve. I was impressed every time with the ability to rapidly connect to people in Jayapura. There is a particular skill at conducting fieldwork "under the radar," when researchers are not welcomed by local authorities, as was my case. I appreciate interviewees' willingness to meet, even though we had to all be aware of surveillance. I am particularly grateful to Anum Siregar for her advice and to staff at the Aliansi Demokrasi untuk Papua (ALDP), who offered some workspace as well as access to their incredible resource bank of local newspaper articles. In Cotabato city (Mindanao), I am very grateful for the exceptional welcome and help from the Institute for Autonomy and Governance (Notre-Dame U.), especially Attny Benny Bacani, who provided office space, helped with contacts, but most importantly offered generosity with his time and hospitality. I very much enjoyed our long discussions, and those brief but intense ones with "Bong" Montesa. I appreciated as well the support from several other staff at the IAG, including Jacque Fernandez, who provided assistance in setting up a few meetings. In Baguio city, I would like to thank Delfin Tolentino and Ray Rovillos for their help in making my brief research visit productive. They were not only helpful but also very welcoming. The staff of the Cordillera Studies Centre were also very helpful and, in particular, Alice Follosco was incredibly kind in helping to arrange a few interviews. In Pattani, the fieldwork proved particularly challenging when escalating tensions and recent deployment of additional military troops made foreigners such as myself particularly unwelcomed. Nevertheless, I am grateful to those informants who were willing to meet with me, in spite of the fact that discretion had to be exercised at a much higher level than what is expected even with standard ethical procedures to protect human subjects. In particular, I am grateful to one local Muslim leader who must remain anonymous and who braved the troops that disembarked at his home to "protect" me as he managed to wave them away dismissively and without hesitation. Many thanks to Warathida Chaiyapah, who accompanied me and helped with translation and local logistical communication. There were numerous colleagues, informants, and organizations in Jakarta, Manila, and Bangkok who also provided enormous support, useful insight, and assistance throughout the years. I cannot name them all but would like to acknowledge, in no particular order, Steve Rood from the Asia Foundation; Rizal Sukma, Kristiadi, Christine Tjhin, and other staff at CSIS; Ruth Lusterio-Rico from UP Diliman; Chaiwat Satha-Anand at Chulalongkorn University.

I am also grateful to a number of colleagues who, over the years, provided some useful suggestions, comments, or criticism that contributed to making this a better book. Michelle Ann Miller, Tony Reid, Tom Pepinsky, John Sidel, Lotta Hedman, Duncan McCargo, and Don Horowitz helped shape some of my thoughts in early conversations, discussions, and comments. Although it delayed the book, I am grateful to all my colleagues in the Ethnicity and Democratic Governance Major Collaborative Research Project with whom I enjoyed engaging on themes related to my book. I embarked on that five-year project to exchange ideas and undertake collaborative work with colleagues who worked on similar issues across different regions and subfields. They were a tremendous source of inspiration and feedback. I particularly benefitted from work with my co-editors, André Laliberté and Oded Haklai, on two separate volumes. These edited volumes greatly informed my work, and the workshops leading to them were tremendously useful to bounce off ideas in this book and gain comparative insight from colleagues who participated. I am also grateful for feedback from numerous colleagues over the years at conferences, workshops, and invited lectures. At the University of Toronto, I greatly benefited from the incisive but constructive criticism from colleagues who participated in the informal Comparative Politics workshops. Finally, the two anonymous reviewers of this manuscript were more than generous with their detailed reading and suggestions, for which I am grateful. Although I felt that I had reached the limit of my patience to edit the manuscript after numerous iterations, their comments were really helpful to refine and solidify some of the looser ends.

Over the years, a number of current and former students, several now colleagues and friends, provided invaluable research assistance. Michael Bookman and Caleb Edwards helped with some very preliminary work. Arjun Tremblay and Sanjay Jeram worked on some tremendously useful early research on comparative cases and literature searches. Marie Gagne, Trevor Preston, Isabelle Côté, Irene Poetranto, and Alexandre Pelletier all helped with various requests for some additional literature searches, newspaper searches, and various queries. I am particularly grateful to Jessica Soedirgo, who not only helped me out as others with various searches for information but also proved to be an incredible source of support in the later stages of the manuscript's details, cleaning, and final editing. Many thanks as well to Mark Winward for his willingness to step in and help with final touches.

Many thanks to Lucy Rhymer from Cambridge University Press for her encouragement and support for the project. Thanks go as well to Emily Sharp, Lisa Carter, Malini Soupramanian, and my copyeditor, Rashmi Motiwale, for helping me to respect the deadlines and to guide me through the last steps toward publication.

I was very fortunate to receive generous grants from two funding organizations. I am grateful for generous support from the United States Institute of Peace (grant no. SG-144-04 F) and the Social Sciences and Humanities Research Council of Canada (grant no. 410050834). The findings and conclusions expressed in this book are mine only and do not necessarily reflect the views of the United States Institute of Peace.

Finally, I am grateful for the support and joy provided by my family. They have been hearing about the book more often than they ever hoped for but can now finally see it printed! It is to them, my dearest wife Lisa, daughter Ariane, and son Liam, to whom this work is dedicated.

Abbreviations

ARMM	Autonomous Region in Muslim Mindanao
BBL	Bangsamoro Basic Law
BBMP	United Mujahideen Front of Patani/*Barisan Bersatu Mujahidin Patani*
BJE	Bangsamoro Juridical Entity
BKPG	Financial Assistance for Village Development/*Bantuan Keuangan Pemakmur Gampong*
BNPP	Patani National Liberation Front/*Barisan Nasional Pembebasan Patani*
BRA	Aceh Peace Reintegration Agency/*Badan Reintegrasi-Damai Aceh*
Brimob	Mobile Brigade Corps (Police)/*Korps Brigade Mobil*
BRN	National Revolutionary Front/*Barisan Revolusi Nasional*
BPK	Audit Board of the Republic of Indonesia/*Badan Pemeriksa Keuangan*
BTC	Bangsamoro Transition Committee
CAR	Cordillera Administrative Region
CBA	Cordillera Bodong Association
CBAd	Cordillera Bodong Administration
Con-Com	Constitutional Commission
CPA	Cordillera People's Alliance
CPLA	Cordillera People's Liberation Army
CPM	Civilian-Police-Military Command
CRCC	Cordillera Regional Consultative Commission
DAP	Papua Customary Council/*Dewan Adat Papua*
DAO	Department Administrative Order
DAU	General Allotment Funds/*Danah Alokasi Umum*
DENR	Department of Environment and Natural Resources
DOM	Military Operations Zone/*Daerah Operasi Militer*
DPR	People's Representative Assembly/*Dewan Perwakilan Rakyat*

DPRD	Local People's Representative Council/*Dewan Perwakilan Rakyat Daerah*
FORERI	Forum for the Reconciliation of Irian Jaya People/*Forum Rekonsiliasi Rakyat Irian Jaya*
FPIC	Free Prior and Informed Consent
Fretilin	Revolutionary Front of Independent East Timor/*Frente Revolucionária de Timor Leste Independente*
GAM	Free Aceh Movement/*Gerakan Aceh Merdeka*
GRP	Government of the Republic of the Philippines
IMT	International Monitoring Team
IPRA	Indigenous Peoples Rights Act
ISOC	Internal Security Operations Command
JDP	Papua Peace Network/*Jaringan Damai Papua*
KIA	Kachin Independence Army
KNPB	National Committee for West Papua/*Komite Nasional Papua Barat*
KPA	Aceh Transition Committee/*Komite Peralihan Aceh*
Lakas-NUCD	*Lakas Ng Tao*-National Union of Christian Democrats
LGU	local government units
LIPI	Indonesian Institute of Sciences (Jakarta)
LoGA	Law on Governing Aceh
LNG	liquefied natural gas
MARA Patani	Patani Consultative Council/*Majlis Syura Patani*
MILF	Moro Islamic Liberation Front
MNLF	Moro National Liberation Front
MoA-AD	Memorandum of Agreement on Ancestral Domain
MoU	Memorandum of Understanding
MPR	People's Consultative Assembly/*Majelis Permusyawaratan Rakyat*
MRP	Papuan People's Assembly/*Majelis Rakyat Papua*
MUBES	Congress/*Musyarawah Besar*
NAD	Nanggroe Aceh Darussalam
NAP	New Aspiration Party
NCIP	National Commission on Indigenous Peoples
NGO	non-governmental organization
NPA	New People's Army
NRC	National Reconciliation Commission
NUC	National Unification Commission
OIC	Organisation of Islamic Conference
OPAPP	Office of the Presidential Advisor for the Peace Process
OPM	Free Papua Movement/*Organisasi Papua Merdeka*
Otsus	special autonomy

PA	Aceh Party/*Partai Aceh*
PDI-P	Democratic Party of Indonesia for the Struggle/*Partai Demokrasi Indonesia Perjuangan*
PDP	Papua Presidium Council/*Presidium Dewan Papua*
Perdasi	provincial regulations/*Peraturan Daerah Provinsi*
Perdasus	regulations/*Peraturan Daerah Khusus*
PULO	Patani United Liberation Organization
RDC	Regional Development Council of the CAR
RUU	draft law/*Rancangan Undang Undang*
SAF	Special Action Force (Police)
SBPAC	Southern Border Provincial Administration Center
SBY	Susilo Bambang Yudhoyono
SIRA	Aceh Referendum Information Centre/*Sentral Informasi Referendum Aceh*
SPCPD	Southern Philippines Council for Peace and Development
SRA	Social Reform Agenda
TAO	Tambon Administrative Organization
TNI	Indonesian National Army/*Tentara Nasional Indonesia*
UN WGIP	United Nations Working Group on Indigenous Populations
UP4B	Accelerated Development Unit for Papua and West Papua Provinces/*Unit Percepatan Pembangunan Provinsi Papua dan Papua Barat*

1 Introduction

Tamils, Acehnese, Moros, Tibetans, Abkhazians, and Basques seek more power and control over their territorial homeland. Over time, some groups have gained new institutions and financial resources while others remain embroiled in episodes of violent conflict. All of these groups are territorially concentrated and seek self-determination. As a result, these nationalist conflicts strike at the core of a state's identity, its boundaries and its unity. They pose deep challenges to a state's territorial integrity.

The deep divide between nationalists and the state often appears unbridgeable. The gap separating the Sinhalese-dominated Sri Lankan state and Tamils, for example, appears just as wide even after the Tamil Tigers' defeat.[1] Papuans in Indonesia feel marginalized and excluded while migrants threaten to outnumber them in their claimed homeland.[2] Civil war in Sudan ended with the creation of a new state of South Sudan, but it caused thousands of deaths and vast destruction while laying the basis for new territorial claims.[3]

States jealously guard their territorial boundaries and unity. Whether freed from colonial rule, or shaped out of the ashes of crumbling empires, modern states lay claim to rule over their internationally recognized territory, project power through security forces and institutions, and create an overarching identity to legitimize their integration of various groups under their authority.[4] International law recognizes state sovereignty over its territory and sanctions measures to protect it.[5]

---

[1] Ahmed Hashim, *When Counterinsurgency Wins: Sri Lanka's Defeat of the Tamil Tigers* (Philadelphia: University of Pennsylvania Press, 2013).

[2] Jacques Bertrand, "Autonomy and Stability: The Perils of Implementation and 'Divide-and-Rule' Tactics in Papua, Indonesia," *Nationalism and Ethnic Politics* 20, no. 2 (2014).

[3] Richard Cockett, *Sudan: The Failure and Division of an African State* (New Haven and London: Yale University Press, 2016).

[4] Hendrik Spruyt, *The Sovereign State and Its Competitors: An Analysis of Systems Change*, Princeton Studies in International History and Politics (Princeton, NJ: Princeton University Press, 1994); Stephen D. Krasner, *Sovereignty: Organized Hypocrisy* (Princeton, NJ: Princeton University Press, 1999); Daniel Philpott, *Revolutions in Sovereignty: How Ideas Shaped Modern International Relations* (Princeton, NJ: Princeton University Press, 2001).

[5] Francis Harry Hinsley, *Sovereignty*, 2nd ed. (New York: Cambridge University Press, 1986); James Crawford, *The Creation of States in International Law* (New York: Oxford University Press, 2006).

As a result, these dual claims to territory and group identity often clash and yield conflict. More than other forms of ethnic conflict, those involving nationalist groups are deeper and more endemic. Once launched on a path of seeking self-determination, they aim for independence or claim rights to govern their territory. Such conflicts often lead to civil war.[6] They are even more profound when the state is founded on the basis of a competing nationalist frame that lays claim to one, single nation.[7]

Democratic regimes offer in theory a more flexible context that is conducive to resolving such conflicts peacefully.[8] Their institutions mediate how political actors interact with one another under situations of heightened tension. Through formal political channels, such as the legislative assembly and sometimes the executive, representatives of different groups can voice concerns and grievances. They may seek redress through the courts, which are expected to play an unbiased role.[9] Elections test the political system's capacity to provide ethnic groups with significant representation and power. Nationalist groups can negotiate institutional arrangements, such as territorial autonomy or power-sharing, which represent them and ascribe powers to manage their affairs, within the boundaries of existing states.

Yet, in practice, even well-established democratic states are often saddled with intense nationalist conflicts, including violent ones. In Northern Ireland, the Irish Republican Army and Sinn Fein claimed self-determination.[10] Basques and Catalans claimed nationhood and independence from Spain.[11] Among newer democracies, Czechoslovakia broke up after the resurgence of claims to nationhood from Czechs and Slovaks, respectively.[12]

---

[6] James D. Fearon and David D. Laitin, "Ethnicity, Insurgency, and Civil War," *American Political Science Review* 97, no. 1 (2003): 75–90; Paul Collier and Nicholas Sambanis (eds.), *Understanding Civil War: Evidence and Analysis, Volume 2: Europe, Central Asia, and Other Regions* (Washington, DC: World Bank, 2005).

[7] See for instance, on Indonesia, George McTurnan Kahin, *Nationalism and Revolution in Indonesia* (Ithaca, NY: Cornell University Press, 1955).

[8] Andrew Reynolds, *The Architecture of Democracy: Constitutional Design, Conflict Management, and Democracy* (Oxford: Oxford University Press, 2002); Sujit Choudhry, *Constitutional Design for Divided Societies: Integration or Accommodation?* (Oxford: Oxford University Press, 2008); Tom Ginsburg, "Constitutional Afterlife: The Continuing Impact of Thailand's Postpolitical Constitution," *International Journal of Constitutional Law* 7, no. 1 (2009).

[9] Choudhry, *Constitutional Design for Divided Societies.*

[10] John McGarry and Brendan O'Leary, *The Northern Ireland Conflict: Consociational Engagements* (Oxford and New York: Oxford University Press, 2004).

[11] Sebastian Balfour and Alejandro Quiroga, *The Reinvention of Spain: Nation and Identity since Democracy* (Oxford: Oxford University Press, 2007); André Lecours, *Basque Nationalism and the Spanish State* (Reno: University of Nevada Press, 2007); Montserrat Guibernau, *Catalan Nationalism: Francoism, Transition, and Democracy* (London and New York: Routledge, 2004).

[12] Eric Stein, *Czecho/Slovakia: Ethnic Conflict, Constitutional Fissure, Negotiated Breakup* (Ann Arbor: University of Michigan Press, 1997).

Democratic contexts, therefore, produce an array of outcomes. Violent nationalist conflicts have occasionally erupted at the time of a transition to democracy.[13] In other instances, democracy has allowed conflicting parties to reach ceasefire agreements, negotiate settlements, and new institutional arrangements.[14] Sometimes, nationalist groups have even participated in deliberations for a new constitution, as in the case of Spain.[15] More often than not, the pattern is mixed. Periods of violent conflict might be followed by negotiated settlements. Conversely, violence might decline in intensity but be followed by occasional rioting, demonstrations, and public displays of discontent.

Does democracy reduce or exacerbate nationalist conflict? What explains the variance in conflict outcomes? I argue that democracy matters and it generally does reduce violent nationalist conflict. Yet, the outcome is neither linear nor simple. New structural constraints and incentives tend overall to limit violent conflict, yet the pattern as suggested in the literature can lead to heightened violence in the short term. As a result, while violence tends to be reduced and less frequent over time, it does not disappear under democratic rule, nor is the conflict easily resolved. It opens up more options for nationalist groups to choose to pursue violence, seek negotiated settlements, or accept offers of accommodation. The democratic context multiplies the available options and, more importantly, increases the state's accountability. But the democratic context does not necessarily resolve conflict. Resolution of conflict entails not its absence, but its channelling through formal institutional processes of a democratic regime. This book provides an explanation for the varied pattern of nationalist conflict under democratic rule.

Southeast Asia constitutes the empirical terrain for this study. In Indonesia, the Philippines, and Thailand, five nationalist groups have sought recognition and territorial self-determination: Acehnese and Papuans in Indonesia; Moros and peoples of the Cordillera in the Philippines; and Malay Muslims in Thailand. All these groups are territorially concentrated and have made claims to self-determination.

Nationalist conflicts across Southeast Asia first emerged in authoritarian regimes. The nature of grievances, modes of mobilization, and episodes of violence transformed and shifted over time. Under recent authoritarian regimes, groups that saw themselves as "nations" with secessionist ambitions

---

[13] Jack Snyder, *From Voting to Violence* (New York: W.W. Norton and Company, 2000).

[14] Roland Paris, *At War's End: Building Peace after Civil Conflict* (Cambridge and New York: Cambridge University Press, 2004).

[15] Michael Keating, "Rival Nationalisms in a Plurinational State: Spain, Catalonia, and the Basque Country," in *Constitutional Design for Divided Societies: Integration or Accommodation?*, ed. Sujit Choudhry (Oxford: Oxford University Press, 2008), 316–41; Enric Martinez-Herrera and Thomas Jeffrey Miley, "The Constitution and the Politics of National Identity in Spain," *Nations and Nationalism* 16, no. 1 (2010).

drew on histories of resistance, recast themselves in nationalist terms, and sought to consolidate new forms of mobilization against the state.

Of course, there was nothing natural or inevitable about these groups. While the Acehnese have had a longer history of political and social consolidation, it was far from the case for Papuans, Moros, Cordillerans, or Malay Muslims of Thailand. Papuans have been scattered over a highly mountainous terrain with difficult mobility across the land. Papuan subgroups, speaking their own language, mostly evolved with few contacts among each other. The same is true of the Cordillera, mainly a highland mountainous area where different ethnic groups have been divided by the difficult terrain, with specific local cultures and languages. Moros shared Islam as a religion, but their local ethnolinguistic identities as Tausug, Maranao, and Maguindanao have often been stronger, and they are concentrated in different parts of Mindanao and the Sulu archipelago. Malay Muslims were divided among different sultanates prior to colonial conquest and share close affinities with groups across the border in Malaysia. Nevertheless, nationalists built movements and tapped into overarching common grievances to build more unified identities that have remained important sources of their mobilization.

Once states began to democratize, paths diverged significantly: one group, the Acehnese, enjoys wide-ranging autonomy that has been fairly well implemented while another, the Malay Muslims of Thailand, have neither obtained significant accommodation nor seen a reduction in state repression. Others fall somewhere in between. The following sections introduce my framework for explaining the impact of democratization and how it manifested in the region.

Patterns of Nationalist Conflict under Democratic Rule

Democracy reduces violent nationalist conflict but has a poor record of resolving it. Authoritarian regimes do not resolve conflicts; they generally tend to repress them.[16] Democratic regimes offer the only credible alternative framework by which conflict can be channelled through formal institutions but, in the case of nationalist conflicts, they rarely do. Nationalist conflicts, relative to other forms of ethnic or identity-based conflicts, strike at the core of the state's territorial claim and require a separate analysis to understand how they evolve under changing institutional frameworks.

This book challenges the argument that the establishment of a new democratic regime fuels nationalist violence. While such outcomes occur, they are usually rare or relatively brief. Instead, I argue that democratic regimes create

[16] Christian Davenport, "Multi-Dimensional Threat Perception and State Repression: An Inquiry into Why States Apply Negative Sanctions," *American Journal of Political Science* 39, no. 3 (1995): 690–91, 701; "State Repression and the Tyrannical Peace," *Journal of Peace Research* 44, no. 4 (2007).

conditions that reduce nationalist **violence** but rarely succeed in channelling **conflict** through democratic institutions. Nationalist conflicts are sufficiently deep-seated that negotiated outcomes are difficult to achieve. Mobilization outside of institutional channels occurs regularly. Occasional violent episodes, protests, or other extra-institutional means of making greater claims from the state are part of the landscape of nationalist mobilization and are endemic.

More than any other ethnic or minority conflict, nationalist conflict is the most difficult to resolve because of the wide gap in the preferred outcomes between the state and group. The state is fundamentally concerned with preserving its boundaries and unity. As a result, it views any claims made by nationalist groups as potentially threatening its integrity. As a starting point, its preferred outcome is the dissolution or disappearance of nationalist claims, and the integration and loyalty of the groups making these claims.

Nationalist groups, on the other hand, have strong identities tied to their claimed homeland and a political agenda that includes self-determination and self-governance, irrespective of the grievances that give rise to them. Their preferred outcome includes a range of possibilities, such as full independence in a small minority of cases, some form of recognition of their status, power-sharing, or autonomous institutions. But many other forms of concessions, such as providing more educational or cultural resources, or protecting minority rights, fall short, whereas they will be occasionally sufficient in a number of cases involving ethnic or minority group grievances that are not nationalist in their orientation.

As a result, the gap between nationalist and state objectives is wide. Few institutional solutions can adequately meet the former's claims while reassuring state leaders that their authority and the integrity of territorial borders will be maintained. The fear remains that giving more concessions fuels greater demands, leading ultimately to secession. The structure of the conflict sets, therefore, an equilibrium point that is difficult to achieve.

Why then should democracy reduce violent nationalist conflict? Mostly because it broadens the channels for mobilization, diversifies and dilutes claims to national group representation, and increases the political costs of violence over time. It changes the parameters of repression, increases prospects for negotiated solutions, allows greater representation of interests and claims to resources, and broadens options for mobilization. While the net impact might not eliminate conflict, these processes nevertheless dampen the intensity of conflict, mostly by reducing the conditions fuelling violence. When taking an overall assessment of democracy on such conflicts, therefore, the argument that it fuels violence is tenuous, but the conflict can remain deep, unresolved, and expressed through occasional outbursts that are sometimes violent.

Over the long run, then, there is a tendency for less violent mobilization under democratic regimes but significant variance requires explanation. First, as Snyder and others have suggested, there is an observed tendency for an increase in violent mobilization in some cases of democratic **transition**. Second, the outcomes over time vary significantly, with some cases reaching negotiated agreements that significantly reduce or eliminate sources of conflict while others retain deep grievances and see sporadic violence, protest, or other extra-institutional forms of mobilization.

In order to analyse more deeply this variance, the book considers two different stages of democratization: (i) an early phase of transition from an authoritarian to a democratic regime and (ii) a period of democratic stability. I postulate that there are different structural parameters framing the interaction between the state and nationalist groups in these two stages.

The main differentiating factor between the two stages is that institutions are fluid in the initial phase while they are more set, and therefore stabilize expectations, in the second. First, a transition from an authoritarian to a democratic regime alters the parameters of the conflict by opening up institutional channels to express grievances, and negotiate possible changes to address them. Yet, it also raises uncertainty. The latter heightens the incentive for nationalist groups to mobilize. At the same time, the state is confronted with a strategic choice to signal willingness to compromise, or reaffirm its preferred rejection of nationalist claims. There is a high probability of violence to rise when the state chooses to repress initially, thereby signalling that the new democratic regime is not willing to offer a new basis for negotiation. An initial attempt to offer some accommodation can initially prevent spiralling violence. Such accommodation is typically far less than what groups demand and is usually designed to offer small concessions to move the group away from nationalist demands. Violence tends to increase when the state chooses to continue or increase repression, particularly when the nationalist group is united and well organized.

Second, once democratic institutions stabilize, violence is reduced but conflict tends to remain endemic. I show that as violent mobilization becomes costlier to nationalist groups and the state under democratic rule, both sides have incentives to negotiate, seek new institutional solutions to address nationalist grievances, and attempt to resolve the conflict. Yet, given the deep gap in both sides' preferred outcomes, mutually acceptable negotiated settlements or even the state's establishment of new institutions, powers, and resources to accommodate nationalists often fail and produce, instead, lower violence but ultimately sustained conflict.

A number of factors influence variance across cases. As I explain subsequently, five are particularly important. First, much of the heightened violence is related to nationalist groups' mobilizational capacity. Those with little ability to mount insurgencies produce mostly low-level violence or none at all if state repression is strong. Yet, conflict can remain deep and stalled, with periodic low-level violence resurging. Second, state concessions, particularly in periods of transition, can reduce incentives to mobilize violently, at least in the early stages. Significantly large signals of willingness to concede can even prevent the onset of a civil war altogether. Third, electoral coalitions are key for understanding the degree to which states are willing to make concessions to nationalist groups, particularly if their support is required to maintain a ruling coalition but, more frequently, when there is a shift from a majority reluctant to concede to "secessionists" to one sufficiently tired of continued violence. Conversely, populist leaders might attempt to capitalize on strong armed responses and escalate violent conflicts, but such measures are likely to be short-lived and have high risk of undermining democratic credentials and backfiring politically. Fourth, in presidential systems with highly independent parliaments it is more difficult to resolve conflict and achieve institutional outcomes that address nationalist grievances. As they tend to reflect the majority's reluctance to concede to "secessionists," parliaments will often dilute or thwart peace agreements or legislation that is negotiated with nationalist groups. Finally, the credibility of commitments is important in reaching conflict resolution rather than stalled conflict with low-level violence. Democratic institutions increase credibility mainly because of their greater constraint on the executive's ability to govern arbitrarily and ignore its laws, as well as the greater scrutiny and accountability of state actions. Nevertheless, in the case of commitments to nationalists, they provide only a basic expectation. Constitutionalized recognition of autonomy for nationalists helps to firm up the commitment and make it more credible but requires legislation. The state sometimes crafts it in ambiguous language or with terms that allow it to undermine autonomy and even erode its commitments through regulation. Detailed legislation and negotiated agreements with nationalists help to increase credibility. The combination of these factors, as well as their relative importance, varies according to context but some influence more violence in initial stages and a variety of outcomes, from wide-ranging autonomy that satisfies nationalist grievances to low-level violence and stalled conflict.

This explanation departs from other studies by emphasizing the longer-term patterns of nationalist conflict under democratic rule. As this book shows, the pattern follows a modified version of the inverted U-shaped curve that has been described in the literature. I propose instead that a bell curve more aptly represents the observed tendencies, as it captures a smoothening of the impact of democratization on violence at both ends. Rather than a sudden rise of violence after democratic transition, I suggest that most conflicts have a fairly steady level of violence initially while nationalist groups assess the degree to which new democratic regimes are willing to negotiate or compromise. Initial state concessions also tend to dampen violent mobilization or delay its onset. When democracy stabilizes, there is a tendency for violence to decline but it often remains present, at low levels. In most cases, while democratic stability reduces the incentives for violent mobilization, it nevertheless does not easily resolve conflicts. Grievances remain and nationalist groups continue to use extra-institutional means to voice discontent and make demands, with low-level violence recurring periodically. Nationalist conflicts are much more difficult to resolve as states perceive them to be threats to their foundations. They often remain endemic, stalled, and often sporadically violent. The smoothening of the curve represents this frequent stabilization into low-level violence.

Based on an inductive comparison of five cases and tracing change in two different time periods, I examine why initially similar cases under authoritarian rule produced a wide range of outcomes, both in the first phase of democratic transition and later after democracy stabilized. Relatively low levels of violence as a general observation disguises significant variance in terms of outcomes, from obtaining negotiated special autonomy over a claimed territory to complete absence of accommodation and high levels of state repression. Furthermore, even the most beneficial outcomes to nationalist groups, in the form of special autonomy and detailed legislation, are often subjected to state attempts to dilute and undermine them.

A caveat is in order. While the book traces what I believe to be crucial factors that explain why democratization had varied effects on each conflict, it does not claim to account for all relevant factors in the evolution of secessionist conflicts in the region. Indeed, I weigh the relative importance of factors that explain, domestically, why certain characteristics of democratic change led to more or less violence, and to differentiated outcomes of institutional accommodation. Moreover, I assess how these factors evident in Southeast Asia measure against a broader literature on democratization and ethnic conflict, while providing some general propositions based on this inductive study. Others will analyse better the role of international, regional, or other external factors that might explain some of the patterns observed. I contend, however, that international and regional factors have been far less influential than in other parts of the world, at least with respect to their impact on democratization patterns and their role in the evolution of these conflicts. Finally, the book does not claim to delve in as deep detail as would any particular specialist of each group, but examines carefully the historical and empirical material to engage in a close analysis and dialogue with conceptual factors discussed in relation to the broader theoretical literature.

Southeast Asia: From Violent Insurgency to Autonomy

Southeast Asia has been the locus of numerous forms of nationalist mobilization and violence in the past few decades. Several movements have persisted in Indonesia, the Philippines, and Thailand, in spite of the improvement in democratic governance since the mid-1980s. Yet, the pattern of violent and non-violent mobilization is puzzling, as there are no clear trends across the board toward more or less violence. The most consistent pattern appears to be an ebb and flow between periods of high mobilization and violence, followed by significant troughs, sometimes accompanied by ceasefires or a peace agreement. Only one among these groups, the Acehnese, successfully reached a lasting peace agreement that institutionalized vast autonomy powers.[17] In the four other cases, in spite of a greater democratic environment, conflict has continued, although less violently on the whole.

Over time, as democratization progressed, violence tended to diminish. In many of the cases, there were one or several spikes, mostly during the earlier phase of the transition. When probing at a deeper level, however, there is enough variance that requires explanation. In the initial stages of democratization, there was a wide range among the five cases, with one degenerating into civil war (Aceh), while there was virtually no change in the case of Malay Muslims in Thailand. At a later stage, after democracy stabilized, there was a decline in violence in all cases. But conflict was far from resolved. The range of outcomes was quite broad. There was less violence overall but poor outcomes in terms of conflict resolution, with one case reaching a credible special autonomy agreement (Aceh) and another continuing to be highly repressed (Malay Muslims).

There are several reasons why these five groups can be usefully compared. They share a number of similarities. First, they can be classified as "nationalist" groups, as opposed to ethnic groups more broadly. Second, they are all territorially concentrated and represent relatively small percentages of the overall population. Third, they all had significant periods of armed insurgency during the authoritarian period preceding the democratic opening, with similar kinds of state responses. In addition, as they are all situated in Southeast Asia, they were subjected to similar regional factors. In this case, regional influences are low relative to other regions.

Armed organizations in all cases cast their groups in nationalist terms. They were not only seeking recognition of their ethnic identities and rights associated with that recognition, but they all made claims to a designated homeland and demanded powers and resources to govern their respective groups in that homeland with minimal interference from the central state. They varied in

---

[17] Edward Aspinall, *Islam and Nation: Separatist Rebellion in Aceh, Indonesia* (Palo Alto, CA: Stanford University Press, 2009).

the extent to which some of the groups asked for outright independence and defined their nationalist identities in direct opposition to the dominant majority in control of the state. The Free Aceh Movement (*Gerakan Aceh Merdeka*, GAM) made clear demands for secession from Indonesia on the basis of the long historic control of the Acehnese over their territory and past sovereignty over a local kingdom. Similarly, the Moro National Liberation Front (MNLF) sought secession from the Christian-dominated Philippines, which they rejected on the claimed basis of a long history of territorial control and self-governance under Muslim sultanates that resisted external intrusion from Spanish colonial rule. Several armed groups, including the Patani United Liberation Organisation (PULO), mobilized Malay Muslims in the south of Thailand on the basis of their shared Malay and Islamic identities against the Thai state's long claim to unique "Thai" national identity, while also laying claim to secession on the basis of the territory of the past kingdom of Patani. The Cordillera People's Liberation Army (CPLA) articulated a claim of a shared Cordilleran identity, recognized by Spanish colonizers as "Igorot," and having a long history of resistance to external influence and conquest, and political control over the Cordillera highlands. Finally, Papuans organized under the Free Papua Movement (*Organisasi Papua Merdeka*, OPM) to mobilize against integration to the Indonesian state and to emphasize their distinct racial and ethnic identity from "Indonesians," on the basis of their Melanesian origins. These distinctions laid the basis for a nationalist claim to independence of West Papua.[18]

All five groups are similar in some basic structural features. Acehnese, Papuans, Malay Muslims in Thailand, Moros, and Cordillerans all represent less than four per cent of their country's population. They are also territorially concentrated. The Acehnese occupy most of the Indonesian province of Aceh. Papuans are spread over the western part of the vast island they share with Papua New Guinea, alongside migrants from other regions. They are composed of a large number of different tribal groups. Malay Muslims are

---

[18] There is a vast literature on the history of all these movements. Some useful studies include Aspinall, *Islam and Nation: Separatist Rebellion in Aceh*; Tim Kell, *The Roots of Acehnese Rebellion, 1989–1992* (Ithaca, NY: Cornell Modern Indonesia Project, 1995); Robin Osborne, *Indonesia's Secret War: The Guerilla Struggle in Irian Jaya* (Sydney: Allen and Unwin, 1985); Richard Chauvel, *Constructing Papuan Nationalism: History, Ethnicity, and Adaptation* (Washington, DC: East-West Center, 2005); Wan Kadir Che Man, *Muslim Separatism: The Moros of the Southern Philippines and the Malays of Southern Thailand* (Singapore: Oxford University Press, 1990); Peter G. Gowing, *Mandate in Moroland: The American Government of Muslim Filipinos 1899–1920* (Quezon: New Day Publishers, 1983); William Henry Scott, *The Discovery of the Igorots: Spanish Contacts with the Pagans of Northern Luzon* (Quezon City: New Day Publishers, 1974); Gerard A. Finin, *The Making of the Igorot: Contours of Cordillera Consciousness* (Quezon City: Ateneo de Manila University Press, 2005); Surin Pitsuwan, *Islam and Malay Nationalism: A Case Study of the Malay-Muslims of Southern Thailand* (Bangkok: Thai Khadi Research Institute, Thammasat University, 1985).

concentrated mostly in the contiguous Thai provinces of Pattani, Narathiwat, Yala, and Songklah, where they are a majority with significantly large numbers of Thai Buddhists. The Cordillera is a highland area on the major island of Luzon and is populated overwhelmingly by various ethnic groups that are collectively known as "Igorot." Finally, Moros are a majority in a few districts of the southwest of the island of Mindanao, as well as large parts of the Sulu archipelago, although they are divided among several ethnolinguistic groups: the Tausug, Maranao, Maguindanao, and a few others. They were once a majority on Mindanao but large numbers of migrants from other parts of the Philippines reduced their share of the population on the island, and left them concentrated in relatively limited territory mostly in the southern provinces of Basilan, Lanao del Sur, Maguindanao, Sulu, and Tawi-Tawi. Except for the Acehnese and to some extent the Malay Muslims of Thailand, there were some significant ethnolinguistic and/or tribal differences within each group, and their amalgamation into broader identities was a product of colonial and post-colonial state policies, combined with organizational entrepreneurs that actively pursued a common identity to enhance mobilizational capacity.

Authoritarian regimes shaped the environment for group mobilization and contributed to the development of new grievances. In Indonesia, Thailand, and the Philippines all three authoritarian regimes were military-dominated but varied in terms of their strength and longevity. Indonesia's authoritarian regime first emerged under Soekarno's Guided Democracy in the late 1950s but consolidated after 1965 under the leadership of President Suharto and lasted three decades. Thailand's lasted for decades but was less stable. After the end of monarchical rule in 1932, the regime was mostly authoritarian until the late 1980s, with a brief hiatus between 1973 and 1976. Since the early 1990s, it has wavered between democracy and authoritarian rule, with three instances of military rule after coups in 1991, 2006, and 2014. Under the leadership of Ferdinand Marcos, authoritarian rule in the Philippines was the shortest, lasting only fourteen years from 1972 to 1986.

Nationalist groups sought redress for perceived injustice or mistreatment, and vied for more power and resources for their respective groups, but had few strategic options available to make significant gains. With the exception of some influential Acehnese within the Suharto regime in Indonesia, nationalist groups had almost no access to authoritarian leaders. Moros and Cordillerans in the Philippines, Malay Muslims in Thailand, and Papuans in Indonesia had little or no presence in cabinet or high levels of the armed forces. The respective leadership of provincial administrators had few formal powers and were mostly pawns of the regime. Open expressions of discontent, such as demonstrations, were suppressed. Organizations seeking to promote their interests were either banned or severely curtailed. Consequently, armed resistance was almost the only option where groups were sufficiently aggrieved or organized to confront the state.

During this period, all five groups mobilized mostly in favour of autonomy or secession, although in some cases, such as Cordillerans, they joined forces with other groups seeking to overthrow authoritarian rule. GAM first mobilized in the mid-1970s but then re-emerged in 1989 under Suharto's New Order regime, and went underground after being strongly repressed. The MNLF rose against the Marcos regime in the early 1970s. A small group, which officially became the Moro Islamic Liberation Front (MILF) in 1984, splintered from the MNLF after it had begun to favour reconciliation with the Philippine government. The OPM was formed in 1965 largely in opposition to the forced integration of Papua to Indonesia, through a consultation process that Papuans largely considered to have been rigged. While weak and divided, the OPM sustained its low-key insurgency during the whole period of the New Order regime. In the south of Thailand four organizations were formed in the 1960s: the Barisan Nasional Pembebasan Patani (BNPP), Barisan Revolusi Nasional (BRN), the PULO, and the Barisan Bersatu Mujahidin Patani (BBMP). PULO became the most militant in the 1970s. Cordillerans initially joined the communist New People's Army in 1972, when the latter sought refuge in the Cordilleran highlands and helped to organize resistance against the Marcos regime's large infrastructural projects. In the late days of the authoritarian regime, Cordillerans formed their own resistance organization, the CPLA. These insurgent groups, therefore, all rose during authoritarian rule.

In all cases, the state's main response to nationalist mobilization was repression. The armed forces were regularly deployed to quell domestic strife. Anti-communist rhetoric accompanied some of the justifications. So were accusations of secessionist tendencies, threats to unity, and challenges to the nation. Authoritarian regimes in all three countries varied in terms of their willingness to recognize nationalist groups but overall offered few concessions. At one end of the spectrum, the Thai state denied any recognition to Malay Muslims but provided special state resources for education and development. At the other end, the Marcos administration signed the Tripoli agreement with the MNLF to end violent conflict while promising autonomy in thirteen provinces of the Southern Philippines. In spite of recognizing Moro demands, in fact, the Marcos regime used the agreement to undermine the MNLF while failing to actually implement its promises. The Indonesian government's similar promises of autonomy in Aceh also failed to produce any real powers.

The state's response to mobilization in itself however constitutes one of the factors of subsequent rounds of mobilization. Grievances shift over time, as states respond with military force or choose to accommodate some of the groups' demands. In Aceh, for instance, a strong case can be made that the state's violent and brutal response to the mobilization of GAM in the late 1980s largely contributed in the following decade to further alienating the Acehnese from the Indonesian state and boosting the ranks of the secessionist movement.

While identities were starkly different from other groups or the majority, it is the territorial concentration combined with the state's approach to these groups that fostered and solidified their nationalist objectives. Acehnese in this respect could hardly claim to be much different from most other ethnic groups in Indonesia, with their distinct language and traditions. They perhaps show most clearly how state responses to mobilization contribute to the solidification of nationalist identities and secessionist ambitions. Others, however, were subjected to varying degrees of state exclusion, discrimination, and exploitation of their territory.

Each group's path, therefore, was similar. The identities serve as an initial characteristic of group differentiation. Deep grievances were exacerbated by the repressive policies of authoritarian states. It is the treatment of the group through state policies that fed their political agenda. All groups formed nationalist movements, with varied capacities to mount an armed insurgency.

Finally, regional effects were relatively less significant. In other regions of the world, studies that have looked at nationalist rebellion often found regional patterns associated with periods of regime change, accompanied by significant shifts in international processes. In the post-communist countries of the former Soviet Union and Eastern Europe, for instance, there was a peak in nationalist violent conflict in the early 1990s, at moments when states were highly weakened following the fall of communist regimes. As Gurr contends, "regionally specific conjunctions of local and international conditions" explain the rise and decline of most of these rebellions.[19] These patterns were heightened by a number of irredentist movements by which nationalist groups gained support from majorities across their borders while facing weakened states in transition.

Yet, in Southeast Asia, there are no clear regional trends. Democratization has generally been weak and occurred neither with a democratic wave nor with the demise of any regional power.[20] Of the eleven countries of the region, most sailed through the Third Wave of democratization of the 1970s–1990s with very few changes. Only three countries democratized in this period: the Philippines, with the demise of Marcos in 1986; Indonesia in 1998, with the fall of President Suharto; and Thailand remained an ambiguous case. After an

---

[19] Ted Robert Gurr, "Ethnic Warfare on the Wane," *Foreign Affairs* 79, no. 3 (2000): 56.

[20] Mark R. Thompson, "The Limits of Democratisation in ASEAN," *Third World Quarterly* 14, no. 3 (1993); Jacques Bertrand, *Political Change in Southeast Asia*, (Cambridge and New York: Cambridge University Press, 2013); Sorpong Peou, "The Limits and Potential of Liberal Democratisation in Southeast Asia," *Journal of Current Southeast Asian Affairs* 33, no.3 (2014).

extended period of semi-democratic rule in the 1980s, it appeared to become one of the more solid democracies in the region by the late 1990s and early 2000s, only to witness two coups, deep division, and almost perpetual protests after 2004. Only the War on Terror, as well as the links of local Islamist organizations to broader global mobilization of insurgent Islamic groups, constitutes a weak regional link. But there is little evidence that Acehnese and Malay Muslim groups had links with global terror organizations. The MILF had some tenuous links to Jemaah Islamiyah and Al-Qaeda. Only the smaller and more marginal Abu Sayyaf nurtured closer links, and most spectacularly with ISIS during the Marawi siege of 2017.[21] Furthermore, only in the case of Malay Muslims can we speak of a very weak irredentist link with neighbouring Malaysia. All groups rose within domestic borders and made claims only within these territories. Their designated homelands did not spill over borders. Although regional networks and historical connections explain certain aspects of nationalist movements, they had comparatively less impact with respect to varying conflict outcomes in response to democratization.

Democratic Institutions, Divergent Mobilizational Paths, and Varying Outcomes

Given the similarities among nationalist groups in Southeast Asia, their divergence in terms of mobilizational paths and ultimately institutional outcomes begs for an explanation. None of the groups under authoritarian rule obtained significant recognition of their claims or concessions that came close to meeting their demands. Democratization changed the parameters of mobilization and the space for voicing claims. Yet, there are important differences in its impact.

The state was more limited in its ability to use large-scale, military repression. The costs of military operations were much higher as the media and the public could scrutinize them and openly criticize abusive actions. A host of observer organizations, academics, and the media could probe state policy, monitor the implementation of commitments, and voice criticism of their impact.

Nationalist organizations in turn had broader options: they could voice their grievances in public, organize demonstrations, demand referenda, create alliances among civil society organizations, lobby politicians, create new

---

[21] The most publicized link came with the siege of Marawi city in 2017, when the Abu Sayyaf and the Maute group claimed direct relations with ISIS. See Rommel C. Banlaoi (ed.), *The Marawi Siege and Its Aftermath: The Continuing Terrorist Threat* (Newcastle upon Tyne: Cambridge Scholars Publishing, 2020). For an overview of some of the MILF's links, see Zachary Abuza, "The Moro Islamic Liberation Front at 20: State of the Revolution," *Studies in Conflict & Terrorism* 28, no. 6 (2005).

organizations to represent their groups, create international linkages, and organize rebellious activities. The greater democratic space, therefore, made insurgency less compelling and state repression more difficult.

Yet, there were significant differences in the degree of violent mobilization after the initial democratic opening. Democratic transition created uncertainty. The state could choose to repress but was unlikely to do so in an emerging democratic context, although its response to civilian protest and nationalist mobilization was key.

The initial signalling is crucial to show whether the state is willing to negotiate on the basis of nationalist claims, or even to extend some minor concessions rather than repress. The credibility of this initial commitment is also important. In Aceh, the Indonesian state responded with very minor concessions to an initial period of civilian mobilization and demands for a referendum on independence. With the state signalling strong reluctance to meet Acehnese demands, GAM began a new phase in its insurgency, with the Indonesian armed forces responding with strong military repression. Violent mobilization was very high. In Papua, the Indonesian state also conceded very little. In response, Papuans organized large-scale demonstrations, some of which led to a rise in violence mostly from state repression, after it refused to engage in negotiations. In the Philippines, violence rose both in the Cordillera and in Mindanao but was relatively low in intensity and sporadic. The CPLA mobilized strongly against the Philippine state but quickly reduced its insurgency after Corazon Aquino's government both engaged in negotiations and promised constitutional change to recognize autonomy in the Cordillera. This opening, which also included offers of autonomy to Muslims in Mindanao, contributed to very little change in violent mobilization when democratization occurred. Instead, the MNLF was willing for some time to engage in discussions but, when it became clear that its demands would not be met, it continued its violent mobilization, as did the MILF, which had strong reservations regarding the initial signals. Finally, there was initially little change in violent mobilization after a democratic opening in Thailand, despite the absence of new compromises. But Malay Muslims gained more representation in central government institutions.

Overall, then, Southeast Asian cases show generally some rise in violent and non-violent mobilization but only the Acehnese case becomes a large-scale insurgency. Initial willingness to negotiate new institutions or to offer some minor concessions tended to defuse mobilization but if these proved to be ineffectual, insincere, or insufficient, they often led to violent mobilization in response. The credibility of commitment therefore was important. In Mindanao, credibility of commitment was also crucial. The Philippine state signalled willingness to compromise and extend autonomy, but mostly on its terms, and proceeding unilaterally. The Indonesian state did the same in Papua and provided special autonomy in the late phase of the transition but refused to negotiate.

Two factors explain why violent mobilization was generally weak but still quite varied across cases: differences in mobilizational capacity and the restraining effects of democratic institutions. Mobilizational capacity has varied across groups. GAM, the MNLF, and the MILF all had the capacity to organize armed insurgencies, inflict damage on government targets, and engage in armed combat against the armed forces of Indonesia and the Philippines, respectively. They obtained weapons, and were fairly well coordinated and organized. Conversely, Papuans were never able to mount a significant insurgency. The OPM was more an umbrella for otherwise fairly weak, disparate, and scattered organizations under different leadership, with no significant weapons. Armed groups appeared briefly and made claims to represent Cordillerans and Malay Muslims. First under the auspices of the New People's Army, a communist insurgency, Cordillerans fought against the Marcos regime but, subsequently, the CPLA mainly advocated for self-determination of the people of the Cordillera. In Thailand, the PULO and other small groups organized armed resistance in the past, but were very weak and virtually disappeared after they lost support from neighbouring Malaysia. As a structural precondition, therefore, the varying capacity to mount an insurgency certainly had a significant impact on variance in violent mobilization.

Across the board, however, there was a dampening effect of democratization on the strategic decision to mobilize violently. More options became available for nationalist groups to mobilize, voice their grievances, and make claims. Violent insurgency, in the face of a much stronger state, was always a costly choice. Instead, Acehnese initially organized large demonstrations seeking referenda prior to GAM's remobilization. Several civil society organizations, political parties, and the media openly criticized the violence and conflict in Aceh. Papuans organized a large Congress where they made clear demands on the government. The Papua Presidium Council, the Papua Customary Council, and other organizations voiced grievances, made demands, and lobbied the government. Sustained lobbying contributed to keeping Papuan claims on the agenda. In many ways the strategy was more effective than the OPM's sporadic attacks on police stations and other government targets. In the Philippines, a democratic regime enabled first the MNFL, and subsequently the MILF, to attempt negotiation with heightened assurances that agreements would be credible. For the Cordillera, democratic politics offered the space to mobilize and create linkages to the world indigenous peoples movement.

The costs were also higher for the Indonesian and Philippine states to use military repression. It was slightly less so for the Thai state. The military in

Indonesia and the Philippines was on the defensive as democratic movements explicitly removed armed forces from power. They were criticized for past abuses. Acehnese and Papuan organized civilian movements demanding redress for past injustices, as they joined the broader *Reformasi* movement demanding for the military's role in politics to be scaled back. Electoral pressure and widespread criticism reduced the Indonesian state's capacity to wage war on Aceh. Military operations continued in Papua, but on a much more limited and smaller scale, where they were mostly hidden from scrutiny. Similarly, the downfall of Marcos in 1986, after weeks of widespread protests, triggered a process of constitutional reform and democratization. The armed forces were forced back to barracks while Corazon Aquino encouraged broad consultation with many segments of society, including the Moros and Cordilleran peoples.

In Thailand, the nature and timing of the transition were different, with a lesser impact on the armed forces' role in politics. The timing of democratization can be traced to 1992, after a brief coup in 1991 that was followed by elections. Mass demonstrations prevented the junta from legitimizing itself through the electoral process but, while the armed forces retreated, they remained a significant force. The military had itself gradually democratized the country in the 1980s, and so had been partly involved in the gradual instalment of the democratic regime, in spite of launching a brief coup in 1991. It was therefore less clearly constrained by the democratic process it had initiated.

Democratic transition therefore had some similarities across cases, but mobilization capacity, state signalling, and credibility of commitments created varied effects. Uncertainty characterizes the first phase of democratization, and therefore heightens the probability of violent mobilization as the institutional setting is fluctuating. Where the state signals a willingness to compromise or negotiate with nationalist groups, it can defuse incentives to mobilize violently. But if such signals are deemed not credible, it can heighten the group's incentives to react violently.

In the phase of democratic stability, the new parameters of nationalist accommodation were mostly in place. The incentives for violent mobilization were reduced as institutions became more fixed, the costs were much higher for nationalist groups to use violence, and the options for alternative forms of political mobilization were clearer.

Some of the factors influencing outcomes in the transition phase continued to be highly significant and largely determined violence patterns confirming a bell-shape curve. The dampening effects of democratic institutions continued to operate. The new democratic governments were still reluctant to use the armed forces for repressive actions, in order to avoid perpetuating their internal security roles. More mediatized and open politics required much more justification for repressive action. For insurgent groups, the threshold to mobilize violently was also higher as they competed with civilian groups for support and were subjected to greater scrutiny. The space for negotiating more credible agreements was also wider.

The puzzle arising from this broader trend is how to explain the varied outcomes, including some occasionally persistent, low-intensity violence. The cases confirm that nationalist conflict is difficult to resolve even in democratic regimes. While violence overall tends to decline, the outcomes maintain deep grievances, continued mobilization outside of institutional channels, and often seeds of future mobilization in violent forms. Only Acehnese obtained a negotiated agreement on broad autonomy that appeased and satisfied nationalist demands. By contrast, Malay Muslims were actually more repressed. The three middle cases showed important differences as well. Papuans and Moros obtained some forms of autonomy, but they were deemed insufficient, insincere, or ineffective, thereby causing renewed cycles of discontent, deep grievance, protest, and occasionally violent mobilization. Conflict became mostly resolved in the Cordillera because of a strategic shift: exit and reframe. Cordilleran groups abandoned a nationalist agenda and instead reframed their claims as indigenous people, thereby aligning their demands with the rising international movement for indigenous rights.

When examining pathways and varied outcomes, several factors are key. Mobilizational capacity of nationalist groups remains a differentiating factor. It interacts with institutional factors once democracy has stabilized. First, the nature of the electoral pay-off determines whether a government gains from repressing or accommodating nationalist groups. Second, parliamentary independence can hinder the ability to grant significant institutional accommodation to nationalist groups. Third, the credibility of institutional commitments influences national groups' receptivity to concessions made. The credibility hinges on the effectiveness and impact of past institutional compromises, and the degree to which current ones are the product of negotiation and enshrine strong legislative protections. The pathways by which these factors interact vary over time as they can be influenced by electoral cycles, or different sequencing of institutional commitments.

Table 1.1 shows the variance in outcomes and combination of variables for each case. Again, there is no snapshot of a particular moment of democratic stability, but instead I am tracing how these variables changed over time during the period of democratic stability. A static comparison at a certain point in time would not capture how some apparent outcomes, such as a peace agreement, could sometimes be fleeting and temporary while in other cases they have more lasting effects.

High mobilizational capacity continues to be a strong predictor of outcome. If it was associated with the highest incidence of violent mobilization in the

Table 1.1 *Explanatory variables and outcomes*

	Indonesia		Philippines		Thailand
	Aceh	Papua	Moros	Cordillera	Malay
Mobilizational capacity	High	Low	High	Low	Low
Electoral Pay-off	Accommodation	None	Variable	Accommodation	Variable
Independence of parliament	Low	Low	High	High	Low
Credibility of institutional commitment	Constitution: medium 2001 (special autonomy) – low 2006 (Law on Aceh) – high	Constitution: medium 2001 (special autonomy) – low	Constitution: high 1996 (GOP-MNLF agreement) – low 2018 (Bangsamoro Basic Law) – high	Constitution: high 1988 Republican Act 6766 (Organic Act for CAR) – low 1997 (IPRA) – medium	None
Outcome	Wide-ranging Autonomy – demobilization	Contested and ambiguous Autonomy – Cyclical low-intensity violence	Contested and ambiguous Autonomy – Cyclical violence	Exit and reframe	Repression – persistent low-intensity violence

transition phase, interestingly it also appeared to be strongly associated with the most stable and mutually satisfying outcomes under democratic stability. Only two organizations were able to reach peace agreements leading to negotiated and significant autonomy on paper: GAM in Aceh and the MILF in the Philippines. They were also, respectively, the only organizations with strongly significant ability to continue a violent insurgency.

It would however be simplistic to conclude that launching violent insurgencies leads to successful outcomes. While clearly high levels of violence can become costly politically to state leaders, they do not by themselves explain that a negotiated and significant autonomy is achieved. The converse however is indicative of the high degree of suspicion that the state generally has toward nationalist groups. Given that the state usually sees them as threatening its core, it is more likely that it will prefer a disgruntled group with occasional protest and low-level violence to giving deep concessions if the political costs are low.

Southeast Asian cases show how the three factors associated with democratic stability mediate the impact of mobilizational capacity. In Aceh, constitutional amendments enshrining autonomy created a new institutional environment that made credible the possibility of future legislation. But it was combined with the role of Vice-President Jusuf Kalla, who placed his political capital on finding a political solution to the crisis in Aceh, both as a potential gain for his presidential ambitions and as the crisis in Aceh had contributed to the downfall of former President Abdurrahman Wahid. There was a high electoral pay-off to finding a solution. The 2006 Law of Aceh was a highly credible commitment, not only as a result of mediators supporting the process but mostly because the law was a product of negotiation, supported constitutionally, and with sufficient detail to render possible the changes that were promised. Finally parliament's relatively high dependence on the executive ensured that the president could pass a law that reflected closely enough the peace agreement's commitments.

By contrast, while Papuans shared constitutional provisions in support of autonomy, the credibility of institutional commitment obtained was low. The 2002 special autonomy law was neither negotiated nor sufficiently strong legislatively to secure autonomy rights that could accommodate the demands of nationalist Papuans. Instead, the state proceeded with implementing its preferred version of autonomy while undermining some of its provisions, for instance, by splitting the province. While Papuans mounted numerous protests and demonstrations, and violent clashes have occurred regularly, they never produced political costs to the president or major political parties, so there was little political incentive to deliver more significant autonomy.

Moros in the Philippines had three laws or agreements that provided autonomy in parts of Mindanao: the creation of the Autonomous Region of Muslim Mindanao shortly after the transition to democracy; the 1996 peace agreement between the MNLF and the government of the Philippines; and the Bangsamoro Organic Law of 2018, based on a peace agreement with the MILF. Without the MILF's mobilizational capacity remaining high, it is unlikely that the 2018 Law would have been passed. Similarly, the MNLF's continued mobilization after its initial rejection of the Autonomous Region of Muslim Mindanao was certainly a precondition for the 1996 agreement with the Ramos administration. But democratization allowed for a credible peace agreement to be reached with the MNLF in 1996. The political capital of reaching a peace agreement was high, particularly following the very fragile years of the Aquino administration, during which rebellions continued and Ramos capitalized on peace as a pillar of the social contract that he promoted as a winning political strategy. But the short window for adopting a law prevented its proper implementation, as Ramos' successor capitalized on a repressive strategy to seek an electoral pay-off and parliament's relatively high independence created repeated barriers to adopting legislation that reflected the executive's negotiations. Estrada declared an "all-out-war," while Gloria Macapagal-Arroyo also had to respond to the post 9/11 environment, attacks from jihadists and criminal organizations such as Abu Sayyaf that reduced the electoral pay-off of promoting peace. Nevertheless, while partial agreements were reached with the MILF, they repeatedly failed once in parliament, as elected representatives derailed proposed legislation that could enshrine the 1996 agreement and, later, partial agreements with the MILF. Democratic stability created high credibility of commitments by enshrining autonomy for Moros in the constitution and the government's willingness to sign negotiated peace agreements, but the credibility was eroded through these successive failures to pass legislation in parliament. The original Bangsmoro Basic Law failed in parliament after an agreement with the MILF became part of Duterte's campaign, where his origins in Mindanao offered high political capital to capitalizing on passing the law and reaching peace with the Moros. The renamed Bangsamoro Organic Law was passed in July 2018 largely because of the high electoral pay-off Duterte had hoped for, combined with a parliament that backed him after devastating attacks in Marawi city in 2017, led by Abu Sayyaf in conjunction with ISIS. It was this combination that swayed parliament away from past rejection of autonomy to shift its views on supporting the law to reduce the power of more radical groups.

Cordillerans had a very different outcome as the Cordillera People's Alliance mobilized in favour of an exit-and-reframe strategy, shifting away from nationalist mobilization to reframing the struggle as "indigenous peoples." While Cordillerans had benefitted from similar high credible commitment with the constitutional enshrinement of autonomy for the Cordillera, the government's autonomy proposals were rejected as lacking credibility as they were neither based on negotiations nor did they carry sufficient guarantees to Cordillerans that significant autonomy would be implemented. Mobilizational capacity had been reduced after the CPLA joined a temporary autonomy government, merely seen by other groups as serving the organization, rather than broader Cordilleran interests. Cordillerans capitalized on Ramos' desire to support sweeping legislation on indigenous peoples, as part of his broader campaign for peace. The Indigenous People's Rights Act could pass parliament largely because the removal of a nationalist agenda significantly lowered the perceived threat to the state. With low mobilization capacity, low credibility of institutional commitment to secure autonomy, as well as an independent parliament unlikely to agree to a negotiated, deep autonomy for Cordillerans, the strategic shift allowed them to bypass some of those obstacles and obtain credible legislation as indigenous peoples.

Finally, democratic stability yielded few results for Malay Muslims. In spite of numerous changes in the constitution, none of them, including the most democratically drafted constitution of 1997, produced any principle of autonomy or recognition of Malay Muslims. Instead, the long-standing key organizing principle of one Thai nation, with Buddhism and monarchy as supportive of state unity, significantly reduced the space to obtain credible institutional commitment. With relatively low mobilizational capacity, there was little to no political cost to offer development and some representation in the central government during the transition phase. But the deep-seated resentment produced alternative forms of violence, such as increasing anonymous bombings. Thaksin capitalized on a highly repressive approach to increasing electoral support from a majority that worried about escalating violence. He had political incentives to use such an approach and commanded support in parliament from his Thai Rak Thai party that held a majority.

Democracy has therefore shaped conflict between state and nationalist groups in Southeast Asia. It provided greater space for varied political interests and expressions of identity in the public sphere. It allowed groups to advance interests and raise grievances through representative institutions. It opened up negotiating forums to resolve or reduce conflict. Outside of formal political channels, democracy created a more liberalized environment to voice grievances and exert pressure on governments. Groups gained more freedom to create political organizations. They used the media to criticize government policies. When their demands were unheard, they resorted to demonstrations and various forms of protest. Electorates and partners in governing coalitions, worried about continued conflict, violence, instability, and international image placed significant pressure on governments.

There is strong variance nevertheless across cases in terms of both the greater violence in the initial stages of democracy and the outcomes after democratic stability was in place. The book explains why this variance occurs, and why outcomes satisfactory to both the state and national groups have been difficult to achieve. Even in cases where conflict has become channelled through democratic institutions, the depth of state suspicion of nationalist groups often remains strong. The book also examines the implementation of the Law on Aceh, which corresponds to the most conflict-reducing outcome in the five cases. As shown in comparison to the implementation of special autonomy in Papua, and autonomy laws in the Philippines, the central government in all cases consistently uses strategies to dilute commitments made, and to undermine the powers and resources provided, even in the Acehnese case. While the Law on Aceh has sufficiently strong basis for conflict to remain managed through democratic institutions, the state's strategies certainly in the initial stages perpetuated some mistrust. In other cases, as special autonomy in Papua shows, such strategies contribute to an endemic conflict, with occasional low-level violence, and potential for continued deterioration of Papuans' relations to the Indonesian state. The Bangsamoro Basic Law is similarly credible and with strong legislative details, as in the case of the Law on Aceh, but too soon in its implementation to assess the Philippine state's strategy in this respect. Given its past practice, and comparative observations from the region and elsewhere, it is doubtful that it will not also attempt to dilute and undermine concessions made.

The following chapters present the conceptual framework briefly outlined earlier as well as the five cases from Southeast Asia. Chapter 2 discusses why nationalist conflicts are different from other types of ethnic conflict, and how they are particularly difficult to resolve. It then discusses the conditions under which conflicts become violent, but also endemic even when violence subsides. Finally, it presents a framework for comparison across time, as well as across cases. It argues that many cases follow a bell-like curve in the rise and decline of violent nationalist conflict, as democratization first goes through a transition phase before it stabilizes. Then it discusses factors that explain variance across empirical cases, which are developed in Chapters 3–7. Each chapter presents the process of democratization in the country and the origins of nationalist conflicts under authoritarian rule, before proceeding to the analysis of the patterns of conflict under democratic transition and democratic stability. It traces how the factors introduced in Chapter 2 together explain the variance in the conflict paths and outcomes of the five cases, against the backdrop of similar trajectories under authoritarian rule. Finally, it discusses the implementation and realization of institutional outcomes, particularly in cases such as special or broad-based autonomy, which are seen as benchmarks for accommodating nationalist groups. Even then, promises for resolving conflicts and adequately responding to nationalist group grievances are sobering. As the book concludes, nationalist conflicts are particularly difficult to resolve. Democracy helps but is not the panacea that many would hope for.

Nationalist conflict is widespread and often highly violent. Because of its association with secessionist objectives, it triggers fierce responses from central governments. States place the inviolability of their borders at the core of their foundation and are rarely open to negotiating compromises that threaten the status quo.

Democracy regulates conflict through institutional channels and, in theory, can best address deep divisions.[1] Democratic politics allow a plurality of viewpoints to be expressed, a wide range of interests to be represented, policies on a broad set of issues to be debated, and resources deployed to meet demands and needs of a large number of groups and a broad segment of the population. As Schmitter and Karl state: "Modern democracy, in other words, offers a variety of competitive processes and channels for the expression of interests and values – associational as well as partisan, functional as well as territorial, collective as well as individual. All are integral to its practice."[2]

Yet, democracy does not always yield peaceful outcomes, nor does it easily resolve nationalist conflicts.[3] The nature of nationalist conflict sets the parameters against which states manage such claims. The capacity of democratic institutions to offer channels for representation and opportunities to gain resources frames group strategies and ultimately their willingness to compromise.

In this chapter, I explain the variance in the capacity of democratic regimes to resolve nationalist conflicts. I begin with a discussion of why these conflicts

---

[1] There is a very broad debate about the limits of democracy for managing deeply divided societies.

[2] Philippe C. Schmitter and Terry Lynn Karl, "What Democracy Is … And Is Not," *Journal of Democracy* 2, no. 3 (1991): 78.

[3] Snyder, *From Voting to Violence*; Jacques Bertrand and Oded Haklai (eds.), *Democratization and Ethnic Minorities: Conflict or Compromise?* (New York: Routledge, 2013); Donald Rothchild, "Liberalism, Democracy, and Conflict Management: The African Experience," in *Facing Ethnic Conflicts: Toward a New Realism*, eds. Andreas Wimmer, et al. (Lanham: Rowman & Littlefield Publishers, Inc., 2004); Crawford Young, "The Heart of the African Conflict Zone: Democratization, Ethnicity, Civil Conflict, and the Great Lakes Crisis," *Annual Review of Political Science* 9, no. 1 (2006).

are deeper than many other forms of ethnic conflict. I then make a distinction between the transitional phase of democratization and its later one, when democracy is stabilized. I argue that the uncertainty of the transitional phase heightens the probability of violence in nationalist conflict, but when assessing longer-term effects, violence tends to fall. Once democracy stabilizes, nationalist conflict nevertheless remains endemic; while violence might be lower, it remains present in many cases. Aside from structural factors of nationalist groups themselves, I propose that variance in outcomes is partially an outgrowth of institutional mechanisms of stable democracies and the extent to which new institutions create credible commitments that address nationalist grievances.

"Nationalist" Mobilization and the Parameters of Conflict

Nationalist groups[4] have distinct characteristics that differentiate them from other types of ethnic groups and that shape the parameters of conflict. First, they identify as "nations," with political objectives ranging from some form of shared power to autonomy or secession.[5] Second, they are territorially concentrated, which intensifies claims to a homeland and supports their discourse of "nationhood." Third, their conflict is always a struggle against the state. Furthermore, their grievances, while potentially similar to other ethnic groups, usually contain some claim to power over territory and

---

[4] The nomenclature to identify these groups is vague and oftentimes contentious. I explain why there is a distinct political project involved in seeking self-determination over a particular territory, which distinguishes claims of such groups from those of other ethnic groups, or minorities, that might be seeking protection of their rights without contesting either the boundaries of the state or the legitimacy of its rule. The term "national minorities" has been used mostly in the context of the former Soviet Union and Eastern Europe by recovering the categories that were themselves institutionalized by the Soviet Union and other communist countries, and that have generated many studies on the repercussions of crafting such institutional categories. See Rogers Brubaker, *Nationalism Reframed: Nationhood and the National Question in the New Europe* (Cambridge: Cambridge University Press, 1996); Mark R. Beissinger, "A New Look at Ethnicity and Democratization," *Journal of Democracy* 19, no. 3 (2008): 93–96. Connor used "ethnonationalist," which has been sometimes used to characterize such groups, but the nature of ethnic boundaries often shifts as the emphasis becomes the recovery of their "homelands" and territories that usually are far from being ethnically homogenous. See Walker Connor, "Beyond Reason: The Nature of the Ethnonational Bond," *Ethnic and Racial Studies* 16, no. 3 (1993). Finally, "sub-national" is occasionally used. I find such a label misleading as the mobilization of these groups is "nationalist" and therefore also "national" in character. I use "nationalist groups" to identify groups that self-identify as nations, seek self-determination, and lay claim to territory that they identify as their homeland. They are not necessarily seeking independence, and therefore are not necessarily "secessionists," but mainly seek powers and resources to govern aspects of the people they identify as their nation, as well as the territory to which they lay claim.

[5] In some cases, the autonomous institutions themselves are precursors to creating the nationalist claims. See Philip G. Roeder, "Ethnofederalism and the Mismanagement of Conflicting Nationalisms," *Regional & Federal Studies* 19, no. 2 (2009): 210–11.

self-determination.[6] Markers of differentiation involve language, religion, kinship, or other ascriptive attributes, but the articulation of a group identity as a nation adds characteristics of sovereignty and territorial homeland to ethnic attributes. Furthermore, they do not necessarily have an ethnic base but often they do.

Much of the literature subsumes them within analyses of broader categories.[7] On the one hand, studies of ethnic conflict include all groups that mobilize along ethnic lines or that are targeted by the state or other groups based on their ethnic identity.[8] Broad comparisons encompassing different forms of ethnic conflict miss the important condition that differentiates nationalist conflicts and renders them particularly deep, namely the degree to which the state views the group as a threat to its existence.[9] On the other hand, analyses of civil war focus on violent conflict that only in some cases has an ethnic dimension.[10] By doing so, they explain the escalation of violence more broadly, and by extension why some nationalist groups become particularly violent, but these constitute only a small subset of conflicts involving these groups. The emphasis is more on the escalation to large-scale violence, rather than the underlying causes of mobilization that, only in a handful of cases, turn into civil wars.[11] While the

[6] In some circumstances, of course, one ethnic group controls the state, while another positions itself as a nation seeking its own state. In those cases, two ethnic groups are in conflict, with one capturing the state and the other opposing it. If the groups are both large, they might be competing for control of the state, as in the case of Hutus and Tutsis in Rwanda, or Wallons and Flemish in Belgium. While there is a measure of ambiguity, the most important characteristic tends to be the group's own construction as "nation" and its objectives of self-determination.

[7] For a relatively recent discussion of the distinction among ethnicity, race, and nation as conceptual categories, as well as the problems resulting from several decades of fields that were mostly separate from each other, yet sometimes overlapping, see Rogers Brubaker, "Ethnicity, Race, and Nationalism," *Annual Review of Sociology* 35 (2009). See especially p. 29, for a discussion of how the focus should be less on attempting to specify what an ethnic group is and attempt, instead, to determine how they work. My definition here shifts the focus on the political objectives of the mobilization, rather than defining specific criteria for a "nation" or "ethnic group."

[8] Kanchan Chandra, "What Is Ethnic Identity and Does It Matter?," *Annual Review of Political Science* 9 (2006).

[9] There are studies, of course, that emphasize such a threat by specifically focusing on "secession" or "separatism." A related debate emphasizes whether ethnofederalism, autonomy, or decentralization prevents or encourages secession. See Dawn Brancati, "Decentralization: Fueling the Fire or Dampening the Flames of Ethnic Conflict and Secessionism," *International Organization* 60, no. 3 (2006); David S. Siroky and John Cuffe, "Lost Autonomy, Nationalism and Separatism," *Comparative Political Studies* 48, no. 1 (2015); Svante E. Cornell, "Autonomy as a Source of Conflict: Caucasian Conflicts in Theoretical Perspective," *World Politics* 54, no. 2 (2002); Valerie Bunce, "Peaceful Versus Violent State Dismemberment: A Comparison of the Soviet Union, Yugoslavia, and Czechoslovakia," *Politics & Society* 27, no. 2 (1999); Philip G. Roeder, *Where Nation-States Come From: Institutional Change in the Age of Nationalism* (Princeton, NJ: Princeton University Press, 2007).

[10] Nicholas Sambanis, "Do Ethnic and Nonethnic Civil Wars Have the Same Causes?: A Theoretical and Empirical Inquiry (Part 1)," *Journal of Conflict Resolution* 45, no. 3 (2001).

[11] Nicholas Sambanis, "What Is Civil War? Conceptual and Empirical Complexities of an Operational Definition," *Journal of Conflict Resolution* 48, no. 6 (2004).

spiralling violence shares some commonalities with non-ethnic civil wars, however, the nature of the conflict pitting the state against mobilization along "nationalist" lines is missed.[12] The threat for the state is not only in the violent mobilization itself but also in the nature of the claims that are made, namely a rejection of its own identity and a quest for self-determination of a particular group in direct challenge to the territorial boundaries of the existing state.

There are good reasons, therefore, to analyse nationalist groups separately given their identity not only along ethnic characteristics but also as self-proclaimed nations. Their mobilization is specifically directed at the state.[13] Conversely, states are likely to extend offers of territorial autonomy only to groups that are territorially concentrated and that demand greater self-determination.[14] Offers of such autonomy would be irrelevant for territorially dispersed groups that do not define themselves as nations.

Self-determination over a homeland constitutes a core demand of national-ists. They occasionally appeal to international instruments such as Article 1 of the UN Charter to claim their right to self-determination of peoples.[15] Other grievances become funnelled through the prism of the nationalist agenda and frame both their mobilization and the state's perception of their aims.[16] Political, cultural, or economic grievances are filtered through a nationalist frame, expressed as claims to rights of nations, and therefore intrinsically tied to appeals for control over one's homeland and some form of sovereignty.[17]

"Nationalist" leaders tap into grievances and craft a nationalist narrative and its related political objectives of self-determination. As with ethnic groups, nations are constructed and shaped by leaders who define and reinforce group boundaries or modify them as circumstances change.[18] Self-determination, secession, or other means of increasing the nation's control over its territory

---

[12] For a similar point, see Roeder, *Where Nation-States Come From*, 169.

[13] M. Hechter and D. Okamoto, "Political Consequences of Minority Group Formation," *Annual Review of Political Science* 4, no. 1 (2001).

[14] Donald Rothchild and Caroline A. Hartzell, "Security in Deeply Divided Societies: The Role of Territorial Autonomy," *Nationalism and Ethnic Politics* 5, no. 3–4 (1999); Cornell, "Autonomy as a Source of Conflict"; Roeder, "Ethnofederalism and the Mismanagement of Conflicting Nationalisms."

[15] For an interesting discussion of the origins and foundations of such rights, and their evolution in relation to the other rights of indigenous peoples' and other minorities, see Will Kymlicka, *Multicultural Odysseys: Navigating the New International Politics of Diversity* (Oxford: Oxford University Press, 2007), 205–30.

[16] John Hutchinson, "Myth against Myth: The Nation as Ethnic Overlay," *Nations and Nationalism* 10, no. 1–2 (2004).

[17] Monica Duffy Toft, *The Geography of Ethnic Violence: Identity, Interests, and the Indivisibility of Territory* (Princeton, NJ: Princeton University Press, 2003): ch. 2.

[18] The literature long debated assumptions about the nature of ethnic identity and its impact on conflict, with some scholars emphasizing the "primordial" nature of ethnic relations while others instead emphasized "instrumentalist," "situationalist," or "constructivist" factors. This now dated debate came to a consensus over the relatively fluid nature of ethnic identity and national boundaries. See Brubaker, "Ethnicity, Race, and Nationalism." For a recent discussion,

and power over its own people become the leadership's proposed solution to address a whole range of grievances. While leadership is also an important component of explaining how ethnic identities are constructed, the political aims or aspirations differ.

Structural conditions might create disparities and discontent, but these become grievances when leaders present them as such. As Williams argues, a "grievance" involves a sense of victimization by which a group has lost a collective good such as autonomy, territory, political and civil rights, or has been subjected to discrimination. It is not sufficient for groups to feel some sort of dissatisfaction with their economic, social, or political situation. They must also have a sense of moral outrage at an injustice that has been made to them. The more intense this feeling of loss or discrimination, the more likely conflict arises.[19]

Groups perceive injustices or make claims based on a varied set of structural conditions. For instance, economic inequality or competition for resources is often present. Inequality between regions with concentrations of different ethnic groups can lead to systematic discrimination or structures of power.[20] Where a group is disadvantaged socio-economically, conflict may arise from material inequality even if groups are relatively dispersed.[21] Groups with relatively equal socio-economic status may still be in conflict where ethnic mobilization becomes a means of securing scarce resources, such as jobs.[22]

Political or cultural discrimination may cause deep grievances as well. Loss of political autonomy can be a particularly strong source of conflict, as was the case for the Acehnese or Tibetans in the 1950s, but repression, lack of representation in the central government, can also be important. Cultural repression, such as the denial to practice one's religion, can become a powerful incentive to mobilize.[23] Differentiated representation in bureaucratic and political institutions or access to education and services can contribute to grievances and a perceived sense of being treated as "second-class" or "backward." It is less

see John Coakley, "'Primordialism' in Nationalism Studies: Theory or Ideology?," *Nations and Nationalism* 24, no. 2 (2018).

[19] Robin M. Williams, Jr., "The Sociology of Ethnic Conflicts: Comparative International Perspectives," *Annual Review of Sociology* 20 (1994): 59; Sarah Belanger and Maurice Pinard, "Ethnic Movements and the Competition Model: Some Missing Links," *American Sociological Review* 56, no. 4 (1991).

[20] Michael Hechter, *Internal Colonialism: The Celtic Fringe in British National Development, 1536–1966* (Berkeley, CA: University of California Press, 1975).

[21] Ted Robert Gurr, *Why Men Rebel* (Princeton, NJ: Princeton University Press, 1970); Amy Chua, "Markets, Democracy, and Ethnicity: Toward a New Paradigm for Law and Development," *The Yale Law Journal* 108, no. 1 (1998).

[22] Michael Banton, *Racial and Ethnic Competition* (Cambridge and New York: Cambridge University Press, 1983); Susan Olzak, *The Dynamics of Ethnic Competition and Conflict* (Palo Alto, CA: Stanford University Press, 1992).

[23] Ted Robert Gurr, *Minorities at Risk: A Global View of Ethnopolitical Conflicts* (Washington, DC: United States Institute of Peace Press, 1993), 38–42, 126.

the objective differences between groups than relational comparisons that form the basis of grievances.[24]

Nationalist leaders link grievances to the group's status within the existing state, and offer self-determination as a path to overcome perceived injustice.[25] They often trace historically the cumulated injustices resulting from the group's inclusion within the existing state, whether these are based on economic disparities, lack of control over natural resources, denial of linguistic rights, or a host of other possible grievances. Structural conditions and discriminatory practices are clearly present, but they are selectively used in group mobilization. Claims to self-determination become the main focal point of mobilization.

The state generally views these claims as a threat to its territorial integrity and sovereignty.[26] States in Canada, Spain, the United Kingdom, China, Indonesia, India, Russia, and many other countries have considered nationalist claims as a challenge to their sovereignty. They have taken measures to prevent secession while remaining suspicious that devolving too many powers to autonomous units might fuel future secession.[27]

Their grievances and claims, therefore, are typically targeted at the state. While conflict might involve the group as an ethnic "minority" against a majority ethnic group in control of the state, in other cases the conflict will be directed at the state even when no particular ethnic group controls it.[28] Grievances, therefore, are not necessarily linked to interethnic group conflict but are almost always characterized as a conflict between the group and the state.

The choice of mobilization and political action is also directed at the state. Where institutional channels are available, nationalist groups use electoral

---

[24] Donald Horowitz, *Ethnic Groups in Conflict* (Berkeley, CA: University of California Press, 1985).

[25] Michael Hechter, *Containing Nationalism* (Oxford: Oxford University Press, 2000), 113–32; Andreas Wimmer, *Nationalist Exclusion and Ethnic Conflict: Shadows of Modernity* (Cambridge: Cambridge University Press, 2002); Ted Robert Gurr, *Peoples Versus States: Minorities at Risk in the New Century* (Washington, DC: United States Institute of Peace Press, 2000), 66–81, 195–206. For a discussion of circumstances under which grievances actually do lead to new nation-states as a result of nationalist mobilization, see Roeder, *Where Nation-States Come From*, 259–89.

[26] For an approach that emphasizes the different ways in which states and ethnic groups (nations) relate to territory, and its implications for conflict, see Toft, *The Geography of Ethnic Violence*. In particular, she emphasizes how multinational states "view disputed territory as indivisible, thereby increasing the likelihood of war," even if it means strongly defending worthless territory (p. 28). She argues that they are particularly concerned with precedent setting.

[27] These arguments have been advanced in particular in the context of "ethnofederalism" in the former Soviet Union and Eastern Europe. For example, Henry E. Hale, "Divided We Stand: Institutional Sources of Ethnofederal State Survival and Collapse," *World Politics* 56 (2004).

[28] It is not particularly clear, for instance, that states such as Indonesia or India are controlled by any particular majority group. Even in the case of Indonesia, where Javanese are predominant and have a strong presence in the state, it would be erroneous to conclude that it is a Javanese-dominated state.

representation, cabinet-level representation, lobbying, or courts. They form local political parties, sometimes with clearly stated nationalist objectives. When these options are less available or seem to fail, they might use a number of different extra-institutional strategies, such as demonstrations, protests, or sit-ins. Given the generally high reluctance of the state to accommodate nationalist groups and the high degree of threat it perceives, the options available for compromise are often limited.

When Conflict Becomes Violent

Nationalist conflict, although deep-seated, is not always violent. Long, non-violent episodes can follow violent ones, with grievances still strongly present. The absence of violence certainly does not mean that conflict is absent or has been resolved. The state might be able, for instance, to repress violent outbreaks even if tensions are running very high. Yet, recent literature has placed much emphasis on conditions of violent conflict but less on the range of non-violent forms. Factors that explain violent episodes might be quite different from those that explain conflict more broadly.[29]

The observable expression of conflict varies and the range is quite broad. It includes diverse forms such as the vocal expression of an ethnic group's grievances through established political channels, the use of the media or other public forums to advance group claims, and street protests or demonstrations.[30] These can all express conflict and be indicators of deeply entrenched grievances, without the outbreak of violence, which is of course its most visible expression.

Nevertheless, it might also entail less visible forms. Ethnic groups might increasingly limit their interaction with others. They might develop stronger and more loaded stereotypes against each other, or discriminate against members of the other group. Such forms of conflict may be less measurable and observable, yet constitute significant evidence of increasing tensions and potential escalation.[31]

Violence is an indicator of conflict but its spread or intensity is related more to factors that influence violence per se rather than a measurement of the depth

---

[29] For instance, Brubaker and Laitin had outlined excellent trajectories for investigating the specific conditions triggering violence, as opposed to the broader conditions leading to conflict. See Rogers Brubaker and David D. Laitin, "Ethnic and Nationalist Violence," *Annual Review of Sociology* 24, no. 1 (1998).

[30] While the Minorities at Risk data set attempted to code such differences by establishing a useful distinction between "protest" and "rebellion," I suggest that the emphasis placed in recent years on conditions of violent expressions of conflict have tended to neglect the "protest" or less visible forms of resistance. Gurr, *Minorities at Risk*.

[31] Protests and demonstrations also rose in many cases of democratic transition during the 1990s. See Gurr, *Peoples Versus States*, 156–57.

of grievances. It is a particular expression of conflict that, in turn, can vary widely, ranging from riots to civil war.

Nationalist conflicts are much more likely than other forms of ethnic conflict to end up violent. They always involve a confrontation with the state and the latter is well equipped to inflict violence on groups. State leaders tend to see nationalist groups as greater threats than other mobilized ethnic groups. Since claims to sovereignty and self-determination are either expressed or implied, the state often perceives them as "secessionist" threats. It frequently resorts to violent repression, deploying its security forces in the name of safeguarding unity and territorial integrity.[32] Conflict involving nationalist groups, therefore, are much more prone to civil war, insurgency, and state repression than other types of ethnic conflicts where the state might make greater compromises, extend some rights and protections to minorities, or act as arbiter between two ethnic groups clashing with one another.

Rioting of nationalist groups, as in cases of ethnic riots, requires a catalytic event and a small group that enflames and triggers the riot. "Background conditions," or grievances, simmer below the surface. They are present and "ripe" for violence to occur.[33] But riots are not uncoordinated, spontaneous acts. Triggering events and riot entrepreneurs are always present.[34] Perpetrators have some degree of coherent organization and carefully select targets. With sufficient provocation a small trigger can degenerate into a deadly riot. Conversely, some factors, such as the presence of networks of civic engagement, might prevent violence from spreading.[35]

Riots are often sporadic but can be precursors to a higher degree of violence. They can become recurring events or escalate to become more severe. Cycles of violence require more coordination and organization.[36] Riot entrepreneurs often frame state responses as further sources of grievance.

In the case of nationalist mobilization, these entrepreneurs are often linked to organizations claiming representation of the nation. Since nationalism requires a leadership that has framed grievances in terms of claims to self-determination, it is likely that riots will be tied to this leadership. But they can also be products of division between moderates and more radical nationalist organizations, or even peaceful demonstrations over which these leaders lose control.

---

[32] The case of Sri Lanka and the war against the Tamil Tigers is probably the most illustrative example of this trend.

[33] Donald Horowitz, *The Deadly Ethnic Riot* (Berkeley, CA: University of California Press, 2001).

[34] Ibid.

[35] Ashutosh Varshney, *Ethnic Conflict and Civic Life: Hindus and Muslims in India* (New Haven, CT: Yale University Press, 2002).

[36] Stanley Jeyaraja Tambiah, *Leveling Crowds: Ethnonationalist Conflicts and Collective Violence in South Asia* (Berkeley, CA: University of California Press, 1996).

Riots, therefore, are not necessarily indicative of grievances deeper than those expressed through more peaceful forms of mobilization. Peaceful protests or demonstrations are just as likely to be strong indicators of discontent. Riots are related to factors specific to the dynamics of violent escalation, including "sparks," triggers, and the presence of riot entrepreneurs. When they are linked to nationalist grievances, rioters typically target symbols of the state, ranging from courthouses, local parliaments, and agencies to branch offices of various departments. While these are indicators of such grievances, the violence is triggered by the dynamics of the riot itself.

Insurgency is a more common form of nationalist violent mobilization. It involves small bands of armed individuals using military technology, oftentimes from bases in rural areas, and which typically engage in sporadic attacks, bombings, or sabotage with the objective of undermining or overthrowing a political regime.[37] By definition, insurgency falls short of civil war when certain numeric thresholds are not met. Yet, its processes resemble that of civil war, in terms of both organizational or material resources required and background conditions leading to its emergence. On a lower scale, occasional insurgency or skirmishes are proportional to the degree of organization of the insurgents, state repressive capacity, and generally the (im)balance of forces between the state and the insurgent group.[38]

Civil war requires that an insurgent organization have a high degree of organization, mobilizational capacity, and resources to sustain violent attacks against the state over a steady period of time. It is a large-scale conflict

---

[37] Fearon and Laitin, "Ethnicity, Insurgency, and Civil War," 75; Carles Boix, "Economic Roots of Civil Wars and Revolutions in the Contemporary World," *World Politics* 60, no. 3 (2008). I do not make a distinction between "terrorist acts" and other forms of small-scale use of targeted violent acts. In recent years, the modus operandi of several groups has been influenced by the increasing use of terrorism to reach one's objectives. I include such acts in the variety of options that are used by relatively organized groups and that are equipped with some form of military technology, such as bombs. They tend to be more organized than instigators of riots but less so than groups involved in civil war.

[38] See, for instance, Lars-Erik Cederman, Andreas Wimmer, and Brian Min, "Why Do Ethnic Groups Rebel? New Data and Analysis," *World Politics* 62, no.1 (2010); Stefan Lindemann and Andreas Wimmer, "Repression and Refuge: Why Only Some Politically Excluded Ethnic Groups Rebel," *Journal of Peace Research* 55, no. 3 (2018); Håvard Hegre and Nicholas Sambanis, "Sensitivity Analysis of Empirical Results on Civil War Onset," *Journal of Conflict Resolution* 50, no. 4 (2006); P. M. Regan and D. Norton, "Greed, Grievance, and Mobilization in Civil Wars," *Journal of Conflict Resolution* 49, no. 3 (2005); James DeNardo, *Power in Numbers: Political Strategy of Protest and Rebellion* (Princeton, NJ: Princeton University Press, 1985); Jeremy Weinstein, "Resources and the Information Problem in Rebel Recruitment," *Journal of Conflict Resolution* 49, no. 4 (2005). Some studies, however, establish that excessive levels of repression might decrease the incentive to rebel and hence reduce the occurrence of violence. See Mark Irving Lichbach, "Deterrence or Escalation?: The Puzzle of Aggregate Studies of Repression and Dissent," *Journal of Conflict Resolution* 31, no. 2 (1987); Will H. Moore, "The Repression of Dissent: A Substitution Model of Government Coercion," *Journal of Conflict Resolution* 44, no. 1 (2000).

involving the state and insurgents able to mount armed resistance, contestation of the state's sovereignty, which the literature often defines as violent conflicts reaching relatively high thresholds of deaths.[39] Organizational strength, mobilization capacity, and degrees of state repression[40] all contribute to enabling or hindering large-scale, violent ethnic conflict. In addition, calculated rational actions by rebels, as well as some civilians, might engage in civil war in their attempts to secure and maintain control over a particular territory.[41]

Some types of grievances appear to be stronger causes of civil war, but they are also difficult to dissociate from opportunistic calculations of insurgent leaders. Economically based grievances, for instance, are strongly correlated with civil war's onset but can also involve calculations of costs and benefits relating to probabilities of gaining from the war, overthrowing the state and reaping benefits, as well as the material basis that provides opportunities to engage in war in the first place.[42] If so, armed insurgents might be more motivated by personal gain than expressing deeply seated resentment about poverty or inequality for their group.[43]

Supporting the contention that nationalist groups are much more likely to engage in civil war, some scholars show its greater likelihood when ethnic groups are involved.[44] Some reasons include an imbalance in ethnic group representation or support for ethnic parties.[45] Some attributes of ethnicity, such

---

[39] Nicholas Sambanis, "A Review of Recent Advances and Future Directions in the Quantitative Literature on Civil War," *Defence & Peace Economics* 13, no. 3 (2002): 218. See also E. Elbadawi and N. Sambanis, "Why Are There So Many Civil Wars in Africa? Understanding and Preventing Violent Conflict," *Journal of African Economies* 9, no. 3 (2000).

[40] Edward N. Muller and Erich Weede, "Cross-National Variation in Political Violence: A Rational Action Approach," *The Journal of Conflict Resolution* 34, no. 4 (1990).

[41] Stathis N. Kalyvas, *The Logic of Civil War* (Cambridge: Cambridge University Press, 2006).

[42] Paul Collier, "Rebellion as a Quasi-Criminal Activity," *Journal of Conflict Resolution* 44, no. 6 (2000); Cederman, Wimmer, and Min, "Why Do Ethnic Groups Rebel? New Data and Analysis." Nicholas Sambanis discusses the relative role of ethnicity in causing civil wars, but mostly shows that certain regions, and the presence of neighbouring countries that are undemocratic or at war significantly increases the chances of civil war. See Sambanis, "Do Ethnic and Nonethnic Civil Wars Have the Same Causes?" For a review, see Jeffrey Dixon, "What Causes Civil Wars? Integrating Quantitative Research Findings," *International Studies Review* 11, no. 4 (2009).

[43] Collier and Sambanis, *Understanding Civil War*.

[44] Sambanis, "Do Ethnic and Nonethnic Civil Wars Have the Same Causes?"; Paul Collier and Anke Hoeffler, "On the Incidence of Civil War in Africa," *The Journal of Conflict Resolution* 46, no. 1 (2002); Sambanis, "What Is Civil War?"; Boix, "Economic Roots of Civil Wars and Revolutions in the Contemporary World"; Cederman, Wimmer, and Min, "Why Do Ethnic Groups Rebel?"; Ibrahim Elbadawi and Nicholas Sambanis, "How Much War Will We See?: Explaining the Prevalence of Civil War." *Journal of Conflict Resolution* 46, no. 3 (2002); Lars-Erik Cederman, Kristian Skrede Gleditsch, and Simon Hug, "Elections and Ethnic Civil War," *Comparative Political Studies* 46, no. 3 (2013).

[45] Kanchan Chandra and Steven Wilkinson, "Measuring the Effect of 'Ethnicity,'" *Comparative Political Studies* 41, no. 4–5 (2008).

as religion, are more strongly related to civil war than others, such as linguistic differences.[46]

If grievances provide the background conditions that fuel nationalist claims, leaders are crucial, as I have argued, in framing demands to address these grievances. They do so in relation to a quest for self-determination and raise issues in territorial terms, with a view of seeking greater control over this territory. In order to achieve these goals, a number of mobilization options are generally available.

Leadership goals and mobilization resources mostly explain why violent expression of nationalist conflict escalates. Riots tend to be more unpredictable and more sporadic. They often arise from demonstrations and protests. Nationalist leaders who organize demonstrations might not anticipate that a riot will occur. In fact, riot entrepreneurs could be seeking other goals that contradict those of nationalist leaders. Insurgency and civil war require a higher degree of organization. In those cases, violent mobilization is a much more concerted decision, whether leaders seek its opportunistic use or whether they perceive it as defending the group's identity against the state.[47]

I suggest that four factors are particularly salient in mitigating the emergence and maintenance of a violent expression of nationalist groups. They complement other structural factors raised in the literature, such as rough terrain, state weakness, or the availability of natural resources.[48] But they are more likely to explain aspects of *violence* rather than *conflict* more broadly.

Degree of group organization and availability of military technology: Leaders develop a coherent organization that can be mobilized for the purposes of combating the state. They present violence as a means of achieving self-determination and seek legitimacy on the basis of claiming representation as leaders of their nation. The greater the availability of weapons and other military technology, the more they can oppose the state's armed forces and the greater the likelihood the conflict will degenerate into civil war.[49] Among

---

[46] Marta Reynal-Querol, "Ethnicity, Political Systems, and Civil Wars," *Journal of Conflict Resolution* 46, no. 1 (2002); Sambanis, "Do Ethnic and Nonethnic Civil Wars Have the Same Causes?"; Chandra and Wilkinson, "Measuring the Effect of 'Ethnicity.'"

[47] Weinstein, "Resources and the Information Problem in Rebel Recruitment," 619.

[48] For the classic emphasis on weak state and rough terrain as predictors of civil war, see Fearon and Laitin, "Ethnicity, Insurgency, and Civil War." For a discussion of natural resources and civil war, see Michael L. Ross, "How Do Natural Resources Influence Civil War? Evidence from Thirteen Cases," *International Organization* 58, no. 1 (2004). For state weakness and revolutionary movements, see Jeff Goodwin, *No Other Way Out: States and Revolutionary Movements, 1945–1991* (Cambridge: Cambridge University Press, 2001).

[49] For a similar point, using "capability" to describe this factor and its role in nationalist mobilization, see Toft, *The Geography of Ethnic Violence*. See also John McCarthy and Mayer N. Zald, "Resource Mobilization and Social Movements: A Partial Theory," *American Journal of Sociology* 82, no. 6 (1977); Cederman, Wimmer, and Min, "Why Do Ethnic Groups Rebel? New Data and Analysis." For a discussion on technologies of civil war and insurgency, see also

Southeast Asian cases, civil war erupted in Aceh in part because of the presence of a well-organized insurgent group, *Gerakan Aceh Merdeka* (GAM), as well as its ability to obtain weapons, whereas it largely eluded Papua, where no similar coherent organization was formed.

External support: External support for insurgency is often a key factor. Insurgent groups often rely on external support to attain higher levels of organizational capacity, to procure weapons, resources, and training.[50] There are two main forms: political and material. By political support, I mean recognition of the group's identity and claims, as well as an encouragement of its means to reach its goals. This support can come typically in the form of public statements or, in the case of external states, promoting the group's claims in international forums, such as the United Nations. Material support entails the provision of financial resources for the insurgent groups, weapons, aid, or even sheltering the group on its own territory, in the case of a neighbouring state.[51]

State repression: State repression has two different effects on the rise of insurgent groups: (i) it can suppress the rise of the group or eliminate it; (ii) it can fuel insurgency.[52] Although these are diametrically opposed effects, I suggest that the impact is a question of degree and timing. When the state uses high levels of repression but not sufficient military and police resources to suppress or eliminate insurgent groups, nationalists can organize, launch, and sustain insurgency. With very high levels of repression, including the use of military or police forces, as well as intelligence agencies, states are often able to thwart the emergence of insurgent groups.[53] At a lesser degree, state repressive capacity may leave sufficient space for groups to organize and are much more likely to create and maintain an insurgency if repression is high. With low

Stathis N. Kalyvas and Laia Balcells, "International System and Technologies of Rebellion: How the End of the Cold War Shaped Internal Conflict," *The American Political Science Review* 104, no. 3 (2010). For discussion of prior conditions relating economic wealth to the capacity to purchase arms and finance insurgency, see Ross, "How Do Natural Resources Influence Civil War?"; Weinstein, "Resources and the Information Problem in Rebel Recruitment."

[50] Patrick M. Regan, "Substituting Policies During U.S. Interventions in Internal Conflicts: A Little of This, a Little of That," *Journal of Conflict Resolution* 44, no. 1 (2000); Idean Salehyan, "Transnational Rebels: Neighboring States as Sanctuary for Rebel Groups," *World Politics* 59, no. 2 (2007); Idean Salehyan, Kristian Skrede Gleditsch, and David E. Cunningham, "Explaining External Support for Insurgent Groups," *International Organization* 65, no. 4 (2011).

[51] For a similar discussion on technologies of war and the role of military doctrine, particularly in the context of the Cold War and involvement of external powers in training and supporting insurgencies, see Kalyvas and Balcells, "International System and Technologies of Rebellion."

[52] Christian Davenport, "State Repression and the Tyrannical Peace," *Journal of Peace Research* 44, no.4 (2007); Joseph K. Young, "Repression, Dissent, and the Onset of Civil War," *Political Research Quarterly* 66, no. 3 (2013).

[53] As Davenport notes, however, the empirical evidence is weak to demonstrate the net impact of state repression on insurgency. See "State Repression and the Tyrannical Peace." See also Edward N. Muller, "Income Inequality, Regime Repressiveness, and Political Violence," *American Sociological Review* 50, no. 1 (1985).

repression, although the space is wider to organize, the incentives to do so are less.[54]

All three of these factors explain a large part of the variance in levels of *violence*. There are particularly dangerous combinations. For instance, a high degree of repression, high degree of group organization, and the availability of weapons supported by external actors are a particularly explosive mix that often leads to civil war.[55] A high degree of repression combined with low degree of group organization might appear to be stable but could also be toxic over time. When a nationalist group is repressed, has few means of organizing armed resistance, and has little significant external support, the levels of violence will be low or absent. Yet, it is likely to become more aggrieved over time. If significant factors change, such as the sudden availability of external resources, insurgency might rise very rapidly.

When violence is low or non-existent, *conflict* is not necessarily absent. Very high levels of state repression may thwart attempts to organize an insurgent group. Under such conditions, riots might occasionally occur, but otherwise conflict might not express itself through violent means. Even with structural opportunities where state repressive capacity is limited, low violence might not be an indicator of low levels of conflict. Where groups are divided, disorganized, lack organizational structure, or have no source of weapons or other military technology, they will not be able to mount an insurgency even if their grievances are strong, and the conflict is deep.

Figure 2.1 illustrates the mix of mediating factors. Individual effects of grievances are usually difficult to clearly distinguish. Yet, without grievances, there are few reasons why any groups would develop a nationalist agenda.[56] I take them as given, and focus primarily on mediating factors. As illustrated, the three factors of mobilizational capacity, state repression and external support contribute to the degree to which a conflict will become violent. By this perspective, it is incorrect, I contend, to equate high levels of violence with deeper grievances. In many cases, the degree of violence is less a predictor of grievances than these structural features that allow a nationalist group to use violent means, and the opportunity structure of doing so, given a state's repressive capacity.

Another mediating factor, I suggest, is also important: the *availability of alternative institutional channels to express discontent*. Violent mobilization is a costly option for nationalist groups. I hypothesize that the more channels are available to express their discontent and negotiate peaceful outcomes to conflict,

[54] Muller, "Income Inequality, Regime Repressiveness, and Political Violence."

[55] Young, "Repression, Dissent, and the Onset of Civil War."

[56] And they also form the basis of civil wars, although economic, political and cultural grievances are often intrinsically linked in ethnic civil wars, Sambanis, "Do Ethnic and Nonethnic Civil Wars Have the Same Causes?," 266–67.

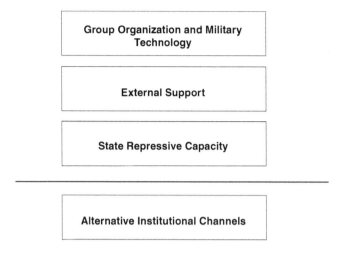

Figure 2.1 Mediating factors affecting violent nationalist mobilization

the less likely groups will resort to violent means of mobilization.[57] Formal institutional channels include cabinet and parliamentary representation, regional or local government where nationalist groups have exclusive or strong representation, the judiciary, or through administrative channels, such as committees or bureaucratic channels where they are consulted. Outside of formal institutional channels, they might use lobbying, protests, demonstrations, and statements in the media. Regime type shapes the parameters of these factors, as the following section contends.

Democracy and Nationalist Conflict

Democratic institutions shape the incentives and constraints of group mobilization. In theory, they offer institutional channels to express grievances and make claims. Parliaments at the national and local levels provide forums for discussion, criticism, and legislative measures to enhance group interests. Laws might extend minority rights, recognize identity claims, and create provisions for power sharing or for carving out exclusive jurisdictions. Autonomous territories, federal units, backed by legislated fiscal and administrative

---

[57] Schneider and Wiesehomeier make a similar assumption in their model testing the impact of institutions and ethnic diversity on civil war. They emphasize the mediating role that political institutions play in multiethnic societies, where the degree of inclusiveness and of fractionalization have a significant impact on conflict. Gerald Schneider and Nina Wiesehomeier, "Rules That Matter: Political Institutions and the Diversity—Conflict Nexus," *Journal of Peace Research* 45, no. 2 (2008): 186.

resources might also offer specific powers.[58] At the very least, democratic regimes create space for freedom of expression and association. Nationalist groups can use such channels to press for favourable policies, resources, or powers.

I argue that democracy matters for relations between nationalist groups and the state. While it might increase violence in an *initial* period of democratization, overall once stabilized, democracy tends to reduce violent nationalist conflict. Nevertheless, conflict often remains deep, difficult to resolve, and prone to renewed violent episodes.

I refer to democratization as a period from the dissolution of an authoritarian regime to the establishment of a relatively stable democratic one. Democratization is "the replacement of a government that was not chosen this way by one that is selected in a free, open, and fair election."[59] Furthermore, democratization is often preceded, or accompanied by liberalization, which is "the partial opening of an authoritarian system short of choosing governmental leaders through freely competitive elections."[60] The definition of a specific time period is often questioned, but liberalization entails the introduction of freedoms of expression and/or of association. In the case of democratization, the announcement of a path toward elections is key, with the criteria of the accountability of rulers to their citizens being the most important distinctive outcome of democratization over liberalization.[61] Although definitions of such a period vary considerably, there is at least

---

[58] Regardless of the mix of institutions, laws, rules, that regulate daily political life, by definition a democratic regime offers a number of political channels that greatly increases the ability to express grievances, make claims, and organize to reach political goals. The debate lies with the ability of ethnic groups to obtain particular kinds of institutional accommodations, and whether the impact of having more freedom to organize and voice grievances raises tensions and conflict, or reduces them. The literature is vast but some key texts include: Arend Lijphart, "Consociational Democracy," *World Politics* 21, no. 2 (1969); Donald Horowitz, "Democracy in Divided Societies," *Journal of Democracy* 4, no. 4 (1993); Larry Diamond and Marc F. Plattner (eds.), *Nationalism, Ethnic Conflict, and Democracy* (Baltimore: Johns Hopkins University Press, 1994); Philip G. Roeder, "Soviet Federalism and Ethnic Mobilization," *World Politics* 43, no. 2 (1991); Brubaker, *Nationalism Reframed*.

[59] Samuel Huntington, *The Third Wave: Democratization in the Late Twentieth Century* (Norman, OK: University of Oklahoma Press, 1991), 9. Huntington's definition remains classic, and establishes useful parameters for our conceptualization.

[60] Ibid.

[61] Guillermo O'Donnell and Philippe C. Schmitter, *Transitions from Authoritarian Rule: Tentative Conclusions About Uncertain Transitions* (Baltimore: Johns Hopkins University Press, 1986), 7–9. There is of course a very large literature on democratization that distinguishes democratic transition and democratic consolidation, as well as a debate over the appropriateness of elections as a benchmark. See also Larry Jay Diamond, "Toward Democratic Consolidation," *Journal of Democracy* 5, no. 3 (1994); Andreas Schedler, "Taking Uncertainty Seriously: The Blurred Boundaries of Democratic Transition and Consolidation," *Democratization* 8, no. 4 (2001); Guillermo O'Donnell, "Illusions About Consolidation," *Journal of Democracy* 7, no. 2 (1996); Timothy J. Power and Mark J. Gasiorowski, "Institutional Design and Democratic Consolidation in the Third World," *Comparative Political Studies* 30, no. 2 (1997); Omar

agreement over what constitutes its character: a phase of institutional change, of crafting and designing a democratic regime, of electoral competition, of building parties and other organizations to compete in the democratic arena.

Violent action is generally risky and costly; therefore, national groups avoid it if other channels are available and deemed promising for attaining their goals. Democratic institutions do so by shaping: (i) the degree to which groups are permitted to express grievances and organize; (ii) varying degrees of accountability in the use of state repression; (iii) formal group representation in institutions; and (iv) the legal environment for jurisdictional divisions and fiscal allocation. At the very least, a democratic environment offers a set of political options that are absent in authoritarian settings. Nationalist leaders, or even riot entrepreneurs, consider strategic alternatives available when deciding on political action.

There has been strong debate on the relationship between democratization and violent ethnic conflict. Many large-N studies have argued that it follows an inverted U-shaped pattern. Violence tends to rise in the initial phase after the fall of an authoritarian regime but then declines when democracy is more firmly established. While most studies compare across static regime types (from autocratic, semi-autocratic to advanced democracies), others infer that single countries would follow a similar pattern as they liberalize. In earlier work, Gurr found greater volatility during a transition but low levels of violent ethnic conflict in advanced industrial democracies.[62] Subsequent studies used more refined methods and confirmed the inverted U-shaped curve. Muller and Weede supported the argument through an analysis of cases in the 1970s. Hegre and others expanded to cases from 1816 to 1992 and confirmed the trend, while Fearon and Laitin later used data starting from 1945 and expanded to include the 1990s.[63] The decade of the 1990s that followed the fall of the Soviet Union and rise of several new civil wars also appeared to validate the trend of rising violence in semi-autocratic regimes or initial phases of democratic transition before declining as democracy consolidates.

Some studies nevertheless have challenged the inverted U-shaped curve. Saideman and his co-authors found a reverse relationship, arguing instead that

---

G. Encarnación, "Beyond Transitions: The Politics of Democratic Consolidation," *Comparative Politics* 32, no. 4 (2000).

[62] Gurr, "Ethnic Warfare on the Wane," 84–87. See also Gurr, *Minorities at Risk*; Demet Yalcin Mousseau, "Democratizing with Ethnic Divisions: A Source of Conflict?," *Journal of Peace Research* 38, no. 5 (2001).

[63] Edward N. Muller and Erich Weede, "Cross-National Variation in Political Violence."; Håvard Hegre, Tanja Ellingsen, Scott Gates, and Nils Petter Gleditsch, "Toward a Democratic Civil Peace? Democracy, Political Change, and Civil War, 1816–1992." *The American Political Science Review* 95, no. 1 (2001); Fearon and Laitin, "Ethnicity, Insurgency, and Civil War." See also Kristian Skrede Gleditsch and Håvard Hegre, "Regime Type and Political Transition in Civil War" in *Routledge Handbook of Civil Wars*, eds. Karl R. DeRouen and Edward Newman (Abingdon, Oxon: Routledge, 2014), 160–64.

violence declines in younger democracies; they explain this finding by postulating that some of the grievances have been addressed as countries became democratic.[64] Elbadawi and Sambanis conclude as well that more democracy leads to lesser risk of civil war, pointing also to poverty and to some degree of ethnic diversity as being important mediating factors. Vreeland tests and rejects the inverted U-shaped curve, and finds that regime type has basically no influence on civil war when correcting for some problems in the data.[65]

Some of these discrepancies reflect methodological differences.[66] Measurement of democratization, as a process, is often defined as a movement from one value to another on the Polity IV scale.[67] When defined, for example, as a three-point gain in the score, there is definitely an improvement in some of the multiple indices compiled to measure authoritarian and democratic features. Nevertheless, in some instances such movements on the scale occur from highly authoritarian regimes to lesser ones, with the endpoint being not a democracy but a semi-authoritarian regime. In other cases, the movement on the scale is nearer to the full democracy point, meaning that democratization entails the implementation of much higher democratic features in already established electoral democracies. Defining both as "democratization" because of the movement on the Polity IV scale can lead to comparisons of very different regimes. Some studies reclassify the scale and categorize scores in the middle position as semi-democracy, or autocracies.[68] Vreeland, however, argues that the use of the Polity index is problematic, particularly since most studies use the aggregate index instead of its components. As he notes, too many studies "blindly" adopt the aggregate scale without looking more deeply at how it is constructed. As regime characteristics in the Polity index might reflect ongoing civil war or political violence, there is a serious risk of a tautological relationship. When isolating political violence, Vreeland then finds that it has greater impact than the regime characteristics themselves, and

---

[64] Stephen M. Saideman et al., "Democratization, Political Institutions, and Ethnic Conflict: A Pooled Time-Series Analysis, 1985–1998," *Comparative Political Studies* 35, no. 1 (2002): 118. Saideman et al. use 10 years as a cut-off point and notes in footnote 23 that the results are not significantly different if they use 5 years.

[65] Elbadawi and Sambanis, "How Much War Will We See?," 329; James Raymond Vreeland, "The Effect of Political Regime on Civil War: Unpacking Anocracy," *Journal of Conflict Resolution* 52, no. 3 (2008).

[66] For a different, yet related, discussion of methodological problems due to the classification of types of ethnic conflict, see Benjamin Reilly, "Democracy, Ethnic Fragmentation, and Internal Conflict: Confused Theories, Faulty Data, and the 'Crucial Case' of Papua New Guinea," *International Security* 25, no. 3 (2000). For problems related to the use of the Polity IV scale and particularly for its interpretation of the middle range scores, see Vreeland, "The Effect of Political Regime on Civil War."

[67] Mousseau, "Democratizing with Ethnic Divisions," 557; Håvard Hegre et al., "Toward a Democratic Civil Peace?," 36; Hegre and Sambanis, "Sensitivity Analysis of Empirical Results on Civil War Onset," 515.

[68] Fearon and Laitin, "Ethnicity, Insurgency, and Civil War," 83.

calls for more precise variables related to particular regimes rather than a broad index.[69] Elbadawi and Sambanis reproduce some of the tests of the Collier and Hoffler civil war studies. While their results are similar in many respects, they show that democracy is associated with less civil war, and therefore argue that economic studies of civil war may have too quickly dismissed its importance. In response to arguments about the inverted U-shaped curve, however, their findings show greater incidence of civil war with political instability but not associated with democratization.[70]

Other diluted or contradictory results from the literature stem from the inclusion of nationalist groups under a broader category of "ethnic groups."[71] As discussed earlier, not all studies agree that ethnic diversity or ethnic mobilization is significant in increasing the risk of civil war. But few studies differentiate by ethnic group type. Yet nationalist groups are much more likely to use violence when opportunity structures shift. Their rejection of state legitimacy carries to the democratic context. They often seek secession or wide-ranging autonomy, and as Robert Dahl has argued "If the unit itself is not proper or rightful – if its scope or domain is not justifiable – then it cannot be made rightful simply by democratic procedures."[72] When studies do include proxies for nationalist groups (e.g., by measuring group concentration in a particular territory), they find much more significant effects of democratization on violent ethnic conflict, as group concentration tends to be associated with secessionist claims.[73] Muller and Weede found a higher degree of violence in "cases of separatism."[74] There is a good case, therefore, to analyse more precisely the effects of democratization on civil war in contexts where nationalist groups challenge the state.

Large-N studies, as discussed earlier, are inconclusive and more research is required to better determine whether democracy or democratization play

---

[69] Vreeland, "The Effect of Political Regime on Civil War"; Lars-Erik Cederman, Simon Hug, and Lutz F. Krebs, "Democratization and Civil War: Empirical Evidence," *Journal of Peace Research* 47, no. 4 (2010).

[70] Elbadawi and Sambanis, "How Much War Will We See?," 324–25.

[71] For a discussion of some of the measurement problems and slippery conceptualization of "ethnic groups", see ibid.

[72] Robert Dahl, *Democracy and Its Critics* (New Haven, CT: Yale University Press, 1989), 207.

[73] Gurr, *Minorities at Risk*; R. William Ayres and Stephen Saideman, "Is Separatism as Contagious as the Common Cold or as Cancer? Testing International and Domestic Explanations," *Nationalism and Ethnic Politics* 6, no. 3 (2000); Saideman and Ayres, "Determining the Causes of Irredentism." Indirectly, Cederman, Wimmer & Min find much higher probability of civil war when ethnic groups are excluded from power. Elbadawi and Sambanis find that ethnic polarization or ethnic dominance amplifies the impact of political development on civil war onset (pp. 329–30). Although the findings are suggestive of conflict process associated with nationalist mobilization, they do not specify the effects of nationalist groups. Cederman, Wimmer, and Min, "Why Do Ethnic Groups Rebel? New Data and Analysis."; Elbadawi and Sambanis, "How Much War Will We See?," 329–30.

[74] Muller and Weede, "Cross-National Variation in Political Violence," 637.

a role in civil war and, if so, through what processes. As Elbadawi and Sambanis concluded in 2002: "Certainly, more attention must be paid to the link between democracy levels and democratization as a process and how they affect societies' proneness to civil violence."[75] Gleditsch, Skrede, and Hegre in a review of the literature on regime type, political transition, and civil war in 2014 called for a more in-depth, fine-grained assessment of the impact of various aspects associated with democratic institutions, regime transitions, and civil war. They point to the fact that many studies use democracy as a proxy that carries too many assumptions about "motives and grievances, ... and various forms of opportunities of conflict" rather than more explicit discussion of these aspects.[76] In his 2014 sole-authored review of the literature on the relationship between democracy and armed conflict, Hegre concludes there is "no consensus of the relative importance of multiple explanations of the empirical observations," pointing to the fact that the large number of studies reviewed tend to use the same, very limited number of data sets, particularly Polity, which has been shown to have problems. He calls for more disaggregation of aspects of democratic institutions. Furthermore, he calls for more research on the "dynamics between socio-economic changes, institutional changes, and the incentives for the use of political violence."

Large-N studies have suggested a number of processes linking democratization and civil war, but are often short on systematically analysing these. They use proxy measurements and develop mostly basic inferences as to what might explain observed empirical patterns. I group some of these processes into three different categories: (i) changes in political opportunity structures; (ii) instability; and (iii) elite interests.

Many emphasize changing political opportunity structures that accompany democratization. In his overview of studies on the inverted U-shaped curve, Hegre points to repression mechanisms that are incomplete and democratic institutions that lack problem-solving mechanisms.[77] Muller and Weede had postulated that the "availability of reasonably effective peaceful means of political action" explained why violence would diminish over time in democracies.[78] Others argue that democracies generally tend to use less repression and less violence against civilians.[79] After its onset, civil war in

---

[75] Elbadawi and Sambanis, "How Much War Will We See?," 325.
[76] Gleditsch and Hegre, "Regime Type and Political Transition in Civil War," 147–48.
[77] Ibid., 163.   [78] Muller and Weede, "Cross-National Variation in Political Violence," 627.
[79] Kristine Eck and Lisa Hultman, "One-Sided Violence against Civilians in War: Insights from New Fatality Data." *Journal of Peace Research* 44, no. 2 (2007); Christian Davenport, *State Repression and the Domestic Democratic Peace* (Cambridge: Cambridge University Press, 2007); Michael Colaresi and Sabine C. Carey, "To Kill or to Protect: Security Forces, Domestic Institutions, and Genocide," *Journal of Conflict Resolution* 52, no. 1 (2008).

democracies tends to be less lethal, again suggesting that democracies tend to be less violent, less repressive overall.[80]

A second process emphasizes instability to explain a possible rise in violence. Hegre points to initial instability, which diminishes over time, to explain the inverted U-shaped curve.[81] Cederman, Hug, and Krebs identified instability rather than a static form of semi-democracy or partial autocracy to explain civil war onset.[82] In a slight variant, Fearon and Laitin had emphasized the underlying conflict over the set-up of the system that leads to violence, in the absence of a sufficient mix of political forces to crush rebels, thereby also reinforcing the changes in the ability to repress.[83] Gleditsch, Skrede, and Hegre also point to power struggles during regime change.[84] Overall, then, this line of explanation sees the rise of violence as temporary, being created mainly by instability that includes, somewhat vaguely, processes relating to power struggles, or the fact of change as increasing the probability of civil war.

Building more precisely from power struggles, the third process more specifically focuses on elites using violence to preserve or gain power at times of change. Snyder's influential study argues that elites from the former authoritarian regime are concerned with retaining power after a democratic opening and might use nationalist rhetoric to mobilize and foster support.[85] Such scenarios tend to heighten violence as they create rising ethnic tensions, in a strategy designed to gain backing from one group while excluding the other. Building from Snyder's original qualitative case comparisons, Mansfield and Snyder find broader validity, and reiterate the pathway of political leaders using nationalist rhetoric that unleashes belligerent politics or military and economic elites seeking to preserve their interests through war.[86] They find that democratic institutions that quickly consolidate avoid such consequences.

In sum, this brief overview inferred in analyses of democratization and civil war suggests several possible processes. First, there is a strong presumption

---

[80] Gleditsch and Hegre, "Regime Type and Political Transition in Civil War," 161; Nils Petter Gleditsch, Håvard Hegre, and Håvard Strand, "Democracy and Civil War," in *Handbook of War Studies III: The Intrastate Dimension*, ed. Manus I. Midlarsky (Ann Arbor, MI: University of Michigan Press, 2009); Bethany Lacina, "Explaining the Severity of Civil Wars." *Journal of Conflict Resolution* 50, no. 2 (2006).

[81] Hegre, Ellingsen, Gates, and Gleditsch, "Toward a Democratic Civil Peace?"

[82] Cederman, Hug, and Krebs, "Democratization and Civil War: Empirical Evidence," 379. See also Kristian Skrede Gleditsch, and Andrea Ruggeri, "Political Opportunity Structures, Democracy, and Civil War," *Journal of Peace Research* 47, no. 3 (2010).

[83] Fearon and Laitin, "Ethnicity, Insurgency, and Civil War," 85.

[84] Gleditsch and Hegre, "Regime Type and Political Transition in Civil War," 149.

[85] Snyder, *From Voting to Violence.*

[86] Edward D. Mansfield and Jack Snyder, "Democratic Transitions, Institutional Strength, and War," *International Organization* 56, no. 2 (2002): 299; see also Gleditsch and Hegre, "Regime Type and Political Transition in Civil War," 149.

that democratization changes the state's calculus over the use of repression. It also offers alternative means of conflict resolution.[87] These align with hypothesized effects of democratization outlined at the outset of this chapter. Second, "instability" appears to be a strong feature, particularly when a regime is still transitional. There are various ways in which it might manifest, such as an opportunity (or defensive) attempt by groups to exploit a window of lower state repressive capacity to mobilize, therefore increasing risks of violence. Third, in some scenarios, certain elites from the previous authoritarian regimes might use nationalist rhetoric in the absence of strong democratic institutions to mobilize, whether for electoral purposes or to preserve their interests. In either case, this heightens the probability of violence. This last process, I suggest, is much narrower and applies to a sub-set of cases where appeals to ethnic identity along exclusivist lines might actually increase elite pay-offs. Competitive environments where ethnic groups might be large and relatively equal in size are certainly a ripe terrain, but where groups are quite different in size, such strategies are rare since factions within the dominant group are likely to be the main contenders for state power. In many cases of civil war, and particularly when secessionist groups are involved, there is no attempt to seize control of the state or compete for power at the centre, but to carve out territorial autonomy or gain independence. As the literature has suggested, but not systematically, such "secessionist" scenarios are much more likely to lead to civil war.

Qualitative studies can offer more detailed, case-based analyses to more precisely determine possible processes linking democratization to civil war, in particular in the context of diverse ethnic societies. As the empirical chapters will show, Southeast Asian cases support the broader finding that transitions from authoritarian to democratic regimes often lead to political instability, even civil war, but mostly in the short term.[88] They also confirm that, over the long run, violence tends to decline as democracy stabilizes. Yet, there is a significant amount of variance that requires explanation. Why, for instance, did civil war re-emerge in Aceh after the democratic opening in Indonesia, while very little violence erupted in Papua? Why were responses to democratization different in the Philippines, when there were insurgencies both in the Cordillera Highlands and in Mindanao? There are some clear cases where new democracies appear

---

[87] Lars-Erik Cederman, Kristian Skrede Gleditsch, and Julian Wucherpfennig, "Predicting the Decline of Ethnic Civil War: Was Gurr Right and for the Right Reasons?," *Journal of Peace Research* 54, no. 2 (2017); Hegre et al., "Toward a Democratic Civil Peace?"; Caroline A. Hartzell and Matthew Hoddie, *Crafting Peace: Power-Sharing Institutions and the Negotiated Settlement of Civil Wars* (University Park, PA: Pennsylvania State University Press, 2007).

[88] Jacques Bertrand, *Nationalism and Ethnic Conflict in Indonesia* (Cambridge; New York: Cambridge University Press, 2004); "Autonomy and Stability: The Perils of Implementation and 'Divide-and-Rule' Tactics in Papua, Indonesia."

less prone to violence initially. We need better understanding of how nationalist groups respond to less repression and more democratic opening. Do they mobilize regardless? Why would they respond violently to states offering to address their grievances or allowing more space to mobilize in non-violent ways?

The following conceptual framework offers a dynamic analysis of regime change over time, while comparing across cases. It is developed from hypothesized factors drawn from existing literature, in conjunction with the inductive analysis of Southeast Asian cases. The starting point is the inverted U-shaped curve hypothesis that is derived not from static comparisons of different regime types but from tracing over time regime change from authoritarian rule to democratic stability.

I propose a modified curvilinear relationship between regime change over time and violent insurgency. As Figure 2.2 shows, a bell curve better represents the trajectory of several cases during a period of democratization. As will be explained, the tails indicate less rapid rise in violence than an inverted U-shaped curve would suggest in the early stages of democratization, while recognizing more persistent yet less intense violence even after democracy stabilizes. While recognizing that both are general and probabilistic representations, the bell curve better captures at both ends certain processes that also explain why there is a fair amount of variance in levels of violence.

Figure 2.2 shows the general progression of violence in the five cases covered in this book. The case of Aceh follows a fairly paradigmatic curve, while others are much flatter, with the peaks of violent insurgency varying quite significantly. The case of Thailand stands out for following a distinct path, which is consistent with the structural limitations of nationalists' violent mobilization. The dark grey line shows a "typical" bell curve and how each case compares to it.

I divide the framework's explanation and subsequent empirical chapters into two stages of analysis. First, I define a period of democratization, which is the stage from the fall of an authoritarian regime to the stabilization of democracy. The second traces change under democratic stability.

Democratization triggers a change in institutional constraints and opportunities; in combination with a high degree of organization, it increases the probability of violence. I emphasize the role of uncertainty in raising the incentives for violence. Rebellions, insurgency, or significantly high degrees of violence require organization, irrespective of the degree of institutional change. Their combination might explain why, in some instances, civil war breaks out whereas in others there might be occasional demonstrations. Yet, at the same time democratic institutions mediate the relationship and help to explain why leaders on either side might refrain from violent mobilization and seek, instead, other

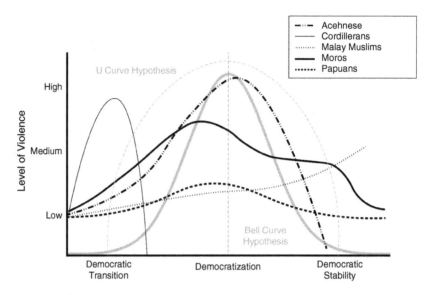

Figure 2.2 Phases of democratization and levels of violent national conflict

forms of reaching their objectives.[89] There is some degree of variance in the response, as well as different patterns leading to violence.

Once stabilized, however, these institutions provide new constraints and opportunities, predictable channels to express discontent and rules regulating relations between nationalist groups and the state. When uncertainty is withdrawn, violence is reduced in part because it takes away the pre-emptive temptation to use violence as bargaining leverage. The costs become higher to mobilize as a challenge to new democratic rules, rather than one of several ways to bargain for some accommodating institutions. Furthermore, as Elkins and Sides contend, the "type of learning process takes place for citizens and especially for minorities, who observe that the political system protects these liberties and that there will be future opportunities to seek power. Democracy will engender more certainty regarding participatory channels, if not outcomes."[90] While opportunities arise to negotiate, the new institutions might also limit the degree to which nationalist groups can make gains.

[89] Beissinger's analysis of nationalist mobilization in the former Soviet Union showed the usefulness of considering agency and nationalist mobilization as an "event" to be analysed alongside structural pre-conditions and institutional constraints. See Mark R. Beissinger, *Nationalist Mobilization and the Collapse of the Soviet State* (Cambridge: Cambridge University Press, 2002).

[90] Zachary Elkins and John Sides, "Can Institutions Build Unity in Multiethnic States?," *American Political Science Review* 101, no. 4 (2007): 694. They are one of a handful of studies that

Early Democratization: The Parameters of Uncertainty

The early phase of democratization produces more uncertain outcomes, and sometimes more violence. During this period, the nature of the institutions themselves are being renegotiated, with many more possible outcomes, ranging from full accommodation of various demands to crisis, breakdown, and a return to some form of authoritarian rule. Nationalist groups might be worried that constitutional negotiations or new democratic institutions fail to provide them with greater self-determination. Whether defensively or offensively, they will seek to make gains. The strategic use of violence depends on how they perceive the state's receptiveness to their claims as well as alternative options to advance their goals.

When authoritarian regimes fall or begin to liberalize, the future path is often indeterminate.[91] A coup can prevent further liberalization, thwart planned elections, or derail the establishment of democratic institutions. Elections might be held yet return to power the previous authoritarian rulers. Aspects of representation might be implemented, while preserving authoritarian features, thereby transforming into a competitive authoritarian regime rather than a democratic one.[92] While an authoritarian regime constitutes a period of stable institutions, when it begins to unravel actors and groups compete for political power and resources.

A critical juncture opens up, during which new opportunities or fears arise. Nationalist groups can negotiate new terms of inclusion in the state.[93] Stakes rise as they attempt to make gains or, at the very least, prevent an erosion of their status.

Uncertainty shapes strategies during a transitional period. Constitutions are open to negotiation, and therefore allow nationalists to seek recognition or self-determination in basic law. Parliaments consider electoral laws, decentralization, fiscal administration, and might adopt new laws to regulate all of these aspects.[94] Parliaments themselves are constituted and the nature of representation is determined during the transitional phase, with nationalist groups sometimes nearly absent. State repression is subjected to scrutiny, to the extent that

---

attempt to assess the short- and long-term impacts of democracy in multi-ethnic states. They find that in the short-term minorities become less attached to the state during a democratic transition, but their loyalties increase as democracy matures.

[91] O'Donnell and Schmitter, *Transitions from Authoritarian Rule.*

[92] Steven Levitsky and Lucan Way, *Competitive Authoritarianism: Hybrid Regimes after the Cold War* (Cambridge: Cambridge University Press, 2010).

[93] Bertrand, *Nationalism and Ethnic Conflict in Indonesia*, 9–27.

[94] In Indonesia, for instance, new laws were passed on elections and decentralization, and negotiations to amend the Constitution on these questions began only months after President Suharto resigned in May 1998, and President Habibie was inaugurated. For more on this period, see Donald L. Horowitz, *Constitutional Change and Democracy in Indonesia* (Cambridge; New York: Cambridge University Press, 2013); Bertrand, *Nationalism and Ethnic Conflict in Indonesia.*

memories of the previous authoritarian regime remain vivid and security forces are often discredited.[95]

Nationalist leaders sometimes use violent mobilization as a means of negotiating new concessions for self-determination, at a time when the state is weak and several other groups are positioning themselves to make gains under new constitutional arrangements. Periods of rapid institutional change open up opportunities to make gains.[96] When constitutions are reopened, representative institutions are modified, the distribution of fiscal resources is reassessed, several groups jockey to increase their share of power. At the same time, others seek to protect past gains, might even feel threatened if the previous authoritarian regime provided special protection or benefits. Mobilization therefore does not reflect deep-seated grievances long repressed under authoritarian rule but a balanced calculus about protecting group interests, making gains, as well as redressing some more recent or more deep-seated grievances. As Beissinger notes, a "quiet" politics of nationalism when state institutions are still dominant and struggles revolve around the imposition of a certain "national order" and resistance to it, is followed by a "noisy" politics of nationalism, "precipitated by a perceived opening of political opportunities, in which the political order and its institutions (including the definition of the boundaries of the community) come under direct challenge and contest."[97]

Democratization shifts some of the parameters of conflict identified earlier and in some circumstances increases the risk of violence. In the immediate fall of a democratic regime, the degree of group organization and availability of military technology will be little changed. Groups that are organized and that have had the capacity to mount an insurgency and obtain weapons will still have them available. The conditions under which they operate changes: they might strike out of opportunity or the fear of greater losses.

Furthermore, there is a risk that democratization can trigger the rise of intra-group competition, with significant impact on insurgency and group

---

[95] There is a debate as to whether democracies are less repressive. Generally, as Davenport contends, most scholars agree that democratization reduces the use of repression. But there are circumstances that make continued use of repression still likely, particularly in "semi-democracies," or transitional regimes. See Patrick M. Regan and Errol A. Henderson, "Democracy, Threats and Political Repression in Developing Countries: Are Democracies Internally Less Violent?," *Third World Quarterly* 23, no. 1 (2002); Jan Henryk Pierskalla, "Protest, Deterrence, and Escalation: The Strategic Calculus of Government Repression," *Journal of Conflict Resolution* 54, no. 1 (2010).

    For a discussion of how constitutions and the legal framework constrain governments and their use of state repression, see Daniel W. Hill and Zachary M. Jones, "An Empirical Evaluation of Explanations for State Repression," *American Political Science Review* 108, no. 3 (2014).

[96] Sidney Tarrow, *Power in Movement: Social Movements and Contentious Politics* (Cambridge: Cambridge University Press, 1998).

[97] Beissinger, *Nationalist Mobilization and the Collapse of the Soviet State*, 26.

organization. When a group splits between more moderate and more extreme groups, violence is much more likely. Oftentimes, insurgent groups have enjoyed strong local support under authoritarian rule as they were seen as the only available representatives. When democratization occurs, restrictions on the formation of political parties, organizations, and associations are lifted. Nationalist groups might form new organizations and political parties to claim representation. Conversely, insurgent groups might split into more moderate and more extreme factions.[98] More extreme groups often attempt to crowd out their competitors or remain relevant by unleashing violence. They often seek to derail and undermine the legitimacy of negotiations. Intra-group competition therefore increases the probability of violence when a group already had the organizational capacity and military technology to mount an insurgency.[99] The split faction continues to tap into supporters of violence and previously available sources of military technology.

External support is little changed in the short term, when an authoritarian regime first declines. External actors that have provided weapons and military technology are still present.[100] One significant exception is when the insurgency and its external supporters have been players in the downfall of the authoritarian regime. In that case, external actors might have a high degree of influence over the direction of the new democracy and its response to nationalist claims.[101] For the most part, however, such circumstances are rare.

State repression and the availability of alternative institutional channels to express discontent are the two factors that begin to change significantly. Democratization reduces the state's ability to repress but within certain limits, as instability remains and the armed forces often still operate independently.[102] Much of the decline in violence over time can be attributed to less state repression, as argued earlier.[103]

---

[98] For a thorough analysis of the impact of fragmentation on the organization of insurgency, see Paul Staniland, *Networks of Rebellion: Explaining Insurgent Cohesion and Collapse* (Ithaca, NY: Cornell University Press, 2014).

[99] Jacques Bertrand and Sanjay Jeram, "Democratization and Determinants of Ethnic Violence: The Rebel-Moderate Organizational Nexus," in *Democratization and Ethnic Minorities: Conflict or Compromise?*, eds. Jacques Bertrand and Oded Haklai (New York: Routledge, 2014).

[100] Regan, "Substituting Policies During U.S. Interventions in Internal Conflicts."; Salehyan, Gleditsch, and Cunningham, "Explaining External Support for Insurgent Groups."

[101] Recent and most glaring examples are the external support from the United States and some of its allies in Iraq, and the subsequent role in crafting Iraq's new political regime after the downfall of Saddam Hussein. See John McGarry, "Asymmetry in Federations, Federacies and Unitary States," *Ethnopolitics* 6, no. 1 (2007).

[102] For an argument regarding the "domestic democratic peace" as a parallel to the democratic peace literature on inter-state war, see Davenport, "State Repression and the Tyrannical Peace."

[103] Muller and Weede, "Cross-National Variation in Political Violence."; Ted Robert Gurr and Will H. Moore, "Ethnopolitical Rebellion: A Cross-Sectional Analysis of the 1980s with Risk Assessments for the 1990s," *American Journal of Political Science* 41, no. 4 (1997).

Following the bell curve in Figure 2.2, there are risks that the relaxation of repression increases the probability, and opportunity, for violent mobilization: under authoritarian rule, repression is high and violent mobilization is low; with democratization, as repression declines, violence sometimes rises but when democracy stabilizes and reaches a higher level, once again violence declines.

Against nationalist groups, state repression might well remain high. As Davenport has noted, state repression is less a function of absolute structural characteristics, such as democratic institutions, and more a result of strategic assessments by state leaders of costs and benefits given certain structural constraints.[104] Because nationalist groups reject the state's legitimacy and are portrayed as secessionist, democratizing regimes are more likely to continue using their armed forces against them and, in particular, when nationalist groups are concentrated in a small territory and far from the broader public view, such as in Thailand. During this transitional period, the armed forces often continue to operate with little civilian oversight, and are more likely therefore to use force, even in disagreement with the new government. It is often over such groups that the armed forces claim their continued independence from civilian rule and cast themselves as guardians of state sovereignty.[105]

Faced with past or still current repression and high uncertainty as to whether their claims will be addressed in constitutional negotiations or new legislation, nationalists have incentive to mobilize strongly. If well organized and armed, they are more likely to continue an insurgency that began under authoritarian rule. State leaders will continue to be suspicious of nationalist group intentions, since the promise of democracy is unlikely to be sufficient in itself to reduce their grievances. As Rustow argued, "national unity," by which he meant the absence of secessionist tendencies or challenges to the boundaries of the state, is the single-most important background condition, and challenge, for democracy.[106]

The first steps that a state takes toward nationalists, therefore, could be crucial in the early days of democratization. Given the high costs of launching, or continuing, violent insurgency, nationalist leaders are equally likely to search for signals of a change in policy or new approach to their demands. Early state concessions can quickly reduce the uncertainty that fuels

---

[104] Davenport, "State Repression and the Tyrannical Peace," 4.

[105] This behaviour is consistent with what Davenport calls the Law of Coercive Responsiveness, by which the state almost always uses repression to counter significant challenges to the status quo, ibid., 7.

[106] Dankwart A. Rustow, "Transitions to Democracy: Toward a Dynamic Model," *Comparative Politics* 2, no. 3 (1970): 361. For a similar discussion, see also Juan J. Linz and Alfred Stepan, "Toward Consolidated Democracies," *Journal of Democracy* 7, no. 2 (1996): 123. Linz and Stepan refer to problems of "stateness" as the most significant challenge to new democracies.

violence.[107] When the state offers concessions prior to democratizing, or when it first begins to liberalize, then it sends a signal that it is ready to negotiate new terms in response to nationalist demands.[108]

I suggest that this pattern is sufficiently common to produce an initially flatter curve in the relationship between democratization and violence. Whether because potential insurgents wait for a brief time to assess the state's willingness to compromise, negotiate, or provide concessions, or respond positively to initial state gestures, the very first phase of democratization oftentimes shows little to no violence. In the first half of the bell curve, violence rises more rapidly after that initial period of time, if the state does not produce signs of compromise or small concessions made prove to be too little to address grievances.

By "concessions," I mean that the state grants something to groups in response to their mobilization. This can be as little as some form of confidence-building measure prior to some negotiations to passing legislation that meets some of their demands. I conceptualize them here mostly as proactive measures to appease rather than accommodate claims to self-determination. Institutional solutions tend to reduce incentives for mobilization when they respond to demands for some form of territorial control, devolution of power, as well as some form of recognition of group claims to nationhood. While all three are unlikely to be met, significant movement toward responding to such claims helps to avoid violence and channel grievances into more regularized negotiations or institutional processes.[109]

---

[107] Cederman et al. emphasize how regional autonomy, although possibly positive, is often extended too late. They make the point that it tends to work as a preventive measure. Interestingly, they recognize the need for more research on "sequences of claims and concessions", as well as "strategic interaction among peripheral groups." See Lars-Erik Cederman et al., "Territorial Autonomy in the Shadow of Conflict: Too Little, Too Late?," *American Political Science Review* 109, no. 2 (2015): 368. Some scholars are skeptical that concessions reduce violence. Conceding sends signals to other groups that might also increase their demands. See, for example, Erika Forsberg, "Do Ethnic Dominoes Fall? Evaluating Domino Effects of Granting Territorial Concessions to Separatist Groups," *International Studies Quarterly* 57, no. 2 (2013). See also Barbara F. Walter, "Building Reputation: Why Governments Fight Some Separatists but Not Others," *American Journal of Political Science* 50, no. 2 (2006).

[108] Cunningham et al. offer an interesting analysis of dyadic relations and interactions between the state and insurgent groups. Moving away from structural conditions, they emphasize the importance of analysing the characteristics and strength of insurgent groups, and the impact of state concessions. David E. Cunningham, Kristian Skrede Gleditsch, and Idean Salehyan, "It Takes Two: A Dyadic Analysis of Civil War Duration and Outcome," *Journal of Conflict Resolution* 53, no. 4 (2009).

[109] Gurr summarized his findings over the 1990s that showed a decline in violent wars involving nationalist groups; he explained these as a result of greater democratization and accommodation of minority rights, in particular autonomy deals to address demands for self-determination. Cederman and Vogt concur with Gurr and, contrary to many previous findings in the literature, show that granting more autonomy was a strong reason for the decline in ethnic civil wars. They also interestingly show that democratization also reduces violent conflict, but not if it

The symbolic recognition of national diversity and corresponding rights is likely to decrease the probability of heightened ethnic conflict. Democratic constitutions often emphasize legal equality and equal treatment despite the fact that the human rights and cultures of minority groups have historically been repressed and disrespected. If a new constitution promises to secure only individual rights, nationalist groups and other minorities have little reason to expect to participate in the polity on par with the majority group.[110] Doing so may require that minorities forego their traditions and practices (e.g., language, rural life style, religion) in an attempt to fully assimilate into the dominant culture. This is why nationalist groups and other minorities often seek group-specific collective rights to help them participate as individual citizens without giving up their language, culture, religion, or other customs that correspond to their way of life. Accordingly, constitutionally entrenching group-specific rights following the transition decreases the impetus for rebellion and protest against the state.

Most importantly, granting more control over territory and devolving power to the nationalist group contributes to defusing violent mobilization. Some form of "autonomy" often encapsulates demands for both such power and such control. When groups first mobilize to obtain autonomy, the expectations are often low. Specific objectives are often vague and the threshold becomes gaining autonomy, while the latter remains undefined. In some cases, institutional structures associated with group representation are already present, usually in the form of local government with certain defined powers. While the existence of some form of territorial autonomy, even minimal, already provides a platform for mobilization, it also represents a benchmark against which to assess the state's further commitment to autonomy. Mobilization and negotiations then revolve around specific powers and resources, a deepening of already obtained autonomy.

Violence tends to decrease with promises of autonomy. For groups that were denied autonomy under authoritarian regimes, such promises could be sufficient to reduce mobilization, at least temporarily. Offers of more significant autonomy, when it was already in place, have similar effects. The absence of compromises, or concessions that are weak and meaningless, foment violent responses as they increase uncertainty and create doubt that the new institutional environment will accommodate group demands or address grievances.

In essence, democratization creates an environment that generally enhances "credible commitments," but not always automatically so for nationalist

ends only with semi-democracy. These findings are consistent with the framework presented here. Gurr, "Ethnic Warfare on the Wane," 55–58; Lars-Erik Cederman and Manuel Vogt, "Dynamics and Logics of Civil War," *Journal of Conflict Resolution* 61, no. 9 (2017): 269.

[110] Will Kymlicka, *Multicultural Citizenship: A Liberal Theory of Minority Rights* (Cotswald: Clarendon Press, 1995).

groups. As the literature on interstate war has shown, without credible commitments to enforce agreements providing security to both parties, conditions are often ripe for violence to emerge. When external actors broker negotiations, they can ensure that commitments made by warring parties are enforced, and therefore their involvement in negotiations enhances the chance that negotiations will reduce violence and sustain peace.[111] In situations of civil war that occurs in the presence of functioning state institutions and are therefore not operating under conditions of anarchy, the nature of these institutions and their impact on constraining power also has deep effects.

Democracy creates an institutional environment that facilitates credible commitments and can foster a reduction of violence and civil war. It is not easy for state leaders to credibly commit to a policy commitment in the future. In others words, when state leaders make a promise, it is difficult for the recipients to view it as enforceable in the future. As Acemoglu and Robinson argue, it is one of the reasons why state leaders decide to initiate democratization as a means of making credible their commitments to future distribution of power and resources. They wilfully accept to constrain their power in order to make credible the possibility that their promises will be honoured. One powerful incentive is to reduce citizen rebellion and social unrest.[112]

This process applies, however, to the relinquishing of elite powers to the citizens at large, the majority that benefits from democratization and increases its power relative to state leaders. While the regime as whole increases the credibility of commitments, it does not mean that promises made to particular groups will all be equally enforced. The broader contract with the majority might not automatically entail that promises to nationalists will be binding, but it increases the general expectation that they will be, relative to promises made under authoritarian rule.

By extension, under threat of civil war or to end it, state leaders may seek to make their commitments to nationalist groups credible. Certainly, democratization begins the process of constraining state leaders more broadly. As Weingast notes, it is generally more difficult in divided societies for rulers to abide by constraints. It requires an added layer of credibility that can be achieved through such institutional solutions as "the electoral system, decentralization of political power to more homogenous political units, and the

---

[111] David A. Lake and Donald Rothchild, "Containing Fear," *International Security* 21, no. 2 (1996): 43–49; James D. Fearon, "Commitment Problems and the Spread of Ethnic Conflict," in *The International Spread of Ethnic Conflict: Fear, Diffusion, and Escalation*, eds. David A. Lake and Donald S. Rothchild (Princeton, NJ: Princeton University Press, 1998); Barry R. Weingast, "Political Stability and Civil War: Institutions, Commitment, and American Democracy," in *Analytic Narratives*, eds. Robert H Bates, et al. (Princeton, NJ: Princeton University Press, 1998).

[112] Daron Acemoglu and James A. Robinson, *Economic Origins of Dictatorship and Democracy* (Cambridge; New York: Cambridge University Press), 136–37; 175.

imposition of explicit limits on majorities at the national level."[113] It also means that "equal rights to all citizens" is not enough and requires, instead, "institutions that provide for credible limits on the state."[114] Keefer shows that it is particularly difficult in situations of insurgency, as state leaders generally lack credibility, at least in the eyes of the insurgents, so violence still occurs as making binding promises to potential insurgents can prove almost impossible.[115] For this reason, when looking at instances of reconstruction after civil war, Coyne and Boettke add the additional point that political leaders must both "establish constraints *and* send a strong signal to citizens that they are sincere in their commitment to reform."[116] Such a problem, I suggest, occurs also in situations where there is potential insurgency, or after long periods without violence, and requires strong signalling if state leaders are to prevent new or renewed violence.

During the democratization phase, as I have argued, uncertainty sometimes outweighs the credible commitment quality of new democratic institutions. Because their nature, exact configuration, and stability are still in flux, they open up opportunities to use violence to extract greater concessions on accommodating institutions, or defensive reactions if nationalist groups expect a failure to meet their demands. It is a fragile balancing act, therefore, between degrees of uncertainty and the increased credibility that democratic institutions might foster.

Initial state gestures or concessions can be key in tilting expectations that democratization is creating greater credibility of the state's commitments. Initial reluctance to grant meaningful powers or resources, use of repression, or rigid refusal to negotiate may enhance uncertainty and fuel nationalists' pre-emptive use of violence. Initiating negotiations, providing gestures of compromise or concessions, can signal that democratization is changing the state's approach to nationalists. As commitments are made, passed in legislation and implemented, they contribute to building credibility. These gestures and concessions add to the new democratic institutions that are being built and that already make state commitments more credible than under authoritarian rule.

This is quite different, of course, from the scenario by which former elites of the authoritarian regime, oftentimes in control of the state, use nationalist rhetoric and violent mobilization to bolster their support. The argument in this book traces a different path that is mostly conditioned by the relative group size

---

[113] Barry R. Weingast, "The Political Foundations of Democracy and the Rule of Law." *American Political Science Review* 91, no. 2 (June 1997): 257.

[114] Ibid., 258.

[115] Philip Keefer, "Insurgency and Credible Commitment in Autocracies and Democracies," *The World Bank Economic Review* 22, no. 1 (2008).

[116] Christopher J. Coyne and Peter J. Boettke, "The Problem of Credible Commitment in Reconstruction," *Journal of Institutional Economics* 5, no. 1 (2009):7.

of the nationalists and the majority in control of the state, as well as the territorial concentration of the small nationalist group. As discussed earlier, such processes are different from those that Snyder observed, which involved groups more equal in size and more likely to compete for control of the state itself. In those latter cases, as Mansfield and Snyder emphasized, a thick network of civic institutions can defuse belligerent nationalist mobilization, particularly with the promotion of inclusive, civic identities and cross-ethnic political alignments *before* embarking on democratization.[117] Such institutions include the rule of law, an impartial bureaucracy, civil rights, and a professional media that, if adopted prior to freeing the press and organizing elections, will prevent violent mobilization. Civic ties across ethnic boundaries can also effectively reduce violence between ethnic groups, as pre-existing local networks of intercommunal civic engagements foster peace between ethnic groups.[118]

Yet, because nationalists as we have defined them here make claims *against* the state, they seek some form of autonomous control over their own affairs, even if they have close ties to members of the majority ethnic group. By building civic institutions prior to democratization, elites in control of the state might have fewer incentives to mobilize against nationalists but the latter are likely to perceive such institutions as attempts to quell their demands and integrate them within a broader set of centralized political institutions, without conceding to demands for self-determination. In effect, such strategies may well backfire and fuel, rather than prevent, violent outcomes.

In sum, democratization heightens overall the probability of violent conflict between the state and nationalist groups, yet there are also paths that lead to its reduction. Uncertainty over the state's future path, whether the regime will remain democratic, whether a new constitution might address nationalist claims all contribute to raising tensions and provides incentives for nationalist groups to mobilize and clamour for self-determination. Violence is even more likely to rise if the state responds with repression or nationalists split into moderate and radical organizations. Conversely, if the state offers concessions early in the democratization process, violence is less likely. Symbolic recognition of a group's national identity, minority rights, and promises of autonomy can greatly defuse violent mobilization during the democratization phase. While uncertainty opens up opportunities for mobilization as the state is weakened, or conditions groups to mobilize defensively, the path to violence is not inevitable.

---

[117] Mansfield and Snyder, "Democratic Transitions, Institutional Strength, and War"; Snyder, *From Voting to Violence.*

[118] Ashutosh Varshney, *Ethnic Conflict and Civic Life: Hindus and Muslims in India* (New Haven, CT: Yale University Press, 2002).

At a secondary level of analysis, three factors are important in explaining why states might extend particular kinds of concessions and whether the latter lead to a sustained decline in violence. The Southeast Asian cases suggest that electoral alliances and independence of parliaments can explain why concessions are offered. Electoral considerations are rarely key in explaining compromises with nationalist groups that are small. Nevertheless, majority coalitions in support of peace can be important electoral strategies where civil war has affected large parts of the country or when a ruling coalition is blamed for continued violence. In some cases, gaining electoral support of the nationalist minority can contribute to building a coalition government with multiple parties or building majority support in a fractured parliament.

The second factor, parliamentary independence, relates to its role relative to the executive. In presidential systems in which parliaments exercise a high degree of legislative independence and provide a check on the presidency, they can prevent or significantly alter agreements that are reached between insurgents or nationalist groups and state negotiators. Conversely, in parliamentary systems or presidential systems in which the executive exercises a high degree of control over parliament, it is easier to obtain approval for negotiated agreements. Given that parliaments reflect majority preferences, they will be likely supportive of the majority group's interests, often against agreements that will be perceived to favour small nationalist groups that have mobilized violently.

The third factor loops back to the credibility of commitments made and, in this case, can explain whether concessions will lead to more than only a brief hiatus in violence. Where concessions are deemed not credible because they fail to address grievances, then they are often followed by renewed insurgency. But it is also the case if concessions that do address grievances are not deemed credible because of the inability to guarantee that the state will follow through with its promise. In periods of democratic transition, such credibility can be very difficult to establish. Indeed, short of constitutional amendments, it is very difficult for the state, even under new democratic institutions, to convince nationalist groups that it will follow through on its commitment, whether these are negotiations, new powers and laws, or promises of more resources. As a result, extending concessions is itself part of a process of building credibility under the new democratic framework. There are therefore few cases where they might suffice to prevent a re-escalation of violence.

Table 1.1 summarizes these factors. Mobilization capacity has been high in two cases, Aceh and the Moros, where some degree of credible autonomy is eventually obtained. The variability of electoral pay-off contributes, along with a high independence of parliament, to a much more uncertain, cyclical, and murky path toward autonomy in the case of the Moros. With no electoral pay-off and low mobilization capacity among the Papuans, there have been few chances that they could obtain greater gains. The Indonesian state's credibility in the commitments made have been better than in Thailand, but remained relatively weak, leading to an undermining of the lesser autonomy that was extended. In the Cordillera, mobilizational capacity was low except initially. With a willingness to accommodate to some degree, high independence of parliament, and low credibility of commitment to autonomy, Cordillerans chose an exit strategy and support for an alternative set of demands as indigenous peoples. They gained strong support from an executive and parliament that saw the alternative as a low threat. Finally, all factors led to the absence of any form of significant accommodation from the Thai state to address Malay-Muslim grievances, in the presence of few electoral incentives to do so, low mobilization capacity, and low credibility of any potential commitment given the high degree of adherence of state leaders to the concept of a single, Thai nation.

Democratic Stability, Institutionalization, and Its Impact on Nationalist Mobilization

When democracy stabilizes, the parameters of nationalist mobilization become more fixed. With a new constitution in place, or new legislation regulating relations with nationalist groups, the array of possible negotiated outcomes is significantly reduced. Under new rules of the game, the state and nationalists continue to advance their respective interests: the former vies to protect state boundaries and sovereignty, with a preference for reducing the power of nationalist groups. The latter seek to gain concessions to enhance their power and territorial control.

The shift from uncertainty – and perceived greater strategic options – to more stable, democratic institutions enshrines a new set of rules regarding nationalist groups. Three scenarios are possible. First, if the state agreed to large concessions during the transitional phase, it is likely that new rules include a number of institutional arrangements that provide new powers and resources to nationalist groups, either in some form of autonomy or significant power-sharing at the centre. Second, if the state has resisted concessions, the new institutional environment, while more democratic, might have no constitutional or legal provisions that address demands from nationalists. Third, in many cases, the state has provided some accommodation of nationalist group demands but far less than what is sought for self-determination. Each of these three institutional environments have different impacts on nationalist groups, with only the first leading, in some cases, to a resolution or normalization of conflict.

In this section, I argue that overall a stable democratic framework reduces violent conflict, regardless of the three scenarios identified earlier. Yet, conflict remains endemic and sometimes deep, with potential for a resumption of violence in the last two scenarios. First, because it is very difficult to reduce the gap between the state's interests and nationalist claims to self-determination, there are strong incentives for the state to adopt strategies that undermine these groups. Second, both sides face greater costs of mobilizing violently, so they seek alternative strategies to repression and violent mobilization in advancing their goals. I discuss democratic stability as a different phase from transition.

Against the backdrop of these broader parameters, I then trace the impact of the variables associated with democratization. The credibility of commitments made increases under democratic stability only if the state has first made a commitment that addresses deep grievances of nationalists and if the institutional measures taken to implement them are sufficiently strong. These include constitutional clauses, legislation that is sufficiently binding, as well as new institutions that gain legally protected powers and resources. Second, the independence of parliament can remain a constraint as parliamentarians can still override or prevent the adoption of constitutional amendments, legislation, and new institutions, as well as ratification of peace agreements. Finally, electoral coalitions remain an important factor in shaping the commitments that the state makes and the degree to which it accepts binding measures to make these credible.

Defining Democratic Stability

Large-N studies that have attempted to differentiate transitional regimes, or new democracies, from more established ones typically use an arbitrary number of years (often five or ten) that qualify as transitional. Use of an across-the-board number of years allows us to capture a survival rate of democracies, and therefore a certain measure of stability.[119] Yet, it falls short of identifying specific criteria for stability other than longevity.

Studies of democratization, in turn, typically distinguish transition from "consolidation," but the latter often remains a distant objective. Some identify consolidation when democracy has become "the only game in town."[120] An alternative measure uses the "two turnover rule," according to which democracy is consolidated when elections have produced two rotations of power.[121] The emphasis in the former focuses on groups or organizations that might still seek to challenge the state or its democratic rules. In the latter, the time frame might vary considerably depending on whether a single party or presidential

[119] Saideman et al., "Democratization, Political Institutions, and Ethnic Conflict."
[120] Linz and Stepan, "Toward Consolidated Democracies."
[121] Huntington, *The Third Wave*, 266–67.

candidate wins successive elections, or whether the opposition twice replaces them. The criterion of democracy as the "only game in town" is particularly problematic as a benchmark in this study as nationalist groups often reject state authority and its boundaries. Consequently, once they accept democracy, the conflict is most likely resolved or, at least, sufficiently reduced that formal institutions are able to mediate the different views. Therefore, consolidation is unlikely to happen, by definition, without nationalists ending their mobilization.

There is a significant analytical gap, I suggest, between the uncertainty of the initial phase and consolidation in the sense of democracy being the "only game in town." I use the term *stability*, therefore, as a much more restricted meaning than consolidation, but more specific than only longevity. There is a difference between a new democratic regime whereby the main pillars are being crafted, and the regularization of a regime once constitutional changes have been made, new institutions established, and elections are held regularly (and free and fair), while only fringe elements threaten the new democratic order. O'Donnell and Schmitter identified transitional periods as ending with the first election, but this benchmark only works when there is a relatively long preparatory period and set of negotiations before these elections are held.[122] In cases where elections are held soon after the demise of an authoritarian regime, such elections might indicate mainly the beginning of a process of transition rather than its end. As a result, Huntington's "two-turnover rule" better captures a certain regularization of democracy, and an acceptance of the new rules of the democratic order.

To identify a more stable, yet still unconsolidated democracy, I relax this rule and identify one turnover as indicating at the very least a willingness on the part of the ruling party to cede power to the opposition. Furthermore, the armed forces should accept the new civilian order and not challenge executive authority.[123] Coup attempts are clear signs of a still unstable democracy but it could also mean that the armed forces engage in operations that override cabinet-level decisions. Finally, constitutional and legislative tools to regulate the new democratic institutions should be in place, including laws administering political parties, elections, provincial/regional authority, and fiscal authority.

---

[122] O'Donnell and Schmitter, *Transitions from Authoritarian Rule*.

[123] Of course, such a condition might be temporary. In Thailand, for instance, it appeared during the 1990s that the armed forces had accepted to relinquish a role in politics but the coup of 2004 and subsequent events in the country have certainly revealed that it was not the case. By contrast, it is clear in Myanmar that the armed forces continued to remain independent after elections in 2015 and maintained an influence over several aspects of governance.

Institutional Constraints and Democratic Stability

A relatively more stable period creates a different set of institutional constraints and opportunities for mobilization than an initial one of instability and uncertainty following the dissolution of an authoritarian regime. The length of time of a transitional period before this level of stability can be reached varies from case to case.

The most important difference is the effect of a more predictable institutional environment and the reduction of uncertainty. Once the period of uncertainty has passed, the new constitution, electoral system, and legislative foundations of the new democracy enshrine a certain type of recognition (or non-recognition) of nationalist groups. Both the state and nationalists reposition themselves within the new institutional framework that creates different parameters to negotiate future concessions. Nationalist groups assess the extent to which they have lost or gained in the new environment, while state leaders strengthen their control and legitimacy over the new democratic regime.[124] This period does not end mobilization or negotiation, but merely sets new institutional constraints.

A stable democracy also creates institutional and normative constraints on the use of violence. Both the state and nationalist groups have incentives to explore alternatives to violence, while also seeing greater potential costs for the state to use repression and nationalist groups to mobilize violently.

Irrespective of the capacity to do so, the state's use of repression becomes much more difficult to justify. During a transitional phase, state authorities or armed forces leaders might use the military or police force against opponents, in appeals to contain elements threatening the new democracy, particularly if they accused nationalist groups of "secessionist" tendencies. When democracy stabilizes, however, the use of the state security apparatus to quell demands or peaceful protests is likely to be met with accusations of continued authoritarianism and association with the previous regime. The public expects greater justification for repression beyond the normal use of police forces. Parliamentarians, the media, and non-governmental organizations question whether the use of force is appropriate, particularly if the government deploys the armed forces to repress a domestic uprising. State actions are more openly scrutinized and criticized. The use of repression is therefore much more costly.

---

[124] The case of Spain is telling in this respect. As a result of the fragility of the Spanish transition, the Spanish constitution created a category of "historic nationalities," which provided them with rights to negotiate new powers and institutions as a result of this recognition. Of course, with the recognition of rights to autonomy for all regions, the parameters of mobilization for the historic nationalities of the Basque and Catalans changed, but there were also new incentives for other regions to also mobilize for greater autonomy. See Luis Moreno, *The Federalization of Spain* (London: Frank Cass Publishers, 2001).

Meanwhile, nationalist groups also modify their strategies once democracy has been stabilized. A new constitution and set of democratic institutions seal their relationship to the new democratic state. Opportunities for renegotiation are narrower than during the transitional phase. As a result, what they have obtained is likely difficult to change. Some will have obtained large concessions and be assessing implementation, others will have been left without any firm state commitment.

Yet, violence is also costlier for nationalists. Although they might still reject the legitimacy of state boundaries, their use of violence will be less easily justified. In most cases, members of nationalist groups benefit from more freedom to organize, to express their views, to organize political parties, and to voice their grievances broadly. In some cases, they also lose the potential allies they might have had in the past when using violence against an authoritarian regime. Moros in the Philippines allied with communists against the Marcos regime, for instance. Karen insurgents allied with students who formed an insurgency against the military regime in Myanmar after the crackdown in 1990. The alliances of convenience often disappear once democracy has been stabilized. It further reduces nationalists' ability to use violence. Finally, they also must evaluate the sentiment of the majority public. More nationalist violence might turn a majority public in favour of the state using military force to repress the group's mobilization, whereas it might otherwise be critical of the democratic regime's use of military repression. By using peaceful methods of mobilization, nationalists reduce the risk of alienating the majority public that restrains the state's capacity to use violent repression, certainly by comparison to its authoritarian past.

While the institutional environment creates new parameters, some structural features nevertheless remain mostly constant. Mobilizational capacity, for instance, remains equally a structural limitation from the beginning of the transition to a more stable democratic period. Ultimately, if groups do not have the resources to resist violently, they are unlikely to do so. At the same time, the type and scale of violent actions will be mainly determined by the availability of resources and organizational capacity, rather than the nature of grievances.

Overall, then, democratic stability creates new institutional constraints and reduces incentives to use violence. The institutions more clearly define whether nationalist groups are recognized, represented in state institutions, provided with fiscal resources and control over their claimed territory, or provided with power-sharing arrangements in the central government. Stable democracies will vary in terms of the degree to which the new institutional structures accommodate nationalist groups, but the institutional rules will be much more clearly defined and less open to contestation than during the transitional phase. One can assess different degrees of accommodation of nationalist recognition, representation and empowerment, and their impact on their ability to use institutional channels to further negotiate or voice their grievances. Irrespective of the degree of institutional accommodation, the incentives to use violence – either state repression or nationalist violent mobilization – are greatly reduced, due to the lower tolerance of democratic publics for state repression, greater scrutiny and institutional regulation of the use of military force, loss of nationalist allies for violent mobilization, and lesser justification for use of violence in a generally more open, democratic environment.

Varying Outcomes under Democratic Stability

Beyond these broad institutional parameters, there are significant differences in outcomes. Ending violence, as argued previously, does not resolve conflict but only its most severe expression. A reduction or elimination of violence with continued deep grievances is a risky outcome, as it is often followed by renewed mobilization and even resumption of violence in the future. In this section, I account for varying outcomes, looking both at patterns of *violence* and the different possible *conflict* outcomes. The latter range from stagnation to mutually agreeable institutions that address nationalist grievances.

While democratic stability solidifies the institutional environment and therefore reduces the range of options available, it leaves a fairly broad set of possibilities. When conflict remains unresolved, and is not yet fully negotiated through normal institutional channels, it can remain deep, lead to extra-institutional mobilization, and even become violent once again. The legitimacy gap often remains wide, with the democratic state even more confidently maintaining its resolve to resist demands for self-determination, while nationalist groups appeal to democratic principles precisely to strengthen their claim and even cast it as a "right" that a democratic state should uphold.

State concessions carry a number of political risks and are not necessarily perceived as a "win-win" situation, even under democratic stability. The state becomes generally more constrained by public opinion in its use of repression, yet it still prefers to minimize concessions to nationalists. Concessions can greatly defuse nationalist incentives to mobilize, and contribute to a reduction of conflict. Yet, they are generally unpopular with the majority, as they are often perceived as conceding to secessionist demands. It is a careful balancing act to offer enough concessions to appease nationalists and reduce conflict, while also ensuring that the electorate and the majority group does not punish the government for "giving too much to secessionists."

On balance, concessions are more likely in early stages when newly democratic governments are still seeking stability. Later, once institutionalized, they are likely to remain more forcefully entrenched in established concessions and institutions. Further concessions are only likely if the state perceives the costs of the status quo to be too high.

Concessions, as defined in the previous section, refer to a broad range of actions and constitute attempts by the state to provide *some* power and/or resources to reduce nationalists' incentives for mobilization, while maintaining a preference for giving as little as possible. This is why they can vary from granting limited rights or resources aimed at coopting or displacing group demands to negotiating full-fledged fiscal and administrative autonomy that meets many of the nationalists' demands.

As with the initial period of democratization, two main factors influence whether the state will offer or deepen concessions made to nationalists: electoral coalitions and independence of parliament. Electoral coalitions can change over time, so there could be some significant shift away or in favour of extending more concessions, depending on whether an electoral coalition relies on support from small nationalist groups or forms a majority that has grown unwilling to support further state repression leading to violence, thereby supporting greater concessions if peace can be achieved. Similarly, an independent parliament will continue to make it more difficult for the state to enforce peace agreements or offer large concessions if the majority is reluctant to support them. Independent parliaments can often dilute concessions from the executive, or greatly modify peace agreements, in ways that intensify rather than alleviate nationalist resentment. Only in the case where majorities support peace at all costs are independent parliaments likely to provide support for extensive concessions.

The impact of concessions will vary in terms of the degree to which they respond to nationalist demands, as well as the credibility of the promise. Nationalists might reduce their demands and accept lesser concessions under democratic stability, as central government institutions might open up some new channels, and nationalist groups might splinter into several organizations seeking to represent them, as insurgent groups lose the advantage they might have held in closed systems. Nevertheless, overall, their demands are unlikely to shift rapidly or so radically that they would welcome state concessions that were previously deemed to fall well below their demands.

The more important change is the credibility of the promise. While democratic stability increases the credibility of commitments as it binds state elites to rules and institutional constraints, such credibility does not automatically extend to commitments made to nationalists. Concessions and commitments gain credibility through a process of trust building and changing expectations over time. Under democratic stability, there is a stronger expectation that such commitments will be more credible, but much depends on continued steps to convince nationalist groups that the state's general reluctance to concede to "secessionists" nevertheless produces concessions that are implemented.

I argue that there is much variance in this respect as states will try to limit their loss of power and resources from past concessions made. While autonomy or other forms of concessions are highly publicized during negotiated settlements, only their implementation reveals the true nature of powers and resources conceded. States continue to view nationalists as threats to their sovereignty, and therefore attempt to thwart their future ability to mobilize in favour of secession.

The state can use an array of bureaucratic and administrative means to limit or undermine concessions made. As these measures are less visible, they can be powerful tools to reduce concessions while publicly voicing strong support for accommodating nationalist groups and reducing conflict. In the end, what at first glance might appear as strong devolution of power might end up much more diluted.

In effect, we should expect that democratic stability creates an institutional environment that is favourable to more credible concessions, but their depth will largely vary depending on majority preferences as expressed through parliaments and electoral coalitions. Where parliaments are strongly independent but states willing to concede, the resulting struggle is likely to lead to failed commitments, such as dilution of peace agreements, reduction of commitments made, or legislation that remains subject to manipulation and erosion of powers and resources that are granted.

These factors on the state side interact with the effects of democratic stability on nationalist mobilization. Nationalists face a dilemma. If democratic institutions fail to satisfy their claims or to provide them with good opportunities to negotiate further, they will continue mobilizing outside of formal channels. Violent strategies can inflict the greatest cost to the state for failing to respond to group demands, but run the risk of backfiring. Sustained violence can create a justification for the state to use military or police forces, thereby escalating the conflict. More significantly, insurgent groups risk losing their legitimacy by using violence under democratic stability, in particular since they can be challenged by within-group organizations or parties using more moderate approaches. Democratic stability often leads to splintering of nationalist groups into more moderate organizations and political parties once alternative channels multiply. Finally, violence risks alienating organizations in the majority that might have been allies. Under authoritarian rule, nationalists can use violent strategies in alliance with reformers seeking to undermine the regime, but such strategic alliances are lost under democratic rule.

As in the earlier period, violence is ultimately shaped by the changing not only of institutional parameters that democratic stability provides but also of the structural preconditions of mobilizational capacity and state repression. As discussed earlier, state repression is ultimately reduced under democratic stability but still remains possible, particularly if nationalist mobilization remains violent. We should expect insurgency or large-scale violence to only be possible in cases where mobilizational capacity is high, although incentives to do so are greatly reduced.

Figure 2.2 therefore shows, under democratic stability, an expected decline in violence overall. Where it differs significantly from the inverted U-shaped curve, however, is once again a curvilinear smoothening at the tail indicating a general tendency for low-level violence to persist. Given the persistent large gap in preferences between state and nationalists, as well as tendencies for majorities and electoral pay-offs to generally favour less, rather than more concessions, I contend from the discussion earlier that the most likely outcome under democratic stability is significantly lower violence but persistent, deep grievances and endemic conflict. In this state, the likelihood of occasional, low-intensity violence remains, as well as high probabilities of extra-institutional mobilization against the state.

Against this broad trend, outcomes still vary and are worth analysing because of the conditions that lead to more lasting conflict reduction. In some cases, democratic stability will lead to conflict resolution by which violence is eliminated, and concessions allow nationalists to channel and negotiate their demands through regular institutional channels. But as argued, I expect this to be a rare case. Most likely, violence is reduced, some concessions made that are sufficient to thwart nationalists' ability to mobilize violently and still gain broad support, while encouraging movement splits, moderate political organizations to arise, or potential negotiations over future political agreements. While all of these measures can contribute to reducing violence, they can also entrench a status quo that maintains deep grievances and institutions that fail to respond to nationalists' perceived needs. This is the most likely scenario that, I propose, leads to sustained stagnation of the conflict, often accompanied by periods of low-level violence. Some conflicts will disappear over time but others will remain and spike from time to time. The bell-shaped, slow tapering tail of Figure 2.2 attempts to capture what I see to be a fairly generalized outcome in many cases of nationalist conflict, namely that most will remain less violent but unresolved, with periods of low-level resumption of violence and longer periods of deep grievances that manifest as extra-institutional actions such as protests and demonstrations.

Finally, I suggest that, in some cases, nationalists will "exit and reframe," often increasing the chances of long-term conflict resolution. It refers to a strategy of abandoning nationalist demands and recasting group grievances in different terms, which are less threatening to the state. One example is the shift away from demanding autonomy or secession to claiming indigenous peoples' rights. This strategy shifts the state's perceived costs of extensive concessions. Because nationalists are often perceived by states and majority groups as "secessionists," it is difficult to find a level of compromise and concessions that both meet the state's and the majority's general reluctance to extend concessions to nationalists and the latter's ability to satisfy its constituencies' demands. It is most likely to occur in cases where mobilizational capacity is low. The strategic choice to follow such a strategy is context-specific and largely depends on the characteristics of the group itself and alternative options available. While claims to indigeneity might work for some, in many other cases such an option would be unavailable. Furthermore, there are few international instruments, such as the UN Declaration on the Rights of Indigenous Peoples, that disillusioned nationalists might tap into to recast their claims under different political labels.

Most scenarios under democratic stability, therefore, lead neither to renewed violence nor to credible negotiated settlements that address nationalist demands. Given the wide gap between the state's strong resistance to nationalist groups that it views as threats to its territorial integrity and the latter's goals of self-determination, the chances of credible and lasting settlement remain slim, even once democratic institutions become more stable. More often than not, given both sides' increased costs of pursuing violence, the conflicts fall below the radar, become less visible because mostly less violent, but nationalist grievances remain.

Pathways to Conflict Resolution in Southeast Asia

I have identified a number of factors that first set structural parameters of violent conflict, then how they interact with institutional changes that democratization introduces over two distinct stages. At each step, I identified the most significant factors that explain variance. When taken together, one or two factors alone cannot predict levels of violence or conflict outcomes resulting from democratization. Yet, their combination and interaction in different stages produce pathways that are explained by tracing how each factor changes the responses from the state and nationalist groups as institutions change. While in theory there are as many pathways as there might be combinations of factors, I suggest that this is unlikely. Some factors, such as mobilization capacity, set clear limitations to options during subsequent stages.

Figure 2.2 and Table 1.1 show the pathways for Southeast Asian cases. When looking at outcomes, only Aceh can be categorized as resolved in that violence has been eliminated and nationalist grievances have been mostly met. The Law on Aceh (2006) enshrined a peace agreement between the insurgent Free Aceh Movement (*Gerakan Aceh Merdeka*, GAM) and the

Indonesian government, which ended the long civil war and provided Aceh with broad-based autonomy that GAM negotiated and accepted. In the case of the Moro nationalists in the Philippines, while a Bangsamoro Law was adopted in July 2018, also resulting from negotiations with the Moro Islamic Liberation Front (MILF), it came after years of sustained, but less violent insurgency and skirmishes have continued since 2018 with smaller insurgent groups. In Papua, low-level violence has continued, and many demonstrations denouncing government policy in the region, while a state-imposed autonomy law has been in place but largely seen as failing to address local grievances. In Thailand, democracy ended in 2006, but during the period of relative democratic stability prior to the coup, low-level violence had been on the rise and few concessions had been provided. Cordillerans initially mobilized strongly for autonomy but, once obtained, found little meaning in its implementation. Non-insurgent groups opted instead to abandon nationalist claims and pursue a successful strategy of reframing their struggle as "indigenous peoples' rights." They gained strong legislation, the Indigenous Peoples Rights Act (IPRA), that defined and secured a whole new set of rights, protections, and resources. Although not always well implemented, it nevertheless gave Cordillerans strong legislative tools to pursue their demands through democratic institutional channels.

At its origins, all cases began with nationalist groups creating some form of insurgency or violent mobilization accompanying demands for independence or autonomy during a period of authoritarian rule. At the time of democratization, they had somewhat different structural parameters of conflict. The Acehnese and Moro groups had relatively high mobilizational capacity, with well-armed, well-organized insurgent groups. The Cordillera had one well-armed, organized, but limited armed group, the Cordillera People's Liberation Army, which had relatively lower mobilizational capacity as it did not enjoy broad support among the various tribal groups of the Cordillera. Papuans had a clearly identified representative insurgent group, the Organisasi Papua Merdeka, but it had low mobilizational capacity as it was factionalized, poorly organized, and had few weapons. Finally, the Malay Muslims of Southern Thailand once had insurgent organizations but had been severely weakened, or had largely disappeared before democratization. The structural constraints of high and low mobilization capacity had an impact on violent outcomes throughout both periods of democratization and democratic stability, limited available options as nationalist groups had varied capacity to mount insurgencies, and also limited state options when faced with the potential of large-scale violence in some cases with virtually no such threat from others.

State repressive capacity and external support were relatively similar across the board. By comparison to other countries and regions in the world, the Indonesian, Thai, and Philippine states had relatively strong armed forces. The

Indonesian and Thai states had long-standing military-dominated authoritarian regimes, while the Marcos dictatorship in the Philippines built-up the armed forces significantly under martial law and used it extensively to repress insurgent groups. In terms of external allies, few insurgent groups enjoyed the kind of support seen in post-Soviet states, or in other regions of the world with strong irredentist movements. Aside from brief support from the Thai state to Malay-Muslim insurgent groups well before democratization, no insurgent group among these cases enjoyed significant support that altered their strength relative to the state.

Many of the cases follow the expected trajectory of increasing violent mobilization during the initial period of democratization. Again, it shows up most significantly in cases with high mobilizational capacity, as nationalist groups with armed and well-organized insurgent groups respond violently to the uncertainty created by the democratic opening: in Aceh most significantly, but also the Cordillera and Mindanao. Violence rises slightly in Papua, but extra-institutional mobilization increases dramatically. It is not represented by Figure 2.2 as it produces only small-scale violence, yet large-scale dissatisfaction, demonstrations, and protests. No change occurs in the Thai case.

Aside from mobilizational capacity, state concessions and their credibility have a significant influence on the timing and degree of violent mobilization. Aceh obtained early state concessions that delayed violent mobilization until GAM concluded that they failed to respond to their demands and showed instead a state keen on co-optation but not responding to grievances. Violence escalated following the bell curve. In the case of the Cordillera, violence spiked but then declined rapidly in response to state concessions that co-opted the CPLA while failing to address broader grievances. Since no other group had mobilizational capacity, violence remained low. Among the Moro, initial state concessions were sufficient to defuse and delay some violence. It resumed at a lower scale once clear that initial promises were not credibly implemented. The Moro National Liberation Front (MNLF) and Moro Islamic Liberation Front (MILF) continued relatively small-scale insurgencies. In Thailand, state concessions to Malay Muslims in the form of developmental funds and initiatives defused some of the grievances and appeared to thwart violent escalation. Mobilizational capacity, however, was also very low.

The character of state concessions and credibility of the commitment were key. In Indonesia, small concessions delayed violence in Aceh and Papua, but failure to extend significant concessions that responded to demands created violence and resentment after the initial period. Subsequent attempts to defuse violence through unilateral concessions also failed. The piecemeal approach largely followed an electoral coalition and majority that were highly reluctant to provide autonomy to Aceh and Papua, and became highly critical of the government's acceptance to run a referendum in East Timor, which subsequently seceded. In the Philippines, early constitutionalization of autonomy for Mindanao and the Cordillera helped to enshrine and, in theory, raise the credibility of promises to the Moro and the Cordillerans. Aquino's initial broad-based coalition under People Power provided leverage for a constitution with broad ranging concessions to build allies for the new democracy, but quickly narrowed down once the previous elite captured parliament and majority preferences showed clear reluctance to concede to Moros in particular. For Cordillerans, a rapid adoption of an autonomy plan designed to co-opt the CPLA defused violent conflict, but no such plan succeeded with the MNLF or MILF in Mindanao. Instead, the MNLF quickly rejected the Aquino government's policies on the basis that they did not respond to grievances while the MILF rejected them even more so as lacking credibility. Both continued violent strategies. The Thai democratic state, with electoral support from provinces with Malay-Muslim majorities, included influential Malay-Muslim representatives into cabinet and extended large development funds to appease Malay Muslims and nurture support for the centralized state, while completely closing the door to discussions of autonomy or special institutions. No violence nor extra-institutional mobilization appeared initially because of the quasi-absence of mobilizational capacity.

During the period of democratic stability, violence declined in all cases except in Thailand, where low-level violence rose, and the Cordillera, where it declined before democracy stabilized in the Philippines. In Aceh, an electoral coalition in the executive and parliament provided strong majority backing to a peace agreement with the Acehnese, after violent escalation became highly criticized. The legislation that arose out of negotiated settlement allowed the conflict to become channelled through normal institutional channels and led to a mostly resolved conflict. Among the Moro, a first peace agreement with the MNLF during democratic stability lowered violence as the executive was clearly committed to a solution that met Moro demands, but it fizzled and failed to be implemented by a largely independent parliament that reflected majority reluctance to provide large concessions to the Moros. Violence overall declined but remained at a low level, mostly initially with the MILF resuming violent attacks from time to time when negotiations faltered, and the MNLF initiating some violent attacks once it was clear that the autonomous government they negotiated was an empty shell. This stalemate perpetuated low-level violence, with few concessions remaining credible after each round of negotiations with the MILF. It took until 2018, when President Duterte could better muster control over parliament to pass a law that finally enshrined a peace agreement with the MILF, but low-level violence continued. The electoral shift to a president from Mindanao was decisive, alongside the greater control over the independent parliament to render peace promises credible through the Bangsamoro Basic Law.

Among Papuans, Cordillerans, and Malay Muslims, no organization had strong mobilization capacity and violence remained relatively low. In Papua, occasional skirmishes occurred mostly involving demonstrators and security forces. Violence was almost absent in the south of Thailand and was basically over in the Cordillera. The case of the Cordillera was resolved mostly because the strategic shift from a nationalist to an indigenous frame of mobilization removed the deep threat that the state usually has toward perceived "secessionists." As parliament repeatedly offered autonomy that was largely rejected on the basis of its lack of credibility, the move toward indigenous peoples' rights opened up a path to a stronger and more credible concession, the IPRA. The state and parliament supported the act as the majority did not see it as a threat in the same way as if they conceded to autonomy on the basis of a nationalist agenda. Cordillerans widely supported IPRA and considered it credible, particularly since it was backed by the rise of the global indigenous peoples movement. The Philippine government's eventual sponsorship and support for the UN Declaration on the Rights of Indigenous Peoples helped, whereas no equivalent international instrument supports nationalist mobilization.[125] Papuans and Malay Muslims, on the other hand, continued to hold deep grievances, as the state failed to address their demands or negotiate with their leaders. The Indonesian state and parliament extended special autonomy to Papua but on its terms, without negotiations, and largely as a strategy to thwart further mobilization. Furthermore, its credibility was poor as the subsequent implementation of special autonomy was accompanied by measures to undermine it. This was a strategy also employed in the Philippines, and which contributed to the failure of the first 1996 peace agreement with the MNLF. It shows that despite the heightened credibility of commitment that democratic stability generally produces, reaching the right degree of legislative enshrinement, meeting demands through negotiation, and creating regulations and institutions that clarify and reinforce the commitment are key in the process of making it credible over the medium term.

The declining, second part of the bell curve is slightly less accurate if juxtaposed against the three cases but its logic is still evident. The low mobilization capacity clearly flattens the curve as none reached the kinds of peaks seen in Aceh and Mindanao. Yet, among the reasons why democratic stability reduces violent mobilization, there is also the credible institutionalization of alternative channels to express grievances, as well as a reduction in the monopoly of representation by insurgent groups. Certainly, in Papua and the Cordillera, representative groups multiplied with different strategies, some of which supported more demonstrations in the case of Papua while others

---

[125] Will Kymlicka, *Multicultural Odysseys: Navigating the New International Politics of Diversity* (Oxford: Oxford University Press, 2007).

chose existing institutional channels, thereby placing some constraints on large-scale mobilization as seen in the earlier period. It was those channels that Cordillerans used as they reframed their mobilization. Finally, the Malay Muslims at least initially attempted to capitalize on their new-found, minimal representation in central institutions, while development funds were funnelled to the population. While overall it means that the curve smooths out at the tail to reflect continued low-level violence and deep grievances, in the case of Malay Muslims this violence actually increased more steadily. The absence of concessions meeting their grievances, the sudden rise in state repression combined with the loss of representation in the centre reflected a shift in electoral alliances that reduced the Thaksin government's need for Malay-Muslim support while catering to a majority inclined to support a repressive approach toward Muslims in the south.

Table 1.1 summarizes the most important variables that explain the pathways and outcomes in all cases. It shows how high mobilizational capacity is associated with outcomes that, in the end, produce some significant autonomy. In the short term, it also produced the most amount of violence. Democratization heightened violence, however, through the uncertainty it created, even when some concessions were made. Low credibility of commitment prevented concessions from sustained tampering of violence and conflict, particularly in Aceh initially and Papua, as well as Mindanao after the initially high commitment to autonomy enshrined in the Constitution. Electoral pay-offs created incentives from governments in Indonesia to negotiate with GAM, and in the Philippines under Ramos with the MNLF and under Duterte to finalize an agreement with the MILF. In Thailand, it contributed to attempting co-optation by including representatives briefly in cabinet. Otherwise, when little pay-off could be gained, concessions were weak or absent. Similarly in the Philippines, the independence of parliament relative to the executive contributed to expressing a majority reluctance to support agreements reached by the executive, and repeatedly undermined the ability to support negotiations with the MILF. In Indonesia, while occasionally parliament did wrest control over agreements to dilute them, as in the case of special autonomy, it was usually done with the consent of the executive or, at least, with sufficient number of coalition partners within the executive, ultimately reflecting the real or anticipated electoral pay-off. The following chapters present the Southeast Asian cases and explain in more detail the pathways and outcome in each conflict.

3   Aceh

From Violent Insurgency to Broad-Based Autonomy

Democratization in Indonesia was accompanied by an unprecedented surge in Aceh's civil war. Yet, by 2006 Acehnese had obtained broad-based autonomy, secured through the Law on Governing Aceh (LoGA, 2006) that reflected a peace agreement between the Free Aceh Movement (*Gerakan Aceh Merdeka*, GAM) and the Indonesian state. The LoGA was the most detailed and elaborate piece of legislation for autonomous governance in Southeast Asia.

The democratic transition, combined with the state's strategic missteps, created conditions for an escalation of violence. Initial attempts to appease Acehnese through state-led recognition of Islamic law and promises of local investment were poor concessions relative to demands for a referendum on independence. The sequence of poor state concessions, repression in response to heightened civilian mobilization, and uncertainty from the democratic transition rapidly closed the window of opportunity for a peaceful settlement. Combined with GAM's mobilizational capacity to launch a new insurgency, these factors set the stage for the rapid escalation of violence.

The fall of President Suharto in 1998 triggered an almost immediate response from nationalist groups. East Timorese, Acehnese, and Papuans began demonstrating to demand justice for past human rights abuses but soon shifted the emphasis toward new institutional demands. With East Timorese obtaining in February 1999 the promise of a referendum on independence, Acehnese and Papuans also made a similar demand. During the period of crafting new democratic institutions, the Indonesian state was on the defensive and less capable of using repression. Faced with a financial crisis, the newly installed President B. J. Habibie was very keen on showing democratic credentials and improving relations with major donor countries.[1] As East Timor was a major irritant in Indonesia's relations with several countries, he agreed in February 1999 to organize a referendum on independence. From this moment, Acehnese and Papuans were emboldened with the expectation that they could also score political gains and perhaps even hold

---

[1] Jacques Bertrand and André Laliberté, *Multination States in Asia: Accommodation or Resistance* (New York: Cambridge University Press, 2010), 181.

their own referendum.[2] Yet, while conceding on East Timor appeared as a logical strategy to cut Indonesia's losses with international donors, reactions to Habibie's response showed that his electoral coalition and the Indonesian majority strongly opposed negotiating with perceived "secessionists" in Aceh and Papua and, consequently, were not inclined to support deep and broad concessions in Aceh. In fact, Habibie was rapidly losing political support in large part because of his perceived weakness in accepting the "loss" of East Timor.

During the first few months after the demise of the New Order regime, a civilian movement arose and demanded a referendum on independence for Aceh. When the state responded with only weak concessions, it missed the opportunity to send a clear signal that a new policy on Aceh, as well as a response to demands for more self-determination, might be achieved. The transition created uncertainty over the future status of Aceh, and therefore appeared to open a window, at a time of state weakness, for GAM to advance its interests through a resumption of insurgency. With signals from the democratizing state of only small concessions and willingness to repress, GAM lost confidence that the transition offered greater chances of establishing new institutions that would respond to its demands.

The state's decisions to close off the civilian movement's demands for a referendum and to engage in repression were key triggers of GAM's resurgence. Having reorganized, obtained arms, and benefitting from a support network mostly based in Malaysia, GAM was able to mount strong attacks against the Indonesian armed forces.[3] Repeated iterations of military operations followed by GAM retaliation led to spiralling violence in the following years.

Yet, violent mobilization clearly increased the costs to the Indonesian government. If the initial calculus was to escalate and limit concessions, the rapid rise of civil war shifted the political landscape. President Wahid initially extended small concessions to Aceh but was limited by the backlash of his predecessor's approach to East Timor. But when violence escalated, he faced the opposite problem, with the People's Consultative Assembly (MPR) strongly critical of his management of the crisis and escalating civil war. The scale and costs of the violence were in open view under the new democratic regime, and it became difficult to justify that a democratically elected government could wage war against citizens that the majority considered to be fellow Indonesians (and Muslims). The democratic mechanisms caught up to the previously intolerant majority preferences for few concessions and repression.

---

[2] Chauvel, *Constructing Papuan Nationalism.*
[3] Edward Aspinall and Harold A. Crouch, *The Aceh Peace Process: Why It Failed* (Washington, DC: East-West Center Washington, 2003), 10–11.

The government offered larger concessions. The 2001 Special Autonomy Law, which was a large concession relative to previous attempts to appease the Acehnese, granted a large number of powers and fiscal resources to Aceh. But GAM dismissed it. It was deemed to lack credibility, in light of the weak ability of the government to follow through on previous commitments.

When democracy stabilized, the Indonesian government had closed definitively the opportunity to demand a referendum and imposed its own institutional parameters for autonomy, based on the 2001 special autonomy agreement. Yet, President Megawati's government also drew criticism for the continuing violence. The Aceh "problem" became a significant electoral issue, which prompted President Susilo Bambang Yudoyono (SBY), Megawati's successor, to change strategy and negotiate a wide-ranging peace agreement.

When negotiations began, GAM demanded greater legislative detail, more concessions, and guarantees that would reduce ambiguities. The 2001 Special Autonomy bill, and previous recognition of Aceh as a special region, provided a benchmark against which GAM would increase its demands. The lack of credibility of the 2001 Special Autonomy bill was an important consideration in GAM's demands for heightened legislative guarantees as part of its negotiations that culminated in the 2006 Law on Governing Aceh.

In the end, with a coalition now supportive of extending significant concessions as part of negotiations, and SBY's ability to have the agreement passed in parliament without significant amendments, the 2006 LoGA sealed a new commitment that was made credible by the degree of its detail and the stabilization of democratic institutions.

From Revolutionary Allies to Nationalist Resistance

The Indonesian state emerged out of a revolutionary struggle against the Dutch, and was premised on the principle of a single Indonesian nation. The Indonesian nationalist movement, which began in the 1920s, developed a vision of a new state for an emerging "Indonesian" population, united in its resistance against Dutch colonial rule. The Indonesian language, which Indonesian nationalists appropriated and renamed from a dialect of Malay serving as lingua franca across the region, became one of the core components of its cultural characteristics. Mostly youths across several regions of Indonesia joined the nationalist movement and eventually the armed resistance that became known as the Revolution (*Revolusi*). When the Japanese had invaded Indonesia during the Second World War, they had created a small militia, which formed the basis of the nascent Indonesian army after the Japanese defeat, the declaration of independence in 1945, and the return of the Dutch. The militia and other enthusiastic youths joined the armed struggle against the Dutch and fought to defend their newly declared republic. This revolution, combined with imagery of the struggle and common language, provided the basis for the Indonesian nation upon which its crafters built the Indonesian state after the Dutch finally withdrew in 1949.

The consequences of this path were important for diverse groups across the archipelago, particularly if making claims to an alternative nationalist status. For the most part, Indonesian nationalists succeeded in rallying the diverse ethnic groups of the archipelago to the republican cause, and they enthusiastically joined the new state and its nationalist creed, by accepting the need for accompanying homogenous policies on language and education, while allowing ethnic groups to practise their culture and speak their languages locally.

In crafting its institutions, the Indonesian state tended to be centralized and unitary. Nationalist elites had strongly rejected federalism as a divisive option that the Dutch had attempted to create in "federated" states it occupied after 1945. As a consequence, the unitary state became a strong pillar of Indonesian nationalism and state builders. Subsequent constitutions upheld the unitary principle and returned to an original draft constitution of 1945 that clearly spelled out a hierarchical relationship among the central government, provinces, and districts.[4]

Aceh was integrated to Indonesia at the time of the Revolution and most Acehnese participated enthusiastically in the crafting of the new Indonesian state. They too had fought their own war against the Dutch in the late nineteenth century and this resistance formed part of their group's historical identity. They joined the Revolution that Indonesian nationalists launched against the returning Dutch after the Second World War, in the hopes that joining the resistance with other groups from the archipelago could lay the foundation of a unified post-colonial state. It was the later denial of, first, an Islamic character to the Indonesian state and, second, a form of autonomy that turned Acehnese against the republic they had helped to establish.

There were three phases to Aceh's resistance to the Indonesian state and emergence of an alternative nationalist movement. The first occurred under the banner of the Darul Islam rebellion, which sought to establish an Islamic state. The second was a specifically Acehnese resistance movement that was created in the 1970s. GAM was a largely secular armed group that fought mostly against the Indonesian state's overcentralization and exploitation of Aceh's natural resources without benefits flowing to the local population. The third phase, in the late 1980s, was a second emergence of GAM, which was then better organized and with more widespread support. The Indonesian armed forces easily crushed GAM in both instances.

---

[4] Kahin, *Nationalism and Revolution in Indonesia*; A. Arthur Schiller, *The Formation of Federal Indonesia, 1945–1949* (The Hague: W. van Hoeve, 1955).

Acehnese *ulama*[5] and their supporters rebelled under the banner of the Darul Islam movement, which originated in West Java. Acehnese had joined Indonesian nationalists and *ulama* had been particularly strong supporters of the republic. Aceh was also the only region where a double revolution occurred, as *ulama* displaced the local aristocracy (*uleebalang*) and became the dominant elite. The emerging ruling class in Aceh resented Soekarno and the Indonesian nationalists' decision to move away from the establishment of an Islamic state and support, instead, for Soekarno's Pancasila.[6] Furthermore, they resented Aceh's integration in 1950 to the province of North Sumatra. They joined the Darul Islam and fought until the late 1950s, when most rebel leaders accepted a settlement but were essentially defeated by the Indonesian armed forces.[7] As a gesture of reconciliation, the Indonesian government in 1959 gave Aceh provincial status and a designation as "special region" (*daerah istimewa*).[8] Former Darul Islam supporters and Acehnese leaders abandoned the goal of an Islamic state for Indonesia and focused, instead, on increasing the gains for Aceh in the form of wide-ranging autonomy. They continued to ask for Islamic law, but only in Aceh. The government agreed to extend wide-ranging autonomy in religion, education, and customary law, while remaining vague on the application of Islamic law.[9]

Under the New Order regime after 1965, these institutional concessions lost their significance. Tensions escalated between Communists and the armed forces around the country, culminating in an attempted coup in September 1965, which led to the establishment of the New Order regime led by Major General Suharto. The regime began with a vast anti-Communist purge in 1965, hundreds of thousands of people were massacred, and the armed forces asserted their dominance over Indonesia. As a result, repressive tools were intensified, tolerance for opposition was even more greatly reduced, and the state became even more centralized.

The application of Islamic law became void, as the regime viewed Islamists and demands for an Islamic state as a threat. Acehnese demands to reconcile Islamic education with the state's secular curriculum were rejected.[10] The power of the Acehnese *ulama* was sidelined and replaced by a technocratic

---

[5] Islamic scholars or community leaders who are considered guardians of Islamic tradition.

[6] Pancasila, literally five principles, was mostly vague and without controversy. However, its first principle, "Belief in One God" was meant to bridge Islamist demands for an Islamic state by accepting the concept of a religious state without adopting Islam as the official religion.

[7] On the social revolution in Aceh, see Anthony Reid, *The Blood of the People: Revolution and the End of Traditional Rule in Northern Sumatra* (Kuala Lumpur, New York: Oxford University Press, 1979). On Aceh's Islamic rebellion, see Eric Eugene Morris, "Islam and Politics in Aceh: A Study of Center-Periphery Relations in Indonesia" (Ph.D. diss., Cornell University, 1983).

[8] Morris, "Islam and Politics in Aceh," 216–24.

[9] Ibid., 226–34; Nazaruddin Sjamsuddin, *The Republican Revolt: A Study of the Acehnese Rebellion* (Singapore: Institute of Southeast Asian Studies, 1985), 293–94.

[10] Morris, "Islam and Politics in Aceh," 273–81.

elite whose loyalty was nurtured by state patronage.[11] The little autonomy that Aceh had previously obtained and implemented was stripped of substance as the central government increasingly streamlined and centralized its authority and control over fiscal resources. Aceh's administrative structures were essentially identical to those of other provinces. Yet, the special status did allow the technocratic elite to perpetuate a sense of distinctive Acehnese identity that served as a prism through which Acehnese subsequently viewed the Indonesian government's centralizing policies, particularly in the natural resource sector.[12]

A second rebellion emerged in the late 1970s, largely as a response to the regime's centralization. GAM rebelled against government control of the province and newly discovered liquefied natural gas (LNG) in 1971. A first refinery began production in 1977 and an industrial zone was created near Lhokseumawe, in North Aceh, to include spin-off industries, such as fertilizer plants.[13] Almost all of the revenues from these investments accrued directly to foreign investors, their Indonesian partners in Jakarta, and the central government. Few benefits trickled down to local Acehnese, most of whom remained employed in the agricultural sector.[14] This first phase of the GAM rebellion was weak; the Indonesian armed forces easily crushed it.

The re-emergence of GAM in the late 1980s was different. It was the first sign that GAM had the capacity to wage a strong insurgency. It was composed of only a few hundred fighters, but they already had the capacity to obtain arms. Furthermore, they enjoyed much broader support among the local population than in the 1970s. The regional military command considered that supporters were widespread and could be found in every village.[15] Once again, local grievances were focused on the visible wealth in the LNG sector, with few benefits to the local population. Resentment and mobilization were strongest along Aceh's East Coast, where LNG production was located. Many of the skilled workers, and even common labourers, were brought in from Java and lived in small enclaves near the industrial sites. Meanwhile, Acehnese had few other avenues for economic advancement. The Acehnese elite was mostly sidelined, except for the small group of technocrats with connections to the regime.[16]

As a response, the Indonesian armed forces repressed the Acehnese even more strongly than it had in the past. This time, it applied a "shock therapy"

---

[11] Kell, *The Roots of Acehnese Rebellion*, 28–40.
[12] Edward Aspinall, "From Islamism to Nationalism in Aceh, Indonesia," *Nations and Nationalism* 13, no. 2 (2007).
[13] Kell, *The Roots of Acehnese Rebellion,* 14–16.   [14] Ibid., 22–23.   [15] Ibid., 66–74.
[16] Dwight Y. King and M. Ryaas Rasjid, "The Golkar Landslide in the 1987 Indonesian Elections: The Case of Aceh," *Asian Survey* 9, no. 9 (September 1988); Kell, *The Roots of Acehnese Rebellion*, 30; Geoffrey Robinson, "'Rawan' Is as 'Rawan' Does: The Origins of Disorder in New Order Aceh," *Indonesia* 66 (1998): 136–38; Bertrand, *Nationalism and Ethnic Conflict in Indonesia*, 170.

approach. It went beyond counter-insurgency tactics and used torture, arbitrary killings, arrests, detentions, and other means to weed out GAM supporters.[17] Bodies were publicly displayed to instigate fear among the local population and stem any potential support for GAM. By 1993, the armed forces had completely crushed, once again, the rebellion but continued to consider GAM as a potential threat.

Fearing a possible resurgence, the Indonesian government placed Aceh under military occupation until 1998, when the New Order regime collapsed. It officially declared the province a Military Operations Zone (*Daerah Operasi Militer*, DOM). The occupation added additional grievances to already deep resentment in the region. With regular sweeping operations in villages, arbitrary arrests, torture, and numerous other forms of human rights abuses, the Indonesian military managed to turn Acehnese deeply against the Indonesian state and what it represented. As Aspinall sums up:

By the 1990s, it had become central to public discourse that the Acehnese had continually been exploited and abused by Indonesia. This image first emerged in the 1950s, although then the chief complaints centered on the place of Islam and only secondarily on mistreatment of the Acehnese per se. In the 1970s, "neocolonial" exploitation of Aceh's natural resources was added to the mix. In the 1990s, the theme par excellence was human rights abuses. Each layer of grievance built on top of that which preceded it, such that Acehnese identity became one founded in suffering at Indonesian hands.[18]

Before democratization began in 1998, Aceh remained under a tight security seal. The armed forces were present in large numbers, they conducted regular operations to "weed out" GAM supporters, they mostly kept it closed off from media reporting and outside observers/activists, and maintained a climate of fear. There were few signs of GAM, although it would become apparent later that support was spreading and members were organizing clandestinely. Under a deeply repressive policy, the notion of Acehnese suffering was widespread. If Acehnese had once seen their identity as congruent with an Indonesian national one, by then it clearly rejected it and had developed a strong, alternative Acehnese nationalist project.

Democratization and the Rise of Violent Mobilization

Soon after he acceded to power, President Habibie began to relax political controls and moved decisively toward the organization of free elections. He promised constitutional reforms, a rapid reduction in the role of the armed forces, and free and fair elections. Habibie as well as the New Order political

---

[17] Kell, *The Roots of Acehnese Rebellion*, 74–77.

[18] Edward Aspinall, "The Construction of Grievance," *Journal of Conflict Resolution* 51, no. 6 (2007): 962.

elite still controlled the parliament (DPR and the MPR), but showing demo-cratic credentials became essential for political preservation.[19] They sought to prevent an unravelling of existing institutions and a loss of control to relentless waves of demonstrations in Indonesia's major cities. They feared potential consequences of allowing the *Reformasi* (Reform) movement to dictate the degree and direction of political reforms. Under such pressure, they seized the initiative to implement gradual but significant reforms: new laws on political parties, free and fair elections, limits on the terms of the president and vice-president, as well as modifications to existing institutions to make them more democratic.[20]

President Habibie and representatives of the MPR chose to preserve the 1945 Constitution while introducing amendments to democratize the polit-ical system. This gradualist approach allowed them to adjust to evolving circumstances and significantly alter Indonesia's institutions without resort-ing to the riskier approach of a broad constituent assembly. Over the course of three years between 1999 and 2002, the MPR adopted amendments that eliminated the armed forces' reserved seats in the legislature (DPR) and the MPR, introduced direct presidential elections, recognized principles of wide-ranging autonomy for regions, and created a second chamber of regional representatives. As Horowitz has noted, "[t]he incremental, grad-ualist strategy the politicians chose responded unusually well to the circum-stances in which they found themselves, ... The insider-dominated, somewhat unusually sequenced, and unhurried nature of the Indonesian reform succeeded in bringing about a constitutional democracy and steered Indonesia away from the dangers of ethnic and religious polarization and violence."[21]

These political changes were compounded by a weak economy and vulner-ability on the international front. Indonesia was recovering from the worst financial crisis of the previous few decades and relied extensively on credit and goodwill from international donors. East Timor was an irritant in its relations with major donors and blemished Indonesia's attempts to cast a new image as a responsible democracy.[22] Under these pressures and in order to swiftly remove obstacles to external support, in February 1999 President Habibie announced a referendum in East Timor, which was technically on a renewed

[19] Horowitz, *Constitutional Change and Democracy in Indonesia*, 44; 47–48.
[20] For a detailed argument about gradualism and its impact, specifically on the strategy to counter the more radical calls for change from the *Reformasi* movement. See ibid., 46–54.
[21] Ibid., 2.
[22] Harold A. Crouch, "The TNI and East Timor Policy," in *Out of the Ashes: Destruction and Reconstruction of East Timor*, eds. James J. Fox and Dionisio Babo Soares (Canberra: Australian National University Press, 2003), 145–50.

commitment to widespread autonomy but promised independence, should East Timorese reject it.[23]

Meanwhile, the armed forces were on the defensive and their repressive capacity was reduced. They had been criticized for the involvement of some high-ranking officers in the May 1998 riots, particularly Lt General Prabowo Subianto.[24] During the period of political reform, the armed forces remained in the shadows as their central role in the New Order regime created strong resentment and their activities were publicly scrutinized. Although their role remained important, they learned to apply violence much more selectively. As Mietzner noted, "the TNI elite now had to come to terms with the fact that the increased public scrutiny on its actions after May 1998 had changed its interaction with society much more fundamentally than the generals had anticipated."[25] In the peripheries of East Timor, Papua, and Aceh, repression continued but was somewhat less overt, and mostly reactive. The armed forces resented President Habibie's sudden acceptance of a referendum in East Timor and used local militias to create instability. After the August 1999 referendum, the latter launched a punitive campaign of destruction and displacement.

Habibie soon lost the confidence of the political elite and was severely weakened in the last four months of his tenure as president. His Golkar party, with 22.4 per cent of the votes, failed to win a majority in the June 1999 elections. Its rival, the Democratic Party of Indonesia for the Struggle (PDI-P), won 33.7 per cent of votes, while much of the other votes went to a number of Islamist parties. In July, a scandal broadly known as "Baligate" linked Bank Bali to illegal donations to Golkar for Habibie's campaign for president. Finally, he was widely criticized for "losing" East Timor, as the referendum in August 1999 returned results that strongly supported independence.

A new period of openness arose after Abdurrahman Wahid was sworn in as the new president on November 1, 1999. Yet, his government adopted similarly contradictory policies, first appearing accommodating but then retrenching under pressure from parliament and the armed forces. Abdurrahman Wahid's presidency was still transitional, as the armed forces continued to be represented in parliament and constitutional changes were still implemented to stabilize the new regime.

Wahid's position was weak, and his accession to the presidency reflected deep divisions in the political elite. Megawati's PDI-P had won a plurality of

---

[23] Donald K. Emmerson, "Voting and Violence: Indonesia and East Timor in 1999," in *Indonesia Beyond Suharto*, ed. Donald K. Emmerson (Abingdon, Oxon: M. E. Sharpe, 1999), 352–58.

[24] Douglas Kammen, "Notes on the Transformation of the East Timor Military Command and Its Implications for Indonesia," *Indonesia* 67, no. 61–76 (1999): 62.

[25] Marcus Mietzner, *Military Politics, Islam, and the State in Indonesia: From Turbulent Transition to Democratic Consolidation* (Singapore: Institute of Southeast Asian Studies, 2009), 211.

votes in the parliamentary elections but required the support of other parties and groups to back her bid for the presidency. Indonesia retained the existing practice of indirect presidential elections by which the MPR – composed of elected members of parliament, representatives of regions, as well as now reduced but still present members of the armed forces – chose the president. As the incumbent and Golkar candidate, Habibie had been discredited by the Baligate affair and criticized for East Timor's loss. Megawati appeared to be the obvious candidate for president. A coalition of Islamist parties, however, backed by members of the armed forces, brokered enough support to elect the widely respected leader of a traditionalist Muslim organization, Nahdlatul Ulama. Abdurrahman Wahid had established strong credentials as a supporter of democratic values and was widely respected even beyond Muslim circles. Nevertheless, his party had few seats in parliament and therefore Wahid had to cobble together a broad cabinet including members from almost all political parties.

In late 1999, President Wahid took steps to contain the armed forces but did not have sufficient power to fully succeed. His government established a tribunal to investigate human rights abuses perpetrated by the military in the aftermath of the referendum. Furthermore, Wahid promoted military reform. During his brief tenure, an unprecedented number of officers were rotated as he attempted to place reformers in charge of the military.[26] While his overall ability to reform the military was feeble, nevertheless until well into 2000 the armed forces wavered in Aceh and Papua between applying some repression and also mostly tolerating a political process that allowed greater openness.

In sum, several structural and institutional circumstances coalesced and opened a wide space to voice grievances, demonstrate, and make new claims. Restrictions on political parties and the media were lifted, and reforms suggested a clear commitment to democratic change. External pressure, combined with financial incentives, provided further motivation for the transitional regime to fulfill its democratic commitments, which included a decisive shift in its approach to nationalist demands. By allowing a referendum in East Timor on autonomy, or independence, the regime signalled a departure from its prior stance of enforcing a strong Indonesian nationalist project. Gradual modifications of legislation and the constitution to entrench regional autonomy and decentralize fiscal and administrative powers sent strong signals for change. Finally, the state's capacity to repress was severely weakened, as the armed forces remained strong but highly criticized domestically and, in its treatment of East Timorese, internationally.

---

[26] Siddarth Chandra and Douglas Kammen, "Generating Reforms and Reforming Generations: Military Politics in Indonesia's Democratic Transition and Consolidation," *World Politics* 55, no. 1 (2002): 103.

In the first few months after the fall of President Suharto, demonstrations were mainly focused on lifting Aceh's status as a Military Operations Zone. A large number of student groups mobilized for the withdrawal of military troops from the province. By August 1998, armed forces commander Wiranto ended the status as an operations zone, and vowed to withdraw troops outside of regular forces.[27]

Nevertheless, during 1998 and part of 1999, violent incidents occurred, but for some time it was not clear whether there actually was a coherent GAM armed organization. In November 1998, seven soldiers were killed in Lhok Nibong, East Aceh. In retaliation to what it perceived to be an attack from GAM, the Indonesian National Army (*Tentara Nasional Indonesia*, TNI) conducted several raids of villages in search of GAM leaders. Up until May 1999, most of the skirmishes were limited. After a soldier was caught in the crowd during a large meeting of GAM in Cot Murong (North Aceh), however, the local military unit opened fire on a crowd in Krueng Geukueh while searching for him.[28] The Krueng Geukueh incident was a turning point.

Up until then, there was a window of opportunity for civilians to organize, mobilize, and make demands from the new democratic government. A group of forty-two representatives from Aceh, comprising the governor, *ulama*, leaders of the local legislature (DPRD), leaders recognized by customary law (*adat*), and NGO, youth, and student representatives met with Habibie in January 1999 and presented several demands that included, most importantly, the prosecution of human rights abuses during the DOM years; the release and rehabilitation of political prisoners; special autonomy, with 80 per cent of total provincial revenues accruing to the provincial government; specific clarifications about Aceh's status as a special region; and a statement that Aceh remained part of the Republic of Indonesia.[29] Habibie ignored their request and referred them to parliament.

After the government promised a referendum for East Timor, a coalition of organizations began demonstrations to also claim one for Aceh. In February 1999, student groups organized the Aceh Referendum Information Centre (Sentra Informasi Referendum Aceh, SIRA). They began to channel what they perceived as a growing demand for independence among Acehnese who were largely disappointed at the government's lack of response to recognition of past human rights violations.

---

[27] For a detailed account, see Aspinall, *Islam and Nation*, 124–29. See also Robinson, "'Rawan' Is as 'Rawan' Does," 145.

[28] *Tempo* 28, no. 10, 1999; *Gatra* 5, no. 26, May 15, 1999; Ahmad Humam Hamid, Chief Coordinator of Forum Peduli HAM, Gubernatorial Candidate for PPP, and Head of Aceh Recovery Forum, interview by author, May 3, 1999, Banda Aceh.

[29] *Gatra* 5, no. 20, April 3, 1999.

In March, in an attempt to appear conciliatory, Habibie visited Aceh, formally apologized and made promises to victimized families, but they were followed by few concrete actions. In response to demands for a referendum on independence, and demands from more moderate groups for autonomy, he promised merely to provide further funds for the establishment of a few local *madrasah* (Islamic school) and for an extension to the local airport.[30]

It was against this backdrop that GAM revealed itself as coherent and highly organized. Up until the Krueng Geukueh incident, the TNI conducted occasional searches for GAM members, and the actors behind attacks against soldiers were not clearly identified. After May 1999, GAM began to issue public statements. Open clashes between the TNI and GAM also increased. In the following months, the TNI restored an active presence with an increase to 6,000 soldiers, which escalated thereafter.[31]

Habibie finished his mandate with a weak attempt to respond to growing demands for autonomy. The Aceh Governor, Syamsuddin Mahmud, had begun to propose special autonomy but, instead, Habibie supported a law on Aceh's special status. The law, which was passed in September 1999 just before Habibie stepped down from his position, extended Islamic law for religious and economic affairs and mandated the inclusion of Islamic education into the general education curriculum.[32] While addressing demands from some *ulama*, the response misread the broad support for GAM's mobilization in favour of independence, as well as the moderate elite's demands for more powers and fiscal resources under a new autonomous government structure.

The sequence of events in 1998–1999 therefore shows a missed state opportunity to offer concessions that might have set Aceh on a more peaceful path. Habibie's transitional period was marked by heightened expectations as the constitution was being amended, wide-ranging autonomy was discussed, and the referendum on East Timor appeared to open the door to greater self-determination. The uncertainty surrounding the end point of these changes raised the hopes among Acehnese, who joined the broad civilian movement and mobilized to demand a referendum. Yet, the state responded with relatively minor concessions, largely perceived among the Acehnese referendum movement and GAM as failing to meet their demands. And while the armed forces had initially retreated from their forceful approach, the state's refusal to issue an apology for past human rights abuses, let alone any redress, combined with a slow but steady application of repression as skirmishes with suspected GAM members occurred, the conditions were increasingly ripe for violence to resume.

---

[30] *Tempo* 27, no. 15, January 12–18, 1999; *Gatra* 5, no. 20, April 3, 1999.
[31] *Forum Keadilan* 8, no. 16, July 25, 1999.   [32] *Forum Keadilan* 8, no. 31, October 17, 1999.

The trend was confirmed during Abdurrahman Wahid's brief presidency from October 1999 to July 2001, as violent conflict escalated rapidly, although there were some attempts to address grievances and reach a negotiated settlement. As Wahid appeared open to conciliation, SIRA, civil society groups, and even *ulama* saw a brief window of opportunity to make new demands. They advocated again for a referendum. In September, just before Wahid's accession to the presidency, a large meeting of *ulama* from boarding schools across Aceh, and which Wahid attended, adopted a resolution demanding a referendum on independence. In November, SIRA mobilized hundreds of thousands of people in Banda Aceh with the same demands.[33]

Nevertheless, by the end of the year and during 2000–2001, the civil war intensified, and Wahid sided increasingly with a repressive approach. While Free Aceh flags were tolerated in a December 4th public display that GAM promoted, TNI's renewed operations soon overrode Wahid's tolerant approach. Armed forces units accelerated their sweeping operations and GAM increased its attacks as well. A local NGO, Forum Peduli HAM, recorded 960 people killed in 2000 as a result of fighting between rebels and government troops, which was more than double the number of deaths in 1999.[34] By March 2001, Minister of Defense Mahfud had announced a new "limited military operation," which officially reintroduced special troops to Aceh. Wahid confirmed the new repressive approach in April by signing Presidential Decree no. 4, 2001. The new policy focused on six points, including political dialogue and special autonomy, but the main emphasis was the provision of a political and legal umbrella for a new military operation.[35]

Wahid simultaneously attempted a more conciliatory approach through negotiation but, without an actual agreement, found little support from the TNI and parliament. Against criticism from parliamentarians and armed forces generals who were reluctant to negotiate with organizations seeking secession, Wahid had approached GAM, under the mediation of the Henry Dunant Centre in Switzerland, and reached an agreement in May 2000 on a "humanitarian pause," which collapsed only a few weeks later when both parties disagreed over its interpretation. Two subsequent agreements also failed to produce even a limited cessation of violence. In September 2000, the humanitarian pause was renewed until 2 December. Yet, during the first and second phases of the pause, casualties continued to rise steadily.

Wahid's personal power weakened considerably because of his poor performance, of which regional conflicts were only a small aspect. In its annual assembly in August 2000 the People's Consultative Assembly (MPR) rebuked

---

[33] *Gatra* 6, no. 1, November 20, 1999; *Forum Keadilan*, no. 33, November 21, 1999.

[34] *Tempo* 29, no. 37, November 13–19, 2000; *Agence France-Presse*, November 11 and 14, 2000, and January 6, 2001.

[35] *Tempo* 30, no. 7, April 16–22, 2001.

the president over his Aceh policy and noted his failure to prevent "separatist movements" from threatening the unitary state of Indonesia. They disapproved of negotiations with GAM and preferred, instead, to implement special autonomy while using force to eliminate the movement.[36] In his accountability speech at the MPR session in August 2000, he declared that he would "no longer tolerate any separatist movements and would take stern action against separatists."[37] Caving into added pressure from the TNI, he condoned their increased repressive approach against GAM.

An attempt to offer special autonomy also failed to reduce GAM's mobilization. Aceh Governor Syamsuddin Mahmud revived his earlier initiative, which was developed locally, and then forwarded to Parliament. Without negotiating with GAM, however, it was unlikely to succeed. Parliament passed a highly revised version as the special autonomy law for Aceh (2001). It came into effect in early 2002 just as the violent conflict was in full force.[38]

It actually was a significant concession from the state, at least on paper. The special autonomy law provided some important new powers and resources, and some symbolic recognition of Aceh's distinctiveness. The change of name, to *Nanggroe Aceh Darussalam* (NAD), identified it as different from other regions, with *nanggroe*, meaning country or state in the local Acehnese language. While all powers relevant to the exercise of special autonomy were granted to Aceh, specific jurisdictions were to be developed in subsequent regulations. At the time, some important institutional concessions were made, such as elections for the governor and for regency heads (bupati), which would become the norm around the country only in 2004. The "Wali Nanggroe," a new position, would implement and preserve local customs. Finally, the central government extended Syariah law, beyond the realm of religious affairs, but without specifying its reach, as it remained subject to respecting the secular laws of the Republic of Indonesia.[39]

The largest gain was in the fiscal realm. The government of NAD obtained 80 per cent share of tax revenues from forestry, mining, and fisheries to accrue to the provincial government, and 55 per cent of revenues from oil, and 40 per cent from gas, for 8 years.[40] Afterward, these allocations were to be

---

[36] See appendix to *Majelis Permusyawaratan Rakyat Republik Indonesia, Ketetapan MPR-RI Nomor VIII/MPR/2000 Tentang Laporan Tahunan Lembaga-Lembaga Tinggi Negara Pada Sidang Tahunan MPR 2000.*

[37] *Jakarta Post*, August 7, 2000.

[38] See Law no. 10, 2001 on Special Autonomy for the Province of Special Region of Aceh as the Province of Nanggroe Aceh Darussalam *(Undang-Undang Republik Indonesia Nomor 18 Tahun 2001 Tentang Otonomi Khusus Bagi Provinsi Daerah Istimewa Aceh Sebagai Provinsi Nanggroe Aceh Darussalam).*

[39] Ibid. For more detail, see Bertrand, *Nationalism and Ethnic Conflict in Indonesia*, chapter 9.

[40] As with all of the other laws on fiscal allocations, the wording in the law remained very ambiguous, with regulations meant to specify exact amounts and calculations. Revenue from royalties and other non-tax revenue were even less clearly allocated.

reduced to 35 per cent on oil and 20 per cent on gas. It also increased the provincial government's share of total tax revenues relative to what was retained by the central government. It differed from the autonomy laws of 1999 (nos. 22 and 25), which allocated significantly new revenues from natural resources to regencies, whereas the special autonomy law granted these resources to the provincial government. On paper, therefore, the NAD law created a substantially different, and significantly empowered, autonomous region in Aceh.

The concession came too late and, instead, encouraged greater demands from GAM. Had the state offered, and parliament approved, such an autonomy law during the early window of civilian mobilization in 1999, it is entirely possible that it could have been sufficient to allow at least a breathing period during which its effectiveness could have been tested. Instead, the Habibie government's faint attempt to appease local grievances through partial implementation of Islamic law and only a symbolic recognition of Aceh's distinctiveness sent a signal of unwillingness to compromise. The offer of "special autonomy" would subsequently provoke GAM to increase its demands, as the offer of special autonomy without negotiating with GAM came too late, and lost much of its credibility.

The failure was therefore a problem of substance but also of credibility. The Indonesian government showed little interest in negotiating and certainly refused to offer options to consult the population by referendum. The state's reluctance to respond to demands for justice for the decade of human rights abuses contributed to raising suspicions as well. Overall, it left the impression that offers of autonomy were not genuine and could easily be reversed.

Democratic Stabilization

The period of democratic stabilization, which began in 2002, marked the beginning of a clearer set of institutional parameters for Aceh. The TNI and the president had greater convergence in their approach, which included greater repression while insisting on special autonomy as the final solution for Aceh. With his Vice-President, Jusuf Kalla, playing a key role, negotiations were launched and led to a peace agreement in 2005. Once enshrined, the Law on Governing Aceh (LoGA, 2006) went well beyond any previous concessions from the state. The shift from violent conflict to normal, institutionalized channels to manage conflict within the established democratic process was possible because of the state's strategic shift to credible concessions, in response to GAM's sustained mobilization.

Four immediate factors combined to allow a peace agreement to succeed.[41] First, after four years of violent conflict, both sides began to experience combat

---

[41] This section is also based on interviews conducted in Banda Aceh, March–April 2008.

fatigue, as casualties mounted but neither GAM nor the Indonesian armed forces gained the upper hand. GAM's mobilization eventually paid off, but its violent form was costly in human lives and was high risk, given the possibility that the Indonesian armed forces might have crushed and repressed the Acehnese even more than they did. Second, the state's shift in strategy to significant concessions, with presidential support, can be attributed to Vice-President Jusuf Kalla, who played an active role in finding a solution to the conflict. Third, the involvement of a neutral mediator, former President Martti Ahtisaari of Finland, contributed to building confidence and reaching a mutually acceptable agreement that made the concessions credible. Finally, the tsunami in December 2004 destroyed most of Aceh's capital, Banda Aceh. It provided a catalyst for both parties to reach an agreement in order to focus on rebuilding the province. The latter falls outside of my explanatory framework; it helps to explain the timing, but not the outcome, which was set in motion before the tsunami.[42]

The June 1999 election provided the first benchmark of democratic stabilization in Indonesia. The results returned a plurality of seats for the opposition PDI-P, which had been repressed under the New Order regime. In October, the new People's Consultative Assembly (MPR) elected Abdurrahman Wahid as president. Wahid was a respected religious leader who was a long-time critic of the New Order regime.[43] His choice as president, after the incumbent President Habibie was sidelined, confirmed the first turnover of power.

Nevertheless, uncertainty still loomed over the independence of the armed forces and negotiations over constitutional amendments. Wahid tried, but ultimately failed, to force the armed forces toward internal reform. As well, the armed forces still held seats in parliament until 2004.[44] Wahid's presidency was mired in controversy and, as a president with weak support in the legislature, he was unable to stem his critics who managed to impeach him, in spite of dubious procedural rights to do so. He was succeeded by his Vice-President Megawati Sukarnoputri.

By mid-2002, the new democratic regime showed signs of stabilization. Megawati became president in July 2001 and had much stronger support in

---

[42] In his writings on the negotiations leading to peace, Farid Husain points out that Ahtisaari was already identified as potential mediator and had been discussed with GAM. A meeting had already been scheduled before the tsunami occurred. See Farid Husain and Salim Shahab, *To See the Unseen: Scenes Behind the Aceh Peace Treaty* (Jakarta: Health & Hospital, 2007), 668.
  See also Edward Aspinall, *The Helsinki Agreement: A More Promising Basis for Peace in Aceh?* (Washington, DC: East-West Center Washington, 2005).

[43] For a detailed look at these events, see R. William Liddle, "Indonesia in 1999: Democracy Restored," *Asian Survey* 40, no. 1 (2000).

[44] For a detailed account of Wahid's attempts at reforming the armed forces, see Mietzner, *Military Politics, Islam, and the State in Indonesia*. Constitutional amendments in 2002 led to the elimination of reserved seats for the armed forces, which became effective with the election of the new parliament in 2004.

parliament. Although she had been outmanoeuvred in the MPR's selection of a president in 1999, her party, PDI-P had the largest number of seats in parliament. Her ascension to the presidency after Wahid's impeachment came with strong parliamentary support that her predecessor lacked.[45]

She also had better relations with the armed forces; as she shared many of their own perspectives on national unity and security issues, they were much less likely to challenge her authority.[46] As the party that had its roots in the Indonesian National Party (*Partai Nasional Indonesia*) of her late father Soekarno, PDI-P and its supporters were strong believers in the nationalism that had led to the unity of Indonesia. Soekarno had presided over regional challenges that threatened Indonesian unity. With his support, the armed forces had successfully crushed these rebellions and reinforced his concept of national unity under the state ideology of Pancasila.[47] Megawati shared the strong nationalist beliefs of her father, and was not open to accommodating groups seeking greater autonomy or independence.[48] She departed as well from her predecessor who had alienated some of the top echelon of the armed forces by seeking to displace some generals and replace them with reformists.

Finally, the MPR adopted the last set of constitutional amendments that not only confirmed Indonesia's new democratic status but also defined more precisely its principles for accommodating ethnic identity.

For nationalists, the new "rules of the game" were clearer. For several months, Acehnese, Papuans, and even fringe groups in Riau and Kalimantan had thought that referenda on independence had seemed possible as in East Timor. By 2002, chances of break-up were gone, but so were hopes of gaining rights to run referenda.

Autonomy was enshrined as the main principle to accommodate the diversity of regions, while not directly representing ethnic groups. First, constitutional amendments recognized the principle of regional autonomy, while remaining ambiguous with respect to relevant units to which such principles applied.[49] Second, the amendment created a new Chamber of Regions, which gave

---

[45] Edward Aspinall, "Modernity, History and Ethnicity: Indonesian and Acehnese Nationalism in Conflict," *RIMA: Review of Indonesian and Malaysian Affairs* 36, no. 1 (2002).

[46] Mietzner, *Military Politics, Islam, and the State in Indonesia*, 225–35.

[47] On this period, see Herbert Feith, *The Decline of Constitutional Democracy in Indonesia* (Ithaca, NY: Cornell University Press, 1962).

[48] Rodd McGibbon, *Secessionist Challenges in Aceh and Papua: Is Special Autonomy the Solution?* (Washington, DC: East-West Centre Washington, 2004), 43.

[49] Regional units (provinces and regencies) were to exercise wide-ranging autonomy in all realms except those that, by law, were specified to be within the jurisdiction of the central government. The constitution also included sections recognizing the need to respect the "diversity of regions" in adopting laws to regulate regional administration, and creating special units for "regional authorities that are special and distinct." See *Undang-Undang Dasar Republik Indonesia, 1945* (2006) Art. 18, 18A, 18B.

provinces equal representation.[50] The units were administrative territories, not necessarily coincidental with any particular group. Third, Megawati reaffirmed the principles of state unity and the paramountcy of the Indonesian nation, through strong statements, fewer concessions, and support for repression when groups transgressed the new rules. Fourth, through legislation, some of which was already enacted before related constitutional amendments, the government specified powers and resources devolved under this new autonomy framework and confirmed a "special autonomy" status in Aceh and Papua, without explicitly recognizing any particular status to Acehnese or Papuans per se.

There was clearly a break with the uncertainty and perceived opportunity for civilian mobilization that had characterized the transitional periods of the Habibie and Wahid administrations. President Megawati was much more willing to defer to the advice of conservative-minded generals, who espoused a repressive approach against GAM. She was a strong Indonesian nationalist who believed that preserving the integrity of Indonesia's territory justified a renewed use of a strong military approach, despite the traumatic DOM period that continued to inform much of Acehnese's negative perceptions of the Indonesian state. With the TNI and Megawati converging on policy toward Aceh, they left little room for compromise.[51]

From 2002 onward, the government's approach signalled an end to tolerance for any perceived mobilization in favour of independence, and a top-down institutional model for Aceh that conveyed the administration's maximum flexibility in accommodating Acehnese demands. Megawati signed Special Autonomy Law no. 18, 2001 upon acceding to office, thereby enshrining an autonomy model for Aceh that was acceptable to the major political parties in Parliament, and that diluted what had originally been a version developed at the initiative of the Aceh Governor, Syamsuddin Mahmud.[52]

The gamble, from the central government's perspective, was that the release of new powers and fiscal resources to Aceh would bolster the technocratic moderates in control of the province, provide new development funding that would entice Acehnese to support it, and move away from GAM's promises of independence. By stomping out GAM militarily – which was the TNI's favoured approach – or by convincing it to adhere to special autonomy through negotiation, it could still present the package as a significant concession to Aceh that could end the violence. As Jemadu has argued, some of these seemingly contradictory approaches reflected tensions between the TNI's

---

[50] Jacques Bertrand, "Indonesia's Quasi-Federalist Approach: Accommodation Amidst Strong Integrationist Tendencies," in *Constitutional Design for Divided Societies: Integration or Accommodation?*, ed. Sujit Choudhry (Oxford: Oxford University Press, 2008), 220–21.

[51] Edward Aspinall, "Anti-Insurgency Logic in Aceh: Military Policy of Separating Civilians from Guerillas Generates More Resistance," *Inside Indonesia* 76 (Fall 2003).

[52] Bertrand, *Nationalism and Ethnic Conflict in Indonesia*, 182.

strong preference for repression, while cabinet ministers, such as SBY, the coordinating minister for Political and Security Affairs, preferred a negotiated solution.[53] Nevertheless, it could also be interpreted as a much more coherent strategy by which applying strong military pressure on GAM would reduce its options, while offering the "carrot" of negotiating an end to the violence and accepting special autonomy.[54]

Nevertheless, the approach failed to reduce the insurgency and GAM's resolve. GAM's forces grew considerably stronger and its mobilization was more focused and effective. A clearer GAM leadership emerged and replaced the ambiguity of GAM's previous approach and the uncertainty of its re-emergence that had characterized the transitional period. It made frequent use of public statements to attract followers, and "hundreds" of youth joined its ranks, even training openly. Its recruitment reached well beyond its original ideological core and attracted a large swath of Acehnese. It obtained weapons through the Southeast Asian arms black market, mostly based in Thailand. Finally, it raised taxes on all aspects of local business activities, including one of the major fertilizer companies, Iskandar Muda Fertilizer. Consequently, it was able to mount strong resistance to the TNI, at least sufficiently to prevent the latter from winning, even as it increased the intensity of its operations.[55]

With GAM rejecting the law, there was little chance that it could resolve the conflict. From the outset, most Acehnese were suspicious of it, as the state developed it without broad consultation. Critics pointed to past failures of implementing special autonomy, as well as the law's lack of response to some of the Acehnese's most important demands, such as redress for past human rights abuses. The law was vague and incomplete, and required that the provincial government pass regional regulations (*qanun*) to make it oper-able. Aside from one, controversial *qanun* to implement aspects of Syariah law, others were not implemented, budgets were released, they were not allocated to intended services, such as education, and much of the funds were lost in corruption. Most significantly, the government held little control over most of the territory.

Furthermore, the provincial government lost control over much of its territory by the time of the Special Autonomy law's implementation. Between 1999 and 2003, as the insurgency escalated, GAM took over offices previously

[53] Aleksius Jemadu, "Democratisation, the TNI, and Resolving the Aceh Conflict," in *Verandah of Violence: Background to the Aceh Problem*, ed. Anthony Reid (Singapore: Singapore University Press, 2006), 282.

[54] As Miller has argued, Megawati's administration was much less committed to special autonomy as a comprehensive political solution, and prioritized the elimination of GAM, Michelle Ann Miller, "What's Special About Special Autonomy in Aceh?," in *Verandah of Violence: Background to the Aceh Problem*, ed. Anthony Reid (Singapore: Singapore University Press, 2006).

[55] Aspinall, *Islam and Nation*, 162–88.

occupied by Indonesian officials and organized its own bureaucratic structure. In reality, its new bureaucracy merely reflected its claim to establishing a new government, rather than an actual ability to deliver services and development. It neither provided services to the population nor the construction of infrastructure, and therefore government support to the Acehnese population was essentially non-existent.[56] As a result, the Special Autonomy law was essentially meaningless.

Meanwhile, Megawati's government pursued negotiations with the mediating role of the Henry Dunant Centre, eventually signing a Cessation of Hostilities Agreement in December 2002. While not the first such agreement, it included greater provisions for monitoring and international support. But GAM resisted disarmament, and neither side showed strong interest in actually implementing the agreement. Instead, the TNI continually pressured Megawati to authorize a fuller and more intensive military campaign. The government also began a crackdown on civil society organizations, most notably by arresting Muhammad Nazar, SIRA's leader, in February 2003.

Finally, Megawati declared martial law in May 2003, which lasted until May 2004 and was then followed by a civilian emergency. She did so after the Indonesian government insisted on GAM surrendering and dropping demands for independence, but GAM negotiators rejected its demands.[57] During this period, the TNI regained the upper hand to apply its own solution to the Aceh conflict. Restrictions were once again imposed on the media, freedom of movement, and international organizations, while the TNI intensified its operations and publicized its achievements in terms of GAM soldiers killed or captured, as well as its confiscation of weapons.[58] With a stalemate, and war fatigue setting in, both sides were ready for negotiations.[59]

The turning point in the conflict was the election in October 2004 of Susilo Bambang Yudhoyono and Jusuf Kalla as president and vice-president, respectively. A resolution to the Aceh conflict was high on their priority list, and Vice-President Kalla was tasked with seeking a political settlement. "The fact that Megawati's leadership was replaced by SBY and Jusuf Kalla . . . [they] were much more engaged, much more open minded. That was the beginning of the end."[60] They had both played important roles in seeking political solutions

[56] Ibid., 159–60.
[57] For a detailed description leading up to the breakdown, see Aspinall and Crouch, "The Aceh Peace Process." GAM was ordered to surrender unconditionally. When they refused, GAM negotiators were arrested and the COHA collapsed. See Husain and Shahab, *To See the Unseen*, 20.
[58] Jemadu, "Democratisation, the TNI, and Resolving the Aceh Conflict," 282–85.
[59] Aspinall, *Islam and Nation*, 230–32.
[60] Aguswandi, Former Head of the Student Solidarity for the People (Solidaritas Mahasiswa Untuk Rakyat, SMUR) and involved in establishing Partai Rakyat Aceh, interview by author, March 24, 2008, Banda Aceh.

to the conflict in their previous ministerial roles. SBY, as coordinating minister for Political and Security Affairs, had been centrally involved in the cessation of hostilities negotiations with the Henry Dunant Centre, and represented the search within the Megawati administration for a peaceful settlement, even though the armed forces gained the upperhand and pulled the administration in a more repressive direction. Jusuf Kalla also sought to open up dialogue and negotiation with GAM:

In 2003, Jusuf Kalla came to Aceh ... It had already been a long time that ministers no longer came to Aceh ... As Coordinating minister for Social Welfare, Kalla wanted to come to Aceh, and stay overnight .... He wanted to be different [from others who would come for the day only]. He showed his courage to Acehnese, that he was not afraid of them.[61]

He repeatedly made openings to meet informally with GAM representatives and, although he failed, he gained respect among some GAM officials for trying to open up a dialogue.

Their combined election signalled a new era of openness to negotiation before the December 2004 tsunami. The latter represented a catalyst, rather than a cause, of the willingness of GAM and the Indonesian state to negotiate. Kalla had established himself as a peace broker in the Maluku and Poso conflicts. He was assigned to resolve the Aceh conflict and, in turn, dispatched his assistant, Farid Husain, to intensify efforts to create contacts with the GAM leadership. The People's Consultative Assembly adopted a resolution mandating the new president and vice-president to find a resolution to the conflict, but their resolve do so was already strong.[62] GAM and Jusuf Kalla's team had already agreed to meet in January 2005, with Martti Ahtisaari as mediator, a few days before the December 26, 2004 tsunami occurred.[63]

For GAM, the tsunami allowed it to save face and begin some discussions, claiming that they were necessary for humanitarian reasons. GAM had already softened its stance as it sought greater international recognition. As Aspinall argued, the first set of negotiations that led to humanitarian pauses mediated by the Durant centre gave it the recognition that it sought, internationally, at a time when the post-9/11 world increasingly had suspicious eyes on its Muslim identity, and its basis on ethnocentrism. The failure to create a support network similar to that of the East Timorese further stimulated a search for alternative forms of international engagement. The tsunami created a context where Aceh's international image shifted dramatically, as a site of humanitarian

---

[61] Interview, Djohermansyah Djohan, Deputy (Political Affairs) to Vice-President Jusuf Kalla, interview by author, April 1, 2008, Jakarta.

[62] Abun Sanda, "Establishing Emotional Relations," *Kompas (English Translation)*, August 15, 2005.

[63] Husain and Shahab, *To See the Unseen*, 68.

disaster where international organizations and foreign governments now sought to intervene and support.[64]

The combination of strong commitment from the president and vice-president, as well as accepting third-party mediation, considerably augmented the chances of achieving a negotiated agreement. Negotiations in Helsinki, brokered by the Finnish former president, overcame problems with past externally mediated ceasefires, including the failure to narrow the gap in claims from both sides, the underestimation of the ability of "spoilers" to undermine the agreement, the lack of proper external monitoring of the ceasefire, and the fact that the ceasefire agreements were being implemented at the same time as the central government adopted a unilateral, top-down autonomy law.[65] With lessons learned from past mistakes, the "Helsinki process" better succeeded when it became clear that no side had gained any advantage from past resumptions of violence. Key points included the external mediator's insistence on having a full settlement before disarming, agreeing on a detailed template for Aceh's governance rather than only a framework toward reaching such an agreement, and obtaining GAM's abandonment of independence and acceptance of autonomy within Indonesia as a basis for peace.[66] The Helsinki peace accord was signed in December 2005.

While the peace agreement provided for a corresponding parliament act, the path to legislation was fraught with potential obstacles. The agreement was signed against the backdrop of a long-standing suspicion among the Indonesian political elite of "secessionist" movements that threatened the unity of the Indonesian state, and this was well reflected in the policies of previous governments, as well as the position of major national parties on Aceh and Papua. The large dissatisfaction that the independence of East Timor had earlier generated had also solidified the resolve of preventing at all costs such an outcome in Aceh or Papua. Disagreements were strong on whether accommodation and providing broader and deeper autonomy would resolve the conflict, or provide a first step toward independence.

By January 2006, the new draft Aceh law (*RUU Pemerintahan Aceh*) had been submitted to parliament.[67] In spite of an attempt from the government to

---

[64] Aspinall, *Islam and Nation*, 222, 28. There are certainly other ways in which the posturing with international audiences had some effect. In 2002, the central government mostly postured to please international supporters in seeking peace, while the military was keen on a repressive approach. GAM sought international support and distancing from other organizations deemed "terrorist" but could not accept the terms that the government imposed. By 2005, these positions had evolved and the central government was certainly much more keen on finding a solution that would bring "Muslims" back to being loyal to Indonesia, and prevent the spread of more radical Islamist organizations that were attempting to win support through distributing aid after the tsunami.

[65] Ibid.   [66] Aspinall, "The Helsinki Agreement," 6.

[67] "*GAM Tak Persoalkan Keterlambatan UU Pemerintahan Aceh* [GAM Isn't Making an Issue Over Delay in Aceh Governance Law]," *Tempo*, January 21, 2006.

accelerate the passage of the law and meet the March deadline,[68] parliament ended up passing the bill much later. There was a significant amount of resistance from lawmakers to the draft, with strong voices wanting to reduce the Aceh law to resemble the status of other provinces. It created delays in forming a local political party, elections for local head, and other plans such as a truth and reconciliation commission.[69] The law was eventually passed in July 2006.[70] In spite of attempts to strongly dilute it, the Aceh Monitoring Mission (AMM) concluded that the law in principle corresponded to the peace agreement.[71]

Lobbying and convincing strong Indonesian nationalists of siding with a form of enhanced autonomy for Aceh were key for gaining sufficient support. One of the main obstacles was Indonesia's party structure, and the need for the national parliament to sanction any agreement that was reached with GAM. Politicians involved even in the mostly moderate Acehnese government were tied to national parties, and had to pursue intensive lobbying to convince their peers within their own parties at the national level to support negotiations with GAM. A small group close to the Acehnese governor approached key political figures in Jakarta to support the process and subsequent LoGA. Initially, strong Indonesian nationalists such as Megawati rejected their approach and suggested instead that their party in parliament would strike down a law providing too much self-government for Aceh. They also approached former TNI commander Try Sutrisno to gain support and curb the more "ultra-nationalist" tendencies within the TNI. Some politicians within national parties such as Megawati's PDI-P were key in convincing their leaders that compromise was the best approach to reaching peace in Aceh: " . . . they really wanted Aceh to be a kind of model. That is what I see as extraordinary . . . . They formulated Aceh to have those aforementioned powers, and then also to have the authority that we needed . . . in the hopes that Aceh would be a model. That was extraordinary."[72] With a shared political interest in reducing violent conflict, the compromise reached in the Helsinki accord gained support in the parliament.

---

[68] *"Pembahasan RUU Aceh Akan Dipercepat* [Discussion on Aceh Law Accelerated]," *Tempo*, February 18, 2006.

[69] *"GAM Harapkan RUU Pemerintahan Aceh Selesai Akhir Mei* [GAM Hopes Aceh Government Law Finished by End of May]," *Tempo*, April 13, 2006.

[70] *"Undang-Undang Pemerintahan Aceh Disahkan* [Aceh Government Law Formalized]," *Tempo*, July 11, 2006.

[71] "AMM: UU Aceh Sesuai Nota Kesepahaman [AMM: Aceh Law Based on Memorandum of Understanding]," *Tempo*, July 13, 2006.

[72] Abdullah Saleh, Vice Head of Special Committee XVIII and PPP Member of DPRD Aceh, interview by author, March 15, 2008, Banda Aceh. See also *"Tim Advokasi Aceh Melobi Megawati* [Aceh Advocacy Team Lobby Megawati]," *Tempo*, February 2, 2006. Megawati's initial position was to consider the law a first step toward independence.

The 2006 LoGA was much more detailed and broad than the previous special autonomy law, even though much of the content was similar.[73] It had 210 articles, which far surpassed either Aceh or Papua's special autonomy laws. The detail in the law, the explicit spelling out of rights and obligations for various executive and legislative roles, as well as specific clauses on the powers of the police, armed forces, and monitoring roles of the Acehnese government were designed to prevent the ability to subsequently circumvent the law by exploiting vagueness and imprecision.

The Aceh government obtained authority over all sectors except foreign relations, defence, national security, monetary and fiscal policy, and justice.[74] The LoGA also allowed it to implement Islamic law but the central government retained the power to appoint judges to the Islamic court. The Aceh government gained more oversight over security organizations by being consulted on the appointment of the Aceh chief of police or the deployment of military troops. Furthermore, the law spelled out specific requirements for the armed forces to respect human rights and local customs.[75]

In fiscal matters, Aceh obtained 70 per cent from oil and gas revenues and 80 per cent from all other resources in the province. These were similar to the 2001 law. In addition, however, the Aceh government gained the authority to calculate these relative allocations and to administer natural resource exploitation in its territory. "We were able to gain authority over oil and gas since Law no.18. So the total of what we received from oil and gas is 70% for Aceh and 30% for the centre. That was already formulated, put in place in Law no.18. We already gained it in ... 2002."[76] The authority over the fiscal management was important in a context where scheduled disbursements and calculations over industry revenues were often contested.

The most controversial article was the right to organize local political parties, thereby creating an exception to national legislation requiring all political parties to have a national outlook. This article allowed the Free Aceh Movement to turn itself into a political party, and to run for gubernatorial and local legislative elections. "What was most crucial in the MoU, what was agreed upon last, was the issue of the local political party. This was the very last issue. As for fiscal matters, the 70% for oil and gas had already been obtained in UU no 18, 2001."[77]

---

[73] In fact, the government negotiators had deliberately sought to remain within the legal limits of the 2002 Special Autonomy Law. See Husain and Shahab, *To See the Unseen*, 86.

[74] Republic of Indonesia, *Undang-Undang Republik Indonesia Nomor 11 Tahun 2006 Tentang Pemerintahan Aceh* [Law No. 11, 2006 of the Republic of Indonesia on Aceh Government] (2006), art. 6.

[75] On the police, see Ibid., art. 99. On military forces, see Ibid., art. 162.

[76] Abdullah Saleh, interview.   [77] Djohermansyah Djohan, interview.

In sum, the state's shift in strategy to offer credible concessions in response to GAM's sustained mobilization was the most significant factor that contributed to ending violent conflict and paving a path toward a peace settlement. The steady increase of repression in the previous period, combined with GAM's increased mobilization, had mainly led to a spiralling of violence and stalemate. Previous state attempts to soften its approach with its version of special autonomy backfired because it lacked credibility as it was drafted without negotiation or consultation with GAM, and was interpreted by GAM as a divide-and-rule strategy to attract moderates and sideline GAM. When faced with evident failure, and partly motivated both by electoral ambitions and democratic pressures to show progress in settling the conflict, SBY and Jusuf Kalla boldly changed the strategy when they agreed to negotiate fully with GAM under international mediation.

Implementing the LoGA: Testing the New Channels of Conflict Management

With a negotiated agreement in place, state concessions only become meaningful when they are implemented. As discussed in Chapter 2, a common state strategy is to appear to concede by negotiating agreements with nationalists, or passing new laws, but subsequently undermining them at the time of implementation. The aim is to attract moderate allies within nationalist groups and provide incentives for them to support the new institutions, while greatly reducing the powers and fiscal resources that effectively enhance self-determination. This strategy differs from state concessions whose primary goal is to achieve a lasting settlement by allowing nationalist groups to make gains in their demands for self-determination.

As the Aceh case shows, even though the state might have been tempted to diminish the effectiveness of the LoGA, nevertheless it agreed in the end to implement it in a credible way. Removed from public and media attention that reaching a settlement entails, the implementation phase opens up the realm of more subtle negotiation of actual power and resource distribution between the two levels of government. The more detailed legislation, as well as high stakes in preventing a resumption of violent conflict, ensured that the most important aspects of the law were implemented in the spirit of the Helsinki accord. Furthermore, the central government's sense of threat was greatly reduced once GAM gained control over the province's government as the implementation of the LoGA corresponded with its own objectives of accepting a broad and meaningful autonomy in exchange for abandoning the quest for independence. Nevertheless, some tensions arose with delays and perceived attempts of the central government to renege on, or modify, its commitments.

Giving GAM a stake in the new institutions, access to political leadership, and control over credible new state resources, as well as potential business opportunities, all contributed to supporting the implementation of the LoGA. Disarmament, which was one of the primary conditions of the Helsinki accord, made it more difficult for GAM members to reignite the insurgency. As part of the agreements, GAM leaders gained the immediate right to run in elections for Aceh's governor. Finally, GAM leaders and former field commanders eyed lucrative business opportunities and funds from foreign donors that accompanied the new peaceful era.

The implementation of the law took several years, and some of its aspects remained unaddressed. The central government delayed passing implementing regulations.[78] Such delays showed early on some resistance in the central government to supporting broader autonomy or self-government. Some of the delays also occurred in local institutions, where lack of technical support and knowledge of governance were common. The local parliament (*Dewan Perwakilan Rakyat Aceh*), newly elected in 2009 for instance, had not passed a single *qanun* (local regulation) in August 2010.[79] The truth and reconciliation commission, which was a key Acehnese demand for redress of past injustice, was never formed, in spite of repeated pressure on the central government to do so.[80]

Much of the immediate change resulting from the LoGA was the election of a governor and transformation of GAM into a local political party. As soon as the law was passed, much of the focus and energy was on the election, especially since the leadership split. GAM had raised in the Helsinki Accord the right of independent candidates to run in elections for governor and district heads, which the Indonesian parliament resisted and contested. The LoGA failed to specify such a right and, when attempts were made to bar independent candidates, massive demonstrations were held and GAM openly criticized the national parliament. In the end, the central government relented, thereby paving the way for elections to be held in December 2006. Irwandi Yusuf, who was part of the Aceh Monitoring Mission and the *Komite Peralihan Aceh* (Aceh Transition Committee), the transitional organization representing GAM soldiers, ran as an independent and won against Humam Hamid, who was backed by the official GAM leadership but nominated by a national party, the United Development Party, since GAM had not yet been authorized to organize

---

[78] "*Dewan Tuding Pemerintah Hambat Pelaksanaan UU Otonomi Aceh* [Council Accuses Government of Blocking Implementation of Aceh Autonomy Law]," *Tempo*, December 1, 2008.

[79] "*Setahun Bertugas, Belum Ada Qanun Disiapkan Parlemen Aceh* [in Office for One Year, No Regulations Prepared by Aceh's Parliament]," *Tempo*, August 17, 2010.

[80] "*Aceh Tetap Bentuk Komisi Kebenaran Dan Rekonsiliasi* [Aceh Continues to Form Truth and Reconciliation Commission]," *Tempo*, January 24, 2007.

its own. The surprise victory of Irwandi Yusuf raised many worries, as he had openly criticized aspects of the LoGA, had rejected GAM's electoral process, ran on his own, and was critical of the "official" GAM approach of supporting a candidate perceived to be close to the central government. But Irwandi enjoyed large support among GAM's grassroots, and his victory was uncontested.[81] Rather than create instability, the split and weakening of GAM's organizational strength represented the beginning of healthier competition in the electoral realm.

If nothing else, the LoGA attracted GAM's former elite to take advantage of political and business opportunities and personal advancement. The ability of this elite to remain influential in society, to keep former armed members in check, and to satisfy their own ambitions largely explain why conflict subsided.

For a limited time period, foreign donors injected large new funds for Aceh's reconstruction after the 2004 tsunami, in addition to the abundant fiscal resources subsequently flowing to the autonomous province. The Aceh-Nias Rehabilitation and Reconstruction Agency (*Badan Rehabilitasi dan Rekonstruksi*), which was established in 2005 and continued to operate until April 2009, invested over $US 5.9 billion, mostly in infrastructure and housing.[82] While much of the funds were spent on damaged coastal areas, mostly outside of the conflict zones, some of the money flowed to former combatants and their families. It largely reached many of its objectives, even though some corruption and slow results plagued the program in its early days.[83] Its scale, however, was so large that it very strongly boosted the local economy, providing some employment, construction contracts, and further demand for local services. By comparison, the already very large, donor-assisted Reintegration and Peacebuilding fund was much smaller, at $US 365 million. Even though the former was largely targeted at non-conflict zones, a multi-stakeholder review estimated that $US 529.5 million (or around 9 per cent) of the tsunami-related funds contributed to the post-conflict infrastructural and other development needs.[84]

The reintegration of GAM combatants into civilian life was a key component of the Helsinki agreement and one that donors largely supported. The

---

[81] For a detailed account, see Marcus Mietzner, "Local Elections and Autonomy in Papua and Aceh: Mitigating or Fueling Secessionism?," *Indonesia*, no. 84 (2007).

[82] "Multi-Stakeholder Review of Post-Conflict Programming in Aceh: Identifying the Foundations for Sustainable Peace and Development in Aceh," (Banda Aceh, Indonesia: Multi Stakeholder Review, 2009), 68, http://documents1.worldbank.org/curated/en/71660146 8259763959/pdf/556030WP0v20Bo110Report0MSR0English.pdf.

[83] For instance, in 2006, 258.1 billion out of 1.087 trillion rupiah from the Japanese government went reportedly missing in 2006. See "Missing: Rp258.1 Billion of Japan Aid for Aceh," *Tempo*, October 31, 2006.

[84] "Multi-Stakeholder Review of Post-Conflict Programming in Aceh," 68.

assistance flowed through the Aceh Peace Reintegration Agency (*Badan Reintegrasi-Damai Aceh*, BRA). One program, designed to contribute to the rehabilitation of conflict-affected areas, indirectly supported ex-combatants. It distributed $US 25 million to 1724 villages in districts most affected by conflict and spread across a third of Aceh's territory. The funds were channelled through the Indonesian government's sub-district development program. Villages decided for themselves how to allocate the funds, with almost 84 per cent being distributed directly to villagers as cash payments, which a World Bank report showed to have some significant impact on reducing poverty and increasing land use. It also notes that, although tensions were created between ex-combatants and non-combatants, overall the funds were allocated proportionately to their numbers. But the report cast some doubt that the overall effects of the funds, although increasing welfare in targeted villages, reduced ex-combatants' negative perceptions, given their expectations that they should have benefited more from such disbursements.[85]

Four years after the Helsinki agreement, there were many signs that a massive injection of funds contributed to reconstructing conflict zones, rehabilitating ex-combatants, and supporting a return to normal economic activity. A multi-stakeholder review of post-conflict assistance noted that, as of December 2009, around $US 365.26 million was allocated in direct reintegration and peace building activities, consisting of projects intended to benefit ex-combatants, victims of conflict, and communities most affected by the civil war.[86] The Government of Indonesia and Government of Aceh provided the lion's share of these funds (47 per cent), while donors, the private sector and NGOs contributed 53 per cent. Around $US 40 million of these funds were provided directly to GAM members and ex-political prisoners, with most receiving disbursements through the BRA and the Aceh Transition Committee (*Komite Peralihan Aceh*, KPA), which represented demobilized GAM members. The Multi-Stakeholder Review of Post-Conflict Programming in Aceh report noted that much of the direct disbursements, in the form of cash payments, had minimal impact on building sustainable livelihoods as many used the funds for consumption or debt repayment, with little advice or support, but provided assistance that could prevent potential spoilers of returning to violent mobilization. In addition to such direct disbursement, the BRA also spent around $US 61.7 million to build new housing in zones where houses had been destroyed by conflict. A large amount of additional funds supported community infrastructure projects, and other peace building activities. Most importantly, it was noted that ex-combatants benefited more than broader

---

[85] Patrick Barron and the World Bank Office (eds.), *Community-Based Reintegration in Aceh: Assessing the Impacts of BRA-KDP*, Indonesia, Indonesian Social Development Paper No 12 (Jakarta: World Bank, 2009).
[86] "Multi-Stakeholder Review of Post-Conflict Programming in Aceh," 51–58.

conflict victims of overall cash disbursements, reinforcing the point that compensation was provided to prevent their return to combat and their reintegration to civilian life.[87]

Nevertheless, several ex-combatants remained disgruntled, particularly in the first few years, and had little trust in the peace process. In its initial phase, many of the reintegration funds were lost in corruption, while only some of the ex-combatants obtained their cash disbursements. Several had lived in the mountains for years and, when they returned to their villages, found that their houses were burned down. They were given land, which is abundant in Aceh, but often with no capital to till the land.[88] There were perceptions that once guns had been turned in, compensation was slow in coming. "After the peace deal ... the army and police obtained raises but, us, former [GAM] combatants were treated like garbage by the government authorities ... We appeal to foreign journalists so that the Aceh Monitoring Mission return and properly implement the Helsinki peace accord. If not, at some point, for sure conflict will rise again in Aceh."[89] Complaints were high that, although peace had returned completely, several services were not being properly restored, including education and culture. As voiced by former combatants, their trust in the peace process was with third party monitoring, but they had no trust whatsoever in the Indonesian government.[90]

Overall, the massive injections of funds for recovery from the tsunami, both reconstruction and post-war rehabilitation, were supportive factors. The GAM elite and several of its members benefitted from a variety of cash and in-kind foreign-funded programs, which provided incentives to reintegrate normal livelihoods and support the new institutional framework. In spite of some continued disgruntlement from some GAM members, the peace agreement continued to be implemented.

In the first years, the institutional and regulatory framework began to be put into place. Parliamentary elections in 2009 allowed *Partai Aceh* (PA), which represented the former GAM, to gain a majority of seats in Aceh's provincial legislative elections. The formation of a local political party was one of the most contentious issues of the LoGA but, once formed, became the main party in the province. While it was a strong gain for local representation, parliament was slow in performing its duties and adopt provincial *qanun*

[87] The amounts per combatant were estimated to be Rp 25 million, see "*Rp 25 Juta Untuk Bekas Tentara GAM* [25 Million Rupiahs for Ex-GAM Soldiers]," *Tempo*, May 15, 2006.

[88] Muad Jahja Adan Beuransah, Spokesperson of GAM Party, interview by author, March 25, 2008, Banda Aceh.

[89] Tengku Hamzah, Former Commander and Resistance in Banda Aceh Area, interview by author, March 28, 2008, Banda Aceh.

[90] This point was made during a conversation on March 28, 2008 with a number of former combatants, who remained anonymous.

(provincial regulations) to implement various aspects of the LoGA. By August 2010, one year after the election, not a single *qanun* had been passed.[91]

In spite of very strong legislation that specified exclusive jurisdictions and strong resources to support broad autonomy for the Aceh government, central government ministries tended to nibble at these powers, and retain some centralized practices. Among GAM leaders, there were worries that some of the wording in the law could be used to constrain the Aceh government, so the primary concern was how to optimize the space that was provided.[92] There were discussions in parliament and in the executive about how best to allocate funds, and following specific formulas arising from the law in areas such as infrastructure, education, health expenditures, as well as revenue sharing from oil and gas. For instance, there were agreements on retaining 40 per cent of general allocation funds (DAU) at the provincial level, while sharing 60 per cent of funds to the regencies and municipalities.[93]

Yet, control of the funds often remained under the central government:

Aceh should have been able to regulate their own [budget] – to have the authority to really manage their own budget and development and priorities. But right now, it's the same. Aceh is like the rest of Indonesia in the context of managing the budget – except this DAU that Aceh can spend . . . But the national budget, it is the same as the rest of the provinces of Indonesia. So we cannot have priorities. Aceh has a lot of money, but the way to do it is to make a plan on development, send it to Jakarta and Jakarta releases the money . . . even though that's Aceh's money.[94]

The budgetary allocation process shows the problems with delineating powers between the different levels of government. The Aceh government was obliged to follow the regular budgetary practices of all other provinces: it would submit its budget proposal to the Indonesian Home Affairs Ministry by the end of March, each year, before funds would be released. This gave one more layer of leverage to the central government over the Aceh autonomous government.[95]

The same was true with oil and gas revenues, and even mining. The percentages were much more generous than in the past, with 70 per cent of oil and gas revenues reverting to Aceh.[96] But the central government retained power of the

[91] "*Setahun Bertugas, Belum Ada Qanun Disiapkan Parlemen Aceh.*"
[92] Ahmad Humam Hamid, interview.   [93] Abdullah Saleh, interview.
[94] Aguswandi, interview.
[95] Australian National University Enterprise, *Governance and Capacity Building in Post-Crisis Aceh* (Jakarta: UNDP Indonesia, 2012).
[96] A weakening oil and gas sector strengthened this political incentive. In the past, the New Order regime had kept tight control over all natural resources and syphoned its profits away from the regions. Very little of the large revenues from natural gas in Aceh remained there. Large conglomerates, the regime's cronies, parts of the military and the central government all shared these revenues at the expense of the local government and population. Yet, the agreement reversed this tendency by giving the Acehnese government large control over natural resource

management of these funds, whereas the Aceh government considered that it should have a direct role in their administration.[97] As a result, the Aceh government depended on the central government's schedule, and sometimes conditions, before releasing funds. This made planning more difficult and provided the central government with leverage to interfere.

The concern was that, once out of the public sphere and into the bureaucratic realm, the central government used a number of strategies to undermine the autonomy granted in the law, and force a convergence toward practices used in the rest of Indonesia.

We have MoU Helsinki, we have Aceh Governing Law – all is in general terms. We are entering a phase right now in detailed discussions. And the devil is in the details. A lot of devils in details. You look at the new Government proposal on the division of authority between Jakarta and Aceh on every sector ... because it's all general, MoU Helsinki, Aceh Governing Law ... except for points like Syariah, ... Every sector: on tourism, on economy, on trade, on everything, on education. And you look at the bundle that is being sent by Jakarta to Aceh ... and you look at the one that the government has with other provinces. Almost exactly the same, almost exactly the same.[98]

Ten years after the passing of the LoGA, many of the original concerns continued to be raised. Significant divergences remained between the Law and the original Helsinki MoU (Memorandum of Understanding). Some aspects of the LoGA were still not implemented. Finally, some implementing regulations further reduced the scope of Aceh's autonomy.

From the outset, the LoGA had some slight differences with the MoU Helsinki that, later, became much more important once regulations began to be implemented. The MoU had specified clear areas of exclusive jurisdictions for the national government, with other areas being under the Aceh government's power. But the LoGA introduced a small addition by which the central government would manage affairs with "a national character," thereby opening the door for the central government to exercise authority on a broad range of issues.[99]

Several other minor modifications created opportunities for the central government to exercise much greater power than originally anticipated in the MoU. Article 8 of the LoGA, for instance, uses "in consultation with and with

---

exploitation and revenues. It became much easier for the central government to do so as reports began to surface of the near depletion of natural gas and oil fields in the region. Vested interests in continued centralization no longer had the same stakes as in the past. This factor certainly facilitated the process of reaching an agreement with fewer powerful groups lobbying against it. See Aspinall, *Islam and Nation*, 220–47.

[97] Abdullah Saleh, interview.

[98] Aguswandi, interview. A report from the Australian National University several years later came to the same conclusion. See Australian National University Enterprise, *Governance and Capacity Building in Post-Crisis Aceh*, 76.

[99] Ibid., 15–18; 76–78.

the consideration of," instead of "in consideration with and with the consent of" as the MoU specified, thereby removing the ability of the Aceh government to veto a central government act. In the management of fiscal resources, the LoGA (art 186.1) requires that the Aceh government seek permission from the Ministries of Finance and Home Affairs before obtaining external loans. It also stipulates that the central government collect revenues from oil and gas, before reallocating to Aceh its share, at the risk that the revenue accounting will lack transparency.

One of the most significant set of unaddressed grievances was the human rights abuses of the past, and institutions to prevent a recurrence of such abuses. The MoU made provisions for a Truth and Reconciliation Commission to investigate abuses during the conflict. But the central government repeatedly delayed forming such a Commission, with no signs of it ten years after the law's promulgation. After repeated attempts to convince the central government, the Aceh government and parliament moved ahead unilaterally by adopting its own by-law (*qanun*) in December 2013. It called on the central government to establish the Truth and Reconciliation Commission. The act of the Acehnese parliament remained a strong statement of disagreement and complaint of the central government's lack of commitment to fully implementing the MoU.[100] Nevertheless, the Aceh government proceeded with the formation of the Commission but it took three more years before it was set up and, four years later, its commissioners had not yet produced significant work.[101] Furthermore, the central government failed to set up a Human Rights Court, which was specified in the LoGA.[102] Other agreements that had not yet been implemented were less central but still important mostly to the Aceh government's control over the economy and its fiscal resources.

The implementing regulations revealed, to some extent, the central government's ability to dilute the breadth and depth of Aceh's autonomy. While implementing regulations are too numerous to be fully discussed, a few were more controversial. Moreover, some key national regulations were required before the Aceh government could proceed with the establishment of its regulatory framework.

Only a few regulations were passed early on, while several others took more than a decade. The first to be passed was the national regulation on Local Political Parties in Aceh (20/2007), which allowed the formation of Partai Aceh that became the official representative of the former GAM. A couple more regulations gave a broad framework for the functioning of the Aceh

[100] "Aceh Passes Bylaw to Address Past Human Rights Issues," *Tempo*, January 10, 2014.

[101] Zahlul Pasha, "Lemahnya Qanun KKR Aceh [Aceh's KKR Law Weak]," *Serambi Indonesia*, May 9, 2017.

[102] Crisis Management Initiative, *Aceh Peace Process Follow-up Project: Final Report* (Helsinki: Crisis Management Initiative, 2012), 19–20.

government, such as the regulation on the appointment of Aceh's regional secretary (58/2009) and the presidential regulation on mechanisms for consultation and consideration in drafting international agreements, laws, and administrative policies directly related to Aceh (75/2008). Other regulations, passed in 2010, specified mechanisms for the Aceh government to cooperate with foreign institutions and agencies (11/2010) and began to devolve authority for the management of the Sabang Special Zone (83/2010). The latter was subsequently withdrawn, however, after local accusations that it ignored the law and simply imposed national standards in effect in other provinces.[103] While there were dozens of additional regulations required from the Aceh government to implement the LoGA, some were passed during the first five to six years, but many others were still lacking.[104]

Some important, as well as controversial, regulations at the national level were only passed in 2015. In particular, President Jokowi signed the long-awaited regulation on national government authority in Aceh, which confirmed the central government's right to exercise authority on issues of "national character," beyond the six jurisdictions that were specified in the LoGA as being exclusive to the national level. Governor Zaini Abdullah continued to publicly criticize this regulation, which was a point of contention ever since the LoGA was passed in 2006.[105] While Jokowi also adopted a regulation on the joint management of oil and gas in 2015, it was done so against the backdrop of several years of central government management and control of the revenues.[106]

In the end, the flow of money to Aceh was the most significant gain from the LoGA but in the absence of clear delineation of powers between different levels of government, whether these funds supported a stronger independent Aceh government still remained unclear. In line with what was obtained in the previous special autonomy law, Aceh would receive "special autonomy funds" (*dana otsus*) to the amount of 2 per cent of the General Allocation Fund for fifteen years, then 1 per cent for the following five years.[107]

The Otsus funds, and oil and gas revenues, began to flow to Aceh in 2008. Although Aceh had already been provided much larger funds since 2002, under

---

[103] Edward Aspinall, "Special Autonomy, Predatory Peace and the Resolution of the Aceh Conflict," in *Regional Dynamics in a Decentralized Indonesia*, ed. Hal Hill (Singapore: Institute of Southeast Asian Studies, 2014), 471.

[104] Crisis Management Initiative, "Aceh Peace Process Follow-up Project," 20.

[105] "Gubernur Bahas Kendala Implementasi UUPA Bersama Komite I DPD RI [Governor Discusses Obstacles to Implementation of UUPA with Parliamentary Committee I]," *Kanal Aceh*, August 10, 2016.

[106] "DPR dan DPD Awasi Implementasi UUPA [DPR and DPD Oversee Implementation of UUPA]," *Serambi Indonesia*, February 3, 2015.

[107] Australian National University Enterprise, *Governance and Capacity Building in Post-Crisis Aceh*, 83.

special autonomy, the fiscal resources to the province after 2008 were even higher. Around Rp 4 trillion on average (around $US 400 million) was added after 2008 to the Otsus and oil/gas allocations.[108]

Some of the differences in implementation, of course, come from internal disagreement. Within Aceh, there are competing visions over the nature of its autonomy. As the broader Indonesian decentralization laws give strong powers to districts across the country, Aceh's districts rely on a negotiation with the provincial government, even though the decentralization law also applies to them. As a result, many of the tensions over budgetary management occurred between the provincial and district levels of government. In the case of the large Otsus funds, for instance, the Aceh government regulation (*Qanun* 2/2008) stipulates that 40 per cent would be retained at the provincial level, while 60 per cent would be allocated to the districts. But further problems arise with provisions that require districts to seek not only program approvals in their respective local parliaments, but also from the provincial government. In the end, they often miss deadlines, and funds are not distributed on time to properly direct them to selected programs.[109]

Governor Irwandi's administration resisted distributing funds to districts, arguing that the Aceh provincial government was the site of autonomy, and therefore had the responsibility to implement the most significant development initiatives. Politically, it was also useful for him to use Otsus funds to improve the image of his government. As a result, he invested much of the funds into key programs that included the Aceh Health Guarantee (JKA) coverage scheme – an ambitious universal health-care coverage program – financial assistance for village development (*Bantuan Keuangan Pemakmur Gampong*), and a scholarship program.[110] In addition to these programs, the Irwandi administration also invested heavily in road building and basic infrastructure, leaving a legacy that was broadly praised among Acehnese.[111]

The greatest achievement of the peace process, in the end, was GAM's disbanding and acceptance of the democratic process, mostly to its benefit. GAM's leadership was able to seize control of Aceh's political landscape, and therefore ensure not only that it would gain financially from the vast new sums available, but also to reward and mostly keep in check its vast network of ex-combatants and non-combatants.[112] While it certainly attempted to maintain a monopoly over Aceh's governance, it accepted results when its control was challenged.

---

[108] Ibid., 56.   [109] Ibid., 84–87.   [110] Ibid., 86.

[111] Edward Aspinall, "Aceh's No Win Election," *Inside Indonesia* 106 (Fall 2011).

[112] For an argument that emphasizes, in particular, the opportunities for illicit fund raising that maintains GAM supporters' interest in peace, see "Special Autonomy, Predatory Peace and the Resolution of the Aceh Conflict."

As discussed earlier, Irwandi's election as governor was the first challenge to GAM's leadership. His strong victory over Humam Hamid allowed him to govern with good support not only from the Acehnese population more broadly but including GAM members, many of whom benefited from his subsequent policies and programs.

Nevertheless, the former GAM leadership successfully expanded its control over the legislature and subsequently the executive, with a near monopoly over Aceh's political representation. The 2009 elections were the first where a local political party could run. Partai Aceh, which officially represented the former GAM, won 43.8 per cent of the vote, far outdistancing the second party, *Partai Demokrat* (14.3 per cent), the party of former Indonesian President Susilo Bambang Yudhoyono who, along with his Vice-President Jusuf Kalla, from Golkar,[113] was praised for reaching the 2005 Helsinki accord with GAM.

In the 2012 gubernatorial elections, PA's candidate, Zaini Abdullah, a former GAM exile, won against incumbent Irwandi Yusuf. The latter had been widely expected to win because of his popularity but Zaini Abdullah won a landslide victory with 55.9 per cent of the vote against Yusuf's 29.2 per cent.[114] Much of the success of the victory was attributed to the KPA, the post-conflict name for GAM. Its former commanders, also usually local party leaders, played a key role in mobilizing support, with the message that PA leaders needed to win the election in order to finalize the transition from GAM to regular politics, and avoid a return to conflict.[115]

Partai Aceh's near monopoly, however, was short-lived. In the 2014 legislative elections, its support declined from 47.8 per cent in the previous election to 36 per cent. While it still gained a plurality of votes, it lost much of its previous support, most surprisingly to a national party, NasDem. The latter benefitted from being led by an Acehnese based in Jakarta, Surya Paloh, and was able to gain some support on the basis of his broad popularity and some significant financial resources. Some of the other votes went to other national parties, as well as to some newly formed, alternative Acehnese local parties, that did not gain as many supporters as expected.

Many Acehnese were disappointed with Partai Aceh's performance after five years in power. They expected much more development, but saw few changes that affected their lives. Instead of adopting regulations to strengthen governance, PA legislators allocated large sums to pork barrel projects and the party's activities. Schools were built but the quality of education and teachers

---

[113] Golkar obtained only 6.6 per cent of the vote, even though more recognition had been given to Jusuf Kalla, who was the main figure involved in the accord.

[114] International Foundation for Electoral Systems, "Elections in Aceh: Another Step Forward," accessed October 10, 2018, www.ifes.org/news/elections-aceh-another-step-forward.

[115] Sidney Jones, "How Will Partai Aceh Govern?," *Tempo*, April 19, 2012; Cillian Nolan, "Elections in Aceh and Timor Leste: After the Struggle," *Jakarta Oist*, April 19, 2012.

remained low. Roads and infrastructure were built primarily in areas where the PA had strong support and where former GAM commanders benefitted from the allocation of local contracts.[116]

In February 2017, Irwandi won again by a slight margin over Muzakir Manaf. Irwandi obtained 37.15 per cent of the votes against Muzakir, who won 31.80 per cent, whereas the incumbent Governor, Zaini Abdullah, obtained only 6.92 per cent.[117] Zaini had been criticized for poor and weak leadership, while replacing professionals with Partai Aceh supporters as top civil servants.[118] Muzakir, who had been Zaini's running mate in 2012 and subsequent vice-governor, became the Partai Aceh's official candidate for governor, while Zaini parted with the PA and ran his own independent campaign, thereby further dividing the former GAM leadership.

With the 2017 gubernatorial election, there was a regularization of electoral politics that confirmed an acceptance of its process. Divisions among the former GAM elite, and open competition in the electoral realm, had ensured a transition of power between leaders and a loosening of Partai Aceh's dominance. With the inability to establish a monopoly, the PA instead has made readjustments to continue nurturing support from its constituency. Although violence occurred in each electoral contest, the outcome was mostly accepted and governors, and the PA, were held accountable for their performance. These were signs that the democratic process was taking hold ten years after the LOGA's adoption and that remaining conflict was being appropriately channelled through institutional channels.

Conclusion

Why were the Acehnese able to obtain an agreement on wide-ranging autonomy that satisfied many of their demands, and that was mostly implemented? Why was such an agreement possible in spite of a highly violent civil war that accompanied Indonesia's transition to democracy? I have shown in this chapter that the factors leading to an intensification of violent conflict during the transition were different than those allowing for negotiations and peaceful settlement after democratic stabilization. The main difference was the impact of institutional uncertainty during the democratic transition, while democratic stability set institutional parameters against which demands could be more predictably pursued.

The particular combination of institutional uncertainty, the state's minimal and non-credible concessions, and GAM's mobilizational capacity created the

---

[116] Institute for Policy Analysis of Conflict, *Aceh's Surprising Election Results* (Jakarta: Institute for Policy Analysis of Conflict, April 30, 2014), 2–3.

[117] "2017 Aceh Gubernatorial Election Results," https://pilkada2017.kpu.go.id/hasil/t1/aceh.

[118] "Aceh's Surprising Election Results," 3.

conditions for the spiralling violence in 2000. Against the latter structural feature of GAM's capacity to mount an insurgency, the sequence of the other two factors was crucial. Faced with mobilization in the form of a broad civilian protest movement demanding a referendum, the state had a brief window of opportunity when it might have offered significant concessions that would have defused the conflict. Instead, it refused to respond to the protests, while offering minimal concessions that failed to respond to demands for self-determination. It did so because the majority, as expressed in parliament and in cabinet, was highly reluctant to negotiate with perceived "secessionists." With a climate of uncertainty surrounding the constitutional negotiations, and whether a new democratic state would accommodate demands for autonomy or greater self-determination, GAM increased its pressure by launching a new insurgency.

With democratic stability, the new constitutional amendments were in place, and the state had passed a Special Autonomy bill for Aceh. These institutional parameters enshrined in principle a recognition of autonomy, but did not sufficiently meet GAM's demands, nor were the new institutions clearly designed to actually devolve power. They lacked the credibility of the commitment made. While GAM's mobilization was met with increasing repression, civil war continued with neither side able to claim victory.

It was the Indonesian state's shift toward more significant concessions that made a path to a peace agreement possible. Continued war was costly politically to the Indonesian government seeking to bolster its democratic credentials. Furthermore, as the Acehnese shared the Islamic religion with the majority and a foundational role in the formation of the Indonesian Republic, the Indonesian public was more sympathetic to the suffering of the Acehnese, at least in comparison to Papuans or East Timorese. Parliamentarians' reactions to the escalation of violence in the region after 1998 show evidence of the majority's inclination. The government lost support for repressive policies and President Wahid was strongly criticized for his handling of the crisis in Aceh, which created pressure on future leaders to find a solution to the crisis. SBY, as interior minister in Megawati Sukarnoputri's cabinet, had been keen on finding a peaceful solution, but Megawati supported by Indonesian nationalists were still reluctant to concede to "secessionists." Jusuf Kalla, as vice-president in SBY's first cabinet, became a key player in steering the state toward an agreement. The media and public opinion by then had become strongly critical of the violence in Aceh. Kalla's actions reflected both a majority that had become increasingly uncomfortable with the intensity of Aceh's civil war in a democratic context, combined with electoral ambitions that made a final resolution to the Aceh conflict eventually more profitable. Majority preferences as expressed in parliament had shifted away from high reluctance to concede to secessionists, to finding a peaceful resolution to the violent civil war.

Democratic stability helped to increase the incentives to reach an agreement, while making autonomy first more credible, and second implemented meaningfully. A number of supportive factors also made the agreement possible and, eventually, implemented. First, the presence of an external mediator helped to increase the credibility of the state's commitment. But the credibility was reinforced by the democratic context, which would allow the local Acehnese parliament and government to openly criticize and take measures institutionally to pressure the central government into delivering on its commitments. Second, it was helpful that GAM not only disbanded but could also seize the reigns first of the position of governor and then the local parliament. As Aspinall has argued, the 2006 law that allowed GAM to dominate local politics provided opportunities for GAM supporters to seize large portions of government funds to enrich themselves and pursue their private interests.[119] But it also meant that they obtained representation and could articulate Acehnese demands within the new democratic institutions.

Nevertheless, even in this case, which was largely successful in reaching a strong legislation through a negotiated process, tensions around the realization of broad-based autonomy remained strong. The state's commitment was clearly stronger than in any other case in this book, given the willingness to sign a peace agreement that led to very detailed and significant legislative concessions. Yet, the state's attempts to dilute or reduce the reach of the law was evident in the process of implementation and shows the difficulties of overcoming state reluctance to cede power to secessionist groups. In the end, the democratic environment and negotiated nature of the agreement that led to the LoGA enabled conflict to remain managed through the regularized institutional process. In the cases of Papua, and arguably Moros in Mindanao initially, such threshold was not reached, and low-level violence, deep grievances, and renewed conflict outside of institutional channels continued, as the following chapters show.

---

[119] Aspinall, "Special Autonomy, Predatory Peace and the Resolution of the Aceh Conflict." While Aspinall calls this a "predatory peace," there is nevertheless a very substantial devolution of power and resources that has met many aspects of the long-standing demands toward self-determination.

4   Papua

Failed Autonomy and Divided They Stand

The initial period of democratization produced little change in levels of violence, because it had been mostly sporadic, localized, and of low intensity. Aside from occasional larger-scale operations under authoritarian rule, most state violence involved few soldiers in isolated areas, or violent crackdowns on demonstrators in main cities. On the Papuan side, the Free Papua Movement (*Organisasi Papua Merdeka*, OPM) occasionally attacked military outposts or isolated soldiers. The main change, therefore, was a reduction in large-scale operations, except in border areas.[1]

The absence of large-scale violence can be explained in large part by insurgent groups' weak organizational capacity and lack of weapons. Furthermore, along with Papuan organizations more broadly, insurgent groups have been strongly divided. The OPM remained composed of divided factions under competing leadership.[2] These factors remained constant after the change of regime. Civilian organizations however emerged and, for a brief time, were able to unite in support of a single political voice under the Papua Presidium Council (*Presidium Dewan Papua*, PDP) in 2000–2002.[3]

The shift to a democratic environment in Indonesia enabled Papuans to mobilize on a larger scale, through peaceful means. The calculus was that greater political space would allow momentum toward independence, or at least a redress of perceived injustices. From the grassroots, Papuan leaders came together to organize two large congresses, which led to the formation of the PDP. The creation of the presidium was an unprecedented display of group unity. Most importantly, a window of opportunity had opened, particularly under the presidency of Abdurrahman Wahid, who allowed Papuans to openly express their grievances and even supported the organization of the first

---

[1] The military withdrew several KOSTRAD (*Komando Strategic Angkatan Darat*, Army Strategic Command) battalions. Nevertheless, it maintained some of its special forces (Kopassus, Komando Pasukan Khusus, Special Forces Command).

[2] Osborne, *Indonesia's Secret War*, 78–9; 112–13.

[3] McGibbon also makes the important point that the PDP deliberately adopted a strategy of non-violence, which explains why much of the subsequent mobilization remained mostly focused on demonstrations, large meetings, and vocal criticism of government policy. McGibbon, "Secessionist Challenges in Aceh and Papua," 31.

Congress.[4] But with the majority reluctant to concede to "secessionists," Wahid was criticized for allowing such freedoms, and the central government reversed its policy and began to repress the large civilian movement. Given the low-level violence, and fewer historical and cultural ties, the majority was quite comfortable with the degree of state repression applied. No criticism emerged in parliament or among the broader Indonesian public.

Papuan groups tried as well an international strategy without much success. At best, they were able to maintain some attention among a few Congressional representatives in the United States, and obtained some support among nongovernmental organizations (NGOs) abroad to raise awareness of continued human rights abuses, unaddressed grievances, and marginalization.[5] They also created links to the international indigenous peoples movement but were much less united in their rhetorical approach in this respect.[6] Furthermore, they continued to vie for independence as the main expression of self-determination, and therefore refused the indigenous peoples movement's acceptance of a more restricted definition. With weak support abroad, Papuan organizations remained divided on the appropriate strategy internationally.

When the democratic regime began to stabilize and the institutional structures were solidified, the central government took several steps to impose its own solution, while using new forms of repression to weaken Papuan mobilization. It adopted a "special autonomy" law and transferred large amounts of new fiscal resources to Papua, while dividing the province, delaying implementation of new institutions, and undermining Papuans leaders who were most critical. While one can argue that the state provided some concessions, they lacked credibility, particularly in the eyes of Papuans with whom no negotiations were held. By examining the details of the special autonomy law and its implementation, it becomes evident that the state attempted to use the law, subsequent regulations and their implementation to offer concessions that would appease Papuans, but then subsequently sought to undermine them to retain more central government control.

After a decade, Papuans were unable to reconstitute a united front against the Indonesian state, and the conflict remained deep, with occasional violence. Papuans continued to reject "special autonomy," and several groups organized periodic demonstrations demanding independence or renewed dialogue. Meanwhile, grievances remained high and most Papuans saw few hopes that these would be addressed adequately within the existing institutional setting.

[4] Ibid., 24.
[5] Bilveer Singh, *Papua: Geopolitics and the Quest for Nationhood* (New Brunswick: Transaction Publishers, 2008), 169–222.
[6] Jacques Bertrand, "'Indigenous Peoples' Rights' as a Strategy of Ethnic Accommodation: Contrasting Experiences of Cordillerans and Papuans in the Philippines and Indonesia," *Ethnic and Racial Studies* 34, no. 5 (2011).

By contrast to Aceh, therefore, Papua's conflict followed a heightened moment of mobilization but failed to be resolved. It settled in a state of deep grievances, periodic violence, and some repression. Commitments made lacked credibility as the legislation was state imposed and implemented alongside measures to weaken Papuan mobilization and autonomy goals. The majority, as expressed in parliament and in cabinet, had few sympathies for what they continued to view as a "secessionist" movement that needed to be contained.

Forced Integration and Assimilation under the New Order

Under authoritarian rule, mobilization and violence in Papua were relatively low but grievances ran deep. The Indonesian armed forces inflicted most of the violence with campaigns aimed at weeding out supporters of the OPM, which remained a weak, disorganized, and poorly armed group. The OPM operated with small raids on military posts, police stations, or other government targets but without much engagement with the armed forces. Papuans deeply resented the Indonesian state, for the means by which it was integrated and by its strongly centralizing and homogenizing policies, which denied any expression of nationalist demands.

In contrast to the Acehnese, Papuans never agreed to the process and means by which they were integrated into the Indonesian state. Through a largely forced process, they became officially part of Indonesia in 1969 and were given a provincial status equal to all others. The United Nations rubber-stamped the process even though it was flawed, which allowed Indonesia to annex a territory that had few historical links to the rest of the archipelago and its inhabitants shared little history or culture with "Indonesians." Subsequently, the Indonesian state implemented policies designed to integrate and assimilate them. It also considered most of the land to be publicly owned, and therefore conceded mining rights to foreign and domestic firms, with few considerations for local needs. By contrast, Indonesia's later integration of East Timor was largely condemned internationally and was never approved by the United Nations.

At the time of the declaration of independence, Indonesia's first president, Soekarno, supported by most of the new country's tiny political elite, laid claim to West New Guinea. When the Dutch and Indonesia signed a final transfer of territory in 1949, however, the Dutch maintained control over it. In subsequent years, the dispute persisted. Indonesia presented its case to the United Nations, on the basis that West New Guinea had been part of the Dutch East Indies, Indonesia was not based on any particular cultural group, and the lack of participation in the Revolution was due to the fact that Papuans still lived "in the stone age." Meanwhile, the Dutch nurtured the development of a Papuan political elite, with views of preparing them for independence. In 1961, the

Dutch established the first representative body, the New Guinea Council, and proposed to the United Nations that the territory be ceded to an international authority in preparation for self-determination.[7]

There were several months of low-level conflict after December 1961, when Soekarno advanced the notion that Indonesia rejected Dutch attempts to create a puppet state. He appointed a new military command to "liberate" West Irian.[8] After several months of small skirmishes and months of negotiations under UN and US auspices, Indonesia and the Netherlands signed the New York agreement in August 1962. Under this agreement, the territory was transferred to an UN transitional authority and then to Indonesia in May 1963, with the provision that Indonesia would consult Papuans in 1969 on the future status of the territory.[9]

The Act of Free Choice was widely contested on the basis of its process. Between 1963 and 1969, little change occurred in West Irian. When Indonesia integrated West Irian, authoritarian rule was already established under Soekarno's Guided Democracy. By 1969, with Suharto at the helm and the New Order regime consolidating, authoritarian rule intensified. Within this context, it is not surprising that the regime was not sympathetic to allowing the Irianese an actual plebiscite on formally integrating to Indonesia. Instead, after months of intimidation, the regime organized a consultation by which 1,028 representatives were asked whether they agreed to West Irian's formal integration to Indonesia. The representatives unanimously supported integration, and the United Nations subsequently ratified the Act of Free Choice. Papuans overwhelmingly denounced the process and the intimidation that produced its results.[10]

After its integration, West New Guinea, renamed Irian Jaya, was restructured to conform to Indonesia's political and administrative structure, which created strong resentment. It obtained the status of province and its territory was subdivided into regencies, districts, and villages, as specified in the Regional Law of 1974. As in the rest of Indonesia, provinces and districts were implementing arms of the central government, with few powers or resources. Leading officials were selected by regional and provincial assemblies, with the approval of the Ministry of Interior and the president. There were no modifications made to account for the different socio-economic, political, and cultural differences that distinguished the area from the rest of Indonesia.

---

[7] Ikrar Nusa Bhakti and Richard Chauvel, *The Papua Conflict: Jakarta's Perceptions and Policies* (Washington, DC: East-West Center Washington, 2004).

[8] Indonesia referred to West New Guinea as "West Irian".

[9] Bhakti and Chauvel, *The Papua Conflict*, 12–13.

[10] Ibid.; Pieter Drooglever, *An Act of Free Choice: Decolonisation and the Right to Self-Determination in West Papua* (London, UK: One World Publications, 2009).

A parallel military command structure was also created, which conformed with the internal security structure across the archipelago.

The state then implemented strong integrationist policies. Indonesian was adopted as the sole language of education, and the national curriculum was readily imposed on Papuans with basically no local content. The expression of local culture was viewed suspiciously and deemed at times subversive. The government even renamed the province Irian Jaya in 1973 and its capital Jayapura, both of which had no roots or significance locally. Political expression such as the raising of the Morning Star flag was strongly repressed, as well as any indication of calls to revisit the integration of West Irian. The Morning Star flag remained one of the most significant symbols of resistance to the Indonesian state, as it represented Papuans' aspiration to self-determination.[11]

Migration rapidly threatened Papuans' status as a majority in their own land. Irian Jaya became a priority destination for the government's transmigration program in 1977. Spontaneous migrants came in much greater numbers and constituted the greatest threat to Papuans' livelihood. It is estimated that, out of a population of 2.6 million in 2000, 1.6 million were Papuan and 1 million were spontaneous migrants and transmigrants.[12]

The armed forces maintained a constant presence. Military campaigns were regularly waged, especially following local revolts. Throughout the 1980s they were on a smaller scale and most often targeted the OPM after hit and run raids. As reports of human rights abuses increased, the military diminished the scale of its responses but violence against civilians, torture, disappearances, and shootings continued.[13] Finally the armed forces, initially through active duty and subsequently retired officers, controlled the provincial government.

Poverty, combined with the exploitation of Irian Jaya's vast resources, further fed Papuan resentment. In spite of being consistently ranked as one of the richest provinces in Indonesia because of its resource-rich mining economy, Irian Jaya ranked as the poorest in Indonesia.[14] Yet, it is rich in natural

---

[11] Bertrand, *Nationalism and Ethnic Conflict in Indonesia*, 151–53.

[12] Michael Rumbiak, Lecturer and Head of Population Research Centre, interview by author, August 25, 2001, UNCEN, Abepura.

[13] Gereja Kemah Injil Indonesia, Paroki Tiga Raja, and Gereja Kristen Injili di Irian Jaya, *Laporan Pelanggaran Hak Asasi Manusia Dan Bencana Di Bela, Alama, Jila Dan Mapnduma, Irian Jaya* [Report on Human Rights Violations and Atrocities in Bela, Alama, Jila, and Mapnduma, Irian Jaya] (Timika, Irian Jaya).

[14] In 2014, for instance, the poverty incidence was 27.8% for the province of Papua and 26.3% for West Papua, the two highest of all Indonesian provinces. See Priasto Aji, "Summary of Indonesia's Poverty Analysis," in *ADB Papers on Indonesia* (Manila: Asian Development Bank, October 2015), 3. There was no change from 1996, where the (then) province of Irian Jaya was also ranked the poorest, according to the Indonesian Statistical Bureau. See Anne Booth, "Development: Achievement and Weakness," in *Indonesia Beyond Suharto: Polity, Economy, Society, Transition*, ed. Donald K. Emmerson (Armonk, NY: M.E. Sharpe, 1999), 131.

resources, particularly mining. For several decades, Freeport-McMoran controlled and operated one of Indonesia's largest mining operations. Jakarta-based Indonesians had been partners in the project but Papuans had few benefits, particularly during the decades of authoritarian rule. The mining corporation's presence in Papua has been a constant source of grievance in spite of providing some employment opportunities in the Mimika region.

The socio-economic gap between Papuans and other Indonesians certainly fuelled negative perceptions. Indonesians treated Papuans as "backward" because many lived very simple livelihoods, sometimes as hunters and gatherers, and wore very little clothing. Indonesian officials considered them too primitive to manage their affairs. While the socio-economic gap was almost no different than pockets of Dayak groups in Kalimantan, their treatment only strengthened their sense of being Papuan and not Indonesian, by contrast to Dayaks who identified with Indonesia in spite of their marginalization.

But the most fundamental source of grievances in Papua continued to reside in the rejection of the process of integration to Indonesia.[15] Every other source of grievance, including a persistent socio-economic gap with migrants and Indonesians more broadly, were read through the prism of "occupation" from Indonesia. McGibbon emphasizes, for instance, the impact of migration and rapid socio-economic change as a source of grievance, yet recognizes that human rights violations and "institutionalized racism" from Indonesian officials are "central for any understanding of the Papua conflict."[16] During the New Order years, state policies were broadly seen as marginalizing Papuans, threatening their culture and their livelihoods.[17] Occasional military operations, and arrests and intimidation of individuals accused of secessionist activities added to broad resentment. Finally, the continued inflow of migrants created a fear of displacement and further marginalization.[18]

Opposition to the regime was sustained but very weak. Although most Papuans resented the Indonesian state, there was little open resistance. The OPM was the most significant organization that defied the Indonesian state. Otherwise, flag raisings and demonstrations occasionally occurred but were generally quelled without difficulty.

Weak unity and lack of resources were the two main factors that explain why Papuans were unable to mount significant resistance to the Indonesian state. Papuans are divided among a large number of subgroups, with further divisions

---

[15] This was a repeated theme in almost any interview or conversation with indigenous Papuans. The Act of Free Choice is frequently mentioned as a reminder of the continued oppression from Indonesians.

[16] McGibbon, "Secessionist Challenges in Aceh and Papua," 3.

[17] Timo Kivimäki, *Initiating a Peace Process in Papua: Actors, Issues, Process and the Role of the International Community* (Washington, DC: East-West Center, 2006).

[18] Octavianus Mote, "West Papua's National Awakening," *Tok Blong Pasifik* 55, no. 3 (2001).

between the Highland and coastal areas. While the Papuan nationalist vision galvanized the opposition to the regime, their sense of shared identity remained weak.

By 1998, there was little evidence of sustained Papuan opposition to the regime, but the grievances ran deep. At every occasion, and in spite of strong repression by the armed forces, Papuans expressed their sense of alienation from the Indonesian state. But on the surface, the conflict remained at low levels of violence largely because of their weak ability to organize armed resistance.

Papuan Mobilization Amid Indonesian State Weakness

When Indonesia began to democratize, Papuans mobilized more strongly but violent conflict rose only marginally, mostly state-induced and relatively low in intensity. During the initial few years, the Indonesian state was weakened by the transition: security forces were on the defensive and less likely to repress; the government was more responsive to external pressure as it sought support to restore economic confidence following the Asian Financial Crisis of 1997 and Suharto's downfall; and uncertainty surrounded the extent and depth of change ahead. Furthermore, as seen in Chapter 3, the transitional governments of President Habibie and President Wahid, from 1998 to 2001, introduced constitutional and legislative changes that gave considerably more powers to regions and allowed groups to organize and express regional grievances.

In this window of opportunity, Papuans organized and mobilized much more strongly than before. They voiced openly their grievances and demands for independence. Subsequently, they organized from the grassroots to build a broad, non-state representative organization.

Yet, violence remained relatively low. Insurgents, under the umbrella organization of the OPM, remained divided, poorly organized, and poorly armed. While the Free Aceh Movement in Aceh and Fretilin in East Timor could "tax" businesses and local citizens to build an army, Papuans were too poor to provide any resources to an armed movement. Furthermore, with more than 300 tribes, "there were too many generals."[19] Instead, a civilian movement was formed and its leadership was able to unify Papuans to an unprecedented degree.

As early as the end of May 1998, Papuans began to organize and openly voice their demands. In Jakarta, students denounced human rights abuses at the hands of the armed forces. In cities across Irian Jaya, thousands of people in

---

[19] Rev. Herman Awom, Papua Presidium Council (PDP), interview by author, March 31, 2012, Jayapura.

July 1998 raised the Morning Star flag, symbol of the nationalist movement, and asked for a referendum on independence.[20] They began to organize more systematically to denounce and ask a revision of the 1969 Act of Free Choice – the means by which West New Guinea was integrated formally to Indonesia – and demand redress for past injustices. Some of these actions coalesced in the formation of The Forum for the Reconciliation of Irian Jaya People (Forum Rekonsiliasi Rakyat Irian Jaya, FORERI), which became a focal point for Papuans to lobby on these issues. FORERI included representatives from local churches, universities, as well as customary, women's and students' groups.

While the government applied repression in response to some of the mobilization, initially the movement was able to rapidly organize and expand. Armed forces commander Wiranto drew a line and responded strongly to the raising of the Morning Star flag and expressions of support for independence. Some troops opened fire against demonstrators on the campus of Cenderawasih University (UNCEN) in July 1998, as well as in Biak.[21] Nevertheless, by October 1998, Habibie took new steps to move the armed forces away from a repressive approach and attempted instead to explore possibilities for dialogue. He lifted the status of the Military Operations Zone (*Daerah Operasi Militer*, DOM), which had allowed security operations over the course of the previous thirty years. He also agreed to meet with FORERI. Eager to show broad-based representation, FORERI led 100 representatives from different sectors of Papuan society to meet with President Habibie. The group formally requested independence as it denounced the process of integration to Indonesia and subsequent human rights abuses. Taken aback by these bold demands, Habibie ended the meeting and subsequently refused to continue a dialogue.[22]

By April 1999, some repression resumed as the cabinet and the armed forces wanted to prevent more demands for independence. Many Team 100 members were arrested.[23] Furthermore, in September, Habibie appointed governors for the newly created provinces of West Irian Jaya and Central Irian Jaya, while the parliament (DPR) followed in October with law no. 45, 1999, that confirmed the division of the existing province into three.

[20] *Media Indonesia*, July 7, 1998; *Forum Keadilan* 7, no. 8, July 27, 1998; *Gatra*, July 18, 1998.

[21] *Media Indonesia*, July 8, 1998; *Kompas*, July 7, 1998; *Forum Keadilan* 7, no. 8, July 27, 1998; *Gatra*, July 11, 1998. For a detailed account of the events of July and October 1998, as well as a detailed assessment of casualties and arrests, see Human Rights Watch, "Indonesia Alert: Trouble in Irian Jaya," accessed July 20, 2020, www.hrw.org/news/1998/07/06/indonesia-alert-trouble-irian-jaya.

[22] Benny Giay, Lecturer at STT-Walter Post, Jayapura and Head of Team Preparing Terms of Reference for Team 100 Meeting, interview by author, August 22, 2001, Jayapura.

[23] Human Rights Watch, *Indonesia: Human Rights and Pro-Independence Actions in Papua, 1999–2000* (Jakarta: Human Rights Watch, 2000), 16.

This division of Papuans' homeland became an additional grievance. Most Papuans rejected the measure as a ploy to divide them. Protesters occupied the provincial parliament (DPRD) for days. Demonstrations spread to major towns and even Governor Freddy Numberi publicly denounced the province's division.[24]

There was no significant response to these protests, nor new policies in the remaining months of President Habibie's tenure. After the defeat of his party in the June elections, and the rise of "Baligate," his administration lost its ability to govern effectively and the status of Papua remained a low priority.

When President Wahid took office in November 1999, he was keen on being more open to Papuans, as with Acehnese. Wahid had strong democratic credentials and believed that a more accommodative approach would yield positive results. He allowed three new directions: first, he reversed the controversial split of the province; second, he advocated more tolerance toward the use of symbols of Papua nationhood, including the controversial Morning Star flag; third, he supported Papuan efforts to organize a grassroots-based consultative process and selection of representatives. The window of opportunity lasted less than one year, from November 1999 to September 2000.

Widespread protests had accompanied the announcement of Irian Jaya's division into three provinces. While Habibie moved ahead despite the uproar, Wahid proceeded to cancelling it. Only two weeks after his accession to the presidency, Wahid announced on November 18 that the planned split was cancelled.[25]

Wahid also allowed greater freedom to express symbols of Papuan nationalism. Theys Eluay, a prominent Papuan customary leader, called for flag raisings on December 1, which commemorates the declaration of Papuan independence on December 1, 1961.[26] On that day, Morning Star flags were raised across Irian Jaya and some estimated 800,000 people participated in massive gatherings across the province.[27] Finally, Wahid visited the province on December 31 and discussed Papuan grievances with community leaders. As a recognition of the importance of symbols, Wahid announced that the province's name would be changed from Irian Jaya to Papua. The name change was not implemented during Wahid's presidency but nevertheless at the time indicated openness to accommodate some of the Papuans' demands.[28]

---

[24] *Tempo* 28, no. 9, May 4–10, 1999; *Gatra*, October 9, 1999; *Forum Keadilan* 7, no. 29, October 24, 1999.

[25] See *Gatra* 6, no. 3, December 4, 1999.

[26] *Tempo* 28, no. 39, November 30–December 5, 1999; *Gatra* 6, no. 2, November 27, 1999.

[27] The latest figure is from Elsham-Irian Jaya. See Human Rights Watch, "Indonesia: Human Rights and Pro-Independence Actions in Papua," 27–30.

[28] *Jakarta Post*, January 2, 2000. The name change was never officially implemented under Wahid's presidency.

Most significantly, Wahid allowed and even provided Rp 1 billion to finance the two large congresses. The first (*Musyarawah Besar*, MUBES), held in February 2000, brought together representatives from a variety of sectors of Irian Jaya, including youths, women, religious, and customary groups. The discussions concluded with a formal denunciation of the Act of Free Choice, criticism of Indonesia's record of human rights abuses, cultural genocide, and impoverishment of the Papuan people.[29] Finally, the assembly appointed a PDP as a formal representative of the Papuan people.

The Papuan People's Congress (*Kongress Papua*), held from May 29 to June 4, 2000, made explicit demands for independence. Its resolutions focused again on the failures of the international community to revisit the Act of Free Choice, revisit the injustices against the Papuan people, and their right to self-determination. The Congress also sealed the representative role of the PDP.[30] It enjoyed broad appeal among the Papuan people. Not only did chosen representatives attend, but thousands more came to witness the event, and ensure that its resolutions would be broadly representative: "Both the MUBES and Congress were flooded with people. Thousands came to ensure that the organizing committee and the PDP would not be like the Pepera [the Act of Free Choice]."[31] Wahid did not formally recognize the PDP leadership but still met with Theys Eluay, its leader, in early July after the Congress.[32]

The Congress and PDP provided Papuans with strong and clear leadership. Papuan identity was constructed by a small elite that, under the last few years of Dutch colonial rule, developed a nationalist program for self-determination, including the adoption of a national anthem, a representative assembly, and culminating in the raising of the Morning Star flag on December 1, 1961. Its goals were thwarted when the Dutch ceded the territory to Indonesia and, later, the Act of Free Choice sealed the integration to Indonesia. Afterward, the shared experience of domination under Indonesian rule, along with marginalization and mistreatment, contributed to nurturing a broader Papuan identity in spite of deep divisions. Papuans are constituted by a large number of tribal groups, geographically separated and sometimes isolated, given a mountainous and largely inaccessible landscape. Unity under a single leadership was always a challenge. OPM, for instance, always remained an umbrella organization with a number of separate and even competing factions. The Congress and the PDP represented a rare instance when Papuans came together and united under

---

[29] See Komunike Politik Papua, signed by Theys Eluay and Tom Beanal as great leaders of the Papuan people, Sentani-Port Numbay (Jayapura), February 26, 2000.

[30] Agus Alua, Vice Secretary General of the Papua Presidium Council, Secretary of the Mubes Organizing Committee and Head of the Congress Organizing Committee, interview by author, August 23, 2001, Abepura.

[31] Benny Giay, interview. He was named one of three moderators of the PDP at the People's Congress.

[32] *Tempo* 29, no. 33, October 15–22, 2000.

a single leadership. The head of the PDP, Theys Eluay, a customary leader, gained broad support in spite of some controversy regarding his past association with the New Order regime.[33] Even various leaders of the OPM agreed to reduce their armed activities and chose to join the PDP.[34] As Eluay stated: "The OPM already agrees with us. And we have already requested that they cease their hostilities."[35]

Papuans skilfully took advantage of this brief window of opportunity to organize a broad civil movement and place their grievances on the national agenda, press for a redress of past injustices and for a referendum. They used the political space to elect an alternative leadership, the PDP, that united different strands of Papuan society and emerged as a broadly recognized leader.

Such opportunity only arose because of the weakness of the Indonesian state at the moment of democratic transition. First, its repressive apparatus was severely weakened. The armed forces and the police were forced to reduce operations and repressive tactics after they were strongly discredited for mishandling protests that contributed to Suharto's downfall and, in particular, the crackdown in Jakarta. Furthermore, much of the Reformasi movement and protests across Indonesia targeted the military's role in politics and made strong demands to reduce its political interference. Second, the transitional government and the political elite were concerned with reassuring donors and financial markets, overcoming the instability of the 1997 Asian Financial Crisis, and setting Indonesia back on a steady course for growth. President Habibie's concession on a referendum for East Timor sent signals that the Indonesian state might yield further to nationalist claims in Irian Jaya.

At the same time, violence never increased significantly in scale. As McGibbon argues: "the province has not experienced the scale of violence and communal unrest that has plagued neighboring regions, namely the Malukus. One reason for this may be the waning momentum of the independence movement. By the last quarter of 2000, independence leaders were finding it increasingly difficult to maintain mass support as independence seemed as distant as ever and the military was increasingly adopting repressive measures." Furthermore, the PDP had adopted a non-violent approach.[36] There were few options for the OPM to gain more influence as it had recognized the PDP's leadership and, in any case, remained as divided as before the transition. Furthermore, violent options required some organizational capacity and availability of weapons, both of which were absent.

---

[33] Benny Giay, interview. See also Tim SKP Jayapura, *Memoria Passionis Di Papua* (Jayapura: Sekretariat Keadilan dan Perdamaian, 2005), 72–73.

[34] Agus Alua, interview.

[35] Theys Eluay, PDP Chair, interview by author, August 21, 2001, Sentani.

[36] McGibbon, "Secessionist Challenges in Aceh and Papua," 30–31.

Two broader factors also limited violent mobilization in Papua and in many other regions of Indonesia. The political elite that crafted the transition, led by President Habibie, sought a consensual approach to constitutional and institutional changes, to avoid losing control over the pace and degree of reforms to the more radical demands of street protesters. While they competed for office, they refrained from instigating violence, mobilizing along ethnic lines, or fomenting large protests as a means of gaining political power. Also, the issue of East Timor contributed to ending President Habibie's political career and set the stage for the Wahid presidency, which relied on a broad coalitional support from all parties in parliament. Much of the efforts of the political elite centred on adopting constitutional amendments to seal the frame-work for the new democracy, maintain stability while beginning to operate under new democratic rules, and decide on the pace and degree of reforms, including most importantly the armed forces' representation in parliament and its political role. The choice of President Wahid allowed him to preserve a degree of consensual politics and rule by coalition of all major political parties. As a consequence, Wahid was in a position to push for deeper reforms, including a tolerant approach toward Irian Jaya, but was highly constrained by the need to nurture the support from all parties.[37]

In the last few months of President Wahid's presidency, violence did increase while the majority in parliament and the political elite controlling Wahid's coalition became increasingly uncomfortable with the tolerance Wahid had shown for the "secessionist" movement. Security forces advocated more repressive approaches to combat the threat. Backed by parliament, they reas-serted some of their influence, as President Wahid's power diminished and as he failed to assert fully his authority over the armed forces.[38] Security forces defied the president's tendencies for more tolerance. Violence and several deaths were reported in Nabire in February and July, in Merauke (February 2000), in Sorong (August 2000) and, particularly, in Wamena (October 2000), where 37 people were killed and 13,000 people left the area. All these cases involved violence around the raising of the Morning Star flag.[39] There was a consistent reversal from Wahid's previous instructions to tolerate flag raisings as expressions of local culture. The August meeting of the People's Consultative Assembly (MPR) refused to endorse Wahid's proposal to change Irian Jaya's name to Papua and members denounced his ineffectiveness at countering secessionism. After September 2000, the MPR and national

[37] Ibid., 39–40. For more details, see Bertrand, *Nationalism and Ethnic Conflict in Indonesia*, 155–58.

[38] Bertrand, *Nationalism and Ethnic Conflict in Indonesia*, 157–58.

[39] Theo Van den Broek and Alexandra Szalay, "Raising the Morning Star: Six Months in the Developing Independence Movement in West Papua," *The Journal of Pacific History* 36, no. 1 (2001): 87–89.

parliament (DPR) significantly curtailed the president's power, and placed him in a highly defensive stance. While they were most critical of the escalating violence in Aceh, they nevertheless pointed to secessionist threats more broadly, including in Irian Jaya.[40]

In sum, the initial phase of democratization saw rising mobilization but violence remained relatively low by comparison to other cases. While the state still used repression, it was much more restrained. The police and armed forces mainly intervened when faced with overt calls for independence, such as the raising of the Morning Star flag and demonstrations calling for secession. Channels to express discontent were much wider than before and, at the level of state institutions, the new democratic framework kept the political elite united in its quest for national unity. This elite also remained moderate and reluctant to use ethnic or religious forms of mobilization that have destabilized democracies elsewhere. While Papuans failed to be included in any meaningful discussions on the constitution, there were nevertheless provisions to enhance their participation in the new democratic institutions and to implement principles of regional autonomy. Of course, the long-standing divisions among Papuans, weak organizational capacity, and absence of weapons also contributed to the missing of large-scale violent mobilization. Finally, while brief, the united leadership of the PDP deliberately chose a peaceful strategy and convinced the OPM to follow its leadership. Although successful initially to gain legitimacy among Papuans, the strategy failed to deliver the substantive gains that the PDP sought.

Stabilization of Democracy

The stabilization of democracy defined the new parameters under which further state concessions and field of negotiation with Papuans would occur. As in the case of Aceh, the Indonesian state more generally had difficulty in using the armed forces to quell dissent, if the new Indonesian democracy would remain credible. Yet, it could still justify repression, mostly with its police and anti-rioting forces, as it countered mobilization that it deemed to be separatist. The state-imposed special autonomy law became the only framework that allowed the state to attempt some appeasement of Papuan demands while making claims that it corresponded to similar autonomy principles applied elsewhere in Indonesia. It lacked credibility and therefore Papuans rejected it. More significantly the state used regulations and other policies to undermine concessions made, and dilute Papuan autonomy so that it would resemble other provinces over time. Against a majority that continued to favour strong Indonesian unity and a reluctance to compromise or negotiate

---

[40] Bertrand, *Nationalism and Ethnic Conflict in Indonesia*, 157–58.

with Papuans, the conflict stalled. The state's approach instead contributed to dividing Papuans, who were already weakly organized and already inclined to division. With low mobilizational capacity, they continued to protest and demonstrate, violence remained relatively low, but grievances deep.

Papuan groups continued to use the new democratic space to voice their demands, but they became increasingly divided. The PDP became discredited after Theys Eluay's death and the erosion of its capacity to mobilize Papuans effectively. Remaining groups had divergent goals. Some networked abroad to organize international pressure. Others rioted sporadically in protest at the Indonesian government's policies. Finally, a few Papuans ran for election, entered the new institutions, and attempted to maximize gains from within.

The central government fed the division, partly by design, partly by coincidence. When clamours for renewed dialogue were made, the central government dragged its feet. Simultaneously, large amounts of fiscal resources were distributed to the provincial and regency governments under the auspices of the special autonomy law, thereby creating opportunities for graft and corruption. With discredited institutions, corruption became widespread and further contributed to Papuan divisions.

Democratic stabilization produced new parameters of repression but also confirmed its limits. After being on the defensive, security forces reasserted some of their power. With a president keen on drawing a firm line on secessionist activities, security forces took new initiatives to crack down on flag raisings, demonstrations, and riots. While the government more often used special police forces, the Mobile Brigade (*Brimob*, a paramilitary branch of the Indonesian police), it also occasionally still deployed the armed forces' special forces (Kopassus), particularly in less visible areas. More generally, it arrested leaders deemed to be engaged in secessionist activities and curtailed organizations or groups that it judged to be threats to national unity. Overall, levels of violent repression were lower as civil society organizations and the media more closely scrutinized and investigated violent incidents.

In parallel to this repression, the government clamped down on the PDP, which had consolidated strong support among Papuans after the Congress. The local police received orders to eliminate all secessionist activities and gather intelligence on the activities of local NGOs. It was instructed to "eliminate people involved in the separatist movement, followed by efforts to foster among the population a positive opinion so that it increasingly sides with the government of the Republic of Indonesia."[41] Theys Eluay and several members of the PDP were prosecuted and sent to prison for separatist activities linked to

[41] Kepolisian Negara Republik Indonesia Daerah Irian Jaya. Rencana Operasi "Tuntas Matoa 2000" Polda Irja (Confidential). Jayapura, November 2000, No. Pol.: R/Renops/640/XI/ 2000, p. 9.

the December 1, 1999 flag raisings, as well as their roles in organizing the Mubes and Congress. They were jailed for two months.[42] The Papuan movement was paralyzed.

After she became president in July 2001, Megawati reaffirmed the government's uncompromising position on the nationalist movement. With strong party presence in parliament and a close relationship to the armed forces, she confirmed a repressive approach in Papua. There was strong support for this nationalist orientation in parliament, and she faced few criticisms from the majority of Indonesians with respect to her policies toward Irian Jaya. Certainly, there was no similar sentiment on the basis of shared religion, as was the case with Muslims in Aceh, that could sway part of the larger elite toward finding a lasting compromise. Criticisms came primarily from human rights organizations, Papuans themselves, and foreigners.

Her successor, Susilo Bambang Yudhoyono (SBY), took a similar approach after he was elected president in 2004. In fact, SBY had been a highly respected Coordinating Minister of Political and Security Affairs in the last year of Wahid's presidency as well as in Megawati's cabinet. He oversaw much of the shift in policy toward Irian Jaya under Wahid and Megawati's presidencies. Furthermore, as a former general, he commanded the respect of the armed forces and shared their values with respect to low tolerance toward groups deemed a threat to Indonesia's unity.

The total number of troops increased between 2004 and 2006. Operations along the border continued and access to border areas remained restricted. Internal security matters were transferred to the local police but some units, particularly Brimob, frequently over-stepped their powers.[43]

Repeated incidents in Puncak Jaya are illustrative of practices found in other regions as well. The Indonesian Human Rights Commission denounced the involvement of security forces in clashes and incidents that killed dozens of people after 2004.[44] In 2010 alone, it recorded eleven incidents in Puncak Jaya. Such incidents occurred in 2011 as well, with at least four people killed in July of that year alone. The Commission accused the TNI (the Indonesian armed forces) of having secret operations in Papua at least since 2004.[45]

The crackdown against the PDP was sustained, even though the government did not ban it. When Kopassus members assassinated Theys Eluay in 2001, it confirmed the state's willingness to continue using the armed forces to both

---

[42] See Human Rights Watch, "Indonesia: Human Rights and Pro-Independence Actions in Papua"; *Tempo* 29, no. 40, December 4–10, 2000.

[43] International Crisis Group, *Papua: The Dangers of Shutting Down Dialogue* (Jakarta: International Crisis Group, 2006), 10.

[44] "Jayapura's Top Cop Replaced for Mishandling Violent Protest", *Jakarta Post*, May 14, 2005.

[45] "*TNI/Polri Di Puncak Jaya Dinilai 'Mubazir'* [TNI/Police in Puncak Jaya Judged 'Redundant],'" *Bintang Papua*, October 23, 2010.

overtly and covertly target secessionists. Yet, such blatant repression was less frequent and more disguised than in the past. Human rights organizations investigated and successfully publicized and criticized the ploy. Public pressure on such abuse was sufficiently strong that the courts sent the perpetrators to jail, one of the rare instances of partial accountability for such use of violence.[46]

The Indonesian government continued to use repression against Papuans but, overall, there were limits on the ability to deploy it on a large scale. It drew a clear line by which it would use physical violence or arrest demonstrators or activists it deemed to be engaging in "secessionist" activities. While open to the state's interpretation, nevertheless it created some restraint and left wide space for Papuans to demonstrate, organize, and voice their grievances and claims. Media scrutiny of the use of force was much greater than in the past, and church groups, NGOs, and human rights organizations reported openly on abuses.

Special Autonomy: A Concession?

Once democratic institutions were stabilized, the Indonesian government focused on implementing "special autonomy" – its solution for Papua. The special autonomy law and its accompanying provisions constituted very significant concessions on paper, both in terms of providing vast new powers and fiscal resources. Nevertheless, they were accompanied by measures to explicitly divide Papuans and to undermine some of the concessions that were made. Many elements, particularly in the armed forces, were likely to have resented these concessions and sought greater repression, while moderates within the government supported accommodation. The state's commitment lacked credibility, not only because special autonomy lacked sufficient legislative safeguards and implementing regulations to provide the kind of wide-ranging autonomy that Papuans demanded but also its failure to negotiate its content rendered Papuan support difficult to obtain.

The MPR session of 1999 had adopted a motion instructing the government to develop a policy of special autonomy for Irian Jaya and Aceh. In its annual session in August 2000, it reiterated the urgency of implementing special autonomy.[47] In the following months, the governor of Irian Jaya, J. P. Solossa, put together a team to develop a draft law, which was presented to the DPR in April 2001. It included clauses protecting and reinforcing Papuan values and

---

[46] Matthew Moore and Indonesia Karuni Rompies Surabaya, "Kopassus Guilty of Eluay Murder," *The Age*, 22 April, 2003. The argument should not be overblown. The sentences were relatively short, and targeted mainly low-level soldiers, but it was still unprecedented, particularly as a condemnation of Kopassus and its methods.

[47] See section IV-G (2), [MPR 1999] and the instructions to the President in response to the President's report to the MPR (Appendix 1.1) [MPR 2000].

culture, substantially devolving power to the province, and proposing that 80 per cent of revenue be retained by the provincial government. The draft was revised and a special autonomy law was passed by the DPR in October 2001.

Law no. 21, 2001 on special autonomy (Otsus) for Papua provided wide-ranging autonomy for the Papuan provincial government, which obtained jurisdiction over all matters except foreign policy, defence, monetary and fiscal policy, religion, and justice. The law also created a special assembly, the Papuan People's Assembly (*Majelis Rakyat Papua*, MRP), to represent *indigenous* Papuan groups. It included representatives from all sectors of Papuan society, such as religious, women, and customary groups. Its mandate was to promote and protect the rights and customs of Papuan people. It was also given powers of consultation and assent over candidates for the position of governor and over decisions and regulations relating to the basic rights of Papuans. While it did not give the MRP legislative powers, which resided with the Papua provincial legislature (DPRP), the law required that the MRP be consulted and its views taken into account on all matters within its purview. In order to address grievances from the past, the law provided for the creation of a Truth and Reconciliation Commission to investigate past abuses. Finally, Papua was to receive 80 per cent from non-tax revenue in mining, forestry, and fisheries, and 70 per cent from oil and gas exploitation. In addition, a greater proportion of tax revenues were to accrue to the province, as well as special autonomy funds for a limited number of years.[48]

The net effect of fiscal transfers was disappointing. Papuan officials and NGO activists blamed the insufficient level of funds for the poor results. "One of our failures during 2000–2001, we didn't calculate properly the distribution of funds. Special autonomy doesn't change national policy of taxation. That is the reason why we only benefit less than 9% of total profit." Once divided among all the regencies, they contend, the funds earmarked for special autonomy provided insufficient fiscal resources to make significant developmental changes.[49] The bulk of the funds were paid for civil servants' salaries, top officials' housing, and other benefits. Without a proper legal framework to regulate the spending, the funds were mostly spent at officials' discretion.[50]

---

[48] Jacques Bertrand, "Indonesia's Quasi-Federalist Approach". The law gave similar percentages to regions for mining, fisheries, and forestry, but less for oil and gas (15.5% and 30.5 respectively). Law no. 33, 2004 and subsequent regulations, however, were much more specific about fiscal categories, their definition, and precise methods of redistribution than the Special Autonomy Law for Papua.

[49] Agus Sumule, Advisor to the Governor of Papua, interview by author, March 30, 2012, Jayapura.

[50] Fadhal Al Hamid, Head of Customary Governance, Dewan Adat Papua (Papuan Customary Assembly), interview by author, March 31, 2012. Jayapura.

Corruption was also very strong. In 2011, the Badan Pemeriksa Keuangan (BPK, Audit Board of the Republic of Indonesia) found that of the Rp 19.12 trillion audited, Rp 4.12 trillion was misused.[51] While corruption was common across Indonesia, the problem was much worse than elsewhere.[52]

In the 2013 budget, the government announced a total of Rp 513.9 trillion to be transferred to regional governments through various budgetary envelopes. This amount represented an 8.4 per cent increase from the previous year and a clear commitment to local governance broadly. Of these funds, Rp 13.2 constituted special autonomy funds (*dana alokasi khusus*), including Rp 4.3 trillion to Papua and Rp 1.8 trillion to West Papua.[53] In addition, Rp 1 trillion was allocated to both provinces as special funds for infrastructure.[54]

While it is very difficult to assess the degree to which it was a coherent strategy, the state nevertheless significantly delayed or never implemented several aspects of the special autonomy law.

The formation of the MRP suffered many delays. Even though the special autonomy law came into effect in January 2002, the MRP was only formed after numerous criticisms from local groups. On August 12, 2005 more than 10,000 people, led by the Papua Customary Council (*Dewan Adat Papua*, DAP), protested against the failure to implement special autonomy, specifically in relation to the failure to create the MRP while pushing ahead with the creation of the province of West Irian Jaya. The DAP's representatives denounced the planned selection process for the new MRP, its delay, and the failure to properly implement the special autonomy law. Consequently, they contended that the law had to be "returned" to the central government.[55]

By October 2005, the government proceeded nevertheless with the creation of the MRP and selection of its members. As its membership required representation from different segments of Papuan society – including women and tribal groups – the selection mechanism became more complex than simple elections. Tribal and church leaders joined their influential voices to the DAP to denounce the process from the outset, thereby undermining the legitimacy of the newly formed MRP.[56]

---

[51] *"Temuan Dana Otsus Dipakai Melancong Ke Eropa, Dibatah* [Autonomy Funds Used for European Vacations]," *Bintang Papua*, April 19, 2011.

[52] *"Pemprov Papua Dinilai Terus Lakukan Pembohongan Public* [Papua's Provincial Government Continues to Lie to the Public]," *Bintang Papua*, November 23, 2010.

[53] By comparison, Aceh was allocated Rp 6.3 trillion.

[54] *"Transfer Anggaran Ke Daerah Rp 518,9 Triliun, Pemerintah Percepat Pembangunan Di Papua Dan Papua Barat* [518.9 Trillion Rupiah Budget Transfer to Regions, Government Speeds up Development in Papua and West Papua]," http://setkab.go.id/berita-5416-transfer-anggaran-ke-daerah-rp-5189-triliun-pemerintah-percepat-pembangunan-di-papua-dan-papua-barat.html, accessed October 5, 2012.

[55] *"Puji Tuhan, Aman! DAP/MAP Ajukan 6 Tuntutan* [Praise the Lord, Safety! DAP/MAP Forward 6 Demands]," *Cendrawasih Pos*, August 13, 2005.

[56] "Establishment of Papuan Council Runs into More Problems," *Jakarta Post*, October 1, 2005.

More broadly, almost ten years after its official beginning, neither the central nor the provincial government had drafted regulations designed to properly implement the special autonomy law. At least twenty-nine regulations and ordinances (*perdasi* and *perdasus*) were required to implement it properly. During the first five years, only one regulation had been successfully passed. Others took many years. Members of the Papuan government and the DPRP blamed the central government for failing to provide assistance and to pass its own regulation (PP, *Peraturan Pemerintah*) that should be in place prior to moving ahead with provincial level ones.[57] In 2010, the Ministry of Interior stated that it was preparing a regulation to guide the process for the provincial implementation of *perdasi* and *perdasus*. The DPRP adopted a draft *perdasus* and four draft *perdasi* in December 2010, with one for the election of MRP members for the period 2011–2015, others on health, HIV/AIDS, and on the process of drafting and adopting these regulations.[58] By April 2013, the DPRP had adopted seven *perdasus* and eight *perdasi* but still several others were required, especially a regulation on the distribution of special autonomy funds.[59] While local officials shared the blame for failing to exercise their own autonomy, nevertheless central government officials were able to paralyze the process of implementation by frequently objecting to various aspects of proposed drafts.[60]

Furthermore, the central government maintained leverage over the disbursement of funds. Although the budget for Papua was raised every year and reached Rp 4.3 trillion for Papua proper and Rp 1.8 trillion for West Papua (formerly West Irian Jaya) in 2013,[61] the capacity to implement special autonomy was curtailed. The central government distributed funds in three instalments. By doing so, it could retain some influence over the local government and prevent it from supporting policies deemed to be "separatist." It also placed a constraint on the Papuan and West Papuan governments' rational allocation of their budget.[62] Projects could not be implemented because funds would remain in Jakarta and the timing of their release remained uncertain.[63]

---

[57] Muridan S. Widjojo and Sherry Kasman Entus, *Papua Road Map: Negotiating the Past, Improving the Present, and Securing the Future* (Jakarta/Singapore: LIPI, ISEAS, 2009).

[58] "*Disahkan, 1 Raperdasus Dan 4 Raperdasi* [1 Perdasus and 4 Perdasi Approved]," *Bintang Papua*, December 3, 2010.

[59] "*Papua Belum Punya Perdasus* [No Special Law for Papua yet]," *Republika*, April 10, 2013.

[60] Agus Sumule, interview.

[61] Sandro Gatra, "Dana Otsus Papua 2012 Naik [Increase in 2012 Special Autonomy Budget for Papua]," *Kompas*, October 28, 2011.

[62] Sekretariat Kabinet Republic Indonesia, "*Transfer Anggaran Ke Daerah Rp 518,9 Triliun, Pemerintah Percepat Pembangunan Di Papua Dan Papua Barat* [518.9 Trillion Rupiah Budget Transfer to Regions, Government Speeds up Development in Papua and West Papua]".

[63] Neles Tebay, Catholic Priest and Coordinator of *Jaringan Damai Papua* (Papua Peace Network), interview by author, April 2, 2012, Jayapura.

The state's lack of commitment to the law resonated at all levels of the bureaucratic hierarchy and strongly dampened any resolve to making it work. "Because it is not a product of negotiation, ... the government does not have a sense of ownership. Papuan people, because they were not consulted, also don't have a sense of ownership." It creates a commitment problem at every level of government, from the president down to governors and district heads.[64]

As a result, the central government every year transferred to Papua large amounts with little accountability, transparency, or clear mechanism for its distribution and use. According to Foker LSM, in the first three years after the enactment of the law, 70 per cent of funds went to salaries while only 30 per cent went to development purposes.[65] They estimated that not much had changed ten years after. Much of the funds went to perks, including housing and cars for officials, as well as travel to Jakarta and abroad.[66] Corruption ran high, while few results were achieved.

Basic services were still lacking in education and health despite the trillions of rupiah transferred over a decade.[67] There was broad agreement among NGOs and activists that the funds failed to produce visible results in areas for which they were intended. The head of the provincial planning development board (Bappeda) could use the funds without much accountability because there was no plan, no design for educational or developmental goals.[68] After ten years, they contended, Otsus had nothing to show. According to the law, most of the funds are targeted to education, health, infrastructure, and raising the standard of living but on all these measures there were few visible changes. Many of the expenses toward education, health, and people's welfare went into infrastructural investments, such as schools, clinics, or underutilized markets, without the corresponding recruitment of teachers and medical professionals, in part because corruption is easier and less traceable with infrastructural projects.[69] In the words of the PDP leader, "We should arrest the bureaucrats, not demonstrators, because they make special autonomy fail."[70]

One of the basic problems remained the inconsistency of the legal framework. While the special autonomy law provided powers in a large number of jurisdictions, many national laws also extended their reach into those same jurisdictions. Some disputes involved the drafting of regulations that would be acceptable to the Interior ministry and deemed not to contradict national

---

[64] Ibid.
[65] Septer Manufandu, Executive Secretary, Foker NGO, interview by author, April 4, 2012, Jayapura.
[66] Fadhal Al Hamid, interview.
[67] Rev. Herman Awom, interview; Septer Manufandu, interview.
[68] Fadhal Al Hamid, interview.   [69] Ibid.
[70] Thaha Al Hamid, Sekjen PDP (Secretary General of the PDP), interview by author, April 1, 2012, Jayapura.

laws. As Otsus was quite vague, it was subject to much interpretation. For example, the Ministry of Forests rejected some of the Papuan government's proposed regulations on the basis that they violated the national forestry law. With uncertainty surrounding the authority obtained under Otsus the Papuan government often followed clearer directives from national laws, such as the national forestry and mining laws.[71]

The Papuan government has therefore been hesitant to exercise its authority even in jurisdictions that are under its purview. At times, "officials appeal to laws that suit their agendas, and there is no consistency between them."[72] More often than not, they check with the central government before making decisions.[73] The exercise of autonomy, de facto, is therefore very limited.

Some of the development initiatives, while somewhat successful, only showed the weaknesses of the autonomy law, as they proceeded outside of its authority. The governor, Barnabas Suebu, launched a program, the Village Development Strategic Plan (*Rencana Strategis Pembangunan Kampung*) program, to disburse funds directly to each village. Starting with a World Bank pilot program, it involved the distribution of Rp 100 million per village.[74] Launched in 2007, the funds were the most visible evidence of government expenses on development. Suebu boasted of the accomplishments, including the creation of small agricultural businesses, greater access to health services as well as education.[75] The funding rose from Rp 350 billion in 2010 to Rp 400 billion in 2011. Much of the expenses were for infrastructural projects, some of which were therefore covered out of special budgetary funds for infrastructure and some presumably from the special autonomy funds.[76] Overall, these funds constituted only a small portion of the special autonomy funds but, more importantly, they were the only funds with visible developmental impact while not addressing the objectives from Otsus.[77]

The central government recognized even more clearly that Otsus was not reaching its objectives when President Susilo Bambang Yudhoyono (SBY) launched a special program for accelerated development. The program aimed at injecting additional funding into infrastructure and providing more coordination of developmental expenditures to gain maximum effect. It culminated in

[71] Yusak Reba, Program Coordinator, Institute for Civil Society Strengthening (ICS), interview by author, April 5, 2012, Jayapura; Septer Manufandu, interview.

[72] Thaha Al Hamid, interview.   [73] Agus Sumule, interview.

[74] "*Kampung Di Papua Dan Irjabar Dapat Rp 100 Juta* [Village in Papua and Irian Jaya Barat Receives 100 Million Rp]," *Suara Pembaruan*, February 27, 2007.

[75] "*Kebijakan Pembangunan Dimulai Dari Kampung* [Development Begins in the Village]," *Bintang Papua*, February 9, 2011; Agus Sumule, interview.

[76] "*2011 Dana Respek Meningkat Rp 50 Milyar* [2011 Respek Budget Increases by 50 Billion Rp]," *Bintang Papua*, April 28, 2011.

[77] Makawaru Da Cunha, "*Siapapun Gubernurnya, Respek Harus Dilanjutkan* [Whoever Becomes Governor Must Continue Respek]," *Bintang Papua*, June 28, 2011.

the creation of a special unit, UP4B (*Unit Percepatan Pembangunan Provinsi Papua dan Provinsi Papua Barat*; Accelerated development unit for Papua and West Papua provinces). Led by a former general, Bambang Darmono, the unit was an ad hoc structure that, while officially playing a coordinating role, essentially bypassed local institutions.[78] As an NGO leader noted: "UP4B is positive, as it was created by the President, but it means that the President considers the implementation of Otsus to be not effective … The provincial government cannot complain because its work has not been adequate. It would not need UP4B, if it did its work."[79]

Critics acknowledged its small successes but pointed to few concrete developmental results.[80] The program was credited mainly with funding a small number of Papuans to be educated in high schools and universities across Indonesia. In 2013, for instance, 500 were sent to high schools in Bali and Java, while 1,370 students were sent to a variety of universities across Indonesia. A few (64) as well were accepted into the Indonesian Military Academy and into the National Police Academy, whereas 1,875 joined the police. The government also gave Papuan businessmen priority in the bidding for construction projects.[81]

It was broadly perceived among Papuans as an additional attempt to bypass special autonomy. The central government's perceived need to pour more funds as well as interference in development constituted evidence of its recognition that the large funds disbursed to Papua and Papua Barat were not having the intended effect on local development. When Jokowi became president, he was pressured to disband UP4B.

Finally, the law made provisions for the organization of a Truth and Reconciliation Commission to address past human rights abuses. Yet, the commission was never implemented. In spite of several requests to move ahead with its establishment, the government stalled.

Thwarting Mobilizational Capacity and Fomenting Division

In addition to eroding the concessions made, the Indonesian state also attempted to prevent Papuans from unifying and increasing their mobilizational capacity. While couched in terms of efficiency and response to local demands, the division of the province and later the MRP were partly designed to prevent Papuans from regaining the strong unity that had led to the congresses and the formation of the PDP.

---

[78] "*Wapres: UP4B Jangan Tabrakan Dengan Otsus* [Vice President: UP4B Should Not Conflict with Autonomy Funds]," *Bintang Papua*, November 25, 2010.

[79] Yusak Reba, interview.   [80] Thaha Al Hamid, interview.

[81] Margareth S. Aritonang, "Jokowi Told to Disband UP4B in Papua," *Jakarta Post*, September 8, 2014.

The MRP's status came full circle. The Indonesian government under Megawati's presidency had clearly delayed its creation under suspicion that it could serve as a platform to advance secessionist objectives. Under sustained pressure, however, it relented. Once created, the MRP gained respect from Papuans across several divides because of the role of its three prominent leaders, Wospakrik, Alua, and Hikoyabi. The state's strategies to displace them, using an Interior ministry's regulation, however, shows the weakness of the law and the vulnerability of the MRP as an institutional representative of Papuans.

From the outset, the policy to divide Papua into three provinces created suspicion and controversy. The Habibie government had introduced a law in 1999 to divide up Papua into three distinct provinces: West Irian Jaya, Central Irian Jaya, and Papua. Faced with strong local resistance, the Law was not implemented but had not been revoked. When she came to power in 2001, President Megawati revived the law and proceeded to implementing it. While the creation of the province of Central Irian Jaya was cancelled because of strong renewed protests, the government nevertheless proceeded with the creation of the province of West Irian Jaya.

A confidential Ministry of Internal Affairs memo showed a carefully planned response to the 2000 Papuan Congress that included the partitioning of the province.[82] For some officials in the Ministry of Internal Affairs, the armed forces and the intelligence agencies, the government had conceded too much autonomy, which would encourage secessionist tendencies. There were therefore attempts to reverse and undermine some of the concessions made.

The government of Papua as well as many activists rejected the newly created provinces and its legality. Megawati appointed a transitional governor while the dispute was settled. The Constitutional Court eventually confirmed the extension of special autonomy to the West Irian Jaya province. Ironically, it revoked Law no. 45, 1999 on Papua's partition, on the basis that it was unconstitutional. Yet, because the partition had been implemented and representatives had been elected to the West Irian Jaya parliament, it recognized and formalized the establishment of the West Irian Jaya province.[83]

Once the new province was created, the local elite began defending its existence against the protests of elites in the province of Papua. MRP leaders openly rejected it and claimed that it contributed to division. The local parliament (DPRP) of the Papua province as well as several NGOs also continued to protest against the division.[84] In the end, as its provincial status became more

[82] Chauvel, *Constructing Papuan Nationalism*.
[83] Tiarma Siboro, "Government Prepares Regulation on West Irian Jaya Province," *Jakarta Post*, July 22, 2005.
[84] "*Pemerintah Masih Pelajari Rekomendasi MRP Soal Irabar* [Government Still Studying MRP Recommendation on West Irian Jaya]," *Suara Karya*, March 21, 2006.

entrenched, Papuan Governor Barnabas Suebu agreed to meet with West Papua (renamed in 2007) provincial Governor Abraham Atururi and ended the dispute.[85] Finally, the central government confirmed its previous decree with a new law. Law no. 35, 2008 confirmed the creation of the West Papua province and ended the controversy. By then, special autonomy had been extended to West Papua, and dedicated special autonomy funds were distributed according to its proportion of total population in both provinces.[86]

The issue was later revived, when the government proceeded to also splitting the MRP. Although primarily a consultative body, it became vocal to defend the interests of the Papuans, who were increasingly marginalized by the influx of migrants. MRP leaders viewed that mandate as representing all Papuans. A team from UNCEN that included a representative from the DAP had proposed that members represent seven customary areas, rather than regencies, but the Interior ministry rejected the proposal and proceeded with the MRP's division.[87] *Perdasus* no. 4, 2010, which regulated the selection process, had reiterated that there was only one MRP. Yet, later the Minister of Interior issued a letter clarifying that there would be two. In spite of protests against the division, the change was implemented nevertheless.[88]

Furthermore, after the provincial division, several groups began to make claims to the creation of new regencies, a phenomenon also found in other parts of Indonesia ever since decentralization offered more resources at the regency level. The issue of partitions (or *pemekaran*) became widespread across Indonesia in the aftermath of the implementation of administrative and fiscal decentralization laws (nos. 22 and 25, 1999), which indirectly contained incentives to create new regencies and gain new fiscal windfalls. In Papua, these incentives expanded to creating new provinces as well. In February 2007, a group of regents (*bupati*), civil servants, and religious and customary groups declared in Merauke the creation of the province of South Papua.[89] They persisted for several years on the basis that the funds from the existing province did not reach the people and primarily catered to the bureaucracy.[90] Demands for a Central Papua province also rose. In 2011, eight *bupati* signed a request to create a Central Papua province, with Timika as its capital. The central

---

[85] "Papua, West Papua Agree to End Their Bickering," *Jakarta Post*, February 21, 2007.

[86] "*Pemerintah Keluarkan Perppu Otsus Papua Barat* [Government Issues Autonomy Law for West Papua]", *Kompas*, April 21, 2008.

[87] Fadhal Al Hamid, interview.

[88] "*Thaha: Revisi Perdasus = Kejahatan Politik* [Thaha: Perdasus Revisions = a Political Evil]," *Bintang Papua*, January 24, 2011.

[89] "*12 Februari, Deklarasi Pembentukan Provinsi Papua Selatan Di Merauke* [February 12, Declaration for the Formation of South Papua Province in Merauke]," *Suara Pembaruan*, February 9, 2007.

[90] "*Provinsi Papua Selatan Masih Sulit Diwujudkan* [South Papua Province Face Formation Difficulties]," *Bintang Papua*, September 27, 2010.

government refused to yield to these demands, focusing instead on the need to better implement development in Papua and West Papua.[91]

Local efforts to create new regencies also accelerated but were more successful. In the Central Highlands, several *bupati* requested the creation of six additional regencies (Lanny Jaya, Nduga, Yalimo, Mamberamo Tengah, Puncak, and Dogeyai) from the existing three (Jayawijaya, Puncak Jaya, and Nabire). For Interior Minister Ma'ruf, most of the 148 new regencies created between 1999 and 2005 had shown very little improvement; nevertheless those new regencies were approved in 2008.[92] They were followed by several more, such as the creation of Kabupaten Deiyai (2008), Kabupaten Intan Jaya (2008), and Tambrauw (2008); and, in West Papua, Kabupaten Manokwari Selatan (2013) and Kabupaten Pegunungan Arfak (2013).[93]

The increasing divisions of the province contributed to weakening Papuans' unity. As they bickered over provincial or regency boundaries, they lost some coherence in communicating clear and consistent demands. Whether by design or as a by-product of developmental and administrative objectives, the effects of these territorial divisions allowed the central government to gain the upper hand in its attempts to reduce the significance of the secessionist movement. In terms of helping to achieve new development objectives, by its own admission the results were very modest.

Finally, government intervention in the selection of MRP members not only undermined Papuan mobilization but also divided them into loyal and mostly quiescent supporters, while sidelining activists who strongly criticized government policy.

In its first term, the MRP gained some credibility despite its delays, lack of clear mandate, and dubious selection of its members. A former leader of the PDP, Agus Alua, obtained the respectable position of MRP head. The former rector of UNCEN, Frans Wospakrik and Hana Hikoyabi both gained positions as deputy chairs. Already highly respected, they provided strong leadership that turned the MRP into an important critical voice in the defence of Papuans.

Two years after its creation, however, the MRP still struggled to define its role. As Agus Alua argued, the lack of regulations to implement special autonomy made it difficult to actually fulfill its mandate. MRP leaders took

---

[91] *"Pembentukan Provinsi Papua Tengah, Menguat* [Efforts to Form Central Papua Province Strengthens]," *Bintang Papua*, April 28, 2011.

[92] "Enam Kabupaten Di Pengunungan Tengah Minta Segera Dimekarkan [Six districts in the Mountainous Regions Requests Division into New Districts]," *Suara Pembaruan*, February 19, 2007; *"Pejabat Tiga Kabupaten Pertanyakan Pemekaran* [Officials of Three Districts Request Division into New Districts]," *Kompas* February 20, 2007.

[93] *"1 Provinsi Dan 10 Kabupaten Baru Diresmikan* [1 New Province and 10 New Districts Formalized]," *Tempo*, April 22, 2013.

the initiative of preparing six draft regulations and submitted them to law-makers and the governor, even if it was not their role.[94]

In July 2010, leaders of the MRP made their boldest attempt to voice Papuan grievances. They sponsored a bill that rejected the special autonomy law on the basis of its failure to raise the welfare of Papuans. When the bill was passed, supporters organized several demonstrations to continue denouncing special autonomy and requesting its revocation. Most controversially, the Minister of Interior prevented in 2011 the re-nomination of Agus Alua and Hana Hikoyabi. The director general of special autonomy had consulted with the governor's office to inquire on ways of preventing the re-nomination of Hana Hikoyabi. Under pressure from the National Chief of Police, the coordinating Minister of Security, Law and Political Affairs, as well as the head of the State Intelligence Agency (*Badan Intelijen Negara*), the Minister of Interior Affairs relented. Agus Alua died before the new MRP was formed but Hana Hikoyabi was clearly barred from renewing her mandate.[95]

Afterward government officials intervened to influence the outcome. In Puncak Jaya and Mimika, for instance, only members of the local commission and the possible candidates rather than a broader segment of representatives made the selection. In Boven Digul and Merauke, the selected candidate to represent women was clearly the *bupati*'s choice, as other candidates had clearly been selected but did not reach the final list.[96] The number of irregularities became sufficiently widespread that members of the DPRP and church representatives met with the Coordinating Minister for Security, Law and Political Affairs to request that the selection process be halted because of interventions from *bupati*, or the exclusion of candidates on the basis of being "separatists" for having participated in local demonstrations.[97] Over these objections, the process nevertheless continued and the new MRP was in place by September 2011.[98]

The MRP's credibility and legitimacy were seriously undermined after the sidelining of previous vocal leaders and interference in candidate selections. Many people chose not to participate in the election of MRP representatives. Rumours circulated that intelligence officials, police, and civil

[94] "Papua Council Struggles for Significance Two Years On," *Jakarta Post*, November 2, 2007.
[95] "*Ditolak Jadi Anggota MRP: Hana Hikoyabi Siap Tempuh Jalur Hukum* [Denied Membership in MRP: Hana Hikoyabi Prepared to Use Legal Channels]," *Suara Pembaruan*, May 7, 2011; Agus Sumule, interview.
[96] "*Sejumlah Calon Anggota MRP Nilai Proses Pemilihan Tak Jujur* [Some MRP Candidates Not Fairly Chosen]," *Bintang Papua*, February 8, 2011; "*Bupati Boven Digoel Dituding Intervensi Pemilihan Anggota MRP* [Bupati of Boven Digoel Accused of Intervening in MRP Elections]," *Bintang Papua*, February 24, 2011.
[97] "*KPU Provinsi Harus Bertanggung Jawab!* [Provincial KPU Have a Responsibility!]," *Bintang Papua*, February 24, 2011.
[98] "*Agenda Penting, Memberi Persetujuan Perdasus Pilgub* [An Important Agenda, Agreement about Gubernatorial Elections in the Special Region]," *Bintang Papua*, September 16, 2011.

servants recruited poorly educated members from villages and offered large sums of money to become representatives. "The MRP has not been very present since Agus Alua and Hana Hikoyabi were not allowed to join again. Many of its members have low education and seem to be there to enjoy their position, rather than get anything done."[99] As a result, and as expected, the MRP became inclined to support central government policies and offered very little resistance.[100]

In sum, the central government used a number of strategies to divide Papuans and undermine the reach of their acquired autonomy. The division into two provinces undermined the ability of re-creating a strong civilian movement to demand greater concessions and maintain an effective check on the existing autonomy arrangements. Instead, special autonomy became a large source of personal enrichment that fuelled even more demands to divide the territory into additional provinces and regencies. Furthermore, the state deliberately undermined the power of the MRP by first delaying its implementation and, later, by intervening in the selection of its members.

Persistently Weak Mobilizational Capacity

A democratic environment facilitated Papuan organizational coherence, and in fact led temporarily to a high degree of unity and common sense of purpose around independence. The weaker state, combined with the armed forces on the defensive, allowed the political space for Papuans to organize. At its height, the 2000 Papuan Congress, followed by the formation of the PDP, provided a structure that unified Papuans and gave them a strong voice.

A decade later, however, the PDP had disbanded and no single organization managed to gain sufficient legitimacy to represent Papuans as a people. Only six months after the Congress, the PDP's strength and the movement's momentum were rapidly diminishing. As McGibbon concluded: "By the last quarter of 2000, independence leaders were finding it increasingly difficult to maintain mass support as independence seemed as distant as ever and the military was increasingly adopting repressive measures."[101]

Over the following years, the PDP increasingly lost support. It became divided over the appropriate strategy,[102] with some increasingly attempting dialogue instead of open calls for independence. The leadership under Thaha Al Hamid created closer links with Vice-President Jusuf Kalla, who was instrumental in reaching a settlement in Aceh. But the PDP soon found itself

---

[99] *"Ditolak Jadi Anggota MRP: Hana Hikoyabi Siap Tempuh Jalur Hukum* [Denied Membership in MRP: Hana Hikoyabi Prepared to Use Legal Channels]"; Thaha Al Hamid, interview.
[100] Rev. Herman Awom, interview.
[101] McGibbon, "Secessionist Challenges in Aceh and Papua," 30.
[102] Fadhal Al Hamid, interview.

isolated from both sides: criticized by its followers for creating closer relations to the state, and eventually sidelined by the state as the PDP lost access to ministers. According to Thaha Al Hamid, the main issue was the lack of clear structure to the movement in Papua, too many interlocutors whereas in Aceh GAM offered a more unified representation conducive to negotiation. They lacked the resources to sustain an effective domestic strategy or an international lobbying effort.[103] So, the PDP took more of a "behind-the-scenes" approach, supported efforts to create dialogue with the central government, and also communicated with other groups to seek a more united agenda. But it was criticized for creating links to the state.[104] Suspicions rose as some were even "accused of cooperating with the military".[105] Papuans were suspicious that leaders could speak of the goal of secession, and meet with officials in Jakarta, without imprisonment. As with many other conspiracy theories that circulate in Papua, some people concluded that the PDP leadership had become too close to the government and the military.

Over time, the DAP attempted to take over the role of the PDP. At the 2000 Congress, the DAP had been created specifically to address the needs of "indigenous" Papuans, in particular their rights, education, and socio-economic well-being, while the PDP was mandated to pursue political object-ives, in particular to lobby for a revision of the Act of Free Choice and Indonesia's status within Indonesia. After 2002, the DAP played an increas-ingly important role. Government officials regularly consulted with DAP representatives. For example, it even met with Vice-President Jusuf Kalla when, under an operation to save the forests, the police arrested several people for cutting trees. The DAP played a mediating role to find solutions to the problem. When Forkorus became head of the DAP in 2007, however, he pushed further its political role, while abandoning the socio-economic and cultural issues previously being pursued by the DAP.[106]

The organization of a third Congress in 2011 sealed the failure of the DAP's political strategy. The leadership of the DAP split, especially with plans to organize a third Congress.[107] The Congress, which was held in October 2011, was particularly controversial as the DAP made plans to declare Forkorus as president of an independent Papua, against the objections of several of its leaders. Yet, the Congress claimed to have broad participation, as in the 2000 one but it failed to unite Papuans. "The Congress (3rd) was not representative. I was a speaker and, as a leader, I had to be there ... but I cannot say that it was representative."[108] In the end, the Congress elected Forkorus who along with other DAP leaders were subsequently arrested and sent to jail for three years for

[103] Thaha Al Hamid, interview.   [104] Ibid.   [105] Rev. Herman Awom, interview.
[106] Fadhal Al Hamid, interview.   [107] Ibid.
[108] Socratez Sofyan Yoman, Ketua Persekutuan-Persekutuan Gereja Baptis Papua (Head of the Federation of Papua Baptist Churches), interview by author, April 3, 2012, Jayapura.

secessionist activities. While he continued to be considered as president for Negara Republik Federal Papua Barat after his release in July 2014, he nevertheless kept a much lower profile. The DAP never regained its strength, and lost the access to ministers and parliament that it had previously enjoyed. "Before, if we wanted, we could talk with ministers, the governor, the Vice-President, now we are considered separatist, as we declared an alternative government. It's really a problem for us."[109]

No other organization was able to garner broad support. Some thought that the Churches might provide unity but they disagreed over political strategy.[110] They became politically divided as some of Church leaders considered others to be too cooperative with the government. Some supported dialogue, while others were suspicious of negotiating with the government. In return, the state provided some funds from Otsus to more cooperative churches: "I am head of the synod ... .Others get money, but I don't get any from the province. Supposed to be from Otsus. I received only once, and then didn't received because I am critical and I resist."[111]

Other organizations shared the same objective, independence, but the strategies differed. Many of the street demonstrations were organized by the National Committee for West Papua (KNPB), whose leader was Benny Wenda, based in the UK. Their goal was a referendum on independence.[112] One strand also tried to internationalize the Papuan issue further and bring its case to the international court, even though other Papuan leaders argued that such a strategy would be unlikely to succeed.[113] Some international and Church-based NGOs attempted to use the former East Timor network.[114] The strategy was less successful because Indonesia could claim international recognition of Papua's integration, whereas foreign governments had been more willing to pressure Indonesia on the East Timor case, given that most countries had not recognized its integration.

Another organization, the West Papua National Coalition for Liberation, based in Vanuatu, advocated for completing the process of decolonization. They formed a commission and wanted to begin an investigation. But, as the leader of the PDP noted, the PDP already commissioned an analysis of the process of integration and found support in the United Nations as early as 2003. Only a handful of small Pacific states have raised the issue of Papua at the United Nations.[115]

Several organizations coalesced to attempt a new lobbying initiative known as the Papuan Peace Network (Jaringan Damai Papua, JDP). It was

---

[109] Fadhal Al Hamid, interview.   [110] Rev. Herman Awom, interview.
[111] Socratez Sofyan Yoman, interview.   [112] Neles Tebay, interview.
[113] Agus Sumule, interview.   [114] Rev. Herman Awom, interview.
[115] For a discussion of lobbying efforts in indigenous peoples' forums, see also Bertrand, "'Indigenous Peoples' Rights' as a Strategy of Ethnic Accommodation."

a cooperative initiative by Neles Tebay, a Papuan priest, and academics from the Indonesian Institute of Sciences in Jakarta (LIPI). Taking a moderate position, they advocated for renewed political dialogue between Jakarta and Papuans to discuss Papuan grievances. JDP organized consultations in Papua and found broad support among many organizations, including the PDP, but not the KNPB. They also lobbied to obtain support from non-governmental organizations in Jakarta. In November 2011, President SBY acknowledged the need for dialogue. His agreement was reiterated in a meeting with Papuan church leaders in December 2011, but there was little follow-up.[116] The JDP continued with its collaborators in LIPI to push for dialogue after the election of President Jokowi.

The inability to foster dialogue stems in part from the deeply held suspicions on both sides. President SBY had suggested "constructive communication" as a means to discuss issues surrounding the implementation of special autonomy, whereas Papuans insisted on dialogue, with a view of presenting themselves as equal partners. "The mistrust runs deep. Many officials within the Indonesian state fear that dialogue would simply lead to Papuans' reasserting demands for independence."[117] They certainly would not resort to any international mediation, as in the case of Aceh, by fear that it might trigger a re-examination of the international position on West New Guinea's integration to Indonesia.

Conclusion

In this chapter, I showed why democracy in Indonesia neither increased levels of violence nor resolved the long-standing conflict in Papua. The new democratic environment enabled the rise of a civilian movement that mobilized and applied sustained pressure to demand a referendum and self-determination. The relatively low mobilizational capacity of the OPM and the strategic decision by the PDP to support non-violent mobilization explain why violent mobilization did not occur, even when faced with greater violent responses from the state. But the impact of greater uncertainty in the period of democratic transition had a similar effect as in Aceh. There was a perceived window of opportunity to renegotiate how Papuans could govern themselves, given that East Timor had obtained a referendum

---

[116] Rev. Herman Awom, interview; Neles Tebay, interview.

[117] Interview with Papuan government official, reporting discussions with state intelligence officials. The problem was the lack of a coordinated approach, a strategic document, and sufficient financial resources. Papuans remained divided even if most organizations made similar demands. As the leader of the PDP complained: "Whenever Papuans meet to consolidate, they form a new organization. We need to consolidate the agenda" (Thaha Al Hamid, interview).

on wide-ranging autonomy and the Indonesia MPR was working on constitutional amendments. This window allowed the formation of Papuan representative institutions (Congresses and PDP) that mobilized to voice
grievances and express demands for self-determination. In response, the
Indonesian state first allowed the mobilization to occur, and greater freedom
of expression and association to flow. But it eventually used repression
against the PDP and sought to clamp down on the civilian movement,
leading to a rise in low-level violence after the initial peaceful period. In
the late stages of transition, it also offered concessions by adopting a special
autonomy law. Yet, the concessions came too late and, by then, had the
effect of increasing Papuan grievances for having failed to either take some
of their most important demands into account or include them in a process
of formal negotiation over their autonomy.

At the time of democratic stabilization, therefore, the pathway from authoritarian rule had already led to a failed attempt at a resolution of the conflict.
A large gap remained between Papuan nationalist objectives for greater self-
determination and the Indonesian state's position of institutional closure, with
constitutional amendments in place supporting wide-ranging autonomy for
Aceh and Papua, and the special autonomy law that represented the state's
conception of the substance and limits of autonomy. As it lacked credibility,
particularly during its implementation, the special autonomy law was broadly
criticized and most Papuans rejected it. While violence remained low, the
conflict remained deep.

The Indonesian state adopted further policies to undermine the concessions it
had made and to prevent mobilizational capacity among Papuan groups. Its
division of the province was reaffirmed and eventually extended to include
even a split of the MRP, which was designed to represent the indigenous
Papuans. The support for the creation of some further regencies, the implementation of special autonomy in the two provinces, its undermining of rising MRP
leaders, and nurturing of new groups of Papuan beneficiaries of the spoils of
autonomy funding contributed to further dividing Papuans.

5   Moros of Mindanao

The Long and Treacherous Path to "Bangsamoro" Autonomy

After democracy returned to the Philippines in 1986, the Moros and the Philippine state entered into multiple phases of negotiation. The 1996 peace agreement with the Moro National Liberation Front (MNLF) was seen as a landmark, yet its reach and effectiveness were very limited. Subsequent attempts to reach a new peace agreement, this time with the rival Moro Islamic Liberation Front (MILF), proved particularly difficult as the MILF sought even deeper concessions. The MILF finally reached in 2014 a peace agreement with the Philippine government, yet it took four more years before the Comprehensive Agreement on Bangsamoro was enshrined as the Bangsamoro Basic Law (BBL) and ratified by parliament in 2018.

At each stage of negotiation, past commitments were deemed insufficient and lacked credibility. It is characteristic of commitment failures, by which the state obtained written agreements but either failed to implement them or sought to undermine its own commitments through other means.

Two important structural and institutional features created additional constraints on the ability to reach a negotiated compromise and make it credible. First, the Philippine's US style division of powers between the executive and legislature, combined with single-term presidencies, introduce institutional problems for implementing commitments made during negotiations. Presidential offices are the primary state actors, but the initiative, development of negotiations, finalizing deals, and implementing all must occur within the short six-year window of a presidency. Meanwhile, as Congressional representatives are independent from the president, every negotiated agreement requires ratification by Congress, whose representatives have their own set of issues, interests, and political considerations that are usually introduced in accompanying legislation and inevitably depart from what the executive negotiates.[1]

---

[1] Paul D. Hutchcroft and Joel Rocamora, "Strong Demands and Weak Institutions: The Origins and Evolution of the Democratic Deficit in the Philippines," *Journal of East Asian Studies* 3, no. 2 (2003); David Wurfel, *Filipino Politics: Development and Decay* (Ithaca, NY: Cornell University Press, 1988).

Furthermore, political parties are weak and somewhat fluid, therefore increasing the unpredictability of congressional votes.[2] Parliamentary independence has therefore been a very strong factor in explaining some of the difficulties in reducing conflict through negotiated agreements, as it reflected the majority's strong reluctance to negotiate or concede to "separatists" and "terrorists." Second, as democratization began Moros were divided between two main armed organizations: the MNLF and the MILF. This division introduced incentives to bid each other out in order to reach better settlements with the state. In addition to having high mobilizational capacity, therefore, the exercise of armed insurgency reacted not only to the state's actions but also to those of the rival organization.

During the transitional phase, two sets of state actions pulled in different directions, with one dampening conflict while the other fuelled it. In sequential terms, Cory Aquino's transitional government acted early to commit the state to negotiations with the Moros on the basis of autonomy. Early meetings with the MNLF, before even acceding to power, prevented a ramping up of violent mobilization in the early days of the government. The MILF essentially waited to see the outcome of this initial opening. The opportunity to reach a settlement was soon derailed, however, as the Constitutional Commission (Con-Com) significantly narrowed the potential reach of territorially based autonomy by qualifying it as autonomy for "Muslim Mindanao." Although it consulted broadly, the commission could not negotiate with the Moros, and therefore the constitutional process moved ahead prior to Aquino's ability to begin formal negotiations. Both the MNLF and MILF saw the state's enshrinement of this form of autonomy, and the subsequent creation of the Autonomous Region of Muslim Mindanao (ARMM), as an insincere concession designed more to defuse the conflict rather than to respond to Moro grievances. The subsequent uncertainty, and political instability under Aquino's administration, contributed to the MNLF and MILF's continued insurgency.

The period of democratic stabilization, which began with the election of President Fidel Ramos in 1992, led to an overall decline of incentives for violence but settled into a stalled conflict, with periods of spikes in violent clashes, followed by extensive periods of ceasefire and negotiation. The institutional features of parliamentary independence and electoral coalitions that remained highly averse to peace agreements with Moro insurgents created obstacles to peace negotiations and mostly reluctant parliaments. Ramos invested electoral capital into peace as a condition for his Social Reform

---

[2] Allen Hicken, *Building Party Systems in Developing Democracies* (Cambridge: Cambridge University Press, 2009), 150–62; Gabriella R. Montinola, "Parties and Accountability in the Philippines," *Journal of Democracy* 10, no. 1 (1999).

Agenda, and successfully negotiated a peace agreement with the MNLF. But the agreement soon fizzled as it became clear that parliamentarians were strongly averse to extending strong powers and concessions to the Moros. Subsequent presidents, Estrada and Macapagal-Arroyo reflected electoral coalitions that were strongly opposed to negotiation. Estrada in particular used populist rhetoric to escalate the conflict, leading to a resurgence of violent conflict with the MILF. Macapagal-Arroyo defused some of the violence and reopened negotiations, thereby showing the democratic incentives to reduce repression and defuse civil war, but faced continued parliamentary roadblocks. As a result, the credibility of the Philippine state's commitments to peace was very low, and the MILF therefore demanded more guarantees, while the autonomy institutions in place, and the former agreement with the MNLF, became completely discredited. The conflict stalled, low-level violence continued with occasional spikes, and deep grievances remained. Benigno Aquino Jr. again capitalized on peace for electoral gain, but faced a parliament that was reluctant to support it. As the first president from Mindanao, Duterte succeeded in obtaining parliamentary approval because of a strong electoral interest in producing peace in Mindanao, strong populist appeal, and a related influence over parliamentary members.

The Marcos Regime and the Emergence of Moro Resistance

The Moros began to mobilize in the 1970s. From the period of Spanish colonialism, they were differentiated from other peoples of the archipelago by their adherence to Islam. Yet, they were divided into several different groups, with uneven degrees of linkages between themselves and occasional violent conflict against the Spanish colonial rulers. American colonial policies, as well as post-independence policies of the Philippine state strengthened the shared grievances experienced by Muslims but a stronger sense of common identity emerged mainly in the 1960s. Circumstances were ripe by then for an intellectual elite to foster a common identity as "Moro" and reconstruct past history to articulate a past of shared resistance.

As with all Muslim peoples, Moros shared a transcendent identity as part of the *umma*, the broad community of adherents to Islam, yet it is unclear to what extent they saw themselves as sharing a distinct identity as "Moros" or Muslims of the Philippines, even though they were divided among several ethno-linguistic groups. While the nationalist movement of the late 1960s and 1970s mobilized on the basis of "Moro" identity, its offshoot movement most distinctly represented by the MILF throughout the last few decades placed a much clearer emphasis on Islam. Finally, in the most recent agreements with the Philippine state, "Bangsamoro" (literally Moro nation) has re-emerged as the label now being enshrined.

There is some contention on the extent to which Moros had a common identity during Spanish colonial rule. The term "Moro" was first used by the Spanish as early as 1572 to depict the inhabitants of the Philippines, although it was soon used more exclusively to identify the Muslims from "indios," which described local inhabitants converted to Christianity.[3] Some scholars, such as Majul, have argued that Muslims did share a common sense of identity, even if the sultanates in the region were divided and sometimes fought each other. In face of Spanish attacks, many of which targeted mosques, Muslim graveyards, and other symbols of the Islamic faith, a shared sense of resistance emerged.[4] McKenna has questioned this claim and argues instead that such shared identity was still absent under Spanish colonial rule. He finds the evidence scarce to suggest strong religious appeals in conflict pitting the Spanish against the local Muslims, and finds a diverse set of interests guiding attacks on both sides. For McKenna, even the so-called Moro wars provide scant evidence of a pan-Muslim resistance. He finds no instance of a broad alliance across Muslim groups against the Spanish. He also emphasizes that these wars amounted to mainly occasional skirmishes, involving groups sometimes more akin to piracy than to political war, amidst generally peaceful coexistence.[5]

After a brief period of indirect rule, by which local *datus* (traditional rulers) helped to pacify the South, American colonial administrators contributed to strengthening local leadership roles while helping to create some intergroup linkages. Local *datus*, who had collaborated with the Americans, were integrated to new structures of elected political offices (in municipalities and as assemblymen), and a broader Muslim identity encouraged under their leadership as a means, in the end, to integrate the population to the Philippine polity. A "Moro" province was created as the administrative structure including all Muslim areas. The integrative strategy proved elusive, but its consequence was to lay some basis for a self-conscious Moro identity.

During the Commonwealth years (1935–1946), state policies contributed to a deepening of grievances. Americans built political institutions that ensured the perpetual dominance of a Christian landed upper-class, who could control the state by drawing on its massive base among the Christian majority. By doing so, it did not need to build coalitions, or seek support among the Muslim minorities, thereby alienating and marginalizing them. Furthermore, Christians dominated even Muslim areas. Already under American colonial rule, Christians controlled most local administrative positions. After 1935, the government of Manuel Quezon accelerated the appointment of Christians to

[3] C. A. Majul, *Muslims in the Philippines* (Quezon: Asia Center, 1973); Thomas M. McKenna, *Muslim Rulers and Rebels: Everyday Politics and Armed Separatism in the Southern Philippines* (Berkeley, CA: University of California Press, 1998).
[4] Majul, *Muslims in the Philippines*, 95–98.   [5] McKenna, *Muslim Rulers and Rebels*, 82–83.

administrative positions and Christians were encouraged to migrate to Mindanao from Luzon. Unregistered land was declared part of the public domain and therefore denied customary land rights by which Muslim communities had previously governed their territory. Because of suspicions of the government's intentions, high processing fees, and uncertainty about procedures, Muslims failed to register their lands and did not take advantage of new land on offer. The Bureau of Lands did not make much effort to socialize Muslims to this new regime and, instead, favoured migrating Christians. Loans and assistance were also offered to new Christian settlers.[6] Christian migration and related land registration were sufficiently high to marginalize Muslims in many areas of Mindanao where they were once dominant. Muslims in Cotabato declined, for instance, from 64.53 per cent of the population in 1918 to 34.64 per cent in 1960.[7] This geographic dispersal and relative loss of concentration of Muslims in Mindanao and the Sulu archipelago contributed later on to the difficulties of creating a more unified movement and laying claims to a territorial homeland.

After the Philippines obtained its independence in 1946, part of the Moro elite was integrated to the state through elected offices but this had little effect on the broader Moro population. Moro *datus* and other members of the elite gained access to local and regional offices, occasionally gaining seats in the national congress. Yet, the population shared few of its benefits and an overall sense of marginalization remained.

The government structure was based on the American system and gave no special representation for Moros in the central government. While the Philippine state did not explicitly construct a "Filipino nation" as crafters of the Indonesian nation self-consciously did, among Christians nevertheless a common bond and identity had developed and a sense of broader Filipino nationhood had emerged. While it was theoretically inclusive of all groups in the archipelago, Moros never adhered to this broader identity, nor did the constitution and political institutions give Moros any special representation.

The rise of authoritarianism broadened resentment among the Filipino population, but created a catalyst for the formation of a Moro resistance movement. The democratic system had benefited a political class close to the landed elite and agro-industrial business interests with little trickle down to the population. Wealthy families competed for control of the state and institutions, and plundered state resources while the economy became increasingly sterile. Ferdinand Marcos was somewhat of an outsider who, once elected to the presidency in 1965, vowed to implement reforms, break the cycle of family-

---

[6] Peter G. Gowing, *Mandate in Moroland*, 339; McKenna, *Muslim Rulers and Rebels*, 117.
[7] Thomas O'Shaughnessy, "How Many Muslims Has the Philippines?" *Philippine Studies* 23 (1975): 377.

clan control of the state, and steer the country toward a new basis of growth and development. Instead, he increasingly attempted to break the power of established families by nurturing a new class of his business cronies. He declared Martial Law in 1972 to remain in power, using instability from the communist New People's Army (NPA) and the Moros as justification. Yet, it was clear that the main reason was to extend his power and graft opportunities. His policies were designed to benefit himself and his business supporters, while reforms led to deteriorating living standards and growing resentment.[8]

Against this backdrop, an armed resistance movement was formed as a rising intellectual elite tapped into ideological and material resources that had become increasingly available. Young secular-educated Moros formed the MNLF in 1969 and armed resistance began in 1972. By 1973, the MNLF, under the leadership of Nur Misuari, was asking for a withdrawal of government troops from the Southern Philippines, a return of the lands taken away from the Moros, more autonomy, as well as the practice of Islamic law in Muslim areas. In 1974, MNLF demands went even further when the movement declared the establishment of the Bangsa Moro Republic with the stated goal of full independence. The MNLF had developed a very strong-armed insurgency with approximately 30,000 fighters by 1975 and seemed to be growing in strength relative to the Philippine armed forces.[9] It successfully managed to overcome internal divisions among Muslims, at least initially, as Tausug, Maranao, and Maguindanao adhered to the nationalist Moro label that appealed broadly.

In reaction to the escalation of the conflict, the Marcos government, for the first time in the history of the Philippines, agreed to territorial autonomy for the Moros. With an apparent growth in the MNLF's forces, and faced with a number of other internal conflicts, including with the New People's Army, the Marcos government accepted the intervention of the Organisation of Islamic Conference (OIC, which is now Organisation of Islamic Cooperation) to broker an agreement. The OIC, especially Libya, played a key role in bringing the two sides to negotiate a deal. The 1973 oil crisis had shown the Philippines' vulnerability in securing energy sources. While it attempted to diversify its sources by building dams in the Cordillera, this plan backfired as insurgency grew in that region as well, led by the NPA. Marcos saw an interest in reaching an agreement with the MNLF partly to maintain good relations with the Middle East and secure its oil supplies.[10]

---

[8] Bertrand, *Political Change in Southeast Asia*. chapter 3; Benedict Anderson, "Cacique Democracy and the Philippines: Origins and Dreams," *New Left Review* 169, no. 3–31 (1988); Gary Hawes, *The Philippine State and the Marcos Regime: The Politics of Export* (Ithaca, NY: Cornell University Press, 1987).

[9] Ivan Molloy, "The Decline of the Moro National Liberation Front in the Southern Philippines," *Journal of Contemporary Asia* 18, no. 1 (1988): 61–62.

[10] Rudy Rodil, Vice Chairman of the Government Panel, Negotiations with MILF, interview by author, April 29, 2008, Manila.

The Tripoli agreement of 1976 became the first document recognizing Moro rights to political representation on the basis of their distinctive cultural and historical background. It granted autonomy over a region covering thirteen provinces and nine cities in Mindanao, even though Muslims were concentrated in fewer areas and somewhat dispersed, surrounded by majority Christian communities. Foreign policy, national defence, mines, and mineral resources remained under the jurisdiction of the central government. In the autonomous areas, it was agreed that Muslims would establish courts based on Sharia law and would have the right to establish schools and universities, their own administrative, economic and financial systems, as well as Special Regional Security Forces.[11]

The agreement failed, however, because it became clear that the Marcos government never intended to implement it. Negotiations stalled over the details of the accord and Marcos insisted on holding a plebiscite to ratify it. Against the wishes of the MNLF, he unilaterally proceeded with the plebiscite and decreed the creation of two autonomous regions. The MNLF rejected the agreement and fighting resumed. Marcos had used the Tripoli agreement to temporarily defuse the armed conflict and weaken the MNLF, with no intention of actually implementing it.[12]

The MNLF never succeeded in regaining its past strength but, as it began to fade, the MILF was formed in 1984 and would eventually become the main armed group fighting the Philippine military. In spite of the MNLF's rejection of the Tripoli agreement, the Marcos administration nevertheless created two "regional autonomous governments" that were mainly insignificant in terms of providing actual powers and fiscal resources but they provided an incentive for MNLF fighters to defect. By offering an amnesty program and integrating several of them to relatively lucrative positions in these regional government structures, it was able to convince a relatively large number of MNLF members to abandon the struggle. Furthermore, the regime exploited internal divisions in its deployment of development projects and the design of autonomous governments to exacerbate growing divisions between ethnic groups within the MNLF.[13] Hashim Salamat, with a base among the Maguindanao people, had left the MNLF in 1977, partly in reaction to the MNLF's concessions but also because of Nur Misuari and his Tausug following's continued control over the organization. The creation of the MILF was an attempt to shift the broader

---

[11] Agreement between the government of the Republic of the Philippines and the Moro National Liberation Front with the Participation of the Quadripartite Ministerial Commission Members of the Islamic Conference and the Secretary General of the Organisation of the Islamic Conference, Tripoli, December 23, 1976.

[12] McKenna, *Muslim Rulers and Rebels*, 168.

[13] Molloy, "The Decline of the Moro National Liberation Front in the Southern Philippines," 64–67.

appeal among all Philippine Muslims from a nationalist movement based on "Moro" identity and inspired by Marxist ideas to a more explicitly Islamic nationalist thrust, but the tensions between crafting an overarching identity and regional/sub-ethnic ones remained.

At the end of the Marcos regime, therefore, Moro resistance remained constant but then squarely divided into two main organizations. The MNLF, while weakened, still maintained its leading role among the Moros, particularly because of its links to Libya and the OIC. It remained firmly based on Tausug support. The MILF was growing and benefitting as well from disgruntled MNLF fighters increasingly joining its ranks, but it had not yet mounted a significant insurgency against the Marcos regime and remained mostly strong among the Maguindanao. The Philippine state maintained the status quo with respect to its approach to the Moros, as greater military attention was turned toward the dramatic increase in the NPA's strength and capacity to mount an armed insurgency, as well as the growing open expression of discontent among the broader population through protests and demonstrations.

Transition from Authoritarian Rule

The transition from authoritarian rule offered a context that was conducive to a settlement, yet it failed because of regime instability, institutional constraints of the new democracy, and division among the Moros. With strong Moro support to Marcos' removal and early state concessions, further violence was avoided but concessions were insufficient to allow for a peaceful settlement.

The People Power revolution that removed President Marcos in 1986 was based on broad support. Non-governmental organizations, opposition political parties, and the Church united in a mass movement that ended authoritarian rule. The MNLF made clear pledges in support of opposition groups' coalition against Marcos.[14]

Violent conflict was mixed during the transitional period.[15] Initially, clashes with the MNLF declined as the Aquino government took a proactive approach that eliminated much of the uncertainty surrounding the transition, having sent signals that it would negotiate on the basis of territorial autonomy. Furthermore, the armed forces were strongly discredited as a result of their previous support for the Marcos regime, and so military repression against the Moros was mostly halted.

President Aquino moved swiftly to make unilateral concessions and promises of territorial autonomy, with the backing of the large coalition that had

[14] R. J May, "The Philippines under Aquino: A Perspective from Mindanao," *Journal Institute of Muslim Minority Affairs* 8, no. 2 (1987): 348.

[15] Andrew Tan, "Armed Muslim Separatist Rebellion in Southeast Asia: Persistence, Prospects, and Implications," *Studies in Conflict and Terrorism* 23, no. 4 (2000): 273.

supported her People Power accession to power. Initial consultations with the MNLF contributed to defusing its mobilization. Aquino created a Presidential Task Force on Regional Autonomy, headed by Datu Michael Mastura – a respected Muslim leader, former deputy minister of Muslim affairs, and subsequently chief negotiator for the MILF. By mid-March 1986 a ceasefire was achieved but Mastura resigned in June, as he apparently had obtained little response on suggestions to negotiate autonomy on the basis of the Tripoli agreement or to appoint more Moros to the government.[16]

Meanwhile, violence rose partly because Moros were split into two armed groups. The MILF rejected Aquino's initial offers and initiated attacks, against both the MNLF and the armed forces, in an attempt to preserve its claim to represent Moros.[17]

Aquino moved ahead with concessions to the MNLF to build confidence. She allowed a second Bangsamoro National Congress to be held in September 1986, permitted MNLF leader, Nur Misuari, to return to the Philippines to attend the Congress, and finally visited him in Jolo.[18] These initial steps opened the way to what became known as the Jeddah Accord, in which both parties agreed in January 1987 to engage in formal negotiations for territorial autonomy.

The MNLF however raised its territorial demands relative to what it had accepted in the Tripoli agreement, claiming all of Mindanao, Basilan, Tawi-Tawi, Sulu, and Palawan (twenty-three provinces). On the other hand, the state expected to negotiate on the basis of the Tripoli agreement, which limited territorial claims to only thirteen provinces and nine cities.[19] The territorial demands were exaggerated most likely to test the government's willingness to settle at least on broader autonomy and test the credibility of its commitment, given the failed implementation of the Tripoli agreement under Marcos.[20]

Meanwhile, a draft constitution was already being circulated, which contained a clause offering autonomy for "Muslim Mindanao," covering five provinces where Muslims were a majority. It was a much-reduced territorial promise than what the Tripoli agreement stipulated. The Con-Com essentially rejected a position paper from a multisectoral conference of around 500 Muslim representatives from ulama, traditional leaders, students, and

---

[16] May, "The Philippines under Aquino," 350.   [17] McKenna, *Muslim Rulers and Rebels*, 246.

[18] Carmen A. Abubakar, "Review of the Mindanao Peace Processes," *Inter-Asia Cultural Studies* 5, no. 3 (2004): 453.

[19] Federico V. Magdalena, "The Peace Process in Mindanao: Problems and Prospects," *Southeast Asian Affairs* (1997): 245.

[20] The MNLF entered the negotiations without fully appreciating the extent of concessions being made, with one of the most important negotiators even opposed at the outset to a settlement with the government. I am grateful to Carmen Abubakar for this point.

professionals.[21] The paper had based its proposal on the territorial boundaries of the Tripoli agreement. Faced with what appeared to be diametrically opposed proposals, the MNLF broke off talks. The new constitution was adopted nevertheless in February 1987, with the inclusion of the clause.[22]

Congress moved ahead with a bill to implement the constitutional clause, thereby exercising its independence from the Aquino government and without consulting the Moros. Republican Act 6734 created the ARMM, subject to a referendum in the thirteen provinces of the Tripoli agreement, as specified in the Constitution. The referendum was held in 1989 but the MNLF refused to support it, since many of the provinces considered to be the historical territory of the Bangsa Moro (Moro nation) by then were populated by Christian majorities. As predicted, only four voted to join the ARMM, where Muslims were a majority. No other negotiations were undertaken with Moro groups during the rest of Aquino's presidency.[23]

The Constitution, even though drafted according to democratic processes and approved in a nation-wide referendum, reflected the biases of the majority that was unwilling to make large concessions to the Moros. As a result, not only was the autonomy mandated by the constitution ambiguous in its terminology (and surely likely to alienate Christians in potential provinces) but also the requirement of a referendum made almost impossible any basis of negotiation for territory outside of areas with Muslim majorities. Article 10 of the Constitution includes not only wording that restricts the area to Muslim Mindanao, but defines specific powers, and therefore reduces the ability to negotiate any new agreement with the Moros without having to subsequently amend the constitution. Furthermore, parts of the constitution could be used to undermine powers granted under Article 10, for instance, in the management of natural resources over which autonomy is provided yet certain aspects of which are retained at the central level.[24] As a starting point to then negotiate with the MNLF and later the MILF, it left very little room for compromise if constitutional provisions and procedures were to be respected. While enshrinement in the constitution made the state's commitment credible, the strong limit to what was conceded failed to meet the depth of Moro grievances and demands.

---

[21] The Constitutional Commission was formed to draft a new constitution while Cory Aquino established her government and negotiated directly with the Moros. The ConCom was broadly representative and the process largely inclusive, therefore its outcome was mostly unpredictable at the time. See Bernardo M. Villegas, "The Philippines in 1986: Democratic Reconstruction in the Post-Marcos Era," *Asian Survey* 27, no. 2 (1987). For a critical perspective, see James Putzel, "Survival of an Imperfect Democracy in the Philippines," *Democratization* 6, no. 1 (1999): 211–12.

[22] May, "The Philippines under Aquino," 352; Magdalena, "The Peace Process in Mindanao," 250.

[23] Magdalena, "The Peace Process in Mindanao," 250.

[24] Benedicto Bacani, Head of Institute for Autonomy and Governance, interview by author, April 30, 2008, Cotabato City.

Aquino was furthermore paralyzed by several attempted coups, which only reinforced the strong opposition to her administration from within some parts of the military. She could not push strongly in the direction of concessions with the Moros and needed to bow to pressures from Congress, as well as cabinet members who were close to the armed forces.[25]

The initial period of democratization, therefore, had mixed outcomes. The initial, unilateral concessions contributed to defusing violent conflict and mobilization. Yet, two structural factors created opposing tendencies. The most important of these was the Moros' division into two armed organizations competing for legitimate representation. With the MNLF agreeing to discuss autonomy, the MILF rejected what it perceived to be its limited range and resumed violent attacks.[26] In turn, the MNLF sought maximum concessions to maintain its claim to strong representation of Moros' interests, demanding autonomy over the whole of Mindanao and adjacent islands, as opposed to the more limited, yet still broad, territorial autonomy under the Tripoli agreement. Second, the divided Philippine state, mostly among Congress and the executive, sent contradictory signals regarding the state's willingness to negotiate with the MNLF. While presidential representatives seemed ready to use the Tripoli agreement as a basis of negotiation, members of the Con-Com moved ahead with the concept of "Muslim Mindanao," which became enshrined in the Constitution. State commitments were not entirely clear and therefore impaired the initial attempts at defusing the conflict through early concessions. Instead, autonomy for "Muslim Mindanao" was a gamble that it would be sufficient to defuse conflict and attract support among Moros without negotiation. Such a strategy failed: both the MNLF and MILF continued armed attacks.

Democratic Stabilization

The Philippines entered a period of democratic stabilization with the election of President Ramos in 1992. While Thompson considers that "Philippine democracy was consolidated after the May 1992 elections, even if it remains risk-prone,"[27] I consider that "stabilized" more aptly captures the state of its democracy, with some procedural elements functioning well, the absence of

---

[25] David G. Timberman, *A Changeless Land: Continuity and Change in Philippine Politics* (New York: M.E. Sharpe, 1991), 181; Lynn T. White, *Philippine Politics: Possibilities and Problems in a Localist Democracy* (London: Routledge, 2015), 129; Diana J. Mendoza and Maria Elissa Jayme Lao, "Corazon Aquino: The Reluctant First Female President of the Philippines," in *Women Presidents and Prime Ministers in Post-Transition Democracies*, ed. Veronica Montecinos (London: Palgrave Macmillan, 2017), 211.

[26] May, "The Philippines under Aquino," 352; McKenna, *Muslim Rulers and Rebels*, 246.

[27] Mark R. Thompson, "Off the Endangered List: Philippine Democratization in Comparative Perspective," *Comparative Politics* 28, no. 2 (1996): 180.

an anti-system opposition or impending threat of a military coup, yet still some significant weaknesses. It was the second presidential election, but the first under the new constitution of 1987. Attempted coups that had afflicted the Aquino presidency ended, and the military returned to the barracks. The rules of democratic process were established, with the political elite abiding by electoral rules and a legal framework that allowed the development of a vibrant and free media, as well as an active civil society.

The clear reduction in coup attempts marks the most significant benchmark of the Philippines' democratic stabilization. As a former head of the Philippine Constabulary (police), deputy chief of staff of the armed forces under the Marcos regime, and finally chief of staff and Defense Minister in the Aquino administration, Ramos commanded strong respect from the military. Ramos also brokered an unconditional amnesty for military officers who had led the coup attempts and who were being investigated for human rights abuses under the Marcos regime. The new direction, which was a common strategy to secure democratic transitions in Latin America, offered a path for the military to return to the barracks and even for some of its officers to enter politics. One of the leaders of the coup attempts against Aquino, Colonel Gregorio "Gringo" Honasan, was subsequently elected to the Senate.[28]

The election of President Ramos also marked a first turnover of power. Under a presidential system largely modelled on that of the United States, presidential power is most important and there is a clear separation of powers between the executive and the legislature. Political parties are not well institutionalized and are often vehicles to help elect presidents and secure support in the legislature. In this case, the Lakas-NUCD (*Lakas ng Tao*-National Union of Christian Democrats) was established in 1992 by a number of congressmen supporting Fidel Ramos' presidential election. It won a plurality of seats.[29] Although President Aquino supported Fidel Ramos' candidacy, she retained no formal ties to him or to his nascent political party after she left office. Fidel Ramos' election can therefore be considered a first handover of power. Furthermore, Lakas-NUCD, which obtained the most seats, was a new political party. There was strong participation of all parties in the 1992 election, no emergence of an opposition rejecting the democratic process. In fact, there was elite consensus around elections as the main mechanism for gaining power.[30]

[28] James Putzel, *A Captive Land: The Politics of Agrarian Reform in the Philippines* (Philippines: Ateneo de Manila University Press, 1992), 54; Patricio N. Abinales, "Life after the Coup: The Military and Politics in Post-Authoritarian Philippines," *Philippine Political Science Journal* 26, no. 49 (2005): 39.

[29] Samuel C. K. Yu, "Political Reforms in the Philippines: Challenges Ahead," *Contemporary Southeast Asia* 27, no. 2 (2005): 222.

[30] Thompson, "Off the Endangered List," 194.

Finally, the rules of the democratic process were well in place, with respect for individual rights and a number of freedoms. The Constitution of 1987 was highly democratic as it was drafted with the participation and consultation of a vast number of groups and adopted in a plebiscite by a vast majority. Print media, radio, and television quickly expanded after Marcos and became broadly accessible. The space became wide for social criticism and investigative journalism.[31] Associational life developed very rapidly and became the most organized and active civil society in Asia.

The transitional period had put into place a framework under which Moros would be represented. Its confirmation under democratic stabilization offered a strategic quandary. If the state insisted that the 1987 Constitution and creation of the ARMM were the final solution, they risked further alienating the Moros and fuelling the insurgency. The Moros would not accept an institutional framework that had been imposed. While both sides realized that they would likely move away from the existing ARMM, the process to do so was unclear. As a key advisor to the negotiations with the MILF stated:

It's true that there was a gentlemen's agreement before I came in: the MILF would not talk about independence and the GRP should not use the constitution as a framework . . . but whether we like it or not, the GRP cannot get rid of the constitution. We are operating within the constitution whether we say it or not. And we have reached that point that when you talk about minerals, strategic minerals, it says there in the constitution, it's owned by the state. I mean, you cannot get around that.[32]

The issue of constitutionality became an obstacle to implementing several negotiated agreements. The Philippine state, now stabilized under a highly legitimized 1987 Constitution, insisted on following those procedures. While government negotiators sometimes appeared flexible on the issue, Congress often contested agreements on the basis of their constitutionality, or the Supreme Court struck them down. Since the MNLF in the first instance and the MILF, even more so, rejected the Constitution and sought to negotiate as equal partners to the Philippine state, the few agreements reached were diluted once passed into law or failed to be implemented.

With Moros divided into the MNLF and MILF, they continued to compete against one another, while incentives were high to scale up their demands. They both lay claim to legitimate representation of all Moros, and therefore when negotiations proceeded with the MNLF, the MILF continued its struggle.[33] The MNLF initially gained legitimacy as the sole representative of the Moros, boosted by the OIC's support, but the MILF responded to subsequent agreements by continuing its armed struggle and making greater demands.

---

[31] Putzel, *A Captive Land*, 63–64.   [32] Rudy Rodil, interview.
[33] Bertrand and Jeram, "Democratization and Determinants of Ethnic Violence."

Under Fidel Ramos' presidency, the state first appeared to give concessions. Ramos sought to rebuild credibility by enlisting foreign support and making strong, unilateral commitments to negotiating a peace agreement. During his presidential campaign, he visited Muammar Qaddhafi, the Libyan leader who had mediated before between Moros and the Philippine state, and proposed a new phase of negotiations with the MNLF. Given the previous role played by the OIC and its prior recognition of the MNLF as the sole representative of the Moros, Ramos clearly intended to reach an agreement that would attract support from all Moros and undermine the MILF.[34] Ramos sought to break the Philippines' cycle of underdevelopment and considered peace with the Moros and other insurgent groups as a necessary condition for development to proceed and his Social Reform Agenda to succeed.[35]

Soon after his inauguration, he created new institutions to open negotiations with various groups, including the Office of the Presidential Adviser for the Peace Process (OPAPP). With credible promises of peace, as he reigned in the armed forces, rebel groups reduced their violent mobilization and entered negotiations. After the election, a presidential team returned to Libya and met directly with Misuari. A number of similar meetings were held between 1993 and 1996.[36] The role of the OIC, especially Libya, as well as Indonesia was crucial in pressuring both sides.[37]

Negotiations culminated in the 1996 peace agreement with the MNLF. Most significantly, the MNLF agreed to relax its claim to all of Mindanao and the Sulu archipelago, and instead settled on the thirteen provinces and nine cities to which it had previously agreed in the Tripoli agreement of 1976. Yet, they also demanded much more detail and extensive powers before agreeing to sign.

The Tripoli agreement had been a relatively short and vague document. Although it extended autonomy to the specified thirteen provinces and nine cities, there were few details regarding the nature of this autonomy. Foreign Affairs, defence, mines, and mineral resources were spelled out as remaining within the jurisdiction of the central government, while Moros were permitted to implement Sharia law and courts, to establish Special Regional Security Forces, and to create their own schools and universities. Few other jurisdictions were spelled out. The agreement recognized rights to representation in the central government, in the military, and in the Supreme Court, and the establishment of a legislature and executive council in the autonomous region. But in

---

[34] Jacques Bertrand, "Peace and Conflict in the Southern Philippines: Why the 1996 Peace Agreement Is Fragile," *Pacific Affairs* 73, no. 1 (2000): 288; Nathan Gilbert Quimpo, "Options in the Pursuit of a Just, Comprehensive, and Stable Peace in the Southern Philippines," *Asian Survey* 41, no. 2 (2001).

[35] Amina Rasul, Head of Philippine Council for Islam and Democracy and Member of Ramos Cabinet, interview by author, April 29, 2008, Manila; Bacani, interview.

[36] Bertrand, "Peace and Conflict in the Southern Philippines," 40–41.

[37] Amina Rasul, interview; Benedicto Bacani, interview.

other jurisdictions, the relationship between the central government and autonomous regional administrative systems, as well as fiscal issues were to be negotiated later.[38]

The 1996 agreement, although framed as the final implementation of the Tripoli agreement, was actually a much more bonified version. With 154 clauses, it deepened and expanded the Tripoli agreement, even beyond areas that were supposed to be developed further in a subsequent committee. The Tripoli agreement was never implemented, and it was little else than a strategic ploy on the part of the Marcos regime to defuse pressure from the OIC and gain some breathing space in the war against the MNLF and redirect military resources to combat the communist New People's Army.[39] Nevertheless, the MNLF considered the Tripoli agreement as a benchmark and a minimal standard.

While territorial concessions were made, other issues were much more clearly spelled out. The MNLF relaxing its claims to all of Mindanao and the Sulu archipelago was not a large concession, given that Moros had lost their majority in most of the provinces and were a minority even in several of the provinces and large cities of the Tripoli agreement. To negotiate territory on the basis of the Tripoli agreement constituted a potential gain from the limited, four provinces that had joined the ARMM.

The structure of the autonomous region reflected the divisions of power between the executive and the legislature that characterized the broader political system. The chief executive was to be elected and held the power to implement directives from the legislature, but the president retained a supervisory role. He had veto power over legislation, with parliament holding the ability to overturn the veto with two-thirds majority. The legislature obtained jurisdiction over all matters, except those retained by the central government, which included foreign affairs, defence, fiscal and monetary policy, justice (except Sharia), citizenship, immigration, and a few other minor areas. Many clauses specified the rights to promote development, tourism, manage foreign aid in the region, create or reorganize local units, basically spelling out many of the powers that might be expected from the autonomous region. Several clauses spelled out the role of the Special Regional Security Force that had been specified in the Tripoli agreement. Several clauses specified the right to have one cabinet minister from the autonomous region, one Supreme Court justice, as well as judges in other courts.

---

[38] The 1976 Tripoli Agreement between the Government of the Republic of the Philippines (GRP) and the MNLF with the participation of the Organisation of Islamic Conference Ministerial Committee of Six and the Secretary General of the Organisation of Islamic Conference, 1996.

[39] Bertrand, "Peace and Conflict in the Southern Philippines," 39; McKenna, *Muslim Rulers and Rebels*, 168.

A few issues remained ambiguous, particularly with respect to fiscal autonomy. Several rights were extended to the region to establish schools and universities, as well as to adapt curriculum to incorporate "Islamic values," but the national curriculum was retained and the Ministry of Education played a supervisory role. With respect to the management of natural resources, the Tripoli agreement had mainly stated the central government's retention of mining and mineral rights, with some "reasonable" percentage of revenues being devolved to the region. The 1996 agreement went slightly further by granting citizens in the autonomous region the "preferential" right to explore, develop and use these resources. The local legislature could enact rules and regulations over resource industries, but had to take into account national laws and constitutional provisions. Similarly, while the legislature could manage local units in the region, it could not transgress the 1991 law on Local Government Units (LGUs), which granted decentralization of administrative and fiscal power to LGUs. Fiscally, while the regional autonomous government obtained vast powers to manage fiscal resources, the national General Appropriations Act specified allotments to the regional autonomous government, which included income from the value-added tax, taxes on hotels and motels, and a few other sources. Twenty per cent of these revenues, however, were to be allotted to the LGUs. Corporate taxes were to be retained in the province or municipalities where the businesses operated. With few other details regarding fiscal allocations, and some taxation rights granted to the local legislature, the consequence was unclear on the region's ability to gain sufficient resources and sufficient autonomy over the management of those resources to exercise powers that were granted.[40]

The state gained strategic and political benefits, while the MNLF obtained short-term incentives to cooperate, with a promise of significant gains. Ramos gained strong recognition as a peacemaker and an effective leader, which contributed to his ability to further implement his reform agenda. The state had scored a major reprieve in its conflict with the Moros by securing a deal and providing transitional mechanisms for the MNLF's disbandment and reintegration.

Much of the agreement focused on transitional issues. It created a temporary administrative body, the Southern Philippines Council for Peace and Development (SPCPD), to supervise implementation of foreign aid and development programs during a three-year transitional period. The agreement also

---

[40] The Final Agreement on the Implementation of the 1976 Tripoli Agreement between the Government of the Republic of the Philippines (GRP) and the Moro National Liberation Front (MNLF) with the participation of the Organisation of Islamic Conference Ministerial Committee of Six and the Secretary General of the Organisation of Islamic Conference, 1996.

provided for the integration of 7,500 MNLF fighters to the Philippine armed forces and the national police.[41]

Furthermore, in order to re-inject some measure of authority to the temporary ARMM administration, its governance during the transition period was essentially given to Nur Misuari, the MNLF leader, in spite of the MNLF's rejection of the ARMM's legitimacy. It was a temporary compromise before a new law on expanded autonomy could be passed and elections held for a government of the new autonomous region. Misuari, once in power, expected to proceed with making autonomy progress through his control of the autonomous area.[42]

There are three broad reasons why the 1996 agreement subsequently failed and why Moros found themselves still fighting for autonomy.[43] First, state promises failed to be implemented, most importantly because of the nature of the Philippines' political institutions and the weak support received from the Filipino majority. Second, in part because of the legitimacy gap among the Moros, the transitional institutions were highly ineffective, and therefore fed as well the problems with the agreement's implementation. Finally, as the armed struggle shifted to the MILF, the latter increased its claims to Moro representation and denounced the MNLF's compromise, a direct result of the competition between both organizations.

Moreover, under the Philippine Constitution and the clauses of the 1996 agreement, two major steps were required. Congress had to first approve the agreement through the enactment of legislation that reflected its substance. Once the legislation was in place, the government was required to pass within two years a plebiscite in the fourteen provinces and nine cities to determine the final area of the autonomous region. The new autonomous region was supposed to be functional within three years of the signature of the agreement.

Yet, the process stalled in the first phase. Several members of parliament, and their constituencies, were largely opposed to making concessions to the Moros. At the end of 1996, public hearings in Congress saw opposition raised to the granting of autonomy and criticism against Fidel Ramos, who was accused of "selling out" to Muslims. Similar criticisms were voiced in the Senate with calls for withdrawing the SPCPD's powers and excluding LGUs from its purview. One quarter of senators voted against the peace agreement. Other members of parliament attempted to challenge the agreement in the Supreme Court.[44] With such opposition even before the agreement was signed, it was not surprising that Congress continued to be obstructive.

---

[41] Ibid.   [42] Amina Rasul, interview.

[43] For a detailed analysis, see Bertrand, "Peace and Conflict in the Southern Philippines."

[44] R. J. May, "Muslim Mindanao: Four Years after the Peace Agreement," *Southeast Asian Affairs* (2001): 267.

The commitment to passing a new autonomy law became even weaker after the end of Fidel Ramos' presidency. The agreement's strongest advocate, he had already begun to lose support as his mandate was coming to an end and he became mired in controversy, particularly at his perceived attempt to promote constitutional change to expand his mandate.[45]

His successor, Joseph Estrada, had different priorities. Riding a populist vote, Estrada used pro-poor rhetoric to denounce the continued large-scale poverty in the Philippines and won against candidates with stronger middle-class support. Aside from his rhetoric, Estrada had little interest in building a strong program. His administration soon became entangled in corruption scandals and he was ousted by mass demonstrations in 2001. Moros were not part of Estrada's appeal to the rural poor.[46] His erratic behaviour made him more vulnerable to appeals for a strong-handed approach, as the MILF became more significant. He therefore exerted little pressure or leadership to counter Congress' foot-dragging on the new autonomy bill.

Congress was under pressure to adopt a new autonomy law.[47] Nur Misuari had become governor of the ARMM as part of the transitional provisions, but his term as governor was supposed to end in March 1999. Without a new autonomy bill, it was difficult to hold new elections for the ARMM.[48] The MNLF threatened to return to war as it denounced Congress' delays in passing the agreement's three-year deadline for implementation. As a result, the House of Representatives and Senate postponed the ARMM election, while working on their respective bills.

While several versions were presented, the House and Senate eventually settled on two: House Bill 7883 passed in July 1999 and Senate Bill 2129, which culminated eventually in the Congressional Act RA 9054, sponsored by Senator Aquilino Q. Pimentel Jr., the senator for Mindanao. All factions of the MNLF denounced the Organic Act for the ARMM (RA 9054) as an inadequate representation of what was promised in the 1996 agreement. At the same time,

---

[45] Antonio F. Moreno, "Engaged Citizenship: The Catholic Bishops' Conference of the Philippines (CBCP) in the Post-Authoritarian Philippines," in *Development, Civil Society and Faith-Based Organizations: Bridging the Sacred and the Secular*, eds. Gerard Clarke and Michael Jennings (New York: Palgrave Macmillan, 2008), 130; James Marshall Kirby, "Satisfaction and Dissatisfaction with Political Leaders in Indonesia, Korea, the Philippines, and Thailand," in *Incomplete Democracies in the Asia-Pacific: Evidence from Indonesia, Korea, the Philippines, and Thailand*, eds. Giovanna Maria Dora Dore, Jae H. Ku, and Karl D. Jackson (New York: Palgrave Macmillan, 2014), 238.

[46] For Estrada's appeal to the rural poor, see William Case, *Populist Threats and Democracy's Fate in Southeast Asia: Thailand, the Philippines, and Indonesia* (New York: Routledge, 2017), 36. In fact, he even failed to implement those pro-poor promises, with significant impact on the Moro conflict. See Sarah Lumley, *Sustainability and Degradation in Less Developed Countries: Immolating the Future?* (Farnham: Ashgate, 2002), 51.

[47] Benecdito Bacani, interview.

[48] Juliet Labog Javellana, "Estrada Signs Law Resetting ARMM Polls," *Philippine Daily Inquirer*, September 9, 1999.

some members of the MNLF were manoeuvring to remove Nur Misuari from the chairmanship of the MNLF and as head of the ARMM, in part because of his repeated threats to return to war and therefore greatly stalling plans to attract development to the region. When Gloria Macapagal-Arroyo became president, she allowed RA 9054 to "lapse into law," that is, without her signature the law would become effective, without requiring her to take an active role in approving the law. Her administration then organized a plebiscite on expanded autonomy, which was held in eleven provinces and fourteen cities.[49] As predicted, a majority of Christian regions rejected the framework for a new autonomy. Only Marawi city and the island of Basilan voted in favour of joining the existing ARMM.[50] As a result, the ARMM gained a little more territory and a few additional powers, while short of the MNLF's hopes.

The process reflects some of the problems with the Philippines' democratic institutions when attempting to find a meaningful solution to the Moro crisis. The final Act of Congress was supposed to reflect the points reached in the 1996 peace agreement with the MNLF. Yet, provisions of the agreement required that constitutional processes be followed, thereby presenting bills before Congress and subjecting the final bill for ratification by referendum. Several bills were proposed to both Congress and the Senate, with varying degrees of consistence with the peace agreement. Since public hearings were held and congressional representatives were expected to advance the interests of their respective constituents, the final bill would likely diverge from what had been an agreement between negotiators of the OPAPP and the MNLF. The latter having very few representatives in Congress, and even less so after the 1998 elections, they could not influence the outcome. Finally, with legislation failing to pass during the presidential administration that negotiated the agreement, it was difficult to maintain the political support necessary to adhere to commitments made.

Some compromises, but also significant dilutions, were made in these bills. For instance, provisions were included so that members of the ARMM would be required only to vote on amendments of the original bill RA 6734. This way a negative vote would not lead to the withdrawal of the four original provinces from the autonomous region. It also allowed for the clustering of some contiguous municipalities with Muslim majorities before the plebiscite. Yet, several clauses diluted the Agreement. The Bill listed a number of strategic resources that were excluded from the regional government's control,

---

[49] Miriam Coronel Ferrer, "Recycled Autonomy? Enacting the New Organic Act for a Regional Autonomous Government in Southern Philippines," *Kasarinlan* 15, no. 2 (2000): 179–81; Amina Rasul, *Broken Peace? Assessing the 1996 GRP-MNLF Final Peace Agreement* (Manila: Philippines Council for Islam and Democracy, in collaboration with the Konrad Adenauer Stiftung, 2007).

[50] Deidre Sheehan and David Plott, "A War Grows," *Far Eastern Economic Review* 164, no. 40 (2001).

supervision, and use. It nevertheless increased to 50 per cent the proportion of revenues, taxes, and fees from these minerals to be retained by the autonomous government, while also increasing to 70 per cent its share of internal revenue taxes, fees, charges, and taxes on natural resources.[51]

Two other aspects significantly reduced the mechanisms for Moro representation. First, the Agreement had stipulated an increase in representation at the national level, including the cabinet. While the Senate Bill retained Moro representation in the cabinet, it dropped provisions for other forms of representation in national institutions, and even diluted commitments to filling positions of national departments, agencies or bureaus at the regional level. With the mention of "as far as practicable," it allowed the central government to appoint Moros at its discretion. Second, the Bill included a number of checks on the autonomous regional government. Most significantly, it allowed the president to suspend funds for failure to account for these funds or for failure to protect the *lumad* and Christian minorities in the region. It also allowed the president to send the armed forces, without consulting the regional government, in order to prevent or suppress violence or rebellion. These measures gave the president, in fact, enormous leverage and discretionary powers over the autonomous government.[52]

Problems with transitional institutions became a second source of the peace agreement's eventual failure. Corruption strongly undermined both the SPCPD and the ARMM under Nur Misuari. But also, the ARMM was lacking in its ability to manage the region, in large part because of the lack of funding. Even before, under the previous leadership of Zacaria Candao and Lininding Pangandaman, the ARMM was perceived to be inefficient and corrupt.[53] But, once under Misuari and the MNLF's control, the state provided little technical support or training to help the former insurgents become bureaucrats and administrators.[54]

The SPCPD was unable to pursue its mandate adequately because of a lack of funding and state support. To implement the transitional provisions of the 1996 peace agreement, President Ramos signed Executive Order (EO371) that established the SPCPD. It was mandated to temporarily administer foreign aid and other sources of development funding for the newly created Special Zone for Peace and Development. The executive order significantly diluted the powers that had been provided under the 1996 agreement, including the elimination of certain agencies that the SPCPD was specifically designed to supervise and the nomination of forty-four MNLF members to the Assembly.[55] From the outset, the SPCPD's mandate was primarily advisory and depended

---

[51] Ferrer, "Recycled Autonomy?," 179–81; Rasul, *Broken Peace?*.   [52] Ibid.
[53] May, "Muslim Mindanao," 264, 67.   [54] Amina Rasul, interview.
[55] May, "Muslim Mindanao," 267; Amina Rasul, interview.

therefore on influencing and coordinating with line agencies and departments in charge of various departments. So, it was very limited because of little funding, no police powers, no jurisdiction over significant sections of the bureaucracy, nor control over national projects.[56]

Some MNLF insurgents did return to civilian life. Supported by USAID and UNDP, many aid projects were channelled to MNLF communities and run through the structures of the MNLF. Turned into peace and development communities, they provided a structure for the reintegration of the MNLF to civilian and local economic life. But while funds began to be disbursed in mid-1997, there was little follow-up from the government, and therefore the reintegration program remained limited.[57]

Overall, Nur Misurari and other MNLF leaders could be seen as having been inept at running the administration and corrupt, but there is some credence to the perspective that most Moros had never seen the ARMM as a credible form of autonomy and as an entity that was functional, and therefore had little incentive to invest in its success. At the same time, if his administration had demonstrated that the ARMM could be effective without transformation, it would have significantly undermined the argument favouring a new autonomous region and government.[58]

Under RA 9054, the ARMM did not function more effectively. It still lacked much power and had no fiscal autonomy. Every year, it had to request its budget from Congress and lacked legitimacy in light of the continuing negotiations with the MILF. The ARMM did not significantly change as a result. Under a new administration, Muslimin Sema became its leader and former MNLF followers continued to control the government. For the most part, the ARMM retained its primary role as provider of local employment. Its bureaucracy remained bloated, and almost 90 per cent of the budget went to civil servants' pay. Although the ARMM government had the legal ability to exercise more powers, it failed to do so. In budgetary terms, it continued to rely on annual Congressional allocations.[59] As a result, it failed to function as an autonomous government, partly because of inherent constraints and partly because of its own inability to use its jurisdictional autonomy.

A third reason for the agreement's failure was the continued and growing presence of the MILF. The OIC had recognized the MNLF as the sole representative of the Moros, and consequently supported negotiations that led to the 1996 agreement. If the state had hoped that the latter would reduce the MILF's relevance, the strategy backfired. Instead, the MILF gained even more support

---

[56] Bertrand, "Peace and Conflict in the Southern Philippines."
[57] Steven Rood, Representative of Asia Foundation (Philippines), interview by author, April 28, 2008, Makati City, Manila; Rudy Rodil, interview.
[58] Bertrand, "Peace and Conflict in the Southern Philippines."
[59] Benedicto Bacani, interview.

and was an unavoidable force, especially when many disgruntled MNLF rebels joined it as well. The MILF became the stalwart of violent mobilization, which rendered attempts to implement the 1996 peace agreement somewhat meaningless, since lasting peace required ultimately that MILF supporters lay down their arms and also sign a similar agreement. The hopes that the 1996 peace agreement was going to create some momentum in this direction soon fizzled and, instead, its poor implementation became increasing evidence for the MILF to harden its negotiating position.

Commitment Failures, MILF Negotiations, and the Path to Bangsamoro Autonomy

The Philippine government faced a large commitment problem that rendered subsequent negotiations with the MILF and institutional concessions particularly difficult. While the failure of the Tripoli agreement could easily be blamed on Marcos' authoritarian rule, the weak concession that the ARMM represented, its dysfunctional state, as well as the failure to implement the 1996 agreement all contributed significantly to weakening the Philippine state's credibility that it would deliver on its promises and commitments. The Constitution continued to provide a strong, enshrined commitment to autonomy but had been used by a mostly reluctant, independent parliament as argument to undermine some of the past agreements. The majority preference shifted clearly toward more intolerance toward Moros once Estrada gained power and after 9/11 when insurgents became increasingly viewed as "terrorists" in addition to "secessionists." As a result, the parliament was generally reluctant to grant large concessions to the MILF and Moros more broadly, even when presidents such as Benigno Aquino Jr. or the OPAPP were willing to make concessions and negotiate compromises. Although war fatigue and continued violence weighed on the democratic government, after Estrada's "all-out-war" approach backfired, nevertheless it was not sufficient to prompt strong commitments and make them credible. Ironically, it was President Duterte, with strong populist and quasi-authoritarian leanings, who managed to strengthen the state's commitment and convince Congress to pass the BBL. From Mindanao, and with strong electoral influence over a significantly large constituency in parliament, he had a strong electoral interest in peace.

During the 1990s, the MILF positioned itself as an alternative. It had split from the MNLF in 1977, when Hashim Salamat and a few followers objected to signing the Tripoli agreement. It was equally opposed to the 1996 agreement but, by then, was becoming a considerably greater military force. By the early 1990s, it had established two major positions: Camp Abubakar in

Maguindanao province and Camp Bushra in Lanao del Sur.[60] The MILF benefited from MNLF defections, which became greater in the aftermath of the 1996 peace agreement and growing problems with the implementation of even its transitional provisions.

In spite of prioritizing the process with the MNLF, the Philippine state under Fidel Ramos also negotiated a ceasefire agreement with the MILF. In July 1997, the MILF and the Philippine government signed an agreement for a "cessation of hostilities." By 1998, they agreed on a General Framework of Agreement of Intent. The government recognized MILF camps and positions as "zones of peace and development," and even provided some livelihood support to MILF fighters.[61] The government and the MILF subsequently began formal negotiations.

Negotiations were short-lived, as Ramos' presidency ended and Joseph Estrada was elected as president in 1998. They were unsuccessful largely because they were an inheritance from the past administration and Estrada placed little emphasis on them. Negotiations were mainly held at the level of both sides' negotiating panels. Even though many conflicting issues were resolved and negotiations progressed, the new president and several of his advisors had little commitment to their success.[62]

The MILF meanwhile continued to wage attacks to strengthen its position, in violation of existing ceasefire agreements. It had also thrived under these ceasefires that allowed it to protect its main position, Camp Abubakar, and to run virtually its own administration in areas under its control.[63]

In the end, the Armed Forces of the Philippines started a new campaign in February 2000, and President Estrada announced an "all-out war."[64] The repressive approach aligned with more radical views in his administration and in the military, on which he relied for advice.[65] Estrada was also encouraged to pursue this approach to offset mounting criticism of his leadership. Investor confidence plummeted as dubious practices became more frequent. Instead of pursuing sound economic policy, Estrada frequently served the interests of his friends, such as business tycoon Lucio Tan. When the Abu Sayyaf staged a spectacular seizing of hostages on Malaysian soil in May 2000, it only worsened the Philippines' international image and investor

---

[60] May, "Muslim Mindanao," 270.   [61] Ibid.

[62] Moner Bajunaid, Head of Technical Committee, MILF-Government of Philippines Negotiation Panel (1997–2000), interview by author, May 5, 2008, Cotabato City.

[63] May, "Muslim Mindanao," 269.

[64] Mel C. Labrador, "The Philippines in 2001: High Drama, a New President, and Setting the Stage for Recovery," *Asian Survey* 42, no. 1 (2002): 146; Jayson S. Lamcheck, *Human Rights-Compliant Counterterrorism: Myth-Making and Reality in the Philippines and Indonesia* (Cambridge: Cambridge University Press, 2019), 74–75.

[65] Amina Rasul, interview.

confidence.[66] With growing criticism of his cronyism and corruption, Estrada used the offensive against the MILF to make political gains. His strategy worked as his approval ratings rose by 15 per cent as the military won several operations against the MILF. By July, the armed forces seized Camp Abubakar, which was a major military victory.[67]

Although the military approach proved to be initially popular, it became increasingly unsustainable in a democratic context. Two processes contributed to the shift. First of all, the repression backfired, as it fuelled a deepening of the violence and triggered pressures to reduce military operations. Even within cabinet, Vice-President Gloria Macapagal-Arroyo objected to the approach on the basis that it would not resolve the conflict. Furthermore, criticism rose as the "all-out war" seemed excessive.[68] With the costs of the war reaching six billion pesos and casualties rising steadily, the policy contributed to Estrada's downfall.[69] Second, the OIC and major donors, such as the United States, the EU, and Japan exerted increasing international pressure for the Philippines to seek a negotiated solution. Among other factors, the government was concerned about maintaining good relations with Islamic states and advanced democracies to maintain the security of its oil imports as well as its ability to continue exporting labour.[70]

When Gloria Macapagal-Arroyo acceded to the presidency in July 2000, she immediately reversed Estrada's policies and launched a campaign of "all-out peace," even though her reliance on support from the military complicated her policies. With Executive Order 3, she revived the policies of Fidel Ramos, focused on negotiation, created a Government Peace Negotiating Panel, and strengthened the mandate of the Office of the Presidential Adviser on the Peace Process to begin new negotiations with the MILF.[71] But she was surrounded by former military personnel as advisors and could not exercise as much autonomy on security policies as Ramos had.[72] Fighting continued as negotiations

---

[66] Deidre Sheehan, "Estrada's Mindanao: Troubles Grow Worse," *Far Eastern Economic Review* 163, no. 19 (2000).

[67] "Erap's Rebound," *Far Eastern Economic Review* 163, no. 31 (2000).

[68] Nathan Gilbert Quimpo, "Mindanao, Southern Philippines: The Pitfalls of Working for Peace in a Time of Political Decay," in *Autonomy and Ethnic Conflict in South and South-East Asia*, ed. Rajat Ganguly (New York: Routledge, 2012), 122; Rommel A. Curaming, "Historical Injustice and Human Insecurity: Conflict and Peacemaking in Muslim Mindanao," in *Human Insecurities in Southeast Asia*, eds. Paul J. Carnegie, Victor T. King, and Zawawi Ibrahim (New York: Springer, 2016), 130; Joseph Chinyong Liow, *Religion and Nationalism in Southeast Asia* (Cambridge: Cambridge University Press, 2016), 69.

[69] Ayesah Uy Abubakar, *Peacebuilding and Sustainable Human Development: The Pursuit of the Bangsamoro Right to Self-Determination* (Switzerland: Springer Nature, 2019), 103.

[70] Amina Rasul, interview.

[71] "Arroyo's Peacemaking Legacy Leaves a Trail of Blood and Chaos," *GMA News Online*, August 14, 2009.

[72] Carmen Abubakar, Professor, Institute of Islamic Studies at U. P. Diliman, interview (informal conversation) with author, April 28, 2008, Cotabato City.

resumed, which was a significant departure from negotiations under Ramos or Aquino when fighting had basically stopped.

Under Arroyo, [the government] initially continued militarization because she partly relied on military and police to gain votes, in particular in Mindanao, where in conflict areas they could intimidate and pressure voters. Her opponent, Fernando Poe Jr, was very popular in Mindanao, and so vote buying was insufficient to guarantee sufficient votes. So, poles were rigged and the military provided security. So, with the massive fraud in the 2004 election, Arroyo was strongly indebted to the military.[73]

Arroyo's approach was further compromised as a result of the escalating concerns with terrorist groups after 9/11 and the Bali bombings of 2002. The United States increased its technical support to the Philippines armed forces to pursue terrorist groups, especially with suspected links to Al-Qaeda. While Abu Sayyaf became the main target, the MILF was pressured into publicly distancing itself from Al-Qaeda and Jemaah Islamiyah, which was behind the Bali bombings.[74]

The consequence, however, was beneficial as both sides moved toward a ceasefire that involved Malaysia's armed forces as a monitoring force. "Part of the problem with MILF negotiations, although they began in January 1997, is that there was significant fighting until 2003, so [it was] difficult to have successful negotiations. One benefit was reaching a successful ceasefire agreement that included Malaysia (IMT)."[75] In addition to external monitoring, the ceasefire included several mechanisms to prevent a resumption of violence. It lasted until 2009.

Nevertheless, when the MILF began to negotiate on substantive terms with the government, it adopted a completely new set of principles and demands. As Rudy Rodil pointed out:

the issue of governance boils down to how much self-determination they have. They will certainly not be satisfied with having something like the Organic Act; as far as they are concerned, the powers granted in the Organic Act is not enough, so they would like to have more. But the political status, and what to call it, will be difficult because it needs to be consistent with the constitution.[76]

The MILF considered insufficient the 1996 agreement and, in particular, given its poor implementation, it clearly considered that more guarantees needed to be added.

---

[73] Amina Rasul, interview. This information was also confirmed by Rodil.
[74] Amina Rasul, interview; International Crisis Group, *Southern Philippines Backgrounder: Terrorism and the Peace Process* (Brussels: International Crisis Group, 2004); Carolyn O. Arguillas, "Salamat Issues Policy Statement Rejecting Terror; Ermita Welcomes Move," *Mindanews*, June 22, 2003.
[75] Rudy Rodil, interview.   [76] Ibid.

[T]he MILF, trying again to negotiate, and what they are trying to negotiate is not powers that are already granted under [the 1996 agreement] ... but more than that .... [I]f they would just negotiate on what was in the 1996 peace agreement there would be no point in negotiation .... [T]he MNLF's concern is they cannot demand more other than what they have signed. So, this is an opportunity so that [the MNLF and MILF] can cooperate and get more. So, at the end, all of this combined together will be more power to the Bangsamoro. That's how we look at it. We don't look at it as a competition between the MNLF and the MILF but as a complementary effort.[77]

Two main principles drove the MILF's agenda. First, it demanded the establishment of an autonomous government that gives Moros special recognition as a Bangsamoro nation and that obtains status as an equal partner with the Philippine government. Second, it rejected the constitutional process as it considered it biased in terms of the majority.[78]

From the MILF's perspective, several consensus points elevated Moros' status and power much beyond the 1996 agreement. Three aspects to its notion of autonomous government were particularly important: first, the identification and recognition of Bangsamoro identity; second, the demarcation of ancestral domain, thereby recognizing the principle of a homeland; third, the creation of a Bangsamoro Juridical Entity (BJE), which provided Moros with a set of institutions that fall outside of existing structures and recognized a "partnership" between the Moros and the Philippine state on the basis of equality.

In 2006, negotiations led to a breakthrough as the MILF and the government negotiating panel reached a number of consensus points, one of which included the delimitation of the territory to be recognized as a "Bangsamoro" (literally Moro nation) homeland. For the MILF, the recognition as "Bangsamoro" was more than symbolic as past administrations refused to consider Moros as a "nation" but also rejected any concessions that could be used to enhance self-determination.

We're setting up a state. Self-determination itself is nationalist, you see, that's why *bangsa* is about nationality ... Ethnicity itself is a framework that will not work in this assertion of the Bangsa concept because ... there are three major [groups]: Maranao [people of Lanao del Norte and Lanao del Sur], Maguindanao [people of Maguindanao Province] and Tausug [people of Sulu].[79]

---

[77] Abhoud Syed Lingga, Head of Institute of Bangsamoro Studies, MILF Peace Panel Member, and Former Secretary-General of the Moro National Liberation Front (MNLF), interview by author, May 1, 2008, Cotabato City.

[78] Salah Jubair, *The Long Road to Peace: Inside the GRP-MILF Peace Process* (Cotabato City: Institute of Bangsamoro Studies, 2007), 15. Steven Rood also noted in an interview that the government and the MILF had to agree on a trade-off: the MILF would not raise the issue of independence in exchange for the government not raising the issue of the constitutional process.

[79] Datu Michael Mastura, Former Deputy Minister of Muslim Affairs and MILF Chief Negotiator, interview by author, May 2, 2008, Cotabato City.

The recognition of the Bangsamoro, therefore, carried strong connotations of nationhood, and the creation of a state to represent the Bangsamoro. It was not based on ethnicity per se, given the ethnic diversity of the Moros themselves, but on a blend of non-ethnic yet historically grounded sense of Moro, combined with their Islamic heritage.[80]

The demands for such recognition and the state's subsequent acquiescence certainly raised expectations and constituted a significantly deeper concession than what had been previously negotiated:

The concept or the idea of increasing recognition of Bangsamoro groups is not maturing fast enough. It has matured a lot from 1976 . . . there has been autonomy, if you can call it that. But now we are talking about self-determination, now we can talk about Bangsamoro. I remember in 1993, during the '93/'96 peace talks, the use of the word Bangsamoro was not allowed within the government party. Everybody gets slapped. It's very sensitive. You know, that will mean we will recognize Bangsamoro nationhood, no way. But now it is different. Everybody in the government they are talking about Bangsamoro, even in cabinet. But . . . when you're talking about the final political status, that seems to be a little hard to swallow for some people.[81]

A Memorandum of Agreement (MoA) on Ancestral Domain, recognizing and delimiting the territory of the future autonomous government, was to be signed in early August 2008. The MILF had emphasized "ancestral domain" as a principle to recognize a territorial homeland for the Moros. Since the 1970s, and up until recently, the MNLF as well as the MILF considered large portions of Mindanao and the Sulu archipelago to be part of their historical claim.

Negotiations centred around expanding the ARMM to include adjacent territories and other smaller areas where the Muslims were a majority. This was significant as the MNLF had always claimed a much broader territory as a historical claim where Muslims were a majority in the past, rather than reflective of the more disaggregated communities currently scattered across mostly the south west of Mindanao and the Sulu archipelago. In the law that created the ARMM, provinces were the territorial unit that formed the basis of inclusion and exclusion within the autonomous area. As a result, many small areas with strong concentrations of Muslims were left outside of the autonomous region. Both parties therefore agreed to expand on the basis of municipalities and baranguays, which did not dramatically increase the territory of the existing ARMM but contributed to limited expansion to include a greater number of Moros. There was also agreement not only to expand the territory contiguously, but also to provide "juridical" authority over Muslim majority baranguays, even if somewhat separated from the main ARMM territory.[82]

---

[80] Ibid. See also McKenna, *Muslim Rulers and Rebels*, 279–84.   [81] Rudy Rodil, interview.
[82] Rudy Rodil, interview; Benedicto Bacani, interview; Carmen Abubakar, interview. See also Draft Memorandum of Understanding between GRP and MILF, as of Feb 18, 2008.

The MoA agreed on the establishment of the BJE, which would have authority over the ancestral domain.[83] For the MILF, the principle of the BJE, which they proposed, not only recognized institutions specifically designed for the Moro nation but also invested them with powers that raised their status beyond the autonomy that the MNLF previously obtained. The MILF saw the BJE as "a new format or package that should become the umbrella because it's broader and goes beyond autonomy as defined in ARMM." They insisted that the BJE would then have an "associative" relationship with the Philippine Republic, as equal entities, by which they could write their own constitution and jointly amend the national constitution if necessary. This was a strong departure from previous gains, with a much stronger emphasis on the principle of shared sovereignty and equal status with the Philippine state.[84]

During several phases of negotiations, the government had agreed not to raise the constitutional issue in exchange for the MILF consenting to avoid demanding independence.

[W]hen Salamat[85], the former chairman and founder of the MILF [,] got to talk to Ramos ... that means 1997, there was an understanding that the MILF will not invoke its demand for independence. To reciprocate, the Philippine government will not invoke the constitution in the question of sovereignty and territorial integrity. That was an open blank sheet so we could move and discuss the issues in a broad context, free of constraints. Over the years, we succeeded to make the MILF draft, reworking discussion papers, so as a working paper, we had a very brief statement of the problem, the solution.[86]

Nevertheless, just before the government and the MILF signed the MoA, in a surprise move the Supreme Court imposed a moratorium, after a petition from several regional governments.[87] The Supreme Court raised the issue of the constitutionality of the MoA on Ancestral Domain and questioned several aspects of the agreement including the concept of "juridical entity" and its "associative" powers, as well as the implied process that required a change to the constitution in order to be implemented.[88] Once again, an agreement ended because of the limitations imposed by the constitution, this time with the Supreme Court directly involved.

Following the Supreme Court's decision, the two negotiating panels slowly resumed talking but, with presidential elections looming in June 2010, little

---

[83] "Draft Memorandum of Understanding (GRP and MILF, as of February 18, 2008)."

[84] Datu Michael Mastura, interview; Benedicto Bacani, interview.

[85] Hashim Salamat was the founder and leader of the MILF until his death in 2003.

[86] Datu Michael Mastura, interview.

[87] International Crisis Group, *The Philippines: The Collapse of Peace in Mindanao* (Brussels: International Crisis Group, 2008).

[88] For a very detailed discussion of the petition and the court's rationale, see Supreme Court of the Philippines, G.R. No. 183591, http://sc.judiciary.gov.ph/jurisprudence/2008/october2008/183 591.htm, accessed August 1, 2018.

progress was achieved. Negotiations once again hit a familiar roadblock by the end of Arroyo's mandate. In spite of having signed an agreement on ancestral domain, no plan was in place for its ratification. With the Supreme Court moratorium, there were further delays before implementation could be considered or even possible. As Arroyo's term was coming to an end, once again there were few incentives to resume negotiations just before the election of a new president.

Under President Benigno Aquino Jr., negotiations reached new levels. He insisted on ensuring that the negotiations would take place with regular consultation of all parties concerned, including the legislature and local governments, and that the constitution would be respected. He was critical of the Memorandum of Agreement on Ancestral Domain, which had committed the government to recognizing a BJE that would include its own security forces and monetary system, which had been criticized for constituting a state for the Moros. The MILF, however, began negotiations seeking to continue where previous ones had left off.[89]

The main contentious point was related to the MILF's insistence on obtaining a "sub-state," rather than autonomy. In the second half of 2011, the MILF maintained its position for a "sub-state" that would uphold the principles of self-rule and right to self-determination, which had been obtained in the previous round of negotiations under the MoA-AD. The government, in response, proposed "enhanced autonomy" to modify and build on the existing ARMM. By early 2012, both sides agreed on several principles for the creation of an "autonomous political entity" to replace the ARMM, stating concerns on both sides for reaching an agreement before elections scheduled for mid-2013.[90]

The 2012 "Framework Agreement on the Bangsamoro," signed in October 2012, was a breakthrough. While it did not acknowledge a "sub-state" status to the Moros, it formally recognized the Bangsmoro identity, agreed on creating a new "autonomous political entity," which recovered aspects of the MILF's previous concept of "Bangsamoro Juridical Entity." The Bangsamoro was to be governed through an asymmetric arrangement, regulated by the BBL. It created a representative government for the Bangsamoro. It obtained rights to raise its own revenues, including from foreign sources and through a "fair" allocation of revenue from natural resources. The territorial agreement mirrored the past agreement on ancestral domain, as well as the

---

[89] Christian V. Esguerra and Edwin Fernandez, "New Head of Peace Panel with MILF: No Surprises," *Philippine Daily Inquirer*, July 16, 2010.

[90] "MILF Rejects Autonomy Offer," *The Philippine Star*, August 24, 2011; "Gov't Firm on Giving MILF Autonomy Than Sub-State," *The Philippine Star*, August 26, 2011; "Gov't, MILF Agree on Autonomous Entity to Replace ARMM," *Philippine Daily Inquirer*, April 25, 2012.

process by which contiguous areas would join, that is, by majority vote in a plebiscite. Details were to be worked out in the final draft of the BBL.

In subsequent years, much of the negotiations focused on drafting the BBL. A committee comprising government and MILF representatives first signed a Comprehensive Agreement on the Bangsamoro in March 2014 and then concluded a draft of the BBL in April 2014. But President Aquino rejected it for fear that too many of its clauses contravened the constitution. Nevertheless, after significant MILF concessions, a revised draft was submitted to parliament in September 2015.[91]

Once again, electoral considerations and constitutional limitations prevented this new version from being passed. Most significantly, when the Special Action Force (SAF) of the Philippine National Police launched a counter-terrorism attack in MILF-controlled territory against the ceasefire arrangements, what became known as the Mamasapano incident became highly politicized. A video of MILF combatants executing SAF members was broadly circulated, which galvanized politicians from all parties to ask for MILF disarmament before agreeing to resume talks. As a result, the BBL stalled in Congress as elections in 2016 neared.[92]

With the election of President Duterte in May 2016, a new cycle of offers and negotiations began, with a new set of political interests involved. Duterte had mentioned negotiations with the MILF during his campaign. Yet, while he initially agreed to abide by past agreements, he insisted that there might be no need for a BBL, as he had been promoting a federal model for the Philippines.[93]

There was nevertheless a renewed attempt to draft a BBL. Duterte insisted on making it more "inclusive," to take into account all Muslim groups as well as non-Muslims.[94] While he supported a revised version in Congress, it was subjected to scrutiny from House committees and the Senate. As in the past, the MILF insisted that the draft and amendments from the Bangsamoro Transition Committee (BTC), where it had representation, could not be changed. Yet, Congress claimed its constitutional right to do so. It ran the risk again of derailing the agreement by Congress exercising its independent power to draft a law that might contradict what had been agreed with the MILF.

Duterte's resolve remained despite an attempt by marginal Moro groups to escalate the violence and derail the process. The Abu Sayyaf had continued since 2001 to be seen mainly as a fringe group, operating more as a criminal

[91] Zachary Abuza, "Can Duterte Bring Peace to the Philippines?" *The Diplomat*, accessed July 5, 2020, https://thediplomat.com/2016/11/can-duterte-bring-peace-to-the-philippines/.
[92] Ibid.
[93] International Crisis Group, *Philippines Peace Process: Duterte Playing for High Stakes*. (Brussels: International Crisis Group, 2016).
[94] Leila B. Salaverria, "Duterte Meets with MILF Leaders on Supposed Opposition to BBL," *Inquirer News*, March 29, 2018.

gang than a nationalist, insurgent group such as the MNLF and MILF. It had created the closest links to international terrorist groups, such as Al-Qaeda, but the scale of its operations, while disruptive, remained relatively localized and contained. Furthermore, the MILF had clearly remained the main representative of the Moros, along with the MNLF, and developed a mostly distant and brief association with the group. In 2017, however, the Abu Sayyaf along with another marginal group, the Maute group, declared themselves affiliated with ISIS and mounted a five-month siege of Marawi city. They gained sudden worldwide attention and threatened to derail the peace process. The Philippine military's aerial bombings left vast destruction to dislodge the groups, but the latter failed to gain greater support. Their own destruction of many of the city's landmarks, as well as their poor treatment of citizens, created few allies. The siege left deep impressions over the Philippine population, with such a threat elevating risks to democracy and peace, and likely contributed to strengthening the president's resolve and parliamentary support to reach a peaceful settlement.[95]

In May 2018, both houses of Congress passed the new BBL law, which had a number of differences with the original draft that the BTC had submitted. Yet, the Senate and House committed to resolve differences in their respective versions of the bills and to remain consistent with the main points of the BTC draft.[96] In spite of objections from a number of lawmakers in the previous months regarding the powers that were to be conferred to the new Bangsamoro entity, Duterte and allies in Congress were determined to pass the law. For the first time, strong presidential support in Congress allowed for Duterte to reach his objectives in a short period of time.

The new Bangsamoro Law created a Bangsomoro entity to replace the existing ARMM. Its territorial demarcation was determined to be slightly larger than the existing ARMM, with provisions on having various municipalities and districts join the new regional unit. The historic claim to broader parts of Mindanao was now abandoned and replaced with a more realistic territorial demarcation to include Muslim majority communities, even though it would be somewhat disjointed. The entity gained new fiscal powers, by which it would obtain a block grant from Congress to manage according to its own priority and policies, a significant step up in autonomy.[97] While it recovered many of the aspects in the previous MoA-AD, it had primarily evolved to prevent constitutional challenges. Its basis remained the 2012 "Framework Agreement on the Bangsamoro," signed by the Aquino administration.

[95] Banlaoi, *The Marawi Siege and Its Aftermath.*
[96] "Senate, House Approve Proposed Bangsamoro Basic Law," *ABS-CBN News*, May 31, 2018.
[97] Panti Llanesca, "BBL 'Riddled with Unconstitutional Provisions'," *The Manila Times*, May 23, 2018.

The issue of the constitutionality of the new law remained contentious. In the past, the MILF only reluctantly accepted the principle of abiding by the constitution and favoured instead the negotiation of a settlement that would enshrine its principles of autonomy and self-determination, with relevant constitutional changes being implemented subsequently. Duterte took the political risk of insisting on the passage of the bills, and even using his power and influence to ensure their swift passing, in spite of members of the opposition's frequent objections on the basis of the bill's constitutionality. Duterte, who had promoted constitutional change in favour of federalism, sided with the view that the bills should be passed and the constitution amended afterward.[98]

From Vicious Cycle to a Breakthrough?

The apparent breakthrough in 2018 marked a watershed in the long-standing conflict between Moros and the Philippine state. Although not the deep autonomy and recognition as a "sub-state" that they might have sought, on paper the new BBL nevertheless provided recognition of a Bangsamoro identity, an expanded territory, and significant new powers and access to fiscal resources. While showing that it is not impossible to break away from a vicious cycle, the path to a negotiated settlement was certainly riddled with numerous obstacles.

Several institutional features of the Philippines' post-1986 democratic institutions made an agreement especially difficult to reach by comparison to Aceh. In particular, the US-style division of powers between the executive and legislature created strong incentives for the Christian-dominated majority in Congress to reject, dilute, or otherwise delay agreements that the president achieved with the MNLF and the MILF. It reflected a majority, mostly hostile to giving strong concessions to Moros. Combined with single-term presidential mandates, once legislation reached Congress, presidential support was often lost. A newly elected president often changed priorities or saw few political incentives to push strongly for their predecessors' achievements. Fidel Ramos strongly supported the 1996 agreement but it was finally signed at the end of his mandate. Congressional politics in part delayed the implementation of the agreement and, in the end, RA 9054 failed to fulfill the agreement's promises, and during its drafting lacked full support from the Estrada and Arroyo administrations. Without presidential support, it was almost impossible to enact legislation that reflected the agreement.[99] Benigno Aquino's 2012 agreement with the MILF also stalled as Congress did not pass accompanying legislation during his mandate. Agreements were often rushed as negotiators

---

[98] Ibid.; Camille Elemia and Mara Cepeda, "BBL Needs a Push from Duterte to Become Law before Sona," *Rappler*, May 19, 2018.

[99] These points were repeatedly raised in interviews, and most significantly so by Carmen Abubakar and Benedicto Bacani.

eyed the end of presidential mandates and hurried to deliver some results, even though they might subsequently fail.[100]

Constitutional provisions constrained the state and Moros' ability to reach satisfactory settlements. While the Philippine state under some administrations emphasized the need to negotiate within its parameters, others were more willing to relax, or ignore, constitutional provisions to reach a settlement first, and address legislative and constitutional issues next. The constitution, as a result, became a tool for opponents of agreements either to raise problems in Congress and dilute provisions of agreement reached in subsequent legislation or challenge these agreements in the Supreme Court. As Bacani noted, much of the negotiations often times focused on concepts such as "ownership" or "jurisdiction" to finesse constitutional constraints.[101] Nevertheless, constitutional arguments were used in drafting RA 9054 to justify significant changes from the 1996 peace agreement with the MNLF. So were they raised with the MoA-AD and particularly the concept of the BJE, which prompted opponents to challenge the agreement in the Supreme Court and led to the latter's surprise moratorium to prevent its signing. The same discourse surrounding constitutional provisions rose again at the time of signing the 2012 Framework on the Bangsamoro, and might have derailed it as well, were it not for President Duterte's willingness to strongly endorse a revised version, support it through Congress, and publicly call for charter change to allow the BBL to be passed. Presidential support early in the mandate, fuelled by an electoral coalition that could benefit from peace in Mindanao, as well as strong willingness to coordinate actions within Congress, provided an opportunity to break away from the shackles of the constitutional process. In the Philippines, it has been particularly difficult given the very strong legitimacy of the 1987 Constitution, which was drafted with broad popular consultation and across all sectors of society. While it created a strong credible commitment to democracy and adherence to autonomy for Muslim Mindanao in principle, it also created some constraints and ultimately a tool to limit the ability to craft agreements and institutions that responded to the Moros' demands. The credibility of commitment to concessions made to Moros, first the MNLF and then the MILF, was repeatedly undermined.

The Moros' high degree of mobilizational capacity certainly contributed to continued, low-level violence and maintained pressure on the democratic government to reach agreements, as it did in Aceh's case. Concessions were offered to defuse the violence, but more often than not failed to be sufficient to address the Moros' grievances and to be sufficiently credible. Without the MILF's persistence and mobilization after the 1996 agreement, the Moros might well have accepted the diluted RA 9054, with very few gains in terms

---

[100] Benedicto Bacani, interview; Rudy Rodil, interview.   [101] Benedicto Bacani, interview.

of their autonomy. The MILF used this capacity to maintain pressure. As the MILF's foreign affairs representative Ghazali Jafar noted, this was a conscious strategy:

The most effective pressure is our internal capacity. Capacity to fight. Capacity to sustain the war for long, long, long. And capacity to organize the people, so influence the people, meaning our ability to win the hearts and minds of the people. And I think that all these factors are in our hats, because, modesty aside, we are experienced, we have been fighting for I think almost 40 years, and due to the experience we have in fighting and in mobilizing the people, I can certainly say that there is no need for us to invite anybody from outside Mindanao to train us or to, you know, to train us, because we have the experience. As a matter of fact, modesty aside, I think based on our experience in guerilla warfare we can probably train other people on guerrilla fighting yes. And although international pressure is one of the factors but, you know, international pressure can be disregarded by the government, that pressure can be disregarded by the government, but internal factors can never be disregarded by the government, you know?[102]

The strategy worked. The MILF could raise a number of important negotiating points that reached beyond what had been obtained under the ARMM or the 1996 peace agreement. Even in 1996, the MNLF also came with much larger demands, mostly based on territorial demands that matched the thirteen provinces of the Tripoli agreement of 1976. Yet, those territorial demands based on the defunct, and never implemented agreement with the Marcos regime, proved self-defeating, as the territorial reach of the autonomous region could not credibly be expanded beyond a few contiguous areas outside of the four provinces and municipalities of the ARMM. With Muslims having majorities in only few provinces, any plebiscite was sure to reject a greater territorial expansion. The MNLF asked and negotiated successfully a strong autonomy settlement with the Philippine state, but could not fight its subsequent delay in implementation, dilution, and eventual failure to implement meaningful autonomy. When the MILF began negotiating, they therefore raised the bar by rejecting the concept of autonomy enshrined in the constitution and used instead concepts that would enhance Moros' status as a nation, as well the principles of governance that would maximize their self-determination. In the end, they were willing to compromise on territory, relaxed some of their insistence of a juridical entity with equal status to the Philippine state, and agreed to significantly stronger jurisdictional and fiscal powers that were included in the BBL.

---

[102] Gazhali Jafar, MILF Vice-Chair for Political Affairs, interview by author, May 3, 2008, (near) Cotabato city.

6 "Exit and Reframe"

From Cordillera "Nation" to "Indigenous Peoples"

The peoples of the Cordillera developed new forms of mobilization after the end of the Marcos regime. Having previously fought alongside the communist New People's Army (NPA) against authoritarian rule, Cordilleran leaders developed a new sense of Cordilleran "nation," based on shared experience of the various peoples of the region. This new nationalist movement, represented primarily by the Cordillera People's Liberation Army (CPLA) and the Cordillera Peoples' Alliance (CPA) began to make demands for "autonomy."

The movement prompted the state to respond with significant promises. Motivated to show democratic credentials and to consolidate its broad coalition of support for the People Power revolution, the Aquino government agreed to a constitutional clause that enshrined autonomy for the Cordillera, as it also did for Muslim Mindanao. At first therefore the 1987 Constitution heightened the credibility of the state's commitment by enshrining the principle of autonomy, but it became difficult to sustain its credibility with subsequent legislation. Against the democratic institutional environment that supported the principle, the majority remained suspicious of movements deemed "secessionist."

As a result, Cordillerans strongly rejected subsequent legislation on suspicions that the promised autonomy sought to weaken and undermine them. The Philippine state reached a ceasefire and transitional political arrangement with the CPLA, while continuing to reject demands from the CPA. Congress drafted autonomy legislation that was submitted to Cordillerans in a referendum, without reaching any political arrangement with the CPA. This only heightened Cordillerans' suspicion that, as in the Moros' case with the creation of the ARMM, parliament sought to pass an autonomy law that was designed more to stem the violence and coopt the Cordilleran elite without addressing some of the more fundamental grievances and demands for more meaningful and substantive autonomy.

Nevertheless, the concessions made to the CPLA/CBAd (Cordillera Bodong Administration)[1] rapidly defused violence and opened up alternative channels

---

[1] There is confusion between the Cordillera Bodong Association, which was an initiative to regionalize the bilateral system of peace pacts ("bodong") between tribes, in the aftermath of

to seek conflict resolution. While the conflict could have remained deep with low-level violence, as was the case with the ARMM and the MNLF's demobilization in Mindanao, some Cordilleran leaders explored instead an "exit and reframe" strategy. In particular, given the relatively weak ability of Cordillerans to remain united and their limited mobilization capacity relative to the Moros, they chose to develop this new approach. Had they been able to garner stronger capacity to continue an insurgency, they might have followed the path of the MILF. But instead they tapped into an emerging international movement advocating for rights to self-determination for indigenous peoples and found little resistance from the Philippine state to their heightened activities abroad. By joining the movement and contributing to its leadership, Cordilleran leaders refocused mobilization of their peoples in a plea for recognition as indigenous peoples, with similar yet less threatening demands for protection of their territory, way of life, and greater autonomy in their governance.

With democratic stabilization, the strategy succeeded. Cordillerans removed the threat that *nationalist* mobilization otherwise creates for states, including democratic ones. The shift to indigenous peoples opened up a political option that the Philippine state could support and parliament considered non-threatening. International pressure on the democratic state was a contributing factor, but the reduced stakes allowed the Philippine government under Fidel Ramos to capitalize on reaching peace with Cordillerans and channel to parliament a bill that resolved the conflict without seeming to cater to nationalist demands. It also helped that the Indigenous Peoples Rights Act (IPRA), adopted in 1997, granted several rights to Cordillerans and other peoples considered indigenous. Most importantly, they recognized ancestral domains, rights to maintain their culture and modes of governance, as well as consultation on the exploitation of natural resources.

Cordillerans' path contrasts with that of Papuans, who have remained in a stalled conflict with low-level violence. Both regions have had difficulties uniting disparate groups under a single identity. Papuans did achieve a greater nationalist Papuan identity as compared to Cordillerans but the Indonesian state could exploit their tendency for division. In both cases, the state's credibility to commit was weak. Although Cordillerans began with stronger constitutional commitment than Indonesia's vague constitutional enshrinement of autonomy indirectly referring to Papuans, subsequent legislation was unconvincing in both cases. On paper, special autonomy in Papua was stronger than the

the Chico Dam mobilization, and the Cordillera Bodong Administration (CBAd), which was a creation of Father Conrado Balweg, head of the Cordillera People's Liberation Army (CPLA), who attempted to capitalize on the bodong system to justify his own movement for regionalization and autonomy of the Cordillera. Balweg created the CBAd as a breakaway faction from the Cordillera Bodong Association.

legislation proposed for autonomy in the Cordillera, and a less independent parliament could swiftly implement it in Papua without requirement of a referendum, as in the case of the Cordillera. Against weak mobilizational capacity in both cases, the Cordilleran exit strategy and reframing as indigenous peoples certainly allowed for stronger legislative gains. Papuans considered such a course and attended some of the meetings of the world indigenous peoples' movement, but would likely have faced stronger resistance from an Indonesian state with many more diverse cultural groups that could make indigenous claims. Nevertheless, the path was successful for Cordillerans, whereas Papuans continued to present a threat as "secessionist," with a state intent on minimizing concessions.

Reframing Cordilleran mobilization as indigenous peoples had several advantages. First, it overcame difficulties of uniting disparate groups under the Cordilleran label. Second, the remoteness of the Cordillera and different way of life from other Filipinos resonated with the discourse of "indigeneity." Third, and most importantly, it was a less threatening strategy than mobilizing as a "nation" seeking autonomy and self-determination. Finally, by reframing, they hoped to tap into greater international support and create more pressure on the Philippine state.

While such gains were made, however, their implementation was limited. IPRA was one of the most progressive pieces of legislation in the world and became a model for other indigenous peoples. But the gains made in the Cordillera remained limited. Once concessions were made and Cordillerans reduced their mobilization, political pressure to implement promises was reduced and actual gains fell far short than what the legislation offered.

The Emergence of the Cordilleran Movement

Departing from other cases, the "Cordillera" movement was based on a loose amalgamation of groups that did not reflect a single political identity. At least seven distinct groups inhabit the Cordillera mountain range of Northern Luzon. They have shared similar experiences due to their relative geographic isolation, similar livelihoods, and limited contact with the colonial and post-colonial states. Yet, pan-Cordilleran mobilization occurred only after the Philippine state penetrated the region more forcefully to exploit natural resources. It grew mostly as a result of the Marcos regime's incursions. Resistance was first allied to the NPA and would only become more clearly "Cordillera-based" at the eve of the regime's downfall and the People Power revolution.

The Cordilleran peoples became more clearly demarcated during Spanish colonial rule. Historically, they shared many characteristics with the lowlanders of Luzon but became increasingly distinct as missionization was less intense, and they remained relatively isolated and autonomous from colonial administrators. Although some mixing likely occurred as a result of lowlanders fleeing into the mountains to avoid colonial domination, for the most part peoples of the Cordillera retained distinct customs, livelihoods, and access to communal lands.[2] To the Spanish, they were the "Igorots," an identity cast upon them by colonial rulers and with connotations of non-Christian and even "savage." Although sometimes used as an identifier, the term "Igorot" did not capture a clearly formed ethnic identity, and most Cordillerans preferred to be named by their distinctive group identity rather than by this broader term.[3]

When Americans created the Mountain Province in 1908, they contributed to strengthening a shared territorial identity among the dispersed Cordilleran groups. Under successive administrations, local governors built roads and established trading posts and local schools. With more access to the region, various Churches also established schools so that by the 1920s, local leaders began to emerge. One notable figure was Dr Jose M. Cariño, from Baguio city, who became one of the first Cordillerans to study in the United States.[4] The Cariño family became influential and regularly defended the interests of Cordilleran peoples in various administrative forums. In his presentation before the Wood-Forbes Mission in 1921, for example, Dr Cariño denounced the integration of portions of Benguet to La Union province on the basis of the negative effects on lowlander "Igorot." Cariño used the colonial appellation "Igorots" to distinguish the peoples of the Cordillera from lowlanders.[5] Although it would be an exaggeration to make the case that a pan-Cordilleran identity had crystallized at this time period, administrative boundaries, American colonial policies, and interventions from the emerging educated local leadership certainly laid the foundations for a common awareness of shared values and experiences.

The exploitation of natural resources also laid the basis for common resistance to colonial rule, and later the Philippine state. During the decade of the mid-1920s to mid-1930s, the discovery of gold first raised mining issues at the forefront of Cordilleran peoples' resistance. Investors opened new mining operations in several areas, particularly in Benguet and Bontoc. Since local residents had received few titles to land, miners were permitted to explore and open up lands with few restrictions. Governor Dosser argued in favour of considering negative effects on local agricultural practices and water supplies but recognized few legal means by which local residents could challenge

---

[2] June Prill-Brett, "Indigenous Land Rights and Legal Pluralism among Philippine Highlanders," *Law and Society Review* 28, no. 3 (1994): 689.

[3] For an excellent study of the origins of the Igorot identity and its evolution, see Finin, *The Making of the Igorot*. See also Scott, *The Discovery of the Igorots*.

[4] Howard Tyrrell Fry, *A History of the Mountain Province* (Quezon City, Philippines, 1983), 130–31.

[5] Ibid., 115.

mining interests, as they held no legal claims to the land. Nevertheless, several communities did resist and, in Bontoc, even took up arms against prospective miners. This resistance, combined with the Depression and accompanying slump in the price of gold, led a retreat from mining the area but the issue would resurface several years later and constitute the basis of common resistance.[6]

Between 1946 and 1966, Cordillerans remained fairly isolated from state-building efforts of the newly independent Philippine state. The government created separate administrative bodies, along the same lines as the American-created Bureau of Non-Christian Tribes, which administered not only the Cordillera but also the Muslims of the southern Philippines. The Commission on National Integration created in 1957 developed policies to integrate Cordillerans to the broader polity, although in effect its role was very limited.[7]

In 1966, the state implemented two contradictory policies. First, it created a Mountain Province Development Authority in order to stimulate greater investment in the Cordillera. Not only did the administration realize the tremendous untapped mining potential, but it also saw great possibilities for tourism. Yet, at the same time, a case was made to split Mountain Province into several distinct provinces in order to facilitate the administration of this rugged, mountainous region where travelling between different areas was highly con-strained. As a result, a single agency oversaw development for the whole region while it was now being administered as several provinces. Again, although these institutions were created, they led to little more than to reaffirm a long-standing policy of treating Cordillerans as separate from the majority Filipinos. The region remained only marginally penetrated by the state or business interests.[8]

Two parallel factors changed this situation and led to pan-Cordilleran resist-ance. First, a communist guerilla movement expanded its operations into the Cordillera, as its rugged terrain offered an ideal location for some of its operations. Second, the administration of President Marcos showed greater resolve than previous administrations to penetrate the Cordillera and exploit its untapped natural resources.

The Philippines communist movement has deep roots. Inspired by Maoist ideology and the successes of the Chinese Communist Party, an armed resistance movement was first formed to counter the Japanese occupational force. The *Partido Komunista ng Pilipinas* was launched in 1930 and contributed to the organization of the Huk rebellion in 1942 against the Japanese. After the Second

---

[6] Ibid., 177–87.
[7] Charles MacDonald, "Indigenous Peoples of the Philippines: Between Segregation and Integration," in *Indigenous Peoples of Asia*, eds. R. H. Barnes, Andrew Gray, and Benedict Kingsbury (Ann Arbor, MI: Association for Asian Studies, 1995), 345–49.
[8] Ibid.

World War, it formed the first communist insurgency against the Philippine government but was defeated in 1954. Shortly thereafter, in the early 1960s, the Communist movement reorganized with the rise of Commander Dante and the young Jose Maria Sison. In 1969, they created the NPA. For the first few years, the NPA remained fairly weak but it was given a boost with President Marcos' declaration of martial law in 1972. Ironically, Marcos used the presence of NPA resistance as justification for declaring martial law, but the movement was actually weak at that time.[9] As Wurfel mentions: "martial law in 1972 rescued the NPA from oblivion."[10] The martial law's repressive approach sent to the countryside hundreds of young graduates as the NPA's cadres. With stronger military attacks, the NPA dispersed and spread its influence. With greater government corruption and displacement of peasants from their land, the NPA benefitted from the growing disgruntlement.[11]

The expansion of the NPA's activities coalesced with the predatory nature of the Marcos administration to form the Cordillera resistance movement. Prior to 1972, the NPA had no presence in the area. In the early 1970s, the Marcos government began to seize land in the Cordillera for development projects. The Chico dam project was the most controversial one in this respect. Funded by the World Bank and Asian Development Bank, it led to the displacement of 100,000 people. Cordillerans, especially Kalinga, joined the NPA and mounted a successful resistance to the Marcos government.[12]

The Chico dam incident became the symbolic beginning of the Cordilleran resistance movement. The alliance with the NPA was short-lived, as ideological differences separated the Communists attempting to forge linkages across the Philippines and Cordillerans who sought to defend their environment, lands, and livelihood. The resistance was successful, as it led to the postponing of the projected dam and its eventual cancellation after Marcos' downfall. By the end of the authoritarian regime, repression had failed to crush the insurgency and, instead, had provided a catalyst for the creation of a "Cordilleran" identity and aspirations for autonomy.

Mobilizing the Cordilleran "Nation" and Early State Concessions

When the Marcos regime fell in 1986, the transition to democracy was sudden. Cory Aquino became president and immediately sought to defuse past violence

---

[9] Wurfel, *Filipino Politics*, 225–27.   [10] Ibid., 226.

[11] Gregg R. Jones, *Red Revolution: Inside the Philippine Guerrilla Movement* (Boulder, CO: Westview Press, 1989), 18.

[12] Prill-Brett, "Indigenous Land Rights and Legal Pluralism among Philippine Highlanders," 693–94; David Hyndman, "Organic Act Rejected in the Cordillera: Dialectics of a Continuing Fourth World Autonomy Movement in the Philippines," *Dialectical Anthropology* 16, no. 2 (1991): 173.

and consolidate her People Power coalition by extending concessions to the most visibly armed and still violent group, the CPLA. In parallel, other Cordilleran groups organized to lobby the constitutional convention and advocated for autonomy. There was no single Cordilleran movement and therefore the strategies varied. The overall impact in the initial stages of democratization was dramatic reduction in violent mobilization, as the state signed a peace pact with the CPLA and the Constituent Assembly enshrined autonomy for the Cordillera.

The battle against Marcos and the sudden opening of the political space in the last few months of the military regime created new options for mobilization. In the aftermath of the Chico dam victory, several groups had begun to nurture a common consciousness as "Cordilleran," with a nationalist political objective of self-determination. The movement was an elite, educated-class-driven attempt to build a common identity and unity among disparate groups.[13] Local residents close to the dam had developed a common purpose but, afterward, the movement's goal was to use momentum to gain adherence from across the Cordillera.[14] They partly appropriated the term "Igorots," which was a colonial label to identify groups in the Cordillera. But given negative connotations associated with the term, "Cordilleran" or "Kaigorotan" became more commonly used.[15]

Violent armed mobilization had begun to split from the previous alliance with the communist NPA. Father Conrado Balweg[16] created the CPLA in April 1986, only two months after the formation of the Aquino government, and articulated most vocally the armed struggle in terms of the Cordillera being historically separate from the Philippines, and never integrated, therefore seeking freedom from "internal colonialism."[17] Balweg and his supporters also seized the opportunity to reach out to Cordillerans who had opposed the left and sought a new alliance by building on the "bodong" peace pacts that had

---

[13] Raymundo D. Rovillos, Professor, University of the Philippines, interview by author, August 23, 2007, Baguio, Baguio City.

[14] June Prill-Brett, Professor, University of the Philippines, interview by author, August 27, 2007, Baguio, Baguio City.

[15] The Cordillera Peoples' Alliance began to use Kaigorotan, starting with its second congress in 1985. See Athena Lydia Casambre, "The Frustrated Discourse on Regional Autonomy in the Cordillera and Notes toward a Productive Discourse," in *6th International Philippines Studies Conference* (Diliman, Quzon City, 2000).

[16] Balweg was one of the most charismatic and vocal leaders within the NPA in the Cordillera. Others had also sought to organize along indigenous lines, with an earlier attempt to form an Ifugao Liberation Army, for example, but Balweg and his group gained ascendency and were able to seize the opportunity in the immediate aftermath of Marcos' downfall (Raymundo D. Rovillos, interview).

[17] Nela Florendo, "The Movement for Regional Autonomy in the Cordillera from a Historical Perspective," in *Advancing Regional Autonomy in the Cordillera: A Source Book*, ed. Arturo C. Boquiren (Baguio City; Pasig, Metro Manila: Cordillera Studies Center University of the Philippines College Baguio; Friedrich Ebert Stiftung Manila Office, 1994).

expanded in the wake of the Chico dam anti-Marcos movement. The Cordillera Bodong Association (CBA) was an attempt to regionalize what was essentially a local indigenous form of bilateral peace pacts between warring groups.[18]

Other intellectuals and leaders associated with the left sought to create a more political alliance, with similar objectives of unifying Cordillerans around a shared identity and make broader claims to self-determination. They called a regional conference in 1984 to discuss a regional alliance and to confront the regime with local grievances arising from the continued ignorance of land claims and other negative effects of state-supported development projects. The conference ended with the formation of the CPA.[19]

The CPA took a two-pronged approach that used various international and local political instruments to address the long-standing concerns of Cordillerans. It articulated an agenda based on rights to ancestral domain, access to natural resources, economic prosperity, cultural integrity, and regional autonomy.[20] Some of its leaders had begun to frequent the United Nations Working Group on Indigenous Populations (UN WGIP), and had adopted some of the themes around questions of ancestral domain and cultural preservation in particular. But the political focus was primarily on regional autonomy. During the late Marcos years, they focused on articulating a rationale for bringing all of the Cordillera under one region, with more autonomous powers, whereas it had been separated until then, and included into two neighbouring provinces. Well before the People Power revolution, the CPA already demanded regionalization and allied with a group of congressmen, despite their weak and ineffectual status under authoritarian rule.[21]

Marcos' downfall and the creation of a constitutional commission provided the opportunity for the CPA to lobby and push for regional autonomy. The CPA had early meetings with President Aquino where they pressed for regional autonomy and raised concerns regarding the management of natural resources. In spite of reassurances that one of their members would be appointed to the commission, the CPA failed to obtain one as Aquino was concerned about the CPA's left-leaning tendencies. Instead, she appointed Ponce Bonnagen, an academic who took the mantle of the CPA's demands to the Commission. The CPA mobilized and organized an effective lobby in Manila to press both for recognition of indigenous peoples' rights as well as regional autonomy. They found allies with Moros from Mindanao in advocating for the principle of regional autonomy.[22]

---

[18] Raymundo D. Rovillos, interview.

[19] Joan Carling, Former Chairperson, Cordillera Peoples' Alliance, interview by author, August 30, 2007, Baguio City.

[20] Athena Lydia Casambre, "Interpretation of the Debate on Cordillera Autonomy" (1987), 23.

[21] Joan Carling, interview.

[22] Ibid.; Victoria Tauli-Corpuz, Chair, Tebtebba Foundation and Chair, UN Permanent Forum on Indigenous Peoples, interview by author, August 24, 2007, Baguio city; Casambre, "Interpretation of the Debate on Cordillera Autonomy," 11–15.

The Aquino government chose to appease the CPLA, as it still faced violent mobilization from the NPA, as well as the Moros in Mindanao. Informal meetings with Butz Aquino, sent to represent Cory Aquino, resulted in an agreement for representation of Cordilleran interests in the Constitutional Commission, a dialogue between natives of the region, withdrawal of government troops from the Cordillera and the implementation of social projects to spur development. The discussions culminated in a *sipat* (ceasefire) agreement in 1986.[23]

The strategic decision to side with the CPLA and give less support to the CPA had important ramifications. The Aquino government maintained its suspicion of the CPA's left-leaning tendencies, and therefore sought to prop up the CPLA and provide it with a platform to speak in the name of the whole region.[24] Yet, its attempt to prevent the CPA from gaining stronger legitimacy through intervention in the Constitutional Commission failed, and even backfired. The CPA pushed and still obtained significant concessions for regional autonomy within the constitution. But afterward it shifted its strategy as it considered the planned implementation to fall short on genuine self-determination.

After signing a ceasefire agreement with the CPLA, the Aquino government issued Executive Order (EO) 220, which created a temporary Cordillera Administrative Region (CAR), much in the same way that it proceeded with the creation of the ARMM in Mindanao. While the CPA objected to the CAR's creation, the government allowed the CPLA/CBAd to seize control of the new institutions. The CPLA transformed itself into a regional security force, and members of the CPLA/CBAd filled important positions in the newly created administrative region. They also enjoyed the support of the National Economic Development Authority, the regional planning agency whose bureaucrats had already sought a consolidation of planning under the Cordillera region.[25]

With regional autonomy enshrined in the constitution, the government began to prepare an Organic Act. The process involved the creation of a Cordillera Regional Consultative Commission (CRCC), whose members the president appointed. The president mandated the CRCC with the task of drafting the Organic Act, which was then submitted to Congress, and was to be subjected to a referendum, as constitutionally mandated. Again, the president sought to limit the CPA's access, and instead appointed members close to the existing CAR, as well as current Cordillera congressmen. The CRCC produced a draft Organic Act in December 1988, despite criticism that it had not consulted sufficiently broadly and consistently sidelined groups seeking a deeper form of

---

[23] Casambre, "Interpretation of the Debate on Cordillera Autonomy," 25–27.
[24] Raymundo D. Rovillos, interview.
[25] Casambre, "Interpretation of the Debate on Cordillera Autonomy."

regional autonomy. The draft Organic Act was further watered down in Congress, by removing wording on ancestral lands and on self-determination that could provide Cordillerans with tools to prevent business interests from expanding in the region or limiting the reach of the central government's power. It also subjected the Act to "existing national laws and policies."[26] These dilutions satisfied a Congress little inclined to provide autonomy that could lead to the acknowledgement of self-determination and remain mostly within the Philippine frame of regional decentralization rather than deeper autonomy.

Once passed in Congress, Republican Act (RA) 6766 (the Organic Act for the Cordillera Autonomous Region) became law but required ratification by referendum. The CPA directed its efforts against RA 6766. In its view, the Organic Act had been stripped down of significant powers to address issues of ancestral lands, self-determination, exploitation of natural resources, and denounced loopholes that essentially preserved central government power over significant issue-areas. Even the CPLA/CBAd, whose interests had diverged from the CPA's, found common ground against RA 6766. They had demanded that the CPLA be transformed into a regional security force and that the CBAd be retained as a commission in the future government, neither of which were included in the new law. Even some CPCC members complained of their original Act having been "manipulated" and significantly altered.

But the first autonomy debacle was because of the fact that it went to the constitutional regional consultative commission. And then there was a move by the progressives that came out of some reform people in government took cracks and responded to the needs of the time. When it got to Congress it got totally watered down. So, the "No" was a support for the original and not for the watered-down version. That's what the first "No" was all about.[27]

As a result, of the 60 per cent of voters who cast votes 73.5 per cent rejected the Organic Act in the January 1990 referendum.[28]

The democratic environment produced a broad set of interests that found little common ground around regional autonomy. There was no clear common understanding among Cordillerans on the objectives of regional autonomy, and

[26] Joan Carling, "The Cordillera Peoples' Continuing Struggle for Self-Determination," in *International Conference on Indigenous Peoples' Self-determination and the Nation State in Asia* (Baguio, Philippines, 1999).

[27] Zenaida Bridget Hamada-Pawid, activist in Cordillera peace forums, she was later Chairperson and Commissioner of Region I and the Cordilleras and National Commission on Indigenous Peoples Chairman from 2011 to 2013, interview by author, August 27, 2007, Baguio City.

[28] Carling, "The Cordillera Peoples' Continuing Struggle for Self-Determination."; Arturo C. Boquiren, *Advancing Regional Autonomy in the Cordillera: A Source Book* (Baguio City; Pasig, Metro Manila: Cordillera Studies Center University of the Philippines College Baguio; Friedrich Ebert Stiftung Manila Office, 1994); Steven Rood, *Protecting Ancestral Land Rights in the Cordillera* (Diliman, Quezon City: University of the Philippines Press, 1994).

therefore mobilization in favour of an autonomy bill was weak. As a leader of the CPA noted:

[W]hen the constitution was brought to a plebiscite, they had a hard time deciding what position to take. Because, while we had fought for the provisions on ancestral land and autonomy, unfortunately we learned the lesson quite early that beautiful laws do not necessarily mean that you are going to get what you hope for. Because very clearly we had already seen that new structures had been set up to our exclusion. Therefore, we had a difficult time deciding ... There was a big debate, some of us were saying "but we were the ones that fought for it, we should still continue," while others were already saying that "you passed that, we are not going to be part of that; it's just going to be an additional bureaucracy that's going to be controlled by the traditional politicians, the Cordillera People's Liberation Army, etc." And then many people were saying "why don't you people in the Cordillera get your act together and campaign for these provisions so that you will get regional autonomy?" So, the position in the plebiscite ... We were not really very united.[29]

The Aquino government and Congress sought to dilute initial commitments in the Constitution to preserve central government power and prevent, in particular, the instauration of regional autonomy that might implement a much more left-wing agenda on control over land and natural resources. As Vicky Tauli-Corpuz, who would become an internationally recognized Cordilleran leader explained:

But if you expect a Congress, which was a very conservative Congress to begin with, mostly composed of landlords ... I mean it's something that they wouldn't really like. Their political power would be undermined by something called an autonomous region. So, when they were formulating the Organic Act, there was a lot of discontent with what was there. And then, of course, in the Cordillera, especially in the international demo-cratic movement, which is basically a liberation movement to topple the state, having such kind of Organic Act, which basically doesn't change radically the structures and still puts the region within a national development framework which is very pro foreign interests, they don't like.[30]

The Aquino administration found allies within the regional government and congressional representatives, mostly concerned with preserving their existing privileges and interests. The opposition divided along a left-right spectrum. Some groups, associated with a moderate centre, viewed the CPA and associ-ated organizations as too left-leaning and were concerned that their version of regional autonomy would increase the regional power of the left. The CPLA/CBAd sought to preserve its dominant status and acquired privileges through the CAR and secure even greater concessions. Local bureaucrats and officials for their part wanted more power, while preserving existing institutional

---

[29] Joan Carling, interview.   [30] Victoria Tauli-Corpuz, interview.

structures. As a result, there was little momentum to adopt the proposed autonomy, and the Organic Act failed.

One of the Aquino government's last major initiatives was the introduction of the Local Government Code (1991), which implemented significant devolution to the municipalities and local government levels. Local and regional governments had demanded more resources and powers in the aftermath of Marcos' authoritarian regime. The local government code provided for more devolution of revenue from the national government to local government units (LGUs), according to a formula that took into account population and natural resource extraction. It also vastly expanded local taxing powers, the ability to manage local services, such as housing projects, health facilities, agricultural extension programs, and telecommunications.[31]

These powers however were devolved from the national government, rather than defined as autonomous jurisdictions. They fell short of what various constituencies, including the CPA, CPLA/CBAd, and even government officials of the CAR or local development councils sought in terms of regional powers. It nevertheless contributed to a model of decentralized governance that the central government strongly favoured.[32]

Democratic Stabilization: Mobilizing Cordillerans as "Indigenous"

The period of democratic stabilization, which began with the presidency of Fidel Ramos, showed persistent state reluctance to accommodate nationalist claims for self-determination, but allowed Cordillerans to make significant gains as "indigenous peoples." The shift allowed Cordillerans to cast their case alongside a large number of smaller groups across the archipelago to secure legislation that met many of their grievances, while avoiding the autonomy route that the state deemed more threatening. IPRA became a landmark piece of legislation.

Yet, IPRA's implementation showed that the state could still erode the law's effectiveness, through poor implementation and strategies to undermine its commitments. The law provides a benchmark and tool that Cordillerans could use to keep the state accountable, which is more than was ever achieved through seeking autonomy, but its impact has been strongly limited.

The constitution of 1987 enshrined rights for indigenous peoples[33] for the Cordillera. Key to the success of enshrining rights for indigenous peoples had

---

[31] Rocky Molintas, "Advancing Cordillera Autonomy Beyond the Local Government Code," in *Advancing Regional Autonomy in the Cordillera: A Source Book*, ed. Arturo C. Boquiren (Baguio City; Pasig, Metro Manila: Cordillera Studies Center University of the Philippines College Baguio; Friedrich Ebert Stiftung Manila Office, 1994).
[32] Ibid.   [33] See section 22, art. 11; section 5, art. 12; section 6, art. 13.

been the CPA's ability to lobby the Constitutional Commission in alliance with other NGOs. Since much of the subsequent mobilization focused on the autonomy bill, little was done to follow up on this constitutional clause during the last few years of the Aquino presidency.

The defeat of the autonomy bill allowed the CPA to more strongly emphasize mobilization as "indigenous peoples." In the early 1980s, the newly created UN Working Group on Indigenous Populations (WGIP), under the United Nations High Commissioner for Human Rights, became a unique platform for groups to gain international profile. With a principle of broad inclusion, the WGIP and the indigenous peoples' movement grew considerably in the following decade, reaching even 800 groups represented in the 2001 WGIP meetings.[34] Cordilleran representatives for the first time made an appearance before the UN WGIP in 1984, with a statement focusing on ancestral domain, natural resource management, socio-political institutions, and preservation of their cultural identity.[35]

They participated in the WGIP's main activity of drafting the UN Declaration on the Rights of Indigenous Peoples. Most of the draft was essentially written between 1985 and 1993 but encountered subsequently strong resistance from many states. Its central achievement included Article 3, which spelled out a right to self-determination. It was also its main stumbling block as states continued to fear that recognizing self-determination could amount to allowing secessionism.[36] Continued lobbying and campaigns to advance indigenous peoples' rights eventually led to a breakthrough in 2006. The General Assembly adopted the UN Declaration on the Rights of Indigenous Peoples in September 2007.

The victory of Fidel Ramos in the 1992 presidential elections created a strong opportunity for the CPA and its allies in the indigenous peoples' movement to secure legislative gains. Ramos was concerned about gaining sufficient support to govern, as he won with only 20 per cent of the popular vote, in a crowded field of presidential candidates. Furthermore, against the backdrop of political instability and coup attempts during the Aquino

---

[34] Rhiannon Morgan, "On Political Institutions and Social Movement Dynamics: The Case of the United Nations and the Global Indigenous Movement," *International Political Science Review* 28, no. 3 (2007): 276–82; Ronald Niezen, *The Origins of Indigenism: Human Rights and the Politics of Identity* (Berkeley and Los Angeles: University of California Press, 2003), 45–46.

[35] "Review of Recent Developments in the Cordillera Provinces: Northern Luzon; Statement to the UN Working Group on Indigenous Populations," *Center for World Indigenous Studies*, www.hartford-hwp.com/archives/54a/224.html.

[36] Rhiannon Morgan, "Advancing Indigenous Rights at the United Nations: Strategic Framing and Its Impact on the Normative Development of International Law," *Social & Legal Studies* 13, no. 4 (2004); Erica-Irene Daes, "Protection of the World's Indigenous Peoples and Human Rights," in *Human Rights: Concept and Standard*, ed. Janusz Symonides (Ashgate: UNESCO Publishing, 2000); Hyndman, "Organic Act Rejected in the Cordillera."

presidency, Ramos sought to create a strong coalition, rooted in civil society, to strengthen the democratic regime and foster economic development.[37]

Key to his political strategy was his Social Reform Agenda (SRA). While it was broad-based, a core component was the resolution of existing conflicts, partly through the extension of programs and policies to address poverty, inequality, and development needs. As Lusterio-Rico notes, "[the] most critical [factor] in the enactment of IPRA was the strong support provided by the Ramos administration through its Social Reform Agenda (SRA)."[38] Presidential support through the SRA added pressure on legislators to adopt IPRA, which became a "certified administration bill," and therefore obtained strong backing from the president's legislative allies in Congress, and could pass despite numerous objections raised during the debates.[39] In addition to building a broad political coalition through the SRA, President Ramos sought to capitalize on the sufficiently large numbers of votes that indigenous peoples represented: "He was pushing ... a plan for indigenous peoples. Because he knew that indigenous peoples ... were a big voting bloc. So, with the social reform agenda we had a chance to push legislation, so that was one factor that obviously facilitated IPRA."[40]

With such political backing, lobby groups that had long advocated for indigenous peoples' rights could cobble together a legislative strategy that finally obtained majority support in both the Senate and House. Panlipi, a legal-support development NGO, as well as a number of other similar organizations, including the faith-based Catholic Church Indigenous Peoples' Apostolates and the National Peace Conference[41] found support from Senator Juan Flavier, who became a strong and engaged sponsor of the bill that eventually became law.[42] Flavier had been a very well-respected member of Ramos' first cabinet and a supporter of his SRA. He obtained the administration's support to run for the Senate in 1995. As the Chair of the Senate Committee on Cultural Communities, he was in a good position to sponsor a bill.[43]

In the absence of strong presidential support, previous attempts to pass a bill of indigenous peoples' rights had all failed. Gains that were made in the

---

[37] Ruth Lusterio-Rico, Professor, University of the Philippines, Diliman, interview by author, August 20, 2007, Manila.

[38] Ruth Lusterio-Rico, "The Dynamics of Policy-Making: The Enactment of the Indigenous Peoples' Rights Act (IPRA)" (PhD diss., University of the Philippines, 2006), 157.

[39] Ibid., 159–60.

[40] Attny Maria Vicenta De Guzman, Executive Director, PANLIPI, interview by author, August 20, 2007, Manila.

[41] The NPC supported dialogue between the government and armed groups, including those such as the CPLA or the NPA which had been involved in the Cordillera.

[42] Rico, "The Dynamics of Policy-Making: The Enactment of the Indigenous Peoples' Rights Act (IPRA)," 131.

[43] Several parts of Lusterio-Rico's dissertation address these various aspects of the legislative process.

Constitution had yet to be expressed in any legislation. With claims mainly over recognition of communities' ancestral lands, the Department of Environment and Natural Resources (DENR) obtained the authority in 1990 to undertake the delineation and legal recognition of ancestral lands, through regulation, and bypassed the CAR's authority.[44] In 1993, the DENR issued Administrative Order Number 2 (DAO 2), which provided the regulatory framework that defined ancestral domain and ancestral lands and specified how they would be delineated and recognized. While a step in the direction of providing legal guarantees and documentation for land rights, other aspects of indigenous rights lacked legislative support.[45]

DAO 2 differentiated between ancestral land and ancestral domain. Ancestral land included residential lots, agricultural lands, and forests that may be claimed by individuals, families, or clans. Ancestral domain covered ancestral lands and natural resources therein, including nearby areas utilized by the indigenous peoples, and may be claimed by the entire community or tribe. DAO 2 was still based on the 1987 Constitution, which explicitly recognized the state's ownership and sole power to dispense land rights.[46]

Subsequent attempts to pass legislation to more strongly define and enshrine rights to ancestral domain and other forms of protection for indigenous peoples all failed to garner sufficient support in Congress. Between 1987 and 1995, six bills were filed in the House, with several being sponsored primarily by one of the Cordillera representatives, William Claver, who was former CPA chair and a main spokesperson for indigenous peoples in Congress. Despite presenting various versions, however, all his bills failed. So did four others that were presented in the Senate.[47] It was clear, therefore, that Ramos' strong push and his interests in building a political coalition were key.

IPRA[48] became one of the most progressive laws for indigenous peoples. The law adopts the principle of self-identification of indigenous peoples, as was later enshrined in the UN Declaration on the Rights of Indigenous peoples. It

---

[44] Prill-Brett, "Indigenous Land Rights and Legal Pluralism among Philippine Highlanders," 687–97, 707–20.

[45] Rico, "The Dynamics of Policy-Making: The Enactment of the Indigenous Peoples' Rights Act (IPRA)," 97–98.

[46] Rocky Molintas, "The Philippine Indigenous Peoples' Struggle for Land and Life: Challenging Legal Texts," *Arizona Journal of International and Comparative Law* 21, no. 1 (2004): 288.

[47] Rico, "The Dynamics of Policy-Making: The Enactment of the Indigenous Peoples' Rights Act (IPRA)," 100–01.

[48] Republic of the Philippines, Republic Act no. 8371 (The Indigenous Peoples' Rights Act of 1997), 1997. For interesting comments and comparison to ILO 169 and the UN Declaration on the Rights of Indigenous Peoples, see Sedfrey Candelaria, "Comparative Analysis on the ILO Indigenous and Tribal Peoples Convention No. 169, UN Declaration on the Rights of Indigenous Peoples (UNDRIP) and the Indigenous Peoples' Rights Act (IPRA) of the Philippines," *International Labour Organization*, www.ilo.org/wcmsp5/groups/public/–asia/–ro-bangkok/–ilo-manila/documents/publication/wcms_171406.pdf.

specifies that those self-identified peoples must still live in a community, on a territory that they have occupied and used for as long as one can recall. They must also have been differentiated from the majority of Filipinos through a history of political or social resistance.

The law distinguishes between ancestral domain and ancestral lands, and reaffirms the right to a distinct form of ownership. As in the past DAO 2, ancestral land applies to individuals, families, and clans that claim ownership of territory, whereas the domain can encompass a whole community and includes the natural resources associated with the territory.

IPRA requires "Free and Prior Informed Consent" before any outside corporation or government body can use territories or natural resources that are designated as ancestral domains or lands. It also extends to other interactions with the community, such as obtaining cultural materials or transferring responsibility for the management of forests or natural resources.

Participation of indigenous peoples is also required in several instances. They should be consulted in the delineation of ancestral domains and included in projects and programs that are developed in their area. IPRA provides a recognition of indigenous political structures, which should also provide local capacity to participate in other areas such as educational, health, and natural resource management. IPRA emphasizes the responsibility to provide the means for indigenous peoples to govern themselves and take the lead for their development.

Finally, the law creates the National Commission on Indigenous Peoples (NCIP). Composed of representatives from indigenous peoples, the commission is mandated with the task of delineating and issuing certificates of ancestral lands and domains. It also gained the responsibility for the law's implementation and the primary role in formulating policies and programs to enhance the livelihoods of indigenous peoples and fulfill IPRA's mandate.

The adoption of IPRA definitely ended a period of mobilization in the Cordillera. The creation of the temporary CAR had defused the CPLA/CPA's violent mobilization but had failed to address some of the deep grievances held in the region, and about which local organizations continued to advocate both domestically and internationally. The reframing of demands as "indigenous" contributed to defusing congressmen's perceived high stakes in providing "autonomy" to the region, on the one hand and, on the other, Cordillerans' suspicions, particularly among the CPA, that proposed legislation strongly diluted the powers and resources that the proposed legislation provided.

IPRA's Implementation

Over the course of the following years, Cordillerans focused on the implementation of IPRA. NGOs, such as Panlipi and Legal Rights and Natural Resources

Center (Kasama sa Kalikasan/*Friends of the Earth-Pilipinas*), which had been at the forefront of lobbying for IPRA, continued their advocacy to pressure the government into meeting its commitments. New indigenous peoples' organizations were formed in response to the need to participate in advocating for the recognition of particular indigenous identities, and their associated ancestral domains. Building the regulatory and administrative infrastructure to give credence to indigenous rights protection and self-determination removed the issue from Congressional and mediatized debate regarding indigenous peoples and, instead, relegated it to the less visible bureaucratic level. At the same time, some indigenous groups' organizations, most significantly the CPA continued to voice strong objections to government policy as it denounced IPRA as a "sell out."[49]

As in the case of the Moros, once removed from the broader public eye, the response to substantive claims of Cordillerans became diluted, distorted, and undermined when subjected to bureaucratic control. Furthermore, at the beginning, there were strong attempts among IPRA's opponents and their congressional allies to challenge the law in court, and find means of obstructing its implementation. While these failed, it is clear that slow and ineffective implementation eroded the law's original intent.

It is unlikely that the measures to reduce the law's effectiveness or to undermine it constituted a coherent and deliberate state strategy. Nevertheless, it shows how legislative gains are often insufficient to sustain momentum toward achieving the empowerment goals sought by nationalists. In cases, such as the Philippines, where business interests can easily sway bureaucrats, nationalist groups lose their capacity to compete with them in the implementation phase.

At the outset, some bureaucrats and corporations sought to derail the legislation. Initially the DENR resisted the transfer of powers to the NCIP to delineate and recognize ancestral domain. Once regulations were in place, it objected, along with mining industry officials, to aspects that clashed with the 1995 Mining Law. The requirement of "Free Prior and Informed Consent" and its process gave the NCIP new powers and oversight over mining and other development projects, while reducing powers of the DENR.[50] More specifically, the mining industry strongly objected to regulations that provided the NCIP with the power to suspend or stop any project that had violated the process of free and informed consent. Under pressure from the industry, in October 1998 the NCIP passed a modification that exempted from the process

---

[49] Asian Development Bank, *Indigenous Peoples/Ethnic Minorities and Poverty Reduction: Philippines*, ed. Anonymous (Manila: Asian Development Bank; distributed by Independent Publishers Group, Chicago, 2002), 17.

[50] Philippine Center for Investigative Journalism, "New Law on Indigenous Peoples Faces Legal Challenge," (Manila, 1998).

those "leases, licenses, contracts and other forms of concession within ancestral domains" that were in place before the passing of IPRA and its regulations.[51]

The resistance escalated when former Supreme Court Justice Isagani Cruz and Attny Cesar Europa filed a petition with the Supreme Court that challenged the constitutionality of IPRA. They specifically focused on the Constitution's provisions that all mineral and other subsurface resource wealth belong to the state. They contended that IPRA could not vest indigenous peoples with power over these resources once their ancestral domains were recognized. They filed the case in 1998, but the Court settled and closed it on a technicality only in December 2000, without ruling decisively. As a consequence, it left IPRA vulnerable to future challenges on these questions and delayed the law's implementation.[52]

In the first few years, very little was implemented. There were delays in setting up all of the infrastructure under NCIP. Panlipi estimated that, between 2000 and 2005, only seventeen projects were directly related to IPRA. NGOs and indigenous peoples' organizations were more active in addressing issues under IPRA, in particular most of the latter were involved in the delineation of ancestral domain, and supported by international funding and NGOs.[53]

The recognition of indigenous identities and delineation of ancestral domain is a key aspect of IPRA but has been the source of numerous conflicts. As in the case of the UN Declaration on the Rights of Indigenous Peoples, IPRA uses the principle of self-identification. As a result, groups have the right to lay claim to being indigenous and to identify the customary boundaries of their ancestral domains. Indigenous peoples have quite varying systems of political organization, customs, and even concepts of territorial boundaries, and therefore moving to a homogenous system of ancestral domain delineation at the outset creates ambiguities.[54] Furthermore, in the Cordillera, boundary disputes have risen as a result of self-delineation and claims to ancestral domains, especially when related to resources such as access to water for irrigation. Various

---

[51] Asian Development Bank, *Indigenous Peoples/Ethnic Minorities and Poverty Reduction,* 15–16.

[52] Nestor T. Castro, "Ten Years of the Indigenous Peoples' Rights Act: An Assessment," (Manila: University of the Philippines, Diliman, 2007), 7; Panlipi, "Initial Assessment of the Extent and Impact of the Implementation of IPRA," (Panlipi, under the auspices of the International Labour Organization 2005), 7.

[53] "Initial Assessment of the Extent and Impact of the Implementation of IPRA," 52–53.

[54] Steven Rood, "Issues Surrounding Autonomy: Insights from the Work of the University of the Philippines Cordillera Studies Center on Cordillera Autonomy, 1986–1994," in *Advancing Regional Autonomy in the Cordillera: A Source Book,* ed. Arturo C. Boquiren (Baguio City; Pasig, Metro Manila: Cordillera Studies Center University of the Philippines College Baguio; Friedrich Ebert Stiftung Manila Office, 1994), 7–8.

factions and clans are "recreating and re-telling their respective version of their customary laws" in competition for boundary delineation.[55]

Furthermore, since many individuals have already obtained private ownership of land, it must be reconciled with the concept of ancestral domain.[56] As the NCIP acknowledged:

> The issuance of the title is more of a recognition that since time immemorial they have been the owners of the land. So that's how it translates into how the IPRA is working for them. However, there are communities that may not want to have the titles. We cannot force those on a community . . . . But, . . . I think NCIP is succeeding in the issuance of the title, at least for the ones who want to title. Because we are able to issue almost one million hectares.[57]

The relative assessment of success in delineating ancestral domain was questioned, but was also related to criticisms of the NCIP's lack of sufficient budgetary and staffing resources. The NCIP issued twenty-nine certificates of ancestral domain titles between 2002 and 2004, covering a total land area of 604,143 hectares. In 2003–2004, however, there were fifty-six applications involving an additional 1,091,151 hectares. As of January 10, 2005, only one of these applications had been approved. And there were an additional thirty-two that fell into an alternative category, and for which only three had been approved in early 2005. Given the large number of applications and territory covered, it constituted a relatively small accomplishment. As a World Bank report noted, the NCIP faced major problems with lack of expertise, lack of financial resources, and an overly reactive approach to identifying ancestral domain claims.[58]

NCIP officials sought to create links to local governments and NGOs to compensate for lack of resources and issue more titles, in spite of very limited resources: "we network with local governments, we network with NGOs, we network with whoever assists in the titling. Because if we do not do that we will never title, issue the title. It needs money. Titling here needs money."[59]

The ambiguity in determining what is an ancestral domain and how it relates to existing land titles and administrative boundaries, however, has given rise to new conflicts. In particular, under the 1991 local government code – a fiscal and administrative decentralization law – LGUs are the primary beneficiaries of

---

[55] Molintas, "The Philippine Indigenous Peoples' Struggle for Land and Life: Challenging Legal Texts," 297.

[56] Attny Maria Vicenta De Guzman, interview.

[57] Grace Pasqua, Director, Planning, Policy and Research of NCIP (National), interview by author, August 21, 2007, Manila.

[58] Josefo B. Tuyor et al., "Indigenous Peoples Rights Act: Legal and Institutional Frameworks, Implementation and Challenges in the Philippines," in *Discussion Papers, East Asia and Pacific Region: Social Development, and Rural Development, Natural Resources and Environment Sectors* (Washington, DC: World Bank, 2007), 48.

[59] Grace Pasqua, interview.

revenue allotment from the central government. As a result, LGU officials often interfere with the delineation process and, as members sharing the same community as those leaders supposed to participate in the delineation process, they often compete for control and seek to make boundaries coincide with administrative ones. They fear overlapping claims and reduced powers and revenue.[60]

Private property rights clash with the notion of community claims to land as well. Some entrepreneurs or farmers have invested large sums of capital in land areas in the Cordillera and are concerned about the implications of granting ancestral domain rights, when they primarily wish to secure titles for their lands and their investment.[61] Under the Torrens titling system and the Philippines' Comprehensive Agrarian Reform Law, precedence is given to privately held titles over ancestral lands.[62] But these different principles of land titling create some ambiguities and disputes that have been obstacles to IPRA's implementation.

The law's provision for "Free Prior and Informed Consent" (FPIC) has created the most amount of controversy, especially in relation to mining projects. In its initial stages, mining corporations complained that the process was too cumbersome and subject to outside organizations raising objections once a certification was obtained. Certainly, in the first few years, most approved projects and certificates fell outside of ancestral domains. Because much of the territory was not yet delineated as ancestral domain, every project was subjected to field investigation and the FPIC process, even though it was estimated that 17 per cent of land in the Philippines might end up being identified as ancestral domain. As a result, between 2004 and 2006, more than 90 per cent of projects issued with certification preconditions, a required step in the FPIC process, were outside ancestral domain areas. This constituted large amounts of resources devoted to the process in areas where it might not be required.[63]

Until 2012, there were mounting concerns that the FPIC process was flawed and mining interests prioritized. Gloria Macapagal-Arroyo declared mining as a priority for her economic policy and, as a result, reduced the relative power of the NCIP. Already, disputes between the mining industry and the NCIP led to regulations that reaffirmed the exemption of the need for FPIC in the case of mining rights obtained before the passing of IPRA.[64] Once in power, Arroyo transferred the NCIP to the control of the Department of Agrarian Reform and later moved it under the DENR. The DENR maintains responsibility for issuing mining concessions, so that the transfer created a conflict of interest, reduced

---

[60] Recto Alawas, Chief, Technical Management Division, NCIP-CAR, interview by author, August 29, 2007, Baguio.
[61] June Prill-Brett, interview.   [62] Tuyor et al., "Indigenous Peoples Rights Act," 28–29.
[63] Ibid., 41.   [64] Ibid., 31.

the NCIP's power, and undermined indigenous peoples' trust in the NCIP's capacity to implement IPRA in their favour.[65] Since most of the mining resources remain in areas populated by indigenous peoples, Arroyo's policy intensified the conflict with local communities:

The Arroyo administration basically is more interested in … bringing in foreign investments … And of course that means that mining, for instance, has been a flagship project, and that means more manipulation in terms of obtaining free and prior informed consent. And many of the mining areas are in our communities anyway. The last remaining mining resources are in indigenous peoples' communities. So, you can see that that kind of contradiction is very glaring.[66]

In a study of the implementation of IPRA, the World Bank praised the empowerment gained from the FPIC process included in the law, but raised concerns regarding the way it was conducted. The process has been compromised by

the ability of the NCIP to effectively and efficiently facilitate the process; the capacity of the IPs to assert their rights to meaningful participation and informed decision-making; charges of manipulative actions and corrupt practices by big corporations to secure the consent of the IPs; misrepresentation of some IP groups/organizations claiming to represent the IPs; the different interpretations of what constitutes consent; and the instability of the consent even after the memorandum of agreement has been signed.[67]

Arroyo developed a National Mining Policy that targeted up to 30 per cent of the country's land for mining purposes. It was a key component of its Medium-Term Development Plan (2004–2010). Since most land available for mining is situated in the Cordillera and other areas identified with indigenous peoples, the government expected the NCIP to amend its procedures to simplify and accelerate the granting of Certification Precondition/FPIC. The objective was to better "harmonize" IPRA and make it more responsive to the 1995 Mining Act.[68]

Officials from the NCIP themselves recognized that pressure from the presidential office often impeded their ability to fulfill their mandate:

In one instance, there was someone from Malacañang [the residence and workplace of the President of the Philippines] saying that since the president had opened mining in the Philippines, we as NCIP, because we are a government agency, had to support the president on that particular program. But, as NCIP, our role, then, is to be neutral. That is, just to facilitate the consultation through the free and prior informed consent processes from the NCIP and we really have to be in between the company and the

[65] Oxfam America, *Free Prior and Informed Consent in the Philippines: Regulations and Realities* (Boston, MA: Oxfam America, 2013), 13.
[66] Victoria Tauli-Corpuz, interview.   [67] Tuyor et al., "Indigenous Peoples Rights Act," 46.
[68] "Philippines Indigenous Peoples ICERD Shadow Report," (Committee on the Elimination of all forms of Racial Discrimination, 2009), 34–35.

community, ... But here comes another office saying that we should support the president. So, at times, there are things that I think we really have to also define between the office of the president as well as the NCIP so that IPRA will be implemented smoothly.[69]

There were a number of cases where mining corporations, in alliance with some state officials, were either able to circumvent the FPIC process or disregard it altogether. A 2010 report concluded, on the basis of a random survey, that consent of the communities was freely given in only 41.2 per cent of studied cases, while 35.4 per cent gave consent without sufficient information to properly assess the request, and 23.6 per cent had not gained consent freely.[70] In 2005–2006, Anglo American and Oxiana Gold both had mining applications for areas under the Isneg ancestral lands in the Cordillera. In Anglo American's case, indigenous communities twice rejected proposals for Anglo American to mine copper. When they boycotted a third consultation, the NCIP interpreted the community's absence as indicating a lack of opposition.[71] In at least one case, the "elders" selected to represent the Isneg and other indigenous peoples settled in the community were chosen by local officials, instead of consulting traditional leaders. The chosen representatives were not recognized as legitimate leaders and the process went ahead in spite of the objections from the legitimate community leadership.[72] In Oxiana Gold's case, the Kankaney and other IPs in the region of Benguet, rejected by 90 per cent in 2006 its request through an FPIC process. Yet, the NCIP returned again in 2007 with an application from Royalco, a company that had acquired Oxiana's assets, and attempted to divide the FPIC process into three phases, in order to manipulate the outcome.[73]

Cordillerans and other indigenous peoples attempted to resist the Arroyo administration's strong emphasis on mining and apparent disregard for the legislated protections of indigenous peoples. In one manifestation of their opposition, Cordillerans picketed the 2005 Asia Pacific Mining Conference and Mining Exhibit in Manila, where Gloria Macapagal Arroyo was scheduled to give a keynote address. The CPA led the mobilization of several peasant, tribal elder, and people's organizations from the Cordillera.[74]

Yet, the administration's aggressive mining policy continued and was backed up with increased militarization of the Cordillera and other IP areas.

---

[69] CAR NCIP, interview.

[70] Oxfam America, *Free Prior and Informed Consent in the Philippines*, 5. A 2008 nationwide study of holders of Certificates of Ancestral Domain Title (CADT) reported that 70 per cent of the mining and logging operations on their lands were being conducted without their FPIC. And those where the consultation had been held, several did not follow the required procedures.

[71] "Fight in Philippines," *The Observer*, April 22, 2007.

[72] "Philippines Indigenous Peoples ICERD Shadow Report," 47.   [73] Ibid., 50.

[74] AT Bengwayan, "Igorots Picket ASPAC Mining Meet, Condemn Arroyo's Mining Agenda," *Bulatat*, October 16–22, 2005.

UN Special Rapporteur on Indigenous Peoples, Professor Rodolfo Stavenhagen, reported in 2007 that the Lepanto Consolidated Mining Company commissioned the military and paramilitary forces and ensured that members of the CPA were branded as insurgents. It later supported further use of police and paramilitary groups to confront worker strikes and demonstrations.[75]

Under Benigno Aquino's presidency, some of the Arroyo policies were reversed. Most importantly, the NCIP's independence was restored as it was removed from the DENR and placed under the office of the president. It also received a greater budget allocation. Finally, Aquino appointed Zenaida Bridget Pawid as Chairperson. Pawid had been one of the most influential civil society leaders from the Cordillera and had participated actively in the lobbying and crafting of IPRA during the social reform movement of President Ramos.[76]

Some changes after 2012 strengthened aspects of IPRA's procedures. Indigenous peoples were to be more directly included in field investigations of proposed land use and project impact before seeking FPIC. They strengthened their right to non-consent and clarified a number of procedures that were used to manipulate outcomes. They also ensured further FPIC at each major phase of a project, rather than only at its outset. Finally, they elaborated much more on the mandatory aspects of the process that should include community assemblies to present the project, provide dispute mechanisms, and clearly lay out the costs and benefits of the project. Finally, they required the organization of a "validation assembly" before FCIP could be official.[77]

Autonomy or Indigenous Rights?

In parallel to the pursuit of indigenous peoples' rights, some groups in the Cordillera continued to vie for autonomy. The defeat of the 1990 referendum still left the Constitution with a clause mandating autonomy for the Cordillera. It also left the Cordillera under the governance of a transitional authority, the CAR. At least two more attempts were made to revive the autonomy agenda, with a second referendum that also met with defeat in 1998.

Since 1990, much of the initiative for autonomy has come from state agencies and local politicians. From 1992 to 1995, several initiatives were taken to form a new consultative body to draft once again an organic act for Cordilleran autonomy. Congressmen from the Cordillera, CAR officials, and the CPLA-CBAd group remained divided on a number of issues. Ramos favoured a more accelerated approach to developing an autonomy law, rather

---

[75] "Philippines Indigenous Peoples ICERD Shadow Report," 56.
[76] Oxfam America, *Free Prior and Informed Consent in the Philippines*, 13.   [77] Ibid., 14–18.

than reinstating the broad consultation that had driven the first attempt. As a result, Congress passed in July 1997 RA 8438 (the second Organic Act for the Cordillera), which required approval by referendum.

Once again, Cordillerans strongly rejected autonomy. While some observers attributed the failure to a lack of information, there are political forces that have worked against it. Visions for autonomy have been markedly different, for instance. Organizations, such as the CPA, which continued to wield strong influence among some groups in the Cordillera proposed much more radical autonomy and socio-political transformation in accordance with its ideology on the left, which was therefore unwilling to agree to more compromise positions on autonomy. The CPLA was espousing a vision of autonomy based on federalist and socialist principles.

Overall, however, moderate proponents of autonomy had difficulty in articulating the value-added of autonomy, and to make a clear case for the alleged "common and distinctive cultural heritage" that binds the region together. Certainly, there have been worries that some particular groups in the Cordillera would gain advantage over others.[78]

There were several attempts in the following years to draft new autonomy laws. The Regional Development Council of the CAR (RDC) took the initiative, and found allies among congressional representatives of the Cordillera, as well as local politicians. The RDC began to develop its strategy around 2006 to 2007. It built on the existence of the Cordillera Administration Region as a temporary entity (through EO220), as well as the constitutional clause requiring autonomy for the Cordillera:

There is a legal basis for doing this and it is the constitution. We have the EO220 that is in force and in effect. We have the IPRA, Indigenous Peoples' Rights Act, that is in force and in effect. Therefore, that is the translation of the legal framework to pursue all of this ... So the people, the officialdom, who are the managers, they have to respect all this legal framework.[79]

The RDC sought to mobilize large segments of the Cordilleran population by seeking to research what people "wanted" from autonomy. They obtained significant budgetary allocation from Congress to pursue the mandate of consulting Cordillerans and drafting a new autonomy bill.[80]

The RDC's consultations and planning for a third referendum took several years, in part because of fear of a lack of sufficient political support. In spite of

---

[78] Athena Lydia Casambre, "The Failure of Autonomy in the Cordillera Region, Northern Luzon, Philippines," in *1st National Conference on Cordillera Research* (Baguio City: Cordillera Studies Centre, 2000), 6–11.

[79] Rodolfo La Barinto, Chief Economic Development Specialist, National Economic and Development Authority – Cordillera Autonomous Region, interview by author, August 29, 2007, Baguio City.

[80] Ibid.

the fact that Congress was the appropriate body to lobby to prepare a bill on autonomy, presidential support is often most important in creating the necessary momentum for bills to pass and be implemented. The RDC began its autonomy initiative under President Gloria Macapagal-Arroyo, who early on clearly sided with mining interests and placed them at the core of her development strategy. She clearly stated her position on a third referendum at an RDC sponsored meeting in 2006, when she declared that two rejections of autonomy showed that Cordillerans were not favourable to autonomy.[81]

Nevertheless, the RDC persisted in its quest. With the election of Benigno Aquino III, it increased its momentum. The years of planning and consultation resulted in the announcement of five "core principles" for the Cordillera. Chaired by Mayor Mauricio G. Domogan, the Third Autonomy Act Drafting Committee planned the draft legislation, first, on the idea of a permanent regional identity, with jurisdiction of all matters devolved to it, including "administrative organization; creation of revenue sources; ancestral domain and natural resources; personal, family and property relations; regional urban and rural planning development; economic, social and tourism development; educational policies; preservation and development of cultural heritage." This included repatriating powers and administrative tasks from line agencies of the national government in the Cordillera. The second principle specified, however, that existing units, including the Local Government Units would retain existing powers and benefits. Paid employees of the national government, under the third, would continue to be paid by the national government but under the direct supervision of the regional provincial governor. The last two principles focused on the national provision of a special subsidy for development as compensation for past neglect of the region, as well as commitment for continued budgetary support for autonomous development.[82]

The subsidy became a key component of the bill, and its subsequent iterations. The autonomous region would receive P10 billion for the first five years and P5 billion for the succeeding five years of the ten-year subsidy period to fast-track development in the region. The subsidy was to be equally divided among the seven provinces of Abra, Apayao, Benguet, Ifugao, Kalinga, Mountain Province, the City of Baguio, and the regional autonomous government. Municipalities and component cities would also receive P10 million share from the subsidy of the province where they belong, while *barangays* would obtain P1 million each.[83]

[81] Juan B. Dait Jr, "Arroyo Douses Cold Water over Cordillera Autonomy," *Manila Bulletin* Online, June 25, 2006.

[82] "Autonomy Issues Heat up in Mountain Province," *Targeted News Service*, January 12, 2011.

[83] Dexter A, "Draft Cordillera Autonomy Law to Go Thru Consultations," news release, May 27, 2011, http://car.neda.gov.ph/draft-cordillera-autonomy-law-to-go-thru-consultations/.

Various versions of the bill remained similar but most ended up failing to be passed before Congress was adjourned. Senator Aquilino "Koko" Pimentel III filed Senate Bill No. 3115 in February 2012.[84] In the House, several congressmen filed Bill 5595. After two years of consultations and deliberation, a summit was organized on April 30 to consolidate input from pre-summits held in all Cordillera provinces and cities. The summit aimed at providing a national front to President Aquino. As Baguio City Mayor Mauricio Domogan argued: "The best bet we have in winning the President's approval is to show our solidarity, something which the Manifesto for the Creation of the Cordillera Autonomous Region will show and the outputs of the Cordillera Summit on Autonomy."[85]

Regional leaders sought to capitalize on President Aquino's strong commitment to reaching a new autonomy law in Mindanao and make the case for autonomy in the Cordillera, as equally prescribed by the Constitution. Yet, the Mindanao case itself continued to the end of Aquino's presidency, without final passage in Congress.

Bills 5595 and 3115 died with the end of the 15th Congress, but were soon after revived. Once again House representatives from the Cordillera presented House Bill 4649, which led to a whole new series of consultations in various provinces and municipalities of the Cordillera.[86] The House Committee on Local Governments passed the bill in February 2016, without objections, so the expectation was that the bill could easily pass in the full House.[87] Nevertheless, the bill died once again when the 16th Congress ended in June 2016. With the election of a new Congress and Rodrigo Duterte as president, the autonomy bill was once again revived.[88]

The CPA, in turn, has repeatedly rejected the proposed autonomy bills on the basis that they represented mainly a form of decentralization, rather than an actual realization of self-determination. The CPA long discarded its strong support for autonomy enshrined in the constitution and denounced every version presented in Congress on the vague premise that autonomy could not be achieved before a substantial reform of democracy. They pointed to the experience of Muslims in Mindanao to show how, in spite of obtaining an autonomy agreement, little actual self-determination and genuine autonomy was achieved:

---

[84] Antonio Siegfrid O. Alegado, "Bill Seeking Autonomous Region Filed," *Business World*, February 7, 2012.

[85] Marilou Guieb, "Hb 5595 Seeks to Create Autonomous Cordillera Region," *Business Mirror*, May 11, 2014.

[86] "Act Establishing Cordillera Autonomous Region Filed," *Philippines News Agency*, June 17, 2014; Thom Picana, "Cordillera Autonomy Consultation Starts," *The Manila Times*, July 10, 2015.

[87] "House Fails on Cordillera Autonomy Bill," *The Manila Times*, February 8, 2016.

[88] "Council Wants Pending Cordillera Autonomy Bill Certified as Urgent," *Philippines News Agency*, September 12, 2016.

Twice is enough. The people have spoken. And they should not underestimate the Cordillera peoples' wisdom in rejecting the two organic acts … we really learned from our own struggle, that the Cordillera region, which is a very rich region, that the government would just not offer us on the silver platter what we want. Because the Cordillera, even as early as the colonial times, had been treated by the colonial masters and the succeeding Philippine republics, as a resource base for extraction. Precisely what we need is regional autonomy but the putting up of the regional autonomous government again is not seen within a political vacuum. It is seen within a whole range of political developments in our country and international trends regarding indigenous peoples."[89]

The CPA's strategy, therefore, relies on pursuing more fundamental reforms to the Philippines' democratic system, before agreeing to any form of autonomous government.

Conclusion

The case of the Cordillera shows that a strategy of "exit and reframe" can remove some of the perceived threat that national mobilization produces. Cordilleran activists abandoned the quest to unify as a "Cordilleran nation" and, instead, articulated their claims as indigenous peoples. They seized on the opportunity to lobby Congress in favour of legislation that would enshrine indigenous peoples' rights rather than continue to seek autonomy for the Cordilleran people, which entailed a degree of power and resource devolution that Congress would likely not support.

IPRA attained in legislation many of the objectives that had been sought. It defined rights over ancestral domain, self-governance and self-determination. Indigenous peoples gained the power to maintain their cultural practices and indigenous political structures. They were also to be consulted on the development of major projects in their ancestral domain, including those linked to natural resources. The principle of Free Prior and Informed Consent was enshrined in the law. While it applied much more broadly, to all indigenous peoples in the Philippines, it was Cordillerans who were at the forefront of mobilizing in favour of the legislation and lobbied most strongly for its adoption.

Cordillerans were particularly suspicious of the Philippine government's sincerity in enshrining autonomy, thereby confirming a strong commitment problem that the Philippine state faced both in Mindanao and in the Cordillera. The CPA, in particular, denounced multiple versions of autonomy that were initiated by members of Congress. They successfully campaigned for Cordillerans to twice turn down the proposed autonomy proposals. While they had been strong advocates of enshrining autonomy in the Constitution,

---

[89] Windel Bolinget, Secretary General, Cordillera Peoples' Alliance, interview by author, August 27, 2007, Baguio City.

the CPA articulated a position from the left that sought first to change fundamentally the governance structures of the Philippines before supporting autonomy legislation. While such a position lay at one end of a continuum of views, nevertheless they adequately pointed to numerous examples of legislation that were never properly implemented. As such, they were also critical of IPRA, which they viewed as another attempt to undermine, rather than empower, Cordillerans and other indigenous groups.

Mobilization of Cordillerans has certainly been defused. IPRA has moved the conflict to the normal democratic process. Combined with more power to local government units, Cordillerans have gained more power and resources. The strategy enabled Cordillerans to craft a path to more control over their region than, by comparison, Papuans could by continuing to frame their mobilization in nationalist terms in Indonesia. It lowered the threat that enabled an electoral coalition under President Ramos to capitalize on indigenous rights in relation to a broader SRA that could pass a parliament otherwise keen on exercising its independence to minimize concessions and reduce autonomy to administrative decentralization.

Nevertheless, the gains have been mixed. The state has poorly implemented IPRA, in particular in the management and exploitation of natural resources, and the process of free prior and informed consent. The legislation provides a standard against which the use of land and resources in the Cordillera can be assessed and problems raised. Indigenous groups and NGOs have maintained the pressure to denounce practices that violate the spirit of self-determination and right to consultation embedded in the law. They even obtained some modifications to the legislation that closed some of the loopholes used, in particular, to circumvent rules for mining projects.

7   Malay Muslims in Thailand

During the last three decades, the pattern of mobilization in Thailand shows an unclear relationship to democratization. In the first instance, "democratization" itself is somewhat difficult to pinpoint, since there were periods of more open politics followed by military coups. A long decade of semi-democratic rule gradually eased Thailand toward a full electoral democracy and, while many strong characteristics of democracy prevailed for several years, nevertheless it faltered as the armed forces repeatedly intervened to prevent deep reform.[1] Second, Malay-Muslim mobilization has been weak, and even somewhat difficult to identify, as unknown perpetrators were the most frequent instigators of violent attacks, against the backdrop of an apparently quiescent Malay-Muslim majority. The worst violence, after 2002, coincided with a relatively stable period of democratic governance when the Constitution of 1997 had made possible the election for the first time of a majority government led by Thaksin Shinawatra's Thai Rak Thai in 2001.

State repression, combined with very low Malay-Muslim mobilizational capacity, explains the sporadic and somewhat anonymous violent attacks that characterized Malay-Muslim resistance. The question of autonomy, or responding to nationalist aspirations, was completely closed off under all regime types, in favour of nurturing the concept of one Thai nation. With a strong institutionalization of this identity also embedded in the monarchy, there were no channels to pursue demands for accommodation of a Malay-Muslim nationalism. State concessions reflected attempts to coopt the elites, bring them minimally into central institutions, and provide development funding to appease some of the broader grievances. While an electoral coalition

---

[1] Case speaks of "democratic quality," and assesses its degree, particularly after 1997, noting that democracy can persist despite executive abuses and corruption (as it did for some time in Thailand). See William Case, "Thai Democracy 2001: Out of Equilibrium," *Asian Survey* 41, no. 3 (2001). Phongpaichit and Baker, in looking at the rise of "business populism" under Thaksin, nevertheless see Thailand as having undergone a "generation-long period of democratic development that culminated in the 1990s [and] created some impressive formal achievements"; see Pasuk Phongpaichit and Christopher John Baker, "'Business Populism' in Thailand," *Journal of Democracy* 16, no. 2 (2005): 70.

briefly relied on some support for Malay Muslims in the 1990s, Thaksin's majority and his populist appeal had no such need. His tough stance toward the Deep South appealed much more to his constituency.

Because the initial phase of democratization occurred over more than a decade, its effects were not as strong as elsewhere. During the period of semi-democratic rule under the leadership of Prem Tinsulanond a in the 1980s, the state introduced small concessions that included some limited measures to accommodate Malay-Muslim grievances in language use and education, but mostly in the form of social welfare benefits. Such concessions reduced some of the levels of grievance among Malay Muslims more broadly, and were continued as the regime became an electoral democracy in 1988 and reaffirmed in 1992, after a very brief military coup. Ironically, throughout this period, the relatively gradual, even if bumpy, transition to electoral democracy as well as continuity in the policies toward Malay Muslims likely attenuated some of the uncertainty that usually surrounds democratic transition, especially by comparison to the more sudden transitions in the Philippines and Indonesia. Conversely, under democratic stabilization, the government of Thaksin Shinawatra used repression and removed previous concessions. His repressive approach appealed to the Thai majority that, with the first signs of violence in the South, quickly supported what he articulated as the need to crush criminals and "terrorists." The degree of repression largely explains why, subsequently, there was little evidence of a well-coordinated and organized movement to oppose the Thai state. Instead, the movement remained underground and launched sporadic attacks. Its weakness also determined its choice of methods, using occasional bombings, rather than any direct contact with the armed forces.

By comparison to other cases of weak mobilizational capacity, the Thai state's complete closure to adopting principles of autonomy contrasted with Indonesia and the Philippines which, with more sudden and vulnerable new democratic regimes, constitutionalized principles of autonomy. They did so of course largely because they also respectively faced violent insurgents with high mobilization capacity. It made the establishment of credible commitment to democracy more precarious if a path to peace was not devised, while not necessarily in the end committing to implementing the kind of autonomy that nationalist groups sought. Brief electoral coalitions allowed such principles to be adopted and, in cases of Aceh and Mindanao, autonomy to be passed in parliament. But Thailand's democracy was not as fragile given its gradual development, and the electoral coalitions of the 1990s relied more heavily on sustaining the Thai nation than on the need to extend much more than minimal concessions to Malay Muslims that did not challenge that central notion.

Malay-Muslim Resistance to the Thai State and "Nation"

Malay Muslims constitute a small group, territorially concentrated alongside the Thai border. They are the majority population in four provinces of southern Thailand, namely Pattani, Yala, Narathiwat, and Satun, and represent an important proportion in parts of Songkla. All together they constitute only 3 per cent of the population but they have long resisted the Thai state. A Malay-Muslim nationalist movement emerged in the 1960s but was defeated by the 1980s. The Thai state applied mostly repressive and assimilationist policies, while gradually offering small concessions. Nevertheless, it maintained its strong unitary state and concept of a single Thai nation, which made any significant recognition and accommodation of Malay Muslims difficult.

Thai nationalism constructed an image of Thailand as homogenous, around three pillars of Nation, Religion, and Monarchy. Beginning with King Chulalongkorn in the nineteenth century, the Siamese state launched a vast program of reform and state consolidation to resist external pressures from expanding British and French colonial ventures. This effort became intrinsically tied to fostering and deepening a sense of Thai identity. The 1932 coup that ended absolute monarchy and established a constitutional monarchy did not significantly change these foundational principles of the Thai state. Successive regimes, whether authoritarian, semi-democratic, or democratic retained the three pillars that the King has symbolically represented. This path has had deep consequences for the Thai state's approach to ethnic minorities, where the emphasis on state centralization and strengthening of a Thai identity has collided with aspirations, particularly from Malay Muslims, of recognition and accommodation of their distinct identities and cultures, with a concomitant demand for greater self-governance.[2]

Before the consolidation of the Siamese state in the nineteenth century, the areas occupied by Malay Muslims were largely small sultanates with loose tributary relations with the Siamese court. The Siamese state resisted the expansion and consolidation of the British colonial occupation in Malaysia by consolidating its power and presence in Malay-Muslim areas it occupied. Under the Anglo-Siamese agreement of 1832, the Thai state obtained guarantees of less intrusion from the British. In 1909, the border was consolidated and the current territory of Thailand confirmed. The Thai state removed the existing political leadership and structure and began to build infrastructure and introduce administrative reforms and taxation.[3]

Resentment in the region grew as the Thai state increased its presence. Few Thai Buddhists lived in the area, with the exception of a few government

---

[2] Thongchai Winichakul, *Siam Remapped: A History of the Geo-Body of a Nation* (Honolulu: University of Hawaii Press, 1994).

[3] Ibid., 233.

officials. The region remained geographically isolated from the rest of Thailand, with most Malay Muslims living from small-scale farming and fisheries. But when the Thai state expanded its administrative presence and control of daily lives, resentment became stronger. Religious leaders organized tax boycotts. A large rebellion burnt down several public offices in 1910. Former Malay nobility and religious leaders organized another major uprising in 1922, partially led by Abdul Kadir, a former leader of Patani living in the northern part of Malaysia. The rebellion successfully prompted the Thai state to ease some of its policies, by removing regulations that contradicted Islam and levelling taxation to remain in line with that of the Malay population across the border under British rule.[4]

In the 1930s and 1940s, the state's policies were strongly assimilationist. The Phibun Songkhram administration strongly emphasized the "Thaification" of ethnic minorities, which included regulations over language, education, dress, and religious practice. It eliminated previous attempts to accommodate aspects of Malay local culture. The interference with religious practice was a particularly strong source of grievance, specifically since Thai Buddhist officials were placed in charge of regulating and overseeing Islamic religious practice. The government even made strong efforts to convert Malay Muslims to Buddhism, through the compulsory educational curriculum. The repressive power of the state along with its strong assimilationist policies were sufficiently strong that Malay Muslims were mostly paralyzed in their response.[5]

While the post-war period initially saw a relaxation once again of forced assimilation, nevertheless the broader policies of the Thai state remained. After the fall of Phibun's government, the subsequent administration adopted the Patronage of Islam Act (1945), which created a new relationship between the Thai state and the religious leadership. It integrated *ulama*, madrasah, and mosque councils into the state's official administration and elevated the position of Chularajamontri as the highest official representing Islam in Thailand. It also created the Central Islamic Committee and Provincial Islamic Committees. Yet, it also explicitly folded Malay Muslims into a broader category of Thai Islam and placed the committees under the control of the Ministry of Interior. The state gained greater leverage over the appointment of religious leaders in religious schools and in the newly created institutions, therefore adapting its strategy by giving recognition to local institutions and religious culture, while attempting to extend the state's reach.[6]

As a consequence, the *ulama* increasingly played a central role in the leadership of Malay-Muslim communities. Previous nobles had been

---

[4] Surin Pitsuwan, *Islam and Malay Nationalism*, 65–69.
[5] Astri Suhrke, "Irredentism Contained: The Thai-Muslim Case," *Comparative Politics* 7, no. 2 (1975): 195; Pitsuwan, *Islam and Malay Nationalism*, 86–89.
[6] Pitsuwan *Islam and Malay Nationalism*, 105–08.

displaced, many exiled in Malaysia, or otherwise repressed when the Thai state abolished their roles. *Ulama* moved into the leadership vacuum, particularly after their role was legitimized under the Islamic Patronage Act, and several took up formal positions in the Islamic Committees.

The Haji Sulong-led rebellion in 1947 gave new direction to the Malay-Muslims' resistance movement. It drew inspiration in part from the rise of Malay nationalism, and also the international decolonization movement. Haji Sulong, who was Chair of the Patani Provincial Islamic Council became the informal spiritual leader of Malay Muslims. He was an influential *ulama* who gained respect in part from his ability both to create links to the Thai state, as well as resisting the high degree of its interference. In 1947 he proposed a seven-point plan for an autonomous state, including a new high commissioner for the greater Patani region, replacement of most officials with Malay Muslims, recognition of the local language, and full authority over religious affairs. When the Thai state refused to negotiate or to make any significant changes to its policies, Haji Sulong organized a boycott and mass uprising, but was arrested and the violent movement was crushed by the end of 1948. His resistance remained nevertheless an important symbolic turning point for Malay-Muslim nationalism.[7]

It was only in the 1970s that a much more organized insurgency emerged, after another period of restructuring of relations between the Thai state and Malay Muslims. Year 1973 marked a key transition, with the removal of the military regime and its replacement with a first, brief period of democratic rule. The political opening allowed Malay Muslims to better organize and launch more effective resistance to the state.

In the previous decade or so, the Thai state had modified slightly its integrative approach. More emphasis was placed on socio-economic development rather than cultural assimilation. Field Marshall Sarit Thanarat's administration (1957–1963) launched a vast program of growth and development, which began its first decade as a new economic miracle. Education was a cornerstone of the government's strategy in the South, with the objective of creating a new elite that could fill official positions and be the agents of the region's economic development. In 1961, a new program targeted the *pondok* (traditional religious schools) to become new vanguards of modernization. They were registered, regulated, and given public funding on condition that they would integrate aspects of the Thai educational curriculum. In the following years, they were forced to abandon the teaching of Malay, and increasingly teach Thai values and morality that were mostly based on Buddhism. By the 1970s, it created a quota system to allow Malay Muslims to enter Thai

---

[7] Ibid., 141–62.

universities and bypass normal procedures, with the hopes that graduates of national universities would become loyal citizens and government supporters.[8]

Four main organizations nevertheless rose against the Thai state and intensified their violent mobilization in the 1970s: the Barisan Nasional Pembebasan Patani (BNPP), Barisan Revolusi Nasional (BRN), Patani United Liberation Organization (PULO), and the Barisan Bersatu Mujahideen Patani (BBMP).[9] The BNPP was formed in 1959, mostly reorganizing from the past defeat of the Haji Sulong rebellion. Its main strategy of guerrilla warfare aimed at obtaining full independence or autonomy within the federation of Malaysia. It formed close connections to the Islamic Party of Malaysia (*Partai Islam Se-Malaysia*), and formed some linkages with Arab states. The BRN, formed in 1963, was more forward-looking as it disagreed with the BNPP's aspiration for a return to a past sultanate, and instead dreamed of an independent Republic. It was more urban based, promoted a program of Islamic socialism, and created links with the Communist Party of Malaysia. It also mostly eschewed violent mobilization and used instead a political strategy focused on gaining support from the *pondoks*. A group of Patani students formed PULO in 1968 and recruited among students abroad in Mecca and elsewhere, with an emphasis on secular nationalism. It was formed originally as an umbrella organization for various insurgent groups. It was most practical, broader in its appeal, and better organized.[10] The BBMP was formed from a split in the BNPP and remained less significant than others.

In the 1970s, all three groups (BRN, PULO and BNPP) used more frequent violent attacks against the Thai state. Although they could never organize a systematic insurgency, they frequently attacked government targets and continued to mobilize villagers as a "hidden force." The political opening between 1973 and 1976 allowed for a large, unprecedented demonstration to be held at the Pattani Central Mosque. Thousands met daily for forty-five consecutive days, thereby showing the degree of support for resistance against the Thai state.[11] PULO was central in organizing the coalition of religious leaders, student organizations, and Malay-Muslim government officials that led the protest movement.[12] PULO was the most militant in terms of its use of guerrilla tactics, and gained most prominence as well from its continued active leadership from its base in Mecca. It also nurtured a much larger network in the Middle East and Southeast Asia, and used this support to maintain a presence in

---

[8] Ibid., 188–208.

[9] These organizations are most well known under these acronyms. BNPP is the National Liberation Front of Patani; BRN, the National Revolutionary Front; PULO is also known as the *Perubuhan Perpaduan Pembebasan Patani* in Malay, while the BBMP is the United Front of Patani Fighters.

[10] Kadir Che Man, *Muslim Separatism*, 98–101; Pitsuwan, *Islam and Malay Nationalism*, 228–40.

[11] Che Man, *Muslim Separatism*, 101.   [12] Pitsuwan, *Islam and Malay Nationalism*, 237–40.

the news worldwide. Nevertheless, BNPP also participated in insurgent activities, while BRN's were on a smaller scale. Several attempts were made to unify the fronts but all failed because of ideological or strategic divisions.[13]

While the insurgent activities remained relatively strong for over a decade, they fizzled away by the early 1980s. There are three main reasons for the decline in violent mobilization. First, the movement's inability to form a united front and increase the intensity of its insurgency offered only sporadic attacks, difficult and uneven support from the Malay-Muslim population, and relatively little threat to the Thai state and its much more powerful armed forces. Second, there was a shift in the 1980s from Malaysia actively supporting Malay-Muslim resistance organization operating from its territory to increasing its cooperation with the Thai state, both on economic joint interests and to more greatly secure the border.[14] There had been border agreements between the two states, and even joint operations, for instance, against Malaysian communists, particularly in the aftermath of the end of the Vietnam war, but tensions between both states remained because of the Malaysian government's prevention of a reciprocal ability of Thai security forces to enter Malaysian territory in the pursuit of Malay-Muslim insurgents. Greater cooperation nevertheless occurred between both countries in the 1980s, culminating in the 1989 cooperative agreement that led to the disbanding of the Communist Party of Malaysia. An informal quid-pro-quo was the expectation that Malaysia, although less formally, would help to reduce cross-border activities of Malay-Muslim insurgent groups.[15]

Third, there was a change in approach toward the south in the 1980s that contributed to a reduction of violent mobilization. Under a "New Hope" campaign, the government offered amnesty to insurgents. A large number of PULO members and supporters of other insurgent organizations grabbed the incentives that were offered. Furthermore, the formation of the Southern Border Provincial Administration Centre (SBPAC) in 1981, with patronage from the monarchy, helped to reduce grievances as it invested resources in the local economy and created better relations with local Malay Muslims. It was reinforced by an active policy of developing more sensitivity to officials' approach to local grievances and mechanisms to manage local tensions.

By the last decade of "softer" authoritarianism, the persistent low-level insurgency had diminished. For several decades, occasional rebellions and later formation of insurgent groups were signs of deep grievances among Malay Muslims. What originally began as a protest against intrusions from

[13] Che Man, *Muslim Separatism*, 106–09; Pitsuwan, *Islam and Malay Nationalism*, 228–40.
[14] John Funston, "Malaysia and Thailand's Southern Conflict: Reconciling Security and Ethnicity," *Contemporary Southeast Asia* 32, no. 2 (2010): 240.
[15] David Carment, "Managing Interstate Ethnic Tensions: The Thailand-Malaysia Experience," *Nationalism and Ethnic Politics* 1, no. 4 (1995): 12–15.

the Thai state in local lives became more clearly channelled as a Malay-Muslim nationalist movement, initially more irredentist in its orientation but becoming more clearly secessionist under PULO's leadership. The Thai state varied in terms of its degree of repression, but exerted strong military presence while shifting to very few concessions during some periods. Most of these were cosmetic changes, allowing for greater recognition of Islamic schools, for instance, merely to facilitate greater integration to the Thai educational objectives and curriculum. The Thai state remained strongly focused on maintaining a homogenous Thai identity, around principles of Nation, Religion, and Monarchy, with corresponding centralization of its administrative structures. There were few signs before democratization that the state was willing to accommodate Malay Muslims or even loosen its bureaucratic control over the four provinces where they were a majority.

Democratization in Thailand: Half Steps Forward, One Step Back

Thailand's path toward more open and democratic politics can be best characterized as a gradual process periodically interrupted by crises. After several decades of primarily authoritarian rule, the decade of the 1980s marked a period of semi-democratic rule, followed in 1988 by a free and fair election that led to the formation of a government with a prime minister responsible to parliament. I consider the period 1988–1995 as representing a transition to democracy, with the period 1995–2004 representing its stabilization, notwithstanding several caveats discussed later. During this time, Malay Muslims showed very few signs of mobilization, whether violently or through political protest. Instead, the state's concessions allowed the group first to obtain new benefits, including a new university and recognition of some of its Malay language demands. Furthermore, the democratic transition allowed a small group of Malay-Muslim politicians to form a representative group within parliament, and access the government via a small number of ministerial positions. These pre-emptive state concessions, begun under the period of semi-democratic rule, reduced the incentives to mobilize and, instead, appeared to set a new direction of accommodation that departed from the long-lasting repressive and assimilative approach of the Thai state.[16]

Under the leadership of former general Prem Tinsulanonda, from 1981 to 1988, the semi-democratic regime remained under military control. General

---

[16] For a relatively recent analysis of the historical evolution of Thai national identity and the limits of its accommodation of diversity even under democratic rule, see Michael Kelly Connors, *Democracy and National Identity in Thailand* (Abingdon, Oxon: Taylor & Francis, 2004).

Prem was appointed as prime minister and he, in turn, appointed several non-party ministers to the cabinet. At the same time, elections were held, parliament was functional, and the media and civil society organizations operated mostly without constraint. General Prem's government was widely recognized for its technocratic management that contributed to another period of economic prosperity and growth.[17]

Elections in 1988 established the first fully accountable government. Prem's authority had been challenged in previous years as criticism rose over alleged corruption among some of his government's ministers. In spite of his attempts to dissolve parliament and regain his authority, Prem resigned in 1988 after elections returned inconclusive results. The government of Chatichai Choonhavan, who was an elected politician, marked the beginning of the transition. Nevertheless, scandals soon rose as corruption became endemic and visible. A faction of the armed forces launched a coup in February 1991 to remove the Chatichai government, which much of the business and established elite celebrated. When the new junta organized elections the following year, and attempted to manipulate the outcome in favour of its party and candidate, mass demonstrations in Bangkok and Thailand's major cities broke out. While the armed forces cracked down, the King's intervention contributed to resolving the crisis, and new elections were held in September 1992.[18] With the accession to power of the Democrats, under a new coalition government led by Prime Minister Chuan Leekpai, the democratic transition resumed. The Chuan Leekpai government managed to remain in power until 1995.

Although interrupted by a military coup, the period from 1988 to 1995 can be seen as transitional. It was still fragile but free and fair elections were held. Political parties operated without constraints. The media flourished and numerous civil society organizations were formed and were, by some measures, the most important check on governmental power.[19] Snitwongse wrote of the "trials of transition" in 1994, but pointed to the opposition's ability to successfully push for reforms toward a fairer and more effective parliamentary system, and greater accountability.[20]

---

[17] Chai-Anan Samudavanija and Parichart Chotiya, "Beyond Transition in Thailand," in *Democracy in East Asia*, ed. Larry Diamond and Marc F. Plattner (Baltimore, MD and London: Johns Hopkins University Press, 1998).

[18] For a more nuanced explanation of the coup and its aftermath, see Maisrikrod Surin, *Thailand's Two General Elections in 1992: Democracy Sustained* (Singapore: Institute of Southeast Asian Studies, 1992).

[19] William Case, "Democracy's Quality and Breakdown: New Lessons from Thailand," *Democratization* 14, no. 4 (2007): 627–28; James Ockey, "Political Parties, Factions, and Corruption in Thailand," *Modern Asian Studies* 28, no. 2 (1994).

[20] Kusuma Snitwongse, "Thailand in 1994: The Trials of Transition," *Asian Survey* 35, no. 2 (1995).

There is strong reluctance among scholars of Thailand to periodize transition or consolidation of democracy, for good reason. McCargo, for instance, casts a skeptical view of democracy in Thailand. While he acknowledges the positive steps of introducing more civilian rule, new institutions, and legal processes, he notes the severe limitations in terms of looming military intervention and close relations between business and politicians that challenged, even at the height of the 1990s reforms, the view that democracy was more than a veneer.[21] Connors has also been critical of Thailand's democracy, viewing instead the Thai state's use of democracy as one of many tools to preserve elite dominance.[22] Nevertheless, most scholars acknowledge the gradual process of democratization through the electoral process and political freedoms, while casting doubt on other aspects of democracy. By comparison to other cases that I consider, Thailand in this period was subjected to similar pressures of politicians seeking voter support and also to greater public scrutiny than in the past.

The new democratic context offered little in terms of renegotiating the fundamental features of the Thai nation. The armed forces were the greatest source of uncertainty, in particular once they intervened to remove the government of Chatichai Choonhavan in 1991. They continued to operate autonomously from civilian rule. Nevertheless, after their very brief time in office and subsequent failure to control the outcome of the first 1992 election, they appeared to accept a non-political role, which greatly strengthened democratic expectations after 1992. The monarchy continued to embody the symbols of unity of the Thai nation and its close relationship to Buddhism. At the same time, a commission was created to draft a new constitution, which would eventually be adopted in 1997. In principle, given the broad consultation surrounding the drafting process, the constitution could have allowed Malay Muslims to renegotiate their status, but their weak position and the continued, strong consensus surrounding Thai-ness provided little space for them to make demands. As Ginsburg noted: "In Thailand, the monarchy is permanent, while constitutions are ephemeral. Constitutions may not regulate the monarchy; nonetheless, they *are* used to legitimate temporal power-holders."[23] Not a single article of the 1997 Constitution mentioned the Malay Muslims, or any special provision for autonomous government or recognition that could apply to them, except articles emphasizing the freedom of religious practice.

State concessions prior to the emergence of full electoral democracy contributed to appeasing some of the Malay-Muslim demands, and consequently

---

[21] Duncan McCargo, "Democracy under Stress in Thaksin's Thailand," *Journal of Democracy* 13, no. 4 (2002).

[22] Connors, *Democracy and National Identity in Thailand*.

[23] Ginsburg, "Constitutional Afterlife."

the relatively weak mobilization during the 1990s.[24] Most significantly, the Thai government and armed forces regional command adopted a more open approach to listening to local grievances and created a new mechanism for channelling targeted development funding.

The concessions were very small but, given how repressive Thai policies had been in the past, they were a sign of change that could possibly benefit the local population. In the early 1980s, General Harn Linanond organized the *tai rom yen* (peaceful south) campaign, urging all southerners to participate in the elimination of communist and Muslim guerrillas. He was largely credited for successfully implementing an amnesty program and restoring some stability to the south of Thailand.[25] In 1982–83, 450 guerrillas surrendered themselves to the Thai army.[26] By 1984, one of the factions of the BRN, the BRN *Ulama*, called for the whole movement to stop fighting and dedicate themselves to finding a peaceful solution.[27] The change in approach from the armed forces certainly contributed to defusing some of the insurgency, in the hopes that the semi-democratic, more open regime, would work toward addressing the Malay-Muslims' long-standing grievances.

As part of this new strategy, the government created the SBPAC in 1981. The main purpose of SBPAC was to provide a communication channel between the southern provinces and an advisory body in Bangkok, while also educating the Thai population about the culture of Malay Muslims.[28]

Under the leadership of SBPAC, at that time, the assimilation policies were flexible because the leaders of SBPAC . . . realized that the assimilation policies or the Thai-ness policy didn't work. Couldn't win the hearts and minds of the local people. So they became more flexible in some policies and spent more money on the development of the local schools, the *pondok* schools, things like that and try to buy the hearts and minds of the local Malay Muslim leaders in the process. And to a certain extent it was a successful policy.[29]

When problems arose between the local population and government officials, they often appealed to the SBPAC, which usually resolved the issues. Furthermore, the leadership of SBPAC, through the National Security Council,

---

[24] Liow came to a similar conclusion by noting that the creation of SBPAC and greater Malay-Muslim representation as a result of democratization "contributed in no small measure to a rolling-back of the expansion of separatist ideology that was so prominent up until the 1970s." See Joseph Chinyong Liow, "The Security Situation in Southern Thailand: Toward an Understanding of Domestic and International Dimensions," *Studies in Conflict and Terrorism* 27, no. 6 (2004): 535.

[25] Rodney Tasker, "A More Peaceful South," *Far Eastern Economic Review* 126 (1984).

[26] Michel Gilquin, *Les Musulmans de Thailande* (Paris: L'Harmattan, 2002).

[27] A new group, the Barisan Bersatu Mujahiddin Pattani (United Mujahaddin Front of Pattani) tried to relaunch the conflict with little success. Ibid.

[28] Liow, "The Security Situation in Southern Thailand," 535.

[29] Srisompob, Professor, Prince of Songkla University and Director, Deep South Watch, interview by author, January 30, 2009, Pattani.

had close access to the Privy Council and to General Prem.[30] SBPAC officials took a proactive role in communicating directly with the commander of the fourth army and the prime minister, who would in turn direct ministries and provincial officials of the changes in approach and policy. SBPAC would further provide assistance to these officials to understand the new policies that the central government was implementing in the region. These were significant changes.[31]

SBPAC also played a role in the coordination of new initiatives to develop the region socio-economically. It was "the front office of the government in the South" and functioned as a de facto governmental administrative unit, as other formal governmental structures were basically inoperative because of the security threat. In education, it supported projects designed to reform some of the local *pondok* schools by having them teach more of the secular curriculum alongside their own, as well as intensify the teaching of the Thai language. It both allowed the *pondok* schools as well as *Tadika* (pre-schools) to operate but also supported them financially as long as they followed educational reforms.[32] General Prem, himself originally from the South, took special interest in its development and supported special infrastructural projects, such as a four-lane highway.[33] Furthermore, SBPAC and its officials gained greater respect from the local population by being more attentive to local customs, religion, and way of life.[34]

There were however significant limitations in terms of the government's willingness to accommodate Malay Muslims, even on relatively small issues. A prime example is its response to the *hijab* movement of the 1980s. As in other parts of Southeast Asia and the Islamic world, growing Islamic consciousness and changing aspects of religious practice led to a broad-based movement of women to wear the *hijab*.[35] In southern Thailand, the movement culminated in the "Yala Teacher Training College Incident." Students confronted the college administration over its refusal to allow them to wear the *hijab*. The confrontation reached a high point when, in February–March 1988, 10,000 people demonstrated against the ban at Yala's central mosque. While the college yielded under pressure, it took

---

[30] High-Level Official, National Security Council, 1980s and 1990s, interview by author, January 26, 2009, Bangkok.

[31] Piya Kitthaworn, Professor, Prince of Songkla University, interview by author, January 29, 2009, Pattani.

[32] High-Level Official, National Security Council, interview.   [33] Ibid.

[34] High-Level Official, Government Affairs Coordination Division, Provincial Affairs Bureau (Ministry of Interior), interview by author, February 2, 2009, Bangkok.

[35] For more detail about veiling in Thailand during this time, see Chaiwat Satha-Anand, "Hijab and Moments of Legitimation: Islamic Resurgence in Thai Society," in *Asian Visions of Authority: Religion and the Modern States of East and Southeast Asia*, eds. Charles F Keyes, Laurel Kendall, and Helen Hardacre (Honolulu: University of Hawaii Press, 1994).

several more years, until 1997, before the government changed its policies and allowed the *hijab*.[36]

The period of transition to an electoral democracy, from 1988 to 1995, was characterized first by continued accommodation of Malay Muslims. Nevertheless, there were some small violent incidents that indicated continued dissatisfaction with the Thai state's policies, at least among a segment of Malay Muslims.

The SBPAC continued its previous policies and role in large part because it was somewhat independent from elected governments, under the King's sponsorship. During this period, funds for Muslim religious education increased and the government began to provide assistance to attend the Haj. The government also ran a pilot program for the teaching of Malay in secondary schools.[37]

The most important impact of the transitional period to democracy was the increase in Malay-Muslim representation both in parliament and in cabinet. The *wadah* group, a political faction of Malay-Muslim politicians, joined coalitions that could secure more benefits for their constituency and, as a result, successfully wielded more influence than at any point in the past. They shifted their loyalty to the political party that could best secure their interests.

Wadah was the creation of Den Tohmena, who in 1986 proposed the alliance between Malay-Muslim representatives. Tohmena was the son of a famous Islamic teacher in Pattani, and became the most influential Malay-Muslim politician from the 1970s onwards. He created a network of support around local imams and religious teachers that was effective first at securing electoral victories in bids for parliamentary seats and, after 1997, at securing control over the newly created Pattani Islamic Council.

From 1986 to 2001, the *wadah* group managed to secure six parliamentary seats in each election, and some of their members gained cabinet seats. The 1986 election was a mixed success. The *wadah* group joined the Democrat party, and used Islamic rhetoric to secure seats in the three provinces of Pattani, Yala, and Narathiwat, where Malay Muslims were a majority. Yet, in spite of their demands for a ministerial position, they failed to obtain one. According to McCargo, it is likely that security agencies had vetoed the promise made to Den Tohmena that he would obtain a position as deputy minister. As a result, the *wadah* group

---

[36] Preeda Prapertchob, "Islam and Civil Society in Thailand: The Role of NGOs," in *Islam and Civil Society in Southeast Asia*, eds. Mitsuo Nakamura, Siddique Sharon, and Omar Farouk Bajunid (Singapore: Institute of Southeast Asian Studies, 2001), 109.

[37] Gordon Fairclough, "Hidden Hands: Politicians and Army Blamed for Bombings in the South," *Far Eastern Economic Review*, June 9, 1994; Rodney Tasker, "Southern Discomfort: Muslim Separatist Violence Raises Its Head Again," *Far Eastern Economic Review*, 1993.

dropped their support for Democrats and, from then on, never again allied with the party.[38]

Instead, the group allied itself with the New Aspiration Party (NAP) of former general Chavalit Yongchaiyudh. The alliance proved to be a winning strategy. In the cabinet of Chatichai Choonhavan, from 1988 to 1991, Den Tohmena gained a cabinet seat as deputy health minister in a coalition that included the NAP. After the resumption of democratic governance that followed the 1991 coup, Tohmena again gained a cabinet position, as deputy interior minister. The NAP had secured cabinet representation in a coalition with the Democrats. In 1994, Wan Nor, another Malay-Muslim MP who became leader of the *wadah* group, succeeded him as deputy interior minister, as Den and Wan had previously agreed.[39]

As a result of the power they wielded, the *wadah* group managed to broker some concessions. For example, by 1993, religious freedom was stronger, and women and schoolgirls could wear Islamic veils more freely than before.[40] Funds for Muslim religious education increased and the government provided new assistance to attend the Haj. Finally, the government also introduced a pilot program for teaching Malay in secondary schools.[41]

Although the *wadah* group by no means held substantial leverage with any coalition government, they nevertheless delivered a few solid seats in the Deep South, and provided some additional parliamentary support for often fragile coalition governments. In this respect, their ability to form a block and make targeted demands to address Malay-Muslim grievances, at least enabled some modest relaxation of previous neglect and repressive policies.

Violence nevertheless rose during the early 1990s. While low in intensity, the occasional incidents were more frequent than during the semi-authoritarian period of the 1980s. In August 1993, thirty-four schools were burned down, and Muslim guerrillas ambushed a train in Narathiwat and a detachment of Thai army engineers in Yala province.[42] Over the following months, there were more than thirty cases of arson, shooting, and bombings in Southern provinces. No organization claimed responsibility, but speculation ran high of PULO's revival or conspiracy theories that disgruntled military officers might be fomenting instability.[43] It would become clearer later that underground Malay-Muslim groups were using sporadic attacks and anonymity given their weakness in the face of the well-organized Thai armed forces.

---

[38] Duncan McCargo, *Tearing Apart the Land: Islam and Legitimacy in Southern Thailand* (Ithaca, NY: Cornell University Press, 2008), 63–69.

[39] Ibid., 70–75.

[40] Rodney Tasker and Michael Vatikiotis, "Troubled Frontier: Thai Muslim Violence Concerns Malaysia as Well," *Far Eastern Economic Review*, September 16, 1993.

[41] Fairclough, "Hidden Hands."   [42] Tasker, "Southern Discomfort."

[43] Fairclough, "Hidden Hands"; Tasker, "Southern Discomfort."

In the first period of democratic transition after the failed coup of 1991, therefore, we see two somewhat contradictory trends. First, it appeared that Malay Muslims obtained greater accommodation partly in response to the *wadah* group's ability to make gains in exchange for parliamentary support. But in relation to the more long-standing demands of previous insurgent groups for recognition and secession, the small concessions were likely perceived, at least by some Malay Muslims, as too little. The Thai state made no clear commitments toward the Malay Muslims and the *wadah* group itself showed some frustration with the Democrats, as shown by their later support for the NAP. Second, therefore, that violence rose at the same time as a strategic attempt to use democratic institutions for further gain is not surprising. There was little organized movement among Malay Muslims and, instead, splinter groups and members of the religious elite deployed a variety of strategies in the hopes that the more open and changing institutional context might secure some gains.

Democratic Stabilization? Downward Spiral into Violence

It is difficult to assess the Thai case in terms of the evolution of its democratic period. With hindsight, many Thai scholars would argue that there never really was a democratic period.[44] Nevertheless, it could also be argued that, as Thailand entered a period of greater democratic stability it could have persisted, given that new and better institutions were in place.

I begin the period of relative stabilization of democracy in 1995, with the change of government led by the Chart Thai party. By one argument, it was a changeover of power from the more established Democrats to an opposition that represented the rise of new, rural-based politicians allied with provincial business elites. It therefore fulfilled the requirement that I set out for the end of a transition, whereby a changeover of power to the opposition occurs. At the same time, there are strong limitations to this characterization. As pointed out by several scholars, it was precisely the frequent changeover of coalitions that created instability, and that was one of the reasons for changes introduced in the 1997 Constitution that ensured greater party consolidation. It was certainly hardly stable in that respect, given the Banharn Silpa-Archa led government lasted barely one year, followed by a coalition led by Chavalit Yongchaiyudh of the NAP, again lasting only one year and falling under pressure from the 1997 Asian Financial Crisis. I am less concerned, however, with the stability of coalition governments than of the democracy itself, which was nevertheless resilient in spite of the very significant stress of the 1997 crisis. As Case noted,

---

[44] Connors, *Democracy and National Identity in Thailand*; Duncan McCargo, "Network Monarchy and Legitimacy Crises in Thailand," *The Pacific Review* 18, no. 4 (2005).

1997 "was a good test of democratic resilience" as it offered a significant juncture when military intervention could well have occurred.[45]

The constitution of 1997 helped to confirm a more stable democratic period. It was the first one that arose out of an inclusive process. Its main features addressed endemic problems of vote-buying and money-politics that eroded the credibility of electoral democracy. The constitutional committee succeeded in making constitutional reform a public issue that gained media attention and widespread support. Parliament passed the new constitution at a time when the government of Chavalit Yongchaiyudh collapsed as a result of the 1997 Asian Financial Crisis.[46]

The constitution led to more stable governments. The Democrats finished their mandate without the instability that had characterized the late 1980s and early 1990s. The 2001 election produced a majority government and clear turnover of power from the Democrats to the newly created Thai Rak Thai of Thaksin Shinawatra. Although there were some reports of vote-buying and money-politics, the process mandated by the 1997 constitution was followed and violations investigated. Finally, it appeared that the armed forces had finally accepted to stay away from politics. In spite of writing about "democracy under stress," McCargo sums up:

There could be no simple reversion to the top-down rhetoric of earlier times. Politicians and bureaucrats alike are now always on the defensive, aware that their wrongdoings can be exposed to public scrutiny. The 1997 reforms handed some of the most salutary and forward-looking people and organizations in Thailand an opportunity to forge a new rights-based political consciousness. It is now clear that 1997 was not a single decisive moment in Thailand's political history; rather, it was an important juncture for a continuing and highly contested process of change.[47]

More stable democratic institutions ironically produced fewer state concessions toward Malay Muslims and contributed, instead, to an escalation of violence. The sequence is not entirely clear. Bombings and sporadic attacks had already occurred prior to 1997, and so one can argue that subsequent repressive approaches were a response, given the unidentified opponent and the armed forces' perception of a growing underground movement. Yet, at the same time, the few concessions that were made to Malay Muslims were withdrawn and the government subsequently increased its repression.

During the Democrats' mandate from 1997 to 2001, the main change was the creation of the Tambon Administrative Organizations (TAO). The TAOs were a very limited form of decentralized governance across Thailand, without the

---

[45] Case, "Thai Democracy 2001," 531.

[46] It is possible that the King, operating through his proxy General Prem Tinsulanonda, played a role in the removal of Chavalit's government and the subsequent palace support for the Democrats (see McCargo, "Network Monarcy and Legitimacy Crises in Thailand")

[47] McCargo, "Democracy under Stress in Thaksin's Thailand," 125.

scale or autonomy vested in similar initiatives in the Philippines and Indonesia. Essentially local level administrations, the TAOs had very limited taxation powers and were subsumed under provincial government authority. Nevertheless, almost all of the TAO's leading officials were Malay Muslims in the Deep South and elected, which represented a gain in the south where many of the provincial governors or district officials were appointed by Bangkok, and oftentimes Buddhist.[48]

The *wadah* group maintained representatives throughout the period and participated in the coalition government that the Democrats led. Wan Nor, who became the group's leader in 1995, was appointed as communications minister and then house speaker.[49] Nevertheless, it would become clearer that such gains were advantageous mainly to the politicians involved, with few visible benefits accruing to the community.

The election of Thai Rak Thai and Thaksin Shinawatra's government dramatically shifted the relationship between the Thai state and Malay Muslims. Attacks against government targets increased, and the central government, in turn, intensified its repressive approach rather than increasing accommodation for Malay Muslims.

Soon after gaining power, Thaksin abolished two key institutions. Partly in an attempt to break the previous alliance the Democrats held with the "south," as well as the direct influence of the Privy Council, Thaksin eliminated the SBPAC in May 2002. SBPAC had continued since the 1980s to represent the most positive state presence in the region. It maintained its reputation of reducing conflict between the local community and state officials. It implemented a variety of projects such as help for fish production, infrastructure, or scholarships for education. The funds bypassed the bureaucracy and were provided directly to village accounts.[50] Thaksin also dissolved the CPM-43, which had previously coordinated activities between the military and the police, and gave instead to the police the responsibility of providing security in the south. CPM-43 had maintained good relations between the two security branches, often in competition with one another, particularly in the Deep South where a number of side-businesses flourished.

Violence dramatically escalated in the following years. Attacks against police and other government targets had continued but, in 2002, seventeen policemen were gunned down. There was some speculation that disgruntled

---

[48] McCargo, *Tearing Apart the Land*, 80–83.; Boonarong, Deputy Mayor, Municipality of Narathiwat District, interview by author, January 27, 2009, Narathiwat.

[49] McCargo, *Tearing Apart the Land*, 76.

[50] Anonymous, Coordination Manager, Bureau of Education, Culture and Religion, SBPAC, interview by author, January 28, 2009.

military officers might have targeted police as retribution for their reduced control over the region.[51] The escalation after 2004, however, clearly pointed to militias that remained somewhat anonymous. In January 2004, Thaksin's government declared martial law after a spectacular, coordinated attack on twenty schools and an assault on an army camp, where militias managed to steal 300 weapons.[52] More than 240 hit-and-run assaults against government officials and security personnel marked a new threshold in violent attacks, leading to a large number of Bangkok-based bureaucrats, judges, and teachers to flee.[53] In response, the security forces became increasingly careless in their approach. On April 28, 107 Islamic militants and 5 members of security forces were killed in clashes in three southern provinces when youths attacked police and army posts. In a subsequent raid, security forces stormed the Kru-ze mosque and killed thirty-two suspected militants.[54] Later in the same year, on October 24, soldiers dissolved a peaceful protest of more than 3,000 people and arrested 1,300. They piled up prisoners in the back of trucks, which led to seventy-nine people dying of suffocation. These incidents came to symbolize the strong repressive approach under Thaksin and marked a new level as well of Malay-Muslim mistrust.[55]

Thaksin's government dismissed local grievances and dubbed the perpetrators as "bandits," while sending more troops to secure the area. In the next few years, as Srisompob's Deep Watch South reports showed, there were 7,708 incidents between 2004 and 2007, and 4,100 deaths between 2004 and 2010.[56]

There are several explanations for the increase in violence. One view emphasizes Thaksin's sudden decision to abolish the SBPAC and the CPM-43. By doing so, he reduced the army's role while strengthening the police's control over the region's security.[57] As McCargo[58] argued, Thaksin's elimination of the SBPAC, associated with the Privy Council and the army, was part of a broader strategy of loosening the palace's and the Democrats' stronghold

[51] Shawn W. Crispin, "Spotlight: Thai Power Play," *Far Eastern Economic Review* 165, no. 29 (2002).

[52] "Love Vs. War," *Far Eastern Economic Review* 167, no. 20 (2004).

[53] "Gearing up for a Fight," *Far Eastern Economic Review* 167, no. 19 (2004); Sermsuk Kasitpradit and Wassana Nanuam, "Kitti: Separatists, Not Bandits," *Bangkok Post*, Thursday, January 8, 2004.

[54] Crispin, "Gearing up for a Fight."

[55] NRC Thailand, *Overcoming Violence through the Power of Reconciliation* (Bangkok: National Reconciliation Commission, 2006), 47.

[56] Srisompob Jitpiromsri and Duncan McCargo, "The Southern Thai Conflict Six Years On: Insurgency, Not Just Crime," *Contemporary Southeast Asia* 32, no. 2 (2010).

[57] Local interviews confirmed that he was advised that only a handful of people were behind the violence (between 50 and 100) and therefore could easily be controlled by the police. Srisompob, interview.

[58] McCargo, "Network Monarchy and Legitimacy Crises in Thailand."

over the south of Thailand.[59] From this view, the escalation in 2002, and particularly 2004, was partly a by-product of the competition for control between the army and the police.[60]

Another explanation focuses on militias' strategy. PULO and the BRN almost completely disappeared in the 1990s. Furthermore, the resources and community relations role of SBPAC had contributed to reducing support for violent action against the state. But according to Liow, there was a coordinated understanding between both organizations to reduce activities during the 1990s, consolidate and rebuild themselves, while planning to resume violent activities organized around small cells of insurgents after 2000. While the spiraling of violence after the Kru-ze and Tak Bai massacres created greater anger among supporters and fuelled even more attacks than anticipated, nevertheless the underlying strategy was to re-emerge in the 2000s.[61] The timing roughly corresponds with this view. While in its early days, the attacks went unclaimed and were difficult to associate with any particular group, the sustained violent attacks over the following decade or so became identified with the BRN-C (BRN-coordinate),[62] or some other constellation of organizations with the BRN playing a central role, for instance, in later peace negotiations with the Thai state.[63]

But the underlying grievances continue to fuel support for resistance. Thaksin's elimination of earlier accommodations and increased repression certainly intensified this resentment. Malay Muslims felt marginalized and mistreated by Thai government officials. An Asia Foundation survey in 2010 found that Muslims perceived "a failure of the government to understand the local population" as the main cause of conflict (37 per cent), with separatism much less so (17 per cent). Furthermore, 65 per cent considered that ethnic differences between Patani-Malay and Thai are equally more important in the conflict than differences between Muslims and Buddhists, with only

---

[59] McCargo goes further and argues that this was one of several steps to reduce the power of "network monarchy," which he argues was a long-standing pattern, both under authoritarian and democratic regimes, of the King, through the Privy Council, the Democrats and the army to maintain the status quo and its dominance over politics. See also Aurel Croissant, "Unrest in South Thailand: Contours, Causes, and Consequences since 2001," *Contemporary Southeast Asia* 27, no. 1 (2005).

[60] McCargo, *Tearing Apart the Land*, 116.

[61] Joseph Chinyong Liow, *Muslim Resistance in Southern Thailand and Southern Philippines: Religion, Ideology, and Politics, Policy Studies* (Washington, DC: East-West Center, 2006), 35.

[62] There were disagreements regarding the degree of actual coordination and organization, with McCargo estimating that it was more of a loose network rather than a well-coordinated new organization. See McCargo, *Tearing Apart the Land*, 134–81.

[63] Srisompob Jitpiromsri, "An Inconvenient Truth About the Deep South Violent Conflict: A Decade of Chaotic, Constrained Realities and Uncertain Resolution," Deep South Watch, https://deepsouthwatch.org/en/node/5904.

9 per cent and 10 per cent, respectively arguing that one is more important than the other.[64]

The policy of Thai assimilation is decades long, and the liberalization and democratization of Thailand did not reduce the state's strong commitment to this approach. "The local people have resisted the central government for 70 years .... The most important problem is that the government doesn't accept the uniqueness of their identity."[65] According to a former Deputy of the National Security Council of Thailand, the degree of misunderstanding and failure to accept differences runs deep:

> The problem in the South has two layers. The first basic layer is the problem of poverty/ participation/justice of people/low standard of living/education/health. This kind of problem happens in all parts of Thailand, but the South is more sensitive. It is because people in the South have difference in religion causing them to feel that they are second – class people and don't receive attention. The government officials don't know or understand how people feel. People cannot tell the truth or address this feeling, for if they do so, they would be blamed as being disloyal to the country or separatist ... The second deeper layer of the problem is that people would like to protect/ maintain their identity of Patani Malayu Muslim. This feeling is shared by most people in the South.[66]

After 2004, a fragile relationship was ruptured between SBPAC and the local community. SBPAC lost its ability to smoothen relations and reduce misunderstanding. Under Thaksin, instead, the Internal Security Operations Command (ISOC) led soldiers with very little attention to local sensitivities. As a local leader noted: "The military didn't understand and couldn't access the people. At that time hundreds of local people were kidnapped and killed. Lawyer Somchai was also disappeared. During Thaksin, the government didn't use a democratic approach and didn't consult anything with religious leaders. It gave authority to the officials to manage everything here."[67]

Another important source of grievance was the government's approach to education. Traditionally, many Malay Muslims were educated in small religious schools, *pondok*, which were less expensive, managed by the local community, and where education was in Malay. They failed, however, to provide a broad education that prepared pupils for higher education or skilled employment. Conversely, while the public schools offered broader and better-quality education, many Malay Muslims shunned them because the curriculum was conducted entirely in Thai, with no mention of local traditions and customs. With the increase in violence, many teachers were killed or fled,

[64] James Klein, *Democracy and Conflict in Southern Thailand: A Survey of the Thai Electorate in Yala, Narathiwat, and Pattani* (Washington, DC: The Asia Foundation, 2010), 97–99.
[65] Boonarong, interview.   [66] High-Level Official, National Security Council, interview.
[67] Waeduerame Mamingchi, President of Pattani Provincial Islamic Council, interview by author, January 31, 2009, Pattani.

which led to even more families sending their children to *pondok* instead of public schools.[68] Before the election of Thai Rak Thai in 2001, the government had begun to provide funding to some *pondok* schools, with the condition that they would introduce the Thai curriculum. But the quality remained quite poor, with difficulties recruiting Malay Muslims that could teach science, math, and other basic skills.[69] Also, the Ministry of Interior had provided scholarships to attend Thammasat and Chulalongkorn University in Bangkok, but students needed to pass the competitive entrance exams, which generally required mastering the Thai curriculum mostly taught in good public schools. While these measures were partly a government strategy to assimilate them to Thai values, they had provided Malay Muslims with access to higher education that became compromised as the violence rose.[70]

Malay Muslims also resented the lesser status of Islam. Even though the Thai constitution recognized the right of religious practice, it did not treat all religions equally. The government supported Buddhist temples and even provided some funding to Buddhist religious leaders. But there was no support for the building of mosques and very low financial support for local religious leaders.[71]

Meanwhile, employment opportunities in government were low. Higher-level positions even in districts mostly went to Thais from other provinces, whereas local Malay Muslims would only be employed in lower-level ones. The problem was compounded by the low numbers of Malay Muslims who attended Thai public schools, and the poor quality even of religious schools that taught more secular disciplines.[72] There were some noticeable increases of Malay-Muslim personnel such as front-line nurses, teachers (who often replaced Thai teachers who fled), and more employees in the local bureaucracies, when the violence rose, but several of these were temporary jobs. The police and military did not increase the number of Malay Muslims.[73]

Against this backdrop of grievances, Malay-Muslim representation in government lost much of its legitimacy and effectiveness. When the NAP joined Thai Rak Thai for the 2001 election, the *wadah* group also followed. As in the past, they capitalized on the opportunity to gain some influence by joining the governing party or coalition. It was particularly damaging to the group, however, that Wan Nor was Interior Minister during the worst of the government's repressive approach in 2004. Whether he contributed to the decision over the

[68] Boonarong, interview; Alisa Hasamoh, Member National Reconciliation Commission and Prince of Songkla University Lecturer, interview by author, January 28, 2009, Pattani; Prae Sirisakdhamkeng, Professor, Silapakorn University, interview by author, February 2, 2009.

[69] Angkana Neelaphaijit, Human Rights Activist, interview by author, January 25, 2009, Bangkok.

[70] Ibid.   [71] Boonarong, interview.   [72] Ibid.

[73] Srisompob, interview; Prae Sirisakdhamkeng, interview; High-Level Official, National Security Council, interview.

crackdown was unclear, but his role reduced the credibility of the group's representative status in the Deep South.[74] Furthermore, members of the group appeared to be much more benefiting personally from their role in government rather than gaining more resources or benefits for Malay Muslims.[75] As a result, the group lost much of its support among Malay Muslims and most lost their seats.[76]

They lost their status in the Muslim community because people think that the leaders ... failed to act as representatives of their own communities. Because the Wadah group and local politicians fail in terms of morality. Some of them became richer. After you pray, after you get into politics you get richer and richer and you ignore the demands of the local Malay Muslims. You are too obsessive with national politics or personal interests, and so on. They think that these people failed in terms of morality, responsibility.[77]

Thaksin stepped back from his initial assessment of the source problems in the Deep South, but he still failed to address the main sources of grievance. In the aftermath of the armed forces' debacle in the Kru-ze and Tak Bai incidents, he formed the National Reconciliation Commission (NRC) to investigate problems in the Deep South and how to address them. He appointed as its head Anand Panyarachun, a highly respected senior bureaucrat who had overseen a return to democratic rule in 1991–1992.

The establishment of the NRC was an attempt to appease the growing uproar over the escalating violence but its mandate was limited. Anand, for instance, was told that proposing autonomy was "off limits."[78] Nevertheless, the NRC's report flagged the state's structural discrimination against Malay Muslims, and the lack of cultural understanding and respect: " ... they have been perceived as outsiders, marginalized or turned into second-class citizens living in a state bent on the destruction of their language and cultural traditions."[79] They denounced excessive use of repression, lack of access to education, and a restrictive Thai state in which "cultural diversity is viewed by some as a threat to the state and national security instead of a force of strength in Thai society."[80] The report also recognized the existence of a new generation of militants but insisted that its main source of success was popular support because of the local population's perception of injustice. It recommended engaging in dialogue with militants and encouraging officials to increase their understanding of the local socio-cultural context. It also urged the state

---

[74] Chaiwat Satha-Anan, Professor, Thammasat University, interview (informal conversation) with author, January 25, 2009; Piya Kitthaworn, interview.

[75] High-Level Official, National Security Council, interview.

[76] Representative Prasert Phongsuwansiri, Member of Parliament, Yala Province, interview by author, February 4, 2009, Bangkok.

[77] Srisompob, interview.   [78] Chaiwat Satha-Anan, interview.

[79] NRC Thailand, "Overcoming Violence through the Power of Reconciliation," 11.

[80] Ibid., 13.

to adopt reforms in order to strengthen traditional livelihoods and employment opportunities, increase access to justice, maintain diversity in the education system, modify rules on Islamic law and organizations, and promote cultural diversity more broadly.[81] In the end, the recommendations were neither sufficiently bold (such as autonomy) nor sufficiently conservative to be followed, and its impact simply faded.[82]

The democratic period essentially ended in 2006, with a military coup against Thaksin Shinawatra's government. After months of street protests, General Sonthi removed Thaksin from power and installed a temporary military-led government under Prime Minister Surayud Chulanont.

Violent conflict diminished after 2006 but primarily because of a dramatic increase in military repression. The Surayud government apologized to the local people but soldiers used full violence. For instance, it initiated the policy of mass arrests, even reaching sixty to seventy people at times.[83] It forced people to sign a document agreeing to join a "career training" program in military camps. Soldiers offered people 100 baht per day if they chose to join, but the alternative was to be sent to jail, as a local NGO reported.[84] With signatures, the soldiers could not be accused of forcing people to attend what was essentially a re-education effort.

Many of the few Malay-Muslim leaders who participated in the government considered that government policies essentially remained the same, with little understanding of local grievances. As a Senator from the Deep South explained:

There has been no progress [in the situation], clearly only the same thing over and over again. The same issues, same factors, same violence, same misfortunes that happen to local people. No progress, only a little during Surayud, but the armed forces continued their actions: they cannot, don't want, and don't listen ... there is a large budget, but there are no clear results from this budget. The army controls everything.[85]

The democratic period, which essentially ended in 2006, was characterized by a rise of violent mobilization in the Deep South, and a narrowing of concessions to Malay-Muslim groups. The state increased repression under Thaksin, while groups in Pattani remained largely underground. The sporadic violence was mostly anonymous, and showed the weakness of Malay-Muslim organizations.

[81] Ibid.
[82] Duncan McCargo, *Rethinking Thailand's Southern Violence* (Singapore: NUS Press, 2006), 171–72.
[83] Naree Charoenpapiriya, NGO Worker, Peace Witnessing Project, Mahidol University Nakhon Pathom, Thailand, interview by author, January 31, 2009; Chaiwat Satha-Anan, interview.
[84] Naree Charoenpapiriya, interview; Alisa Hasamoh, interview.
[85] Senator Worawit Baru, interview by author, February 4, 2009, Bangkok.

End of Democracy and Persistent Conflict

More than a decade after the end of democratic rule, the conflict in the Deep South remained largely unchanged, but there were signs that the state was willing to discuss potential compromises. Malay-Muslim organizations from across the border in Malaysia responded to openings for negotiation. But in the absence of a democratic framework, and with little influence over the direction of constitutional or political changes, Malay Muslims were limited in their ability to obtain significant gains. Meanwhile, with a state security structure firmly in place, its repressive capacity continued to ensure no widespread mobilization in the Deep South.

Fragile democratic politics returned from 2008 to 2014, but few changes were made. In the brief return of the Democrats to power from 2008 to 2010, Prime Minister Abhisit sponsored two bills to stabilize the conflict in the South. For the most part, these bills consolidated the informal structures already in place and mainly gave more legal leverage for the repressive structures, while reinstating state-sponsored development to appease some of the grievances. The Internal Security Act restored broad authority to ISOC, which had exercised similar powers in the past and placed the Deep South squarely under military command. The law also regularized the restrictions on freedom of movement, as well as the use of the "training camps."[86] It was followed by the Southern Border Provinces Administration Act on December 30, 2010, which was designed to restructure the SBPAC and restore the coordinating and development role that it played up until Thaksin abolished it. The 2010 Act was designed to restore some of the SBPAC's ability to deploy resources for development, which was absent after it was revived in 2006. These laws, however, were added to the already legalized state of emergency in the Deep South, which was reinforced with the State of Emergency decree of 2005.[87]

Yingluck Shinawatra's government, from 2011 to 2014, also failed to change its approach to the South. Largely considered a return of Thaksin's government by proxy, its policies changed little from Thaksin's period, despite the Pheu Thai party's promises made during the election to improve the situation of the Deep South. Remembering the repressive policies of Thaksin's government, the provinces of Pattani, Yala, Narathiwat, and Songkla voted against Pheu Thai in the 2011 elections. Wracked by instability, Yingluck's government placed very little emphasis on the Deep South.[88]

Meanwhile, sporadic attacks continued, with few indications of the movement's leadership. The attacks became bolder, with car and motorcycle bombs

---

[86] "National Security Laws: Key Implications for Thailand," *Bangkok Post*, October 24, 2010.
[87] Ibid.
[88] International Crisis Group, *Thailand: The Evolving Conflict in the South*, Asia Report n. 241 (2012), 1–2.

becoming more frequent, with greater lethal power. Most of these continued to target Thai security officials and symbols of the state. Small groups of insurgents also launched attacks, oftentimes to secure more weapons.[89]

The only significant change was a weak attempt to negotiate with exiled Malay-Muslim insurgent groups. Thawee Sodsong, head of the SBPAC had first attempted secret negotiations in 2012 without success.[90] In February 2013, the government signed an agreement for formal peace talks in Kuala Lumpur. This was an unprecedented breakthrough but nevertheless produced few results. For the most part, insurgent groups issued a number of preconditions for joining the talks, yet they were both unrealistic and actually not enforced as they proceeded in spite of the preconditions not being met. The most significant obstacle remained the lack of clear interlocutors on the Malay-Muslim side. The negotiations proceeded mainly with the BRN-C, which the government considered to be the largest organization, but ignored a number of other long-standing groups, including PULO. Furthermore, it remained unclear to what extent BRN-C directed or even associated with the militants in the Deep South who were responsible for violent acts.[91] While both appeared publicly committed to reducing the violence, there were few changes on the ground. The Ramadan Peace Initiative, to which both sides agreed, initially reduced violence in the first week of Ramadan (July–August 2013), but by the end of the month, new attacks had resumed. It was unclear, again, whether the BRN had withdrawn from the initiative or whether other groups initiated violent attacks to undermine the negotiations.[92]

The coup of 2014 once again returned Thailand to military rule, and policies toward Malay Muslims remained the same. For the most part, the military government ignored the South, while maintaining troop levels, the SBPAC and similar repressive policies as in the past.[93]

Yet, it initiated a new round of negotiations. Malay-Muslim groups joined the talks with a renewed sense of unity. They formed the *Majilis Syura Patani* (Patani Consultative Council, MARA Patani) in March 2015 to serve as an umbrella organization for negotiations. It regrouped many of the organizations

---

[89] For details of these attacks in 2012 alone, see ibid.

[90] Thaksin Shinawatra also attempted to spearhead negotiations ("Thailand: Peace Talks with Southern Insurgents Go Nowhere," *Thai News Service*, December 5, 2012. Prior secret talks between the National Security Council and members of PULO and BRN-C also occurred without much success ("Disunity Puts Southern Peace Process on Its Last Legs," *The Nation*, October 22, 2011; "Thailand Agrees to Historic Peace Talks with Muslim Rebels," *Global Insight*, February 28, 2013.

[91] "Thailand Agrees to Historic Peace Talks with Muslim Rebels."; "Thailand: Source Reveals Conditions of Insurgent Groups at Peace Talks," *Thai News Service*, March 28, 2013.

[92] International Crisis Group, *Southern Thailand: Dialogue in Doubt* (Brussels: International Crisis Group, 2015), 1–6.

[93] Ibid., 11–12.

that had been left behind in the previous negotiations.[94] After a few secret exploratory meetings, both sides met in September 2017 for a "technical meeting" to talk about the narrow objective of a ceasefire and the establishment of a "safety zone." Discussions continued on the safety zone throughout 2018.[95]

The Thai state's uncompromising position, throughout the democratic and authoritarian period, has left few avenues for a resolution of the conflict with Malay Muslims. Repression has occurred across regime types, with the deployment of troops and even the reduction in welfare provisions under Thaksin's government. Although repression has possibly prevented a large-scale insurgency from emerging, it has nevertheless continued to fuel much of the violent attacks that have occurred since 2004. The violence has been sustained and, in some periods, intensified both in terms of geographic location of these attacks – with a few occurring in Bangkok – and also in terms of their boldness and lethal capacity, with the deployment of vehicle bombs and small insurgent attacks. The conflict has been stalled, with sustained low-level violence producing a cumulatively large number of casualties since 2004.

The mobilization of Malay Muslims has been sustained, but with little ability to pressure the government into compromise. The violence remained mostly sporadic, varying in intensity, but not systematic. Perpetrators remained anonymous, rather than linked to a particular organization. In later years, it appeared that the Thai state's contention that BRN-C was behind the violence seemed more credible, as violence appeared to diminish after small negotiated agreements in 2013. Regardless, the movement remained highly fragmented and weak, with no clear line of authority to members on the ground in the Deep South.

Prior structural conditions, therefore, supersede the impact of the institutional change from authoritarian to democratic rule. Mobilizational capacity was generally too weak to change the state's policies in the Deep South. The Thai state, on the other hand, has remained strongly imbued with the sense of one, indivisible Thai nation under a highly centralized state. Despite deep divisions in the Thai state, the country's political elite has remained united behind its strong reluctance to recognize Malay-Muslim difference and deeply averse even to decentralization, let alone autonomy or self-governance. Concessions made were mostly to appease through development schemes, and mostly through structures such as SBPAC that fall outside of regular institutional channels.

---

[94] In addition to BRN, these included Barisan Islam, Pembebesan Patani (Islamic Liberation Front of Patani, BIPP), three factions of the Patani United Liberation Organization (PULO), and Gerakan Mujahidin Islam Patani (Patani Islamic Mujahidin Movement, GMIP) (Ibid., 21).

[95] Razlan Rashid and Pimuk Rakkanam, "Thailand, Mara Patani Hold Technical Talks on Deep South Truce," *Benar News*, September 12, 2017.

8 Conclusion

This book began with a relatively simple question, whether democracy tends to increase or reduce nationalist conflict. Such a question raises a host of objections and qualifications that render its answer immensely complex. Democratic regimes are quite varied in their character and quality; a large number of them can even be questioned on the basis of their democratic credentials or objectionable on the basis of measurable criteria.[1] Similarly, there are no objective criteria to identify nations. As constructivist scholars have conclusively defended, nations are self-identified and mostly recognized by their claims and political goals.[2] Finally, conflict takes on a variety of forms; while the literature more recently focused on its violent expression, there are other modes that are also relevant to assess but more challenging to measure.

Nevertheless, it raises an issue that remains highly relevant to our understanding of groups that mobilize for secession, autonomy, or simply recognition of their distinct status. Some of these, such as the Catalans, mobilize with relatively little violence, yet conflict is clear. Large demonstrations contested the democratic Spanish state that, in turn, responded with legal instruments to reject local claims and demands. In other cases, such as the Uyghurs, demands for independence or autonomy, while present and recurrent, are completely stifled. The Chinese government used strong repressive measures, including re-education camps to suppress any such demands. There is a large number of groups that are concentrated on territory they claim as their homeland and that continue to negotiate with a dominant state for their self-determination.

As I have argued, democracy reduces *violence* but does not eliminate endemic nationalist *conflict*. There is a strong gap between reducing violence and regularizing conflict through normal democratic processes. More often than not, nationalist groups might be less repressed, or find fewer incentives to mobilize violently, yet their claims and grievances often fail to be addressed.

---

[1] Arend Lijphart, *Democracies: Patterns of Majoritarian and Consensus Government in Twenty-One Countries* (New Haven, CT: Yale University Press, 1984); Gerardo L. Munck, "What Is Democracy? A Reconceptualization of the Quality of Democracy," *Democratization* 23, no. 1 (2016).

[2] Brubaker, *Nationalism Reframed.*

Democracy matters in large part because it is the only credible regime in which nationalist groups have any chance of finding a negotiated compromise. Where authoritarian regimes succeed in reducing violent conflict, they do so with strong repressive means as in the case of the Chinese regime's repression of the Uyghurs or Tibetans. In cases where territorial autonomy has been granted, it is usually meaningless.[3]

What aspects of democracy reduce violent nationalist conflict? As has been widely debated in the literature, there are numerous pathways that explain why, in some cases, transitions to democracy have been associated with higher levels of nationalist mobilization and violence.[4] While I do not reject such findings, my analysis of Southeast Asian cases offers some qualifications and alternative explanations.

Southeast Asia: From Secessionism to Conflict Resolution?

Southeast Asian cases suggest that nationalist groups face very difficult pathways towards gaining recognition and accommodation, and the outcomes rarely correspond to their political goals. Acehnese, Papuans, Cordillerans, Moros, and Malay Muslims have all been involved in violent conflict against the Indonesian, Philipine, and Thai states, respectively. All of these cases had significant insurgencies during a period of authoritarian rule. Armed nationalist organizations claimed to represent their respective groups and mobilized violently to oppose authoritarian rule and demand self-determination. Democratization changed the institutional parameters of mobilization as well as the state's ability to repress. The groups diverged considerably in their subsequent paths, with some increasing their violent mobilization while others negotiated peace. The ebb and flow of violence has varied significantly, however, and there are no straightforward outcomes.

Almost all the important episodes of violent insurgency occurred when these states were under authoritarian rule. They all share a baseline of violent mobilization against states that repressed, sought to assimilate, or otherwise undermined nationalist demands. Malay Muslims, under PULO and BRN,

---

[3] Donna Bahry, "The New Federalism and the Paradoxes of Regional Sovereignty in Russia," *Comparative Politics* 37, no. 2 (2005); Brian D. Taylor, "Force and Federalism: Controlling Coercion in Federal Hybrid Regimes," *Comparative Politics* 39, no. 4 (2007): 424; Cederman et al., "Territorial Autonomy in the Shadow of Conflict"; Enze Han and Christopher Paik, "Ethnic Integration and Development in China," *World Development* 93 (2017).

[4] As indicated in Chapter 2, Snyder emphasized the role of ruling elites in violent nationalist mobilization during periods of transition. See Snyder, *From Voting to Violence*. For an interesting counter-argument, discussing how ethnic diversity was useful for democratic change, see Beissinger, "A New Look at Ethnicity and Democratization," 91. He noted that mobilization from below in order to challenge the existing ethnic stratification can actually lead to democratic stability.

fought most strongly against the Thai state in the 1970s. GAM was formed during the New Order regime and organized an insurgency in 1976 and 1989, but was twice crushed. Papuans, under the OPM, were less able to organize significant insurgency, but showed strong signs of resistance to the Indonesian state, which undertook military operations to "weed out" secessionists. The Moro National Liberation Front was formed and fought most actively after President Marcos declared martial law. Cordillerans joined the NPA and rose up against the Marcos regime before forming Cordillera-based organizations.

When authoritarian regimes accepted to negotiate or form institutions to accommodate state nationalist groups, they failed to implement them. The Marcos regime appeared most accommodating by signing the 1976 Tripoli agreement with the MNLF, by which it provided autonomy to thirteen provinces and nine cities in Mindanao, but proceeded to never implement it. The Indonesian government's provision of a distinct status for Aceh in 1959 was meaningless, as it claimed to extend certain particular rights to the Acehnese but in fact gave the same powers and resources as every other province. It mostly retained a strong, centralized state, even more so under the New Order regime after 1965. None of the authoritarian regimes managed to eliminate group demands and mobilization, nor did they offer institutional accommodation that significantly altered the power and autonomy of nationalist groups.

Democracy in all these cases contributed to a reduction of violent mobilization but the relationship is not straightforward. While democracy generally makes institutional power and concessions more credible, particularly if constitutionalized, it does not guarantee that commitments made to nationalists will be implemented or even that significant accommodation will be made to meet their demands.

Initially, democratization can lead to higher violence, as Snyder and others have shown. In Southeast Asian cases under study, the transition to democracy offered at least better promise of finding a negotiated solution, yet the initial outcome was quite varied. Violence rose in Aceh, after a large civilian movement failed to obtain significant gains. Violent mobilization in the Cordillera continued strongly in the initial months after Cory Aquino gained power but subsided dramatically once promise was made to include Cordillerans in constitutional negotiations. Papuans lobbied the new democratic government after 1998 and organized demonstrations, while the OPM moved backstage. The MNLF began discussions with the new Aquino government, but then resumed its mobilization once the government appeared to move away from promises made, while the MILF continued violent mobilization as well. Malay Muslims remained mostly silent and violence did not rise in the initial years of Thailand's return to democracy.

Once democracy stabilized, the outcomes also varied considerably. The Acehnese successfully negotiated a peace agreement with the Indonesian government that led to the Law on Governing Aceh (LoGA, 2006), GAM's demobilization, and the channelling of subsequent conflict through established democratic institutions. The Moros followed a convoluted pathway, with a failed implementation of the 1996 peace agreement, many failed parliamentary bills designed to respond to Moro demands, successive failures of negotiations, but finally a peace agreement with the MILF in 2014 that, even though delayed, led to the Bangsamoro Basic Law (2018). Papuans, Cordillerans, and Malay Muslims failed to obtain state concessions that addressed their demands but had very different outcomes. Papuans maintained demands for independence and self-determination, but obtained state-imposed special autonomy that has been largely contested, while the conflict continues to produce low-level violence and deep resentment. Cordillerans rejected the autonomy that the state offered, largely on the basis of its lack of credibility, and developed an alternative strategy of abandoning a nationalist Cordilleran frame to adopt instead one focused on "indigenous peoples." They obtained significant gains through the Indigenous Peoples Rights Act (1997). Malay Muslims were repressed, autonomy remained off-limits, and only small concessions were made to appease some of the elite. Low-level violence rose during the period of democratic stability.

I have argued in this study that Southeast Asian cases suggest a smoother and somewhat more varied pattern than the literature proposes with the inverted U-curve relationship between regime type and violent nationalist conflict.[5] Agreeing with the thesis, highly repressive authoritarian regimes as well as mature democratic states are most likely to have little *violent* nationalist conflict. In mature democratic states, violent mobilization becomes mostly obsolete once institutions to channel grievances through legal or political means allow nationalist groups to negotiate satisfactory compromises. Highly authoritarian ones use the full strength of the state's repressive apparatus to crush, or even prevent, the rise of violent mobilization. Of course, in less repressive authoritarian states, there is space to organize clandestine organizations, smuggle weapons and mobilize to some degree, so insurgencies do often tend to result from authoritarian suppression of claims, as happened in all Southeast Asian cases. More analysis is required to better understand thresholds of repression after which mobilization becomes possible under authoritarian regimes.

In the middle range of the curve, however, violent mobilization is more likely at the highest point, where regimes undergoing transition are situated. Uncertainty surrounding such transitions, I suggested, heightens the incentives

---

[5] Mousseau, "Democratizing with Ethnic Divisions"; Gleditsch and Ruggeri, "Political Opportunity Structures, Democracy, and Civil War"; Hegre et al., "Toward a Democratic Civil Peace?"

to mobilize offensively or defensively to secure gains, at a time when the state is weakened. The costs of such mobilization, or state repression, diminish when regimes become more stable, consistent with a downward slope of the curve.

Nevertheless, an inverted U-curve is too simple, and I propose instead that a bell curve might better represent the observed patterns. In few cases of nationalist conflict do we see sudden rises in violent mobilization right after democratic transition and subsequently rapid and complete decline once democratic stability is in place. Instead, there is good reason to argue that, in many cases, there is an initial period of low violence associated with a window when the state chooses to signal the willingness to offer concessions and negotiations, and nationalist insurgent groups waiting to see how the transition unfolds. Similarly, once democracy stabilizes, institutional commitments often lack sufficient credibility to address deep grievances, so although the incentives for violent mobilization are reduced, it nevertheless remains present at lower levels, as conflict remains endemic. A bell curve reflects this pattern, with a smoother curve at both ends. Furthermore, certainly in Southeast Asian cases, the curve is often much flatter than this representational design would suggest, with only rare dramatic increases in violence, mostly associated with the degree of mobilizational capacity.

Explaining Variance in Patterns and Outcomes

As the Southeast Asian cases have shown, the pathways and outcomes following democratization varied considerably. While some experienced heightened violence, others had very little. The five cases showed a very broad range of outcomes after democratic stability, from gaining wide-ranging autonomy after a negotiated settlement to state repression and no attempts to accommodate demands for autonomy.

Three broad conclusions can be made across all cases. First, democracy overall reduces the incentives for violence. States repress less as deploying the armed forces or clamping down is difficult to justify in a democratic context. The Indonesian state's military campaigns against Acehnese and Papuans were much more broadly mediatized and eventually contributed to the state's reduction in their use. The same is true of the Philippines, where military repression was associated with the Marcos regime. Only Estrada, with his "all-out war" against the MILF, openly used strong repression but it soon backfired. The Thai state showed relative restraint until democracy was essentially collapsing. Similarly, while insurgent groups have mobilized violently, they have also competed for representation with other organizations under democratic rule. Therefore, the costs of civil war or large-scale violence was higher as they risk losing support, particularly since some conditions improved for their followers under democratic rule. GAM, MNLF, and the MILF all had incentives to negotiate for peace and use violence as little as possible, even though GAM ended up in a spiralling civil war. They were more open to negotiating with a democratic state. Papuans deliberately chose a peaceful path under the Congress and PDP, and requested that the OPM reduce its use of violence. The Cordilleran People's Alliance chose political strategies abroad over organizing an alternative insurgent group to the CPLA, after the latter accepted a peace agreement with the Philippine state. While democracy reduces the incentives for violent mobilization, it still does not mean that the conflict is resolved or violence is completely absent.

Second, states are reluctant to provide concessions or to compromise even under favourable democratic conditions, and often tend to undermine concessions made. As a result, conflict often remains stalled, with low-level violence and without resolution. This outcome is frequent because nationalist mobilization strikes at the core of the modern nation-state system and is seen as a basic threat to its existence. I have argued that we need to distinguish nationalists from other ethnic groups or forms of identity mobilization because their claims to self-determination and identities as nations challenge existing territorial boundaries, or state conceptualizations as single unified nations. States jealously guard their borders and sovereignty, and are backed by an international system that protects these principles. While the right to self-determination enshrined in the UN Charter first appeared after the breakup of empires at the end of the First World War, it never translated into international legal or normative mechanisms by which groups viewing themselves as nations could claim their own states.[6] As a result, regardless of regime type, nationalist groups and their claims are viewed with high suspicion, and states are reluctant to make concessions that meet their demands.

Third, the institutional uncertainty of a democratic transition creates strategic responses that are different than in periods of democratic stability when institutions are more firmly established. The downfall of an authoritarian regime creates both opportunities to mobilize to make gains over previously denied claims and defensive responses to protect one's status against democratic majorities that might be inclined to deny nationalist demands. Violence is more likely because of the uncertainty it produces. Both GAM in Aceh and the MNLF/MILF in the Southern Philippines initially waited to see the new democratic governments' commitment to accommodating demands for self-determination. They remobilized violently when it became clear that constitutional negotiations and public pressure significantly reduced the menu of options in response to their claims. When more stable institutions are in

---

[6] For a good overview of issues and tensions in international law, see James J. Summers, "The Right of Self-Determination and Nationalism in International Law," *International Journal on Minority and Group Rights* 12, no. 4 (2005).

place, including new constitutions, the framework within which groups can advance and negotiate these claims becomes clearer. The more established institutional framework changes the calculus of repression and mobilizational opportunities, as well as the expectations of potential gains. These frame what outcomes become possible.

Against this backdrop, I conclude on a few propositions that explain why we observe a fair amount of variance. The initial stages of democratic transition sometimes produce civil war and other times very little violence. Under democratic stability, the outcomes range from conflict resolution to sustained state repression, with frequent stalled conflict or abandoning nationalist mobilization for alternative strategies.

First, mobilization capacity is a strong structural precondition of violent mobilization but is also associated with successful, credible state concessions. While low-level violence can occur in regions with weakly armed groups, disparate or divided ones, larger-scale violence and civil war usually require a high degree of organization, mobilization, and lethal capacity. Only in Aceh and Mindanao, with high mobilization capacity from GAM, the MNLF, and MILF do we see much higher levels of violence. In many cases, nationalist organizations mobilize either through demonstrations, protests, or other peaceful means when the democratic space allows. In Papua, the Congresses and PDP were the height of peaceful mobilization. Papuans continued to hold occasional demonstrations and protests. Several conflicts will have some degree of instability leading to low-level violence, such as in Papua and Thailand, whether state induced through repressive responses or small-scale attacks requiring very few weapons or numbers of people. As a result, the level of violent mobilization does not provide a good indication of the depth of grievances or degree of conflict. Persistent low-level violence and extra-institutional mobilization can equally strongly reflect deep grievances. Such deep resentment continues to be present throughout Papua, and Malay Muslims certainly held deep grievances that became strongly repressed after the 2006 coup. Civil war and large-scale violence occur mostly because of organizational factors and deployment of lethal weapons. While democratization in many cases reduces the incentives and payoffs of using such large-scale violence, it nevertheless might also produce stalled conflict.

Based on Southeast Asian cases, mobilization capacity also appears to produce greater chances of reaching lasting settlements to nationalist conflict. Given the state's overall reluctance to extend concessions to "secessionists," it rarely extends more than minimal concessions to reduce violence, without addressing deeper grievances. When the costs of violence are high, or the threat from insurgent groups is large, it becomes increasingly difficult for a democratic government to contain the political fallout. While greater repression is an option, it is risky in a democratic context when fragile democratic governments are reluctant to cede more influence to the armed forces. As shown, the initial period was more volatile but, during the period of democratic stability, peace agreements were reached with both GAM and the MILF, followed by credible legislation to enforce them. Only two cases are insufficient to conclude that high mobilizational capacity of nationalist groups is a necessary precondition to reaching lasting settlements to conflict, but further analysis would be useful to determine whether such high political and societal costs are the main or only path to such settlements, certainly not a normatively appealing finding.[7]

Second, early state concessions can avoid spikes in violence but often lead to commitment problems. In many cases, democratic transition opens up expectations that negotiations or compromise will occur, or at least higher hopes that democracy might produce better outcomes for nationalist groups than authoritarian rule. Certainly, Moros, Acehnese, Papuans, and Cordillerans all began discussions with newly democratic governments and withheld violent mobilization initially. In cases where states proactively offer concessions, such as Indonesia for Aceh and the Philippines in Mindanao, they often prevent a surge in violent mobilization that might otherwise occur if the transition's uncertainty creates expectations that grievances will not be addressed. Significant state concessions that meet such grievances do reduce incentives for mobilization. Frequently, however, they prove to be insufficiently deep, fail to be implemented, or they are simply promises without concrete legislation, so they mainly delay the onset of violent remobilization. Initial state concessions were rejected in Aceh, once GAM considered them to fail to address their grievances and later, when special autonomy was deemed to lack credibility. The creation of the ARMM in the Philippines was similarly insufficient to convince the Moros to abandon violent mobilization. Concessions to the CPLA in the Cordillera had mixed effects of convincing the CPLA of accepting the new Cordillera Administrative Region, as well as its benefits, while the CPA and many Cordillerans rejected these as failing to address the demands for significant autonomy. Overall, since states are generally reluctant to concede to secessionists, they are unlikely to offer more than what ends up being short-term attempts to defuse violence and coopt nationalist elites, or otherwise seek to undermine their mobilizational appeal.

Third, electoral coalitions and types of parliamentary systems are key factors explaining state concessions and repression. In rare cases, electoral coalitions will require the support of nationalist groups and might deliver state concessions in return. In Thailand, in exchange for electoral support for broad-based

---

[7] Toft even goes so far as to argue that rebel victory might be the best path to long-term democratic outcomes and peace. See Monica Duffy Toft, "Ending Civil Wars: A Case for Rebel Victory?," *International Security* 34, no. 4 (2010); *Securing the Peace: The Durable Settlement of Civil Wars* (Princeton, NJ: Princeton University Press, 2010).

coalitions in the late 1980s and 1990s Malay Muslims obtained inclusion in the ruling coalition, with some minor concessions on education and religious rights. More often than not, they respond to majority pressure and preferences as expressed through parliamentary support. The degree of violence or repression that tilts majorities in favour of concessions and compromise is difficult to determine and is likely context specific. Electoral systems, such as proportional representation, that produce multiple-party coalitions often give more leverage to small groups, such as nationalists, but this is rare. In Thailand, with changes to the electoral system brought about by the 1997 Constitution, Thai Rak Thai obtained a majority that allowed Thaksin to tap into populist leanings to ignore and then repress the Deep South, where Malay Muslims reside, moving away from inclusion and concessions of previous coalitions. In Indonesia, Acehnese and Papuans enjoyed no such concessions given an electoral system based on large national parties with party coalitions around candidates for President and Vice-President. It proved important in changing support for a peace agreement that Vice-President Jusuf Kalla broadly promoted. Previously a majority in parliament had denounced concessions made by President Wahid to "secessionists," particularly in Papua. The Philippines showed the impact of presidential systems with a high degree of parliamentary independence. It became repeatedly difficult for peace negotiations to yield support or accompanying legislation in parliament, thereby producing several cycles of violent mobilization, ceasefire negotiations, peace agreements, and legislation that collapsed before finally reaching sufficient alignment of presidential electoral incentives and control over parliament under Duterte to pass the Bangsamoro Basic Law.

Fourth, reframing away from nationalist goals can yield better state concessions but there are risks. Given the lack of international support for nationalist groups and the state's reluctance to view them as anything but secessionists that threaten the state's boundaries and sovereignty, a move away from making nationalist claims tends to defuse state repression and violence. For some groups, such as in the Cordillera, adopting a new frame as indigenous peoples allowed them to continue pushing for self-determination and autonomy but on terms and with specific powers and resources that were different from nationalist goals. As a result, in the case of Cordilleran groups, it was easier to obtain parliamentary support for legislation that enshrined indigenous peoples' rights.

Finally, the credibility of commitments highly influences the degree to which violence might be reduced in early stages and conflict resolved once democracy is stabilized. New democratic regimes are generally more credible than authoritarian ones largely because they are supported by constitutions and institutions that tend to be more highly respected, as well as judiciaries that help to enforce laws. But their commitment to nationalist groups often lacks credibility as it often falls short of satisfying grievances, can often be poorly implemented, or later undermined. Without third parties, even democratic states face a certain degree of credible commitment problems, in spite of their institutional checks and balances, and public scrutiny. Constitutional enshrinement of principles of autonomy helped to provide a credible commitment in cases of Acehnese, Papuans, Moros, and Cordillerans as constitutions are difficult to amend in both countries and the principle allowed room to recognize some of their demands, in ways that the reinforcement of the Thai nation and lack of autonomy (or decentralization) in Thailand's constitutions repeatedly closed opportunities for Malay Muslims to legitimately claim autonomy. But later state concessions or legislation often lacked credibility. In the cases of Aceh and Papua, "special autonomy" fell short because it was not negotiated. It fell through in Aceh and was implemented in Papua, but has continually been contested and its parameters undermined by subsequent state regulations and contradictory laws. The Philippine state had huge commitment problems as it repeatedly failed to pass laws in parliament that corresponded to agreements reached, first with the MNLF and then the MILF. The ARMM as well as temporary institutions of the 1996 agreement failed to be implemented as originally committed. Conversely, negotiated agreements between nationalist groups and the state, followed by legislation that largely respects the agreement, heightens credibility, particularly if laws are sufficiently detailed that they become more difficult to undermine through regulation or other legislation. Ultimately, these characteristics helped to make the Law on Aceh (2006), which was more detailed and extensive than the previous special autonomy, and the Bangsamoro Basic Law (2018) much more credible than any other legislation or concessions made to nationalists in Indonesia and the Philippines.

Democracy and Nationalist Conflict

Nationalist conflict is difficult to resolve. States view nationalists as strong threats to their sovereignty and seek to repress them. Nationalists are mostly concentrated territorially and make strong demands for self-determination or independence. While such nationalist groups and objectives are elite driven and constructed, they are rarely abandoned or reframed. Nationalist groups might become less politically active, but they rarely disappear unless they are accommodated and their grievances addressed.

All nationalist groups are constructed, as most of the scholars of nationalism agree. The extent to which they are based on ethnic identity however is debated and contested.[8] Furthermore, identities as nations oftentimes fluctuate, adjust to demographic circumstances, and become more or less inclusive. Nations are

---

[8] The literature and debate is vast on the relationship between nations and ethnicity. See, for instance, Anthony Smith, *The Ethnic Origins of Nations* (Oxford: Blackwell, 1986); Liah Greenfeld, *Nationalism: Five Roads to Modernity* (Cambridge, MA: Harvard University Press, 1992).

sometimes defined in non-ethnic terms but other times could be ambiguously so. For instance, nationalists in Quebec, Catalonia, and Scotland have adapted their definitions of group boundaries under increasing immigration. Nationalist leaders change their discourse and bases of mobilization to keep advancing their political goals.[9]

Regardless of their ethnic ties, nationalists are a threat to the state since they challenge its own national identity and often its boundaries. States therefore try to "make the problem disappear." Authoritarian regimes suppress them in the hopes that they give up their mobilization. They attempt to assimilate, integrate, or transform nationalists to eliminate claims to self-determination. Democratic states display similar propensities. They still repress, sometimes attempt to assimilate, and other times adopt policies to integrate nationalist groups but on terms they most often are reluctant to negotiate. The Indonesian, Philippine, and Thai states all attempted a mix of policies, from military repression to imposed institutions, as a means to crush mobilization and dissuade a resumption of claims to self-determination.

Yet, authoritarian states usually fail to repress nationalists effectively. While they might stifle mobilization, in many other cases, repression fuels it, including in its violent forms.[10] The Chinese state has used strong repressive tools, including forced incarceration, against Uyghurs and Tibetans, but failed to eliminate nationalist claims.[11] Authoritarian states in Indonesia, the Philippines, and Thailand had periods of intensive civil war against nationalist groups. Myanmar experienced sixty years of civil war against several nationalist groups without resolution.[12] Russia continues to repress Chechens, yet their nationalist claims persist.[13] Its predecessor, the Soviet state, failed to eliminate nationalist demands despite decades of ideological indoctrination and repressive policies. Ironically, Stalin and his successors recognized the difficulty of eliminating nationalist claims by institutionalizing "national minorities," albeit

---

[9] Michael Keating, "Stateless Nation-Building: Quebec, Catalonia and Scotland in the Changing State System," *Nations and Nationalism* 3, no. 4 (1997); Matthew Mendelsohn, "Measuring National Identity and Patterns of Attachment: Quebec and Nationalist Mobilization," *Nationalism and Ethnic Politics* 8, no. 3 (2002); Gérard Bouchard, *La Nation Québécoise Au Futur Et Au Passé*, Collection Balises (Montréal: VLB, 1999).

[10] Davenport, "Multi-Dimensional Threat Perception and State Repression," 154–56; Will H. Moore, "Repression and Dissent: Substitution, Context, and Timing," *American Journal of Political Science* 42, no. 3 (1998); Gurr, *Peoples Versus States*; Sambanis, "Do Ethnic and Nonethnic Civil Wars Have the Same Causes?"

[11] Sean R. Roberts, "The Biopolitics of China's 'War on Terror' and the Exclusion of the Uyghurs," *Critical Asian Studies* 50, no. 2 (2018).

[12] Jacques Bertrand, Alexandre Pelletier, and Ardeth Maung Thawnghmung, "First Movers, Democratization and Unilateral Concessions: Overcoming Commitment Problems and Negotiating a 'Nationwide Cease-Fire' in Myanmar," *Asian Security* 16, no. 1 (2018).

[13] Monica Duffy Toft and Yuri M. Zhukov, "Islamists and Nationalists: Rebel Motivation and Counterinsurgency in Russia's North Caucasus," *American Political Science Review* 109, no. 2 (2015).

without real powers. The longer-term consequences of this recognition helped to create a new base for future mobilization.[14]

If so, is democracy's record much better at resolving nationalist conflict? As I have shown on the basis of Southeast Asian cases, the record is mixed. For the most part, only few nationalist conflicts are likely to be resolved with wide-ranging autonomy agreements that are highly credible, implemented fully, and responsive to nationalist grievances. Agreements to secession are even less likely, given the current norms of the international system and states' high reluctance to concede more power to nationalist groups and, particularly, to relinquish territory. It is much more likely that nationalist conflicts remain stalled, with episodic periods of low-level violence, continued deep grievances and mobilization outside of the normal institutional channels to voice discontent with the status quo. In a few cases, this study would expect some comparatively weak groups to abandon a nationalist quest and reframe their demands by reinventing their group identities to tap alternative political, legal, and institutional channels to advance self-determination. The global progression of rights for indigenous peoples, which obtained strong international support with the United Nations Declaration on the Rights of Indigenous Peoples, opened up a new set of opportunities for some groups that could reinvent themselves as "indigenous."

Nationalist conflicts have too often been folded into studies of civil war or ethnic conflict more broadly, yet they should be analysed separately as I have suggested. They differ in at least two important ways. First, the kinds of demands they make differ from conflicts revolving around ethnic identity that are concerned with obtaining minority rights or cultural protection. With self-determination being more centrally part of their political agenda, states approach these conflicts with preferences and strategies that account for their perceived degree of threat. Second, studies of civil war, as well as many studies of ethnic conflict, focus more specifically on conditions of large-scale violence, with ending civil war or violence being the main measure of conflict resolution, rather than outcomes that accommodate nationalist groups and reduce grievances to allow channelling through regular institutional processes.

The scope of the broader propositions, therefore, applies mainly to such groups in the context of democratization, from transition to the establishment of democratic stability. Where regimes are still authoritarian or semi-democratic, state repression is more readily used and available. There is also less scrutiny and accountability of state actions. Nationalist groups remain likely to be suspicious of any state willingness to compromise, as the latter's credibility is very weak. After Turkey became more democratic in the 1980s, the government slowly introduced more concessions for Kurds. The PKK

---

[14] Brubaker, *Nationalism Reframed*; Roeder, "Soviet Federalism and Ethnic Mobilization."

remained active but exercised more restraint as some concessions were introduced. Nevertheless, the government's refusal to introduce much more than minimal changes to allow Kurds some cultural expression maintained their deep resentment.[15]

Electoral coalitions and parliaments become significant mainly in democratic regimes where they begin to be more functional and more openly critical, while reflecting popular preferences and pressures.

Finally, while some processes remain even in advanced democracies, they are less pronounced as judicial recourse and formal institutional processes are highly regularized and credible. Nevertheless, conflicts in Northern Ireland and Catalonia continued to display for long periods of time the characteristics of stalled conflict with low-level violence described in this study. Catalans raised their demands, even after obtaining recognition as "historic nationality," subsequently "nation," and after adopting its own statute of autonomy, in large part because of perceptions that such constitutional guarantees were later undermined through the Spanish state's strategies to steer a segment of the Catalan elites to accept a more centralized Spain. Divisions were fostered through political parties on different points along the spectrum of support for a more autonomous Catalonia.[16] Recent remobilization of the Catalans shows how deep the nationalist conflict remains, despite a flexible constitutional framework that accommodated high degrees of flexibility in crafting autonomy for Catalonia and the Basque country. Violence became politically much less possible among the Basques, leading to ETA's disbanding, but the grievances remain deep.[17]

Two more qualifications are also important. First, this analysis extends mostly to cases where nationalist groups are relatively small and territorially concentrated. When they compete for control of the entire state, their political objectives differ and their access and control of national level institutions are much more significant. It is mostly relevant in cases where nationalists aspire to carving out an independent state or obtaining self-determination through autonomy over their territory, rather than power sharing arrangements at the centre, such as in the former Czechoslovakia, Rwanda, or Burundi. Second, the

[15] David Romano, "The Long Road Toward Kurdish Accommodation in Turkey: The Role of Elections and International Pressures," in *Democratization and Ethnic Minorities: Conflict or Compromise?*, eds. Jacques Bertrand and Oded Haklai (New York: Routledge, 2013).

[16] Josep M. Colomer, "The Venturous Bid for the Independence of Catalonia," *Nationalities Papers* 45, no. 5 (2017); César Colino, "Constitutional Change without Constitutional Reform: Spanish Federalism and the Revision of Catalonia's Statute of Autonomy," *Publius: The Journal of Federalism* 39, no. 2 (2009); Josep M. Colomer, "The Spanish 'State of Autonomies': Non-Institutional Federalism," *West European Politics* 21, no. 4 (1998).

[17] "Asymmetric Governance in Multination States: Rethinking Territorial Politics in Comparative Perspective," workshop, June 12–15, 2018, Agirre Lehendakaria Center for Social and Political Studies, University of the Basque Country.

presence of external actors that intervene in a conflict can highly influence the degree of violence, as well as the nature of state concessions. Contrasting significantly from nationalist movements in the post-Soviet countries, in Southeast Asia there were rare sources of external support, mostly political rather than military or economic.[18] Malaysia provided some shelter and weak economic support to PULO and BRN in the 1970s, but foreign policy interests within ASEAN as well as directly in its bilateral dealings with Thailand superseded its commitment to supporting nationalists. It nurtured closer economic ties, and stable borders, thereby significantly reducing such support by the 1980s, partly contributing to the Malay-Muslim groups' decline. It never resumed such support even when groups appeared to rise again by the 2000s, although some continued to reside in Malaysia with little attempt by Malaysian authorities to detain or prevent them from organizing their activities. GAM benefitted mostly from connections to Acehnese in Malaysia, mostly through illegal arms trade networks. Papuans gained sympathy from external NGO networks that had sustained the East Timor campaign, but with little impact on foreign governments that pressured the Indonesians on the case of East Timor. They ended up with weak political allies, such as Vanuatu, which gave its support in international forums but could not help much more. Cordillerans had no external allies initially, but developed again political support in international forums only when they began to redefine the nature of their mobilization as indigenous peoples. Finally, the MNLF had sustained support from the Organisation of Islamic Conference (OIC), and Libya in particular, mostly to exert political pressure on the Philippines and provide a foreign base for its leaders. The MILF, conversely, had little support as the MNLF retained the recognition of official representative of the Moro people after the signing of the Tripoli Agreement in 1976, that Libya and the OIC helped to broker. Subsequent analyses that made some links between the MILF and international Islamist networks showed very little substantive support or close relations. Overall, then, while external support played a small, mostly political role, in some of these cases, it did not contribute to explaining the rise of violent mobilization in Southeast Asia.

By contrast, many nationalist groups that emerged out of the collapse of the former Soviet Union obtained strong support from kin groups in neighbouring countries. In Georgia, for instance, external support for nationalist mobilization in Abkhazia and South Ossetia contributed extensively to the escalation of violence.[19] External support also increased violence and mobilizational

---

[18] By contrast, external support has much more frequently been relevant in other cases, such as the post-Soviet states.

[19] David Siroky, "The Sources of Secessionist War: The Interaction of Local Control and Foreign Forces in Post-Soviet Georgia," *Caucasus Survey* 4, no. 1 (2016): 63–91; Cornell, "Autonomy as a Source of Conflict"; Carment, "Managing Interstate Ethnic Tensions."

capacity in the Biafran movement against the Nigerian state. But overall, in many cases, external support might in fact be much more marginal than has often been expected, particularly given the world system's normative constraints on intervention.[20]

Regionally, there have been other similar conflicts that fall beyond the scope of this study, as they either had exceptional circumstances or did not occur in democratic contexts. East Timor had a parallel trajectory to Aceh and Papua only in as much as democratization allowed mobilization leading to a referendum on independence. But the pressures from the international community were much stronger than in other cases, largely because the United Nations and most major countries had never recognized the integration of East Timor.[21] In relative terms, such pressures were much more significant than the majority's reluctance to allow the East Timorese to secede. It therefore had an ambiguous status internationally that made domestic factors less relevant.

Myanmar has a large number of similar nationalist cases but is difficult to compare given the uniquely ambiguous nature of its decade-long experience with democratization that led to a military coup in 2021. Certainly, the transition to civilian rule did bring some expectations of negotiation and state concessions that allowed some groups, such as the Karen National Union and the Restoration Council for Shan State, to agree to a nationwide ceasefire and political dialogue. It also created uncertainty and worry that the new democratic state would not address deep grievances. In some cases, this led to breaking ceasefire agreements that were made under authoritarian rule and a new escalation of violence, where mobilization capacity was still strong, as in the case of the Kachin Independence Army after the armed forces launched new attacks in June 2011. The credibility of any commitment made by the state was largely undermined by the military's continued independence and exclusive power to manage border affairs and internal armed conflict. It also held sufficient number of seats in parliament and in the executive to exercise a veto over the civilian government's policies. As a result, even though the government of Aung San Suu Kyi held peace negotiations after 2015, few concrete concessions were made while unilateral measures to decentralize some powers to ethnic states largely failed to show a genuine commitment to meet nationalist demands for federalism.[22]

In sum, the book's argument extends mostly to countries transitioning to democracy until the initial periods of democratic stability, although some of its

---

[20] Alexis Heraclides, "Secessionist Minorities and External Involvement," *International Organization* 44, no. 3 (1990).

[21] Bertrand, *Nationalism and Ethnic Conflict in Indonesia*, 136–43; see also John Roosa, "Finalising the Nation: The Indonesian Military as the Guarantor of National Unity," *Asia Pacific Viewpoint* 48, no. 1 (2007) and Matthew Jardine, "Power and Principle in East Timor," *Peace Review* 10, no. 2 (1998): 195–202.

[22] Bertrand, Pelletier, and Thawnghmung. "First Movers, Democratization and Unilateral Concessions."

observations can be seen in less-than-democratic settings as well as mature democracies. It provides a counterpoint to studies that have predicted state-initiated violent mobilization as a frequent occurrence to defend elite interests and, instead, shown that it is often the uncertainty surrounding the institutional setting that, in several cases, will increase incentives for nationalists in territorially concentrated peripheries to mobilize violently. Initial state concessions, early in the transition, help to defuse mobilization, but are often insufficient mostly because of their lack of credibility. Stable democratic regimes are a necessary but not sufficient condition for conflict between the state and nationalist groups to become channelled through the formal institutional process.[23] More often than not, it reduces violent conflict but grievances remain deep. A resolution of nationalist conflict often requires strong mobilizational capacity, state concessions that meet demands through negotiated processes and detailed legislation, and most likely feasible when there are significantly high electoral payoffs and supportive majorities in parliament to end nationalist conflict. The combination of these factors is rare in nationalist conflicts.

Where Have Nationalists Gone?

As democracy recedes in many regions of the world, what has been the impact on nationalist conflict? States generally attempt to suppress or even eliminate them. While democratic states face institutional and normative constraints to do so, authoritarian states have freer rein. Nationalists have become less visible but have not disappeared. With shifting global political alignments, others have also resorted to "exit-and-reframe" strategies, in both democratic and authoritarian settings.

The changing international environment has further eroded nationalist incentives to mobilize, particularly as insurgent movements. Gurr noted a significant decline in violent mobilization in the 1990s and attributed it to the spread of democracy.[24] The Southeast Asian cases certainly confirmed such a decline in the 2000–2010s, which I also explain by the lesser incentives for violent mobilization under stable democratic periods in each country. Yet, early state concessions were strong predictors of such decline in transitional regimes, with general uncertainly raising the probability of violence when such concessions were absent, as in the case of Aceh. With fewer transitions to democracy

---

[23] This is consistent with findings from other studies, such as ibid.; Beissinger, "A New Look at Ethnicity and Democratization." In an interesting finding, Elkins concurs that democratizing countries might have greater dissatisfaction from ethnic minorities, and therefore democratically consolidated countries fare better, yet these countries also find that they remain somewhat dissatisfied, even when they obtain federalism. See Elkins and Sides, "Can Institutions Build Unity in Multiethnic States?"

[24] Gurr, *Peoples Versus States*, 36.

in the past decade, such sources of mobilization have been reduced. Furthermore, the presence of external support for nationalists continued to decline steadily after the Cold War, while international instruments to claim protection and rights for national minorities remained weak and unchanged. The strong reluctance of most states to support Scots' or Catalans' demands for referenda on independence, even after Spain's repressive approach to Catalan nationalists, further perpetuates the norms of sovereignty of the current state system.

The rise of authoritarian rule, as well as its strengthening in existing regimes, has dampened opportunities to seek negotiated settlements for nationalist groups. In some cases, state repression has increased, as has been the case against Thailand's Malay Muslims since the return of authoritarian rule. The Chinese have steadily intensified their repression against Tibetans and Uyghurs in the past decade. The Russian state under Putin has also steadily repressed Chechens. The Malian state, after having reached a peace settlement with the Tuareg, reneged on commitments and used greater repression after the coup of 2012.

Over the past twenty years, two sets of changes in the international context have created new perceived opportunities for "exit-and-reframe strategies." First, the global movement for rights of indigenous peoples has succeeded in shifting states to support new norms and legal instruments, culminating in the UN Declaration on the Rights of Indigenous Peoples.

While the right for self-determination of nations is enshrined in the UN Charter, nationalist groups have had little success at tapping it to make gains on their claims. Similarly, the protection of minority rights could be used by states to dampen nationalist demands and offer instead cultural or linguistic protection. Since the General Assembly passed the UN Declaration on the Rights of Indigenous Peoples in 2007, an increasing number of groups have sought to self-identify as "indigenous" in order to claim some of the benefits that nationalists often claim, such as territorial recognition, some degree of self-determination and control over natural resources.[25]

Miskitos in the 1980s resisted the Nicaraguan nationalist revolution with appeals to territorial autonomy, and adopting a nationalist frame under the leadership of MISURASATA/MISURA. The democratic opening after 1984, and subsequent negotiations, led to parliamentary enshrinement of an

---

[25] By contrast, as Kymlicka notes, "the prospects for developing global norms on national minorities are non-existent in the foreseeable future" (p. 273) precisely because of the greater threat that they represent to peace and security. He notes how norms at the UN have evolved to assign targeted rights to indigenous peoples, rather than "national minorities" in the European legal and normative context. Consistent with the argument in this book, he notes the security fears that have prevented the ability to address concerns of national minorities, as opposed to indigenous peoples. See Kymlicka, *Multicultural Odysseys*, 265–73.

autonomy statute for the Atlantic Coast regions of Nicaragua. But its implementation and details of Miskito empowerment required further mobilization.
The formation of YATAMA (Children of the Mother Earth) constituted not only
an abandonment of violent insurgency and mobilization as a political party but
also a change in the frame of mobilization to a more explicit "indigenous"
appeal. By 1991, they were mobilizing to pressure Nicaragua to support the UN
declaration.[26]

The Tuareg of Mali mobilized in 1990 by using a Tuareg nationalist frame to
demand *Azawad* independence. The Azawad Popular Movement, Popular
Liberation Front of Azawad, and the Azawad Revolutionary Army all aimed
at creating a united front of the various Tuareg tribes to form an Azawad
nationalist group.[27] After the transition to democracy, the Tuareg obtained
some powers through a form of state decentralization, which led to decreases
in violent mobilization but grievances remained. They then increasingly
coalesced with other African groups under the Indigenous Peoples of Africa
Coordinating Committee which was formed in 1997, and through the following
decade became involved in discussions leading to the UN Declaration on the
Rights of Indigenous Peoples.[28]

Several other groups have explored a shift to an indigenous people form of
mobilization. The Berbers in North Africa have pursued a nationalist agenda as
"Kabyle" but also as "Amazighs" seeking rights as indigenous peoples.[29] So
have the Crimean Tatars, Roma, and even the Kurds. In sum, a new international instrument providing increasing rights that are broadly recognized
greatly motivated some nationalists to reframe their demands and reshape how
they presented their identities.

Second, international *jihadist* networks have provided increasing funds and
logistical support to resist states, thereby offering new sources of both material
and ideological resources. Some nationalists have found fertile ground to shift
their strategies and tap into such opportunities. In particular, where state
repression has increased, the options available have appeared oftentimes
limited. Malay Muslims in Thailand increasingly use the same strategies as
many such jihadist groups, mostly in the form of bombings. They have risked

---

[26] Ethnic minority groups in Nepal, after democratization began in the 1990s, shifted to an
explicitly indigenous frame of mobilization alongside claims for ethnically-based federalism.
See Susan I. Hangen, *The Rise of Ethnic Politics in Nepal: Democracy in the Margins*
(Abingdon: Routledge, 2010), 34–58.

[27] Nigel Crawhall, "Africa and the UN Declaration on the Rights of Indigenous Peoples," *The
International Journal of Human Rights* 15, no. 1 (2011).

[28] Douglas Livermore, "The Case for Azawad," *African Security Review* 22, no. 4 (2013): 288–90;
Andrew Lebovich, "AQIM and Its Allies in Mali," The Washington Institute for Near East
Policy, www.washingtoninstitute.org/policy-analysis/view/aqim-and-its-allies-in-mali.

[29] See Congrès Mondial Amazigh, *Amazighs of Morocco: An Indigenous People Despoiled*,
presented at UN Committee for Human Rights 118th Session, October 17 to November 4,
2016, Geneva.

being linked to global networks, although they have mostly kept their distance. Many Tuareg previously in nationalist organizations joined Ansar Dine ("Defenders of the Faith") using a more jihadist and Islamist frame, later in an uncomfortable alliance with the emerging Al-Qaeda in the Islamic Maghreb movement that quickly spread throughout the region after 2012 and displaced many nationalists mostly organized around the more recent Mouvement National pour la Libération de l'Azawad. Chinese repression of the East Turkestan Islamic Movement, which mobilized in favour of Uyghur independence, eventually laid the basis for some of its fights to create links to Al-Qaeda, with increasing numbers of Uyghurs participating in global jihadist groups as well as mobilizing in Xinjiang. Some Uyghur activists increasingly adopted a jihadist discourse in their struggle against China.[30] While a *jihadist* frame has not offered greater international recognition, it has opened up links to new potential allies and resources, thereby tempting many aggrieved nationalists to seek new mobilization strategies.

Many groups, however, remain less visible than in the past, sometimes enjoying limited state concessions but other times largely repressed and ignored. Many nationalist groups, such as the Acehnese and Moros, have gained some degree of autonomy over their territory but several others, such as Papuans, have found it failed to meet their demands or their powers were diluted. Many more nationalist groups – Biafrans in 2015, Scots in 2016, Catalans in 2017, Sikhs in 2018 – appear to have ended their mobilization only to rear their heads and show that their grievances remain vivid and deep. Their strategies are strongly shaped by the regime in which they operate and the responses of their respective states to their mobilizational approaches.

The resolution of nationalist conflicts is more promising in democratic states but also requires flexibility and accommodation. While the fears of state disintegration are legitimate and oftentimes realistic, more often than not they are exaggerated. Through early concessions, compromise, and negotiation, states can avert or attenuate violent escalation. Providing more meaningful territorial autonomy, alongside guarantees of its credibility, can offer a large number of groups with long-standing grievances some strong incentives to fully endorse the new democratic environment and create more long-lasting stability.

---

[30] Roberts, "The Biopolitics of China's 'War on Terror' and the Exclusion of the Uyghurs."

Glossary

Abu Sayyaf	Islamic separatist organization in the Southern Philippines
Adat	Customary law: a term broadly used to identify the cultural traditions and laws of the vast number of different tribes and ethnic groups across Indonesia
Bangsamoro	Moro Nation
Barangay	Village administrative unit
Bupati	Regency/district head
Chart Thai	Thai Nation Party
Daerah Istimewa	Special region
Darul Islam	House of Islam, rebellion against the Indonesian state between 1949 and 1962
Datu	Traditional ruler
Forum Peduli HAM	Care Human Rights Forum: an Acehnese human rights organization
Golkar	Golongan Karya (functional groups): an organization representing functional groups and effectively operating as a large government party under the New Order regime and as a party in the post-Reformasi era
Hijab	Islamic headscarf/veil
Jihad	Holy war
Kabupaten	District/Regency
Madrasah	Islamic school
Maute	Splinter group of the MILF
Nahdlatul Ulama	Association of Muslim Scholars
NasDem	National Democratic Party
Pancasila	Five principles; Indonesian state philosophy
Panlipi	Legal Assistance Center for Indigenous Filipinos; Filipino NGO
Partai Aceh	Aceh Party, political party associated with GAM
Partai Demokrat	Democrat Party

Partai Islam	Islamic Party
Pemekaran	Division/proliferation (of administrative units)
Pheu Thai	For Thais Party; political party founded by Thaksin Sinawatra after dissolution of his two former parties
Pondok	Islamic school
Qanun	Regional regulations/local laws in Aceh
Reformasi	Reform
Revolusi	Revolution
Sipat	Ceasefire
Tadika	Primary schools run by mosques
Thai Rak Thai	Thais Love Thais Party; party of Thaksin Shinawatra
Thai Rom Yen	"Peaceful South"; amnesty campaign in Thailand in the 1980s
Ulama	Islamic scholars
Uleebalang	Acehnese aristocracy
Umma	Global community of Muslims
Wadah	Political faction of Malay-Muslim politicians in Thailand
Wali Nanggroe	Head of the state of Aceh

Bibliography

Newspapers

"1 Provinsi Dan 10 Kabupaten Baru Diresmikan [1 New Province and 10 New Districts Formalized]." *Tempo*, April 22, 2013.

"12 Februari, Deklarasi Pembentukan Provinsi Papua Selatan Di Merauke [February 12, Declaration for the Formation of South Papua Province in Merauke]." *Suara Pembaruan*, February 9, 2007.

"2011 Dana Respek Meningkat Rp 50 Milyar [2011 Respek Budget Increases by 50 Billion Rp]." *Bintang Papua*, April 28, 2011.

"Aceh Passes Bylaw to Address Past Human Rights Issues." *Tempo*, January 10, 2014.

"Aceh Tetap Bentuk Komisi Kebenaran Dan Rekonsiliasi [Aceh Continues to Form Justice and Reconciliation Commission]." *Tempo*, January 24, 2007.

"Act Establishing Cordillera Autonomous Region Filed." *Philippines News Agency*, June 17, 2014.

"Agenda Penting, Memberi Persetujuan Perdasus Pilgub." *Bintang Papua*, September 16, 2011.

Alegado, Antonio Siegfrid O. "Bill Seeking Autonomous Region Filed." *Business World*, February 7, 2012.

"AMM: UU Aceh Sesuai Nota Kesepahaman [AMM: Aceh Law Based on Memorandum of Understanding]." *Tempo*, July 13, 2006.

Arguillas, Carolyn O. "Salamat Issues Policy Statement Rejecting Terror; Ermita Welcomes Move." *Mindanews*, June 22, 2003.

Aritonang, Margareth S. "Jokowi Told to Disband UP4B in Papua." *Jakarta Post*, September 8, 2014.

"Arroyo's Peacemaking Legacy Leaves a Trail of Blood and Chaos." *GMA News Online*, August 14, 2009.

"Autonomy Issues Heat Up in Mountain Province." *Targeted News Service*, January 12, 2011.

Bengwayan, AT. "Igorots Picket Aspac Mining Meet, Condemn Arroyo's Mining Agenda." *Bulatat*, October 16–22, 2005.

"Bupati Boven Digoel Dituding Intervensi Pemilihan Anggota MRP [Bupati of Boven Digoel Accused of Intervening in MRP Elections]." *Bintang Papua*, February 24, 2011.

"Council Wants Pending Cordillera Autonomy Bill Certified as Urgent." *Philippines News Agency*, September 12, 2016.

Cunha, Makawaru Da. "Siapapun Gubernurnya, Respek Harus Dilanjutkan [Whoever Becomes Governor Must Continue Respek]." *Bintang Papua*, June 28, 2011.

Dait, Juan B., Jr. "Arroyo Douses Cold Water over Cordillera Autonomy." *Manila Bulletin Online*, June 25, 2006.

"Dewan Tuding Pemerintah Hambat Pelaksanaan UU Otonomi Aceh [Council Accuses Government of Blocking Implementation of Aceh Autonomy Law]." *Tempo*, December 1, 2008.

Dexter, A. "Draft Cordillera Autonomy Law to Go Thru Consultations." *News Release*, May 27, 2011, http://car.neda.gov.ph/draft-cordillera-autonomy-law-to-go-thru-consultations/.

"Disahkan, 1 Raperdasus Dan 4 Raperdasi [1 Perdasus and 4 Perdasi Approved]." *Bintang Papua*, December 3, 2010.

"Disunity Puts Southern Peace Process on Its Last Legs." *The Nation*, October, 2011.

"Ditolak Jadi Anggota MRP: Hana Hikoyabi Siap Tempuh Jalur Hukum [Denied Membership in MRP: Hana Hikoyabi Prepared to Use Legal Channels]." *Suara Pembaruan*, May 7, 2011.

"DPR Dan DPD Awasi Implementasi UUPA [DPR and DPD Oversee Implementation of UUPA]." *Serambi Indonesia*, February 3, 2015.

"DPRP Tidak Restui Pemekaran Papua Tengah [DPRP Does Not Approve New Province of Central Papua]." *Bintang Papua*, July 21, 2010.

Elemia, Camille and Mara Cepeda. "BBL Needs a Push from Duterte to Become Law before Sona." *Rappler*, May 19, 2018.

"Enam Kabupaten Di Pengunungan Tengah Minta Segera Dimekarkan [Six districts in the Mountainous Regions Request Division into New Districts]." *Suara Pembaruan*, February 19, 2007.

Esguerra, Christian V. and Edwin Fernandez. "New Head of Peace Panel with MILF: No Surprises." *Philippine Daily Inquirer*, July 16, 2010.

"Establishment of Papuan Council Runs into More Problems." *Jakarta Post*, October 1, 2005.

Fairclough, Gordon. "Hidden Hands: Politicians and Army Blamed for Bombings in the South." *Far Eastern Economic Review*, June 9, 1994, 20.

"Fight in Philippines." *The Observer*, April 22, 2007.

"GAM Harapkan RUU Pemerintahan Aceh Selesai Akhir Mei [GAM Hopes Aceh Government Law Finished by End of May]." *Tempo*, April 13, 2006.

"GAM Tak Persoalkan Keterlambatan UU Pemerintahan Aceh [GAM Isn't Making an Issue Over Delay in Aceh Governance Law]." *Tempo*, January 21, 2006.

Gatra, Sandro. "Dana Otsus Papua 2012 Naik [Increase in 2012 Special Autonomy Budget for Papua]." *Kompas*, October 28, 2011.

"Gereja Dukung Moratorium Pemekaran Papua [Church Supports Moratorium on New Districts]." *Bintang Papua*, May 22, 2010.

"Gov't Firm on Giving MILF Autonomy than Sub-State." *The Philippine Star*, August 26, 2011.

"Gov't, MILF Agree on Autonomous Entity to Replace ARMM." *Philippine Daily Inquirer*, April 25, 2012.

"Gubernur Bahas Kendala Implementasi UUPA Bersama Komite I DPD RI [Governor Discusses Obstacles to Implementation of UUPA with Parliamentary Committee I]." *Kanal Aceh*, August 10, 2016.

Guieb, Marilou. "HB 5595 Seeks to Create Autonomous Cordillera Region." *Business Mirror*, May 11, 2014.

Javellana, Juliet Labog. "Estrada Signs Law Resetting ARMM Polls." *Philippine Daily Inquirer*, September 9, 1999.

Jones, Sidney. "How Will Partai Aceh Govern?" *Tempo*, April 19, 2012.

"Kampung Di Papua Dan Irjabar Dapat Rp 100 Juta [Village in Papua and Irian Jaya Barat Receives 100 Million Rp]." *Suara Pembaruan*, February 27, 2007.

Kasitpradit, Sermsuk and Wassana Nanuam. "Kitti: Separatists, Not Bandits." *Bangkok Post*, Thursday, January 8, 2004.

"Kebijakan Pembangunan Dimulai Dari Kampung [Development Begins in the Village]." *Bintang Papua*, February 9, 2011.

"KPU Provinsi Harus Bertanggung Jawab! [Provincial KPU Have a Responsibility!]." *Bintang Papua*, February 24, 2011.

Llanesca, Panti. "BBL 'Riddled with Unconstitutional Provisions'." *The Manila Times*, May 23, 2018.

"MILF Rejects Autonomy Offer." *The Philippine Star*, August 24, 2011.

"Missing: Rp258.1 Billion of Japan Aid for Aceh." *Tempo*, October 31, 2006.

Moore, Matthew and Indonesia Karuni Rompies Surabaya. "Kopassus Guilty of Eluay Murder." *The Age*, April 22, 2003.

"National Security Laws: Key Implications for Thailand." *Bangkok Post*, October 24, 2010.

Nolan, Cillian. "Elections in Aceh and Timor Leste: After the Struggle." *Jakarta Post*, April 19, 2012.

"Papua Belum Punya Perdasus [No Special Law for Papua yet]." *Republika*, April 10, 2013.

"Papua Council Struggles for Significance Two Years On." *Jakarta Post*, November 2, 2007.

"Papua, West Papua Agree to End Their Bickering." *Jakarta Post*, February 21, 2007.

Pasha, Zahlul. "Lemahnya Qanun KKR Aceh [Aceh's KKR Law Weak]." *Serambi Indonesia*, May 9, 2017.

"Pejabat Tiga Kabupaten Pertanyakan Pemekaran [Officials of Three Districts Request Division into New Districts]." *Kompas*, February 20, 2007.

"Pembahasan RUU Aceh Akan Dipercepat [Discussion on Aceh Law Accelerated]." *Tempo*, February 18, 2006.

"Pembentukan Provinsi Papua Tengah Menguat [Efforts to Form Central Papua Province Strengthens]." *Bintang Papua*, April 28, 2011.

"Pemerintah Masih Pelajari Rekomendasi MRP Soal Irabar [Government Still Studying MRP Recommendation on West Irian Jaya]." *Suara Karya*, March 21, 2006.

"Pemprov Papua Dinilai Terus Lakukan Pembohongan Public [Papua's Provincial Government Continues to Lie to the Public]." *Bintang Papua*, November 23, 2010.

Picana, Thom. "Cordillera Autonomy Consultation Starts." *The Manila Times*, July 10, 2015.

"House Fails on Cordillera Autonomy Bill." *The Manila Times*, February 8, 2016.

"Provinsi Papua Selatan Masih Sulit Diwujudkan [South Papua Province Faces Formation Difficulties]." *Bintang Papua*, September 27, 2010.

"Puji Tuhan, Aman! DAP/MAP Ajukan 6 Tuntutan [Praise the Lord, Safety! DAP/MAP Forward 6 Demands]." *Cendrawasih Pos*, August 13, 2005.

Rashid, Razlan and Pimuk Rakkanam. "Thailand, Mara Patani Hold Technical Talks on Deep South Truce." *Benar News*, September 12, 2017.

"Rp 25 Juta Untuk Bekas Tentara GAM [25 Million Rupiahs for Ex-GAM Soldiers]." *Tempo*, May 15, 2006.

Salaverria, Leila B. "Duterte Meets with MILF Leaders on Supposed Opposition to BBL." *Inquirer News*, March 29, 2018.

Sanda, Abun. "Establishing Emotional Relations." *Kompas (English Translation)*, August 15, 2005.

"Sejumlah Calon Anggota MRP Nilai Proses Pemilihan Tak Jujur [Some MRP Candidates Consider Selection Process Not Fair]." *Bintang Papua*, February 8, 2011.

"Senate, House Approve Proposed Bangsamoro Basic Law." *ABS-CBN News*, May 31, 2018.

"Setahun Bertugas, Belum Ada Qanun Disiapkan Parlemen Aceh [in Office for One Year, No Regulations Prepared by Aceh's Parliament]." *Tempo*, August 17, 2010.

Siboro, Tiarma. "Government Prepares Regulation on West Irian Jaya Province." *Jakarta Post*, July 22, 2005.

Tasker, Rodney. "Southern Discomfort: Muslim Separatist Violence Raises Its Head Again." *Far Eastern Economic Review*, 1993.

Tasker, Rodney and Michael Vatikiotis. "Troubled Frontier: Thai Muslim Violence Concerns Malaysia as Well." *Far Eastern Economic Review*, September 16, 1993, 12.

"Temuan Dana Otsus Dipakai Melancong Ke Eropa, Dibatah [Autonomy Funds Used for European Vacations]." *Bintang Papua*, April 19, 2011.

"Thaha: Revisi Perdasus = Kejahatan Politik [Thaha: Perdasus Revisions = a Political Evil]." *Bintang Papua*, January 24, 2011.

"Thailand Agrees to Historic Peace Talks with Muslim Rebels." *Global Insight*, February 28, 2013.

"Thailand: Peace Talks with Southern Insurgents Go Nowhere." *Thai News Service*, December 5, 2012.

"Thailand: Source Reveals Conditions of Insurgent Groups at Peace Talks." *Thai News Service*, March 28, 2013.

"Tim Advokasi Aceh Melobi Megawati [Aceh Advocacy Team Lobby Megawati]." *Tempo*, February 2, 2006.

"TNI/POLRI Di Puncak Jaya Dinilai 'Mubazir' [TNI/Police in Puncak Jaya Judged 'Redundant']." *Bintang Papua*, October 23, 2010.

"Undang-Undang Pemerintahan Aceh Disahkan [Aceh Government Law Formalized]." *Tempo*, July 11, 2006.

"Wapres: UP4 Jangan Tabrakan Dengan Otsus [Vice President: UP4 Should Not Conflict with Autonomy Funds]." *Bintang Papua*, November 25, 2010.

Interviews

Abubakar, Carmen. Professor, Institute of Islamic Studies at U.P. Diliman. Interview (informal conversation) by author. April 28, 2008. Cotabato City.

Al Hamid, Fadhal. Head of Customary Governance, Dewan Adat Papua (Papuan Customary Assembly). Interview by author. March 31, 2012. Jayapura.

Al Hamid, Thaha. Sekjen PDP (Secretary General of PDP). Interview by author. April 1, 2012. Jayapura.

Alawas, Recto. Chief, Technical Management Division, NCIP-CAR. Interview by author. August 29, 2007. Baguio.

Alua, Agus. Vice Secretary General of the Presidium Dewan Papua (PDP), Secretary of the Mubes Organizing Committee and Head of the Congress Organizing Committee. Interview by author. August 23, 2001. Abepura.

Aguswandi. Former Head of SMUR and Involved in Establishing Partai Rakyat Aceh (Aceh People's Party). Interview by author. March 24, 2008. Banda Aceh.

Anonymous. Coordination Manager, Bureau of Education, Culture and Religion, SBPAC. Interview by author. January 28, 2009.

Anonymous. High-Level Official, Government Affairs Coordination Division, Provincial Affairs Bureau (Ministry of Interior, Thailand). Interview by author. February 2, 2009.

Anonymous. High-Level Official, National Security Council of Thailand, 1980s and 1990s. Interview by author. January 26, 2009.

Awom, Herman. Presidium Dewan Papua (PDP). Interview by author. March 31, 2012. Jayapura.

Bacani, Benedito. Head of Institute for Autonomy and Governance. Interview by author. April 30, 2008. Cotabato city.

Bajunaid, Moner. Head of Technical Committee, MILF-Government of Philippines Negotiation Panel (1997–2000). May 5, 2008. Cotabato city.

Baru, Worawit. Senator. Interview by author. February 4, 2009. Bangkok.

Beuransah, Muad Jahja Adan. Spokesperson of Aceh Party. Interview by author. March 25, 2008. Banda Aceh.

Bolinget, Windel. Secretary General, Cordillera Peoples' Alliance. Interview by author. August 27, 2007. Baguio city.

Boonarong. Deputy Mayor, Municipality of Narathiwat District. Interview by author. January 27, 2009. Narathiwat.

Carling, Joan. Former Chairperson, Cordillera Peoples' Alliance. Interview by author. August 30, 2007. Baguio city.

Charoenpapiriya, Naree. NGO Worker, Peace Witnessing Project, Mahidol University. Interview by author. January 31, 2009.

Djohan, Djohermansyah. Deputy (Political Affairs) to Vice President Jusuf Kalla. Interview by author. April 1, 2008. Jakarta.

Eluay, Theys. PDP Chair. Interview by author. August 21, 2001. Sentani.

Giay, Benny. Lecturer at Stt-Walter Post, Jayapura and Head of Team Preparing Terms of Reference for Team 100 Meeting. Interview by author. August 22, 2001. Jayapura.

Guzman, Attny Maria Vicenta de. Executive Director, Panlipi. Interview by author. August 20, 2007. Manila.

Hamada-Pawid, Zenaida Bridget. Activist in Cordillera Peace Forums. She was later Chairperson, Commissioner of Region I, and the Cordilleras and National Commission on Indigenous Peoples Chairman from 2011 to 2013. Interview by author. August 27, 2007. Baguio city.

Hamid, Ahmad Humam. Chief Coordinator of *Forum Peduli Ham*, Gubernatorial Candidate for PPP, and Head of Aceh Recovery Forum. Interview by author. May 14, 1999. Banda Aceh.

Hamzah, Tengku. Former Commander and Soldier, GAM, in Banda Aceh Area. Interview by author. March 28, 2008. Banda Aceh.

Hasamoh, Alisa. Member National Reconciliation Commission and Prince of Songkla University Lecturer. Interview by author. January 28, 2009. Pattani.

Jafar, Gazhali. MILF Vice-Chair for Political Affairs. Interview by author. May 3, 2008. (Near) Cotabato city.

Kitthaworn, Piya. Professor, Prince of Songkla University. Interview by author. January 29, 2009. Pattani.

La Barinto, Rodolfo. Chief Economic Development Specialist, National Economic and Development Authority – Cordillera Autonomous Region. Interview by author. August 29, 2007. Baguio city.

Lingga, Abhoud Syed. Head of Institute of Bangsamoro Studies, MILF Peace Panel Member, and Former Secretary-General of the Moro National Liberation Front (MNLF). Interview by author. May 1, 2008. Cotabato city.

Mamingchi, Waeduerame. President of Pattani Provincial Islamic Council. Interview by author. January 31, 2009. Pattani.

Manufandu, Septer. Executive Secretary, Foker NGO. Interview by author. April 4, 2012. Jayapura.

Mastura, Datu Michael. Former Deputy Minister of Muslim Affairs and MILF Chief Negotiator. Interview by author. May 2, 2008. Cotabato city.

Neelaphaijit, Angkana. Human Rights Activist. Interview by author. January 25, 2009. Bangkok.

Pasqua, Grace. Director, Planning, Policy and Research of NCIP (National). Interview by author. August 21, 2007. Manila.

Phongsuwansiri, Prasert. Member of Parliament, Representative Yala Province. Interview by author. February 4, 2009. Bangkok.

Prill-Brett, June. Professor, University of the Philippines, Baguio. Interview by author. August 27, 2007. Baguio city.

Rasul, Amina. Head of Philippine Council for Islam and Democracy and Member of Ramos Cabinet. Interview by author. April 29, 2008. Manila.

Reba, Yusak. Program Coordinator, Institute for Civil Society Strengthening (ICS). Interview by author. April 5, 2012. Jayapura.

Rico, Ruth Lusterio. Professor, University of the Philippines, Diliman, Manila. Interview by author. August 20, 2007. Manila.

Rodil, Rudy. Vice Chairman of the Government Panel, Negotiations with MILF. Interview by author. April 29, 2008. Manila.

Rood, Steven. Representative, Asia Foundation (Philippines). Interview by author. April 28, 2008. Makati City, Manila.

Rovillos, Raymundo D. Professor, University of the Philippines, Baguio. Interview by author. August 23, 2007. Baguio city.

Rumbiak, Michael. Lecturer and Head of Population Research Centre. Interview by author. August 25, 2001. Abepura.

Saleh, Abdullah. Vice Head of Special Committee XVIII and PPP Member of DPRD Aceh. Interview by author. March 25, 2008. Banda Aceh.

Satha-Anan, Chaiwat. Professor, Thammasat University. Interview (informal conversation) by author. January 25, 2009.

Sirisakdhamkeng, Prae. Professor, Silapakorn University. Interview by author. February 2, 2009.

Srisompob Jitpiromsri. Professor, Prince of Songklah University and Director, Deep South Watch. Interview by author. January 30, 2009. Pattani.

Sumule, Agus. Advisor to the Governor of Papua. Interview by author. March 30, 2012. Jayapura.

Tauli-Corpuz, Victoria. Chair, Tebtebba Foundation and Chair, UN Permanent Forum on Indigenous Peoples. Interview by author. August 24, 2007. Baguio city.

Tebay, Neles. Catholic Priest and Coordinator of *Jaringan Damai Papua* (Papua Peace Network). Interview by author. April 2, 2012. Jayapura.

Yoman, Socratez Sofyan. Ketua Persekutuan-Persekutuan Gereja Baptis Papua (Head of the Federation of Papua Baptist Churches). Interview by author. April 3, 2012. Jayapura.

Journal Articles and Books

Abinales, Patricio N. "Life after the Coup: The Military and Politics in Post-Authoritarian Philippines." *Philippine Political Science Journal* 26, no. 49 (2005): 27–62.

Abubakar, Ayesah Uy. *Peacebuilding and Sustainable Human Development: The Pursuit of the Bangsamoro Right to Self-Determination*. Switzerland: Springer Nature, 2019.

Abubakar, Carmen A. "Review of the Mindanao Peace Processes." *Inter-Asia Cultural Studies* 5, no. 3 (2004): 450–64.

Abuza, Zachary. "The Moro Islamic Liberation Front at 20: State of the Revolution." *Studies in Conflict & Terrorism* 28, no. 6 (2005): 453–79.

"Can Duterte Bring Peace to the Philippines?" *The Diplomat*, https://thediplomat .com/2016/11/can-duterte-bring-peace-to-the-philippines/.

Acemoglu, Daron and James A. Robinson. *Economic Origins of Dictatorship and Democracy*. Cambridge; New York: Cambridge University Press, 2006.

Aji, Priasto. "Summary of Indonesia's Poverty Analysis." In *ADB Papers on Indonesia*. Manila: Asian Development Bank, October 2015.

Anderson, Benedict. "Cacique Democracy and the Philippines: Origins and Dreams." *New Left Review* 169 (1988): 3–31.

The Spectre of Comparisons: Nationalism, Southeast Asia, and the World. London; New York: Verso, 1998.

Asian Development Bank. *Indigenous Peoples/Ethnic Minorities and Poverty Reduction: Philippines*. Manila: Asian Development Bank; distributed by Independent Publishers Group, Chicago, 2002.

Aspinall, Edward. "Modernity, History and Ethnicity: Indonesian and Acehnese Nationalism in Conflict." *RIMA: Review of Indonesian and Malaysian Affairs* 36, no. 1 (June 2002): 3–33.

"Anti-Insurgency Logic in Aceh: Military Policy of Separating Civilians from Guerillas Generates More Resistance." *Inside Indonesia* 76 (Fall 2003): 23–24.

The Helsinki Agreement: A More Promising Basis for Peace in Aceh? Policy Studies, 106: Washington, DC: East-West Center Washington, 2005.

"From Islamism to Nationalism in Aceh, Indonesia." *Nations and Nationalism* 13, no. 2 (2007): 245–63.

"The Construction of Grievance." *Journal of Conflict Resolution* 51, no. 6 (2007): 950–72.

Islam and Nation: Separatist Rebellion in Aceh, Indonesia. Studies in Asian Security. Stanford, CA: Stanford University Press, 2009.

"Aceh's No Win Election." *Inside Indonesia* 106, no. October–December (2011).

"Special Autonomy, Predatory Peace and the Resolution of the Aceh Conflict." In *Regional Dynamics in a Decentralized Indonesia*, edited by Hal Hill, 460–81. Singapore: Institute of Southeast Asian Studies, 2014.

Aspinall, Edward and Harold A. Crouch. *The Aceh Peace Process: Why It Failed.* Washington, DC: East-West Center Washington, 2003.

Australian National University Enterprise. *Governance and Capacity Building in Post-Crisis Aceh.* Jakarta: UNDP Indonesia, 2012.

Ayres, R. William and Stephen Saideman. "Is Separatism as Contagious as the Common Cold or as Cancer? Testing International and Domestic Explanations." *Nationalism and Ethnic Politics* 6, no. 3 (2000): 91–113.

Bahry, Donna. "The New Federalism and the Paradoxes of Regional Sovereignty in Russia." *Comparative Politics* 37, no. 2 (2005): 127–46.

Balfour, Sebastian and Alejandro Quiroga. *The Reinvention of Spain: Nation and Identity since Democracy.* Oxford: Oxford University Press, 2007.

Banlaoi, Rommel C., ed. *The Marawi Siege and Its Aftermath: The Continuing Terrorist Threat.* Newcastle upon Tyne: Cambridge Scholars Publishing, 2020.

Banton, Michael. *Racial and Ethnic Competition.* Comparative Ethnic and Race Relations. Cambridge; New York: Cambridge University Press, 1983.

Beissinger, Mark R. *Nationalist Mobilization and the Collapse of the Soviet State.* Cambridge: Cambridge University Press, 2002.

"A New Look at Ethnicity and Democratization." *Journal of Democracy* 19, no. 3 (2008): 85–97.

Belanger, Sarah and Maurice Pinard. "Ethnic Movements and the Competition Model: Some Missing Links." *American Sociological Review* 56, no. 4 (August 1991): 446–57.

Bertrand, Jacques. "Autonomy and Stability: The Perils of Implementation and 'Divide-and-Rule' Tactics in Papua, Indonesia." *Nationalism and Ethnic Politics* 20, no. 2 (2014): 174–99.

"'Indigenous Peoples' Rights' as a Strategy of Ethnic Accommodation: Contrasting Experiences of Cordillerans and Papuans in the Philippines and Indonesia." *Ethnic and Racial Studies* 34, no. 5 (2011): 850–69.

"Indonesia's Quasi-Federalist Approach: Accommodation Amidst Strong Integrationist Tendencies." In *Constitutional Design for Divided Societies: Integration or Accommodation?*, edited by Sujit Choudhry, 576–605. Oxford: Oxford University Press, 2008.

Nationalism and Ethnic Conflict in Indonesia. Cambridge; New York: Cambridge University Press, 2004.

"Peace and Conflict in the Southern Philippines: Why the 1996 Peace Agreement Is Fragile." *Pacific Affairs* 73, no. 1 (2000): 37–54.

Political Change in Southeast Asia. Cambridge; New York: Cambridge University Press, 2013.

Bertrand, Jacques, Alexandre Pelletier, and Ardeth Maung Thawnghmung. "First Movers, Democratization and Unilateral Concessions: Overcoming Commitment

Problems and Negotiating a 'Nationwide Cease-Fire' in Myanmar." *Asian Security* 16, no. 1 (2018): 1–20.

Bertrand, Jacques and André Laliberté. *Multination States in Asia Accommodation or Resistance*. New York: Cambridge University Press, 2010.

Bertrand, Jacques and Oded Haklai, eds. *Democratization and Ethnic Minorities: Conflict or Compromise?*. New York: Routledge, 2013.

Bertrand, Jacques and Sanjay Jeram. "Democratization and Determinants of Ethnic Violence: The Rebel-Moderate Organizational Nexus." In *Democratization and Ethnic Minorities: Conflict or Compromise?*, edited by Jacques Bertrand and Oded Haklai, 103–29. New York: Routledge, 2014.

Bhakti, Ikrar Nusa and Richard Chauvel. *The Papua Conflict: Jakarta's Perceptions and Policies*. Washington, DC: East-West Center Washington, 2004.

Boix, Carles. "Economic Roots of Civil Wars and Revolutions in the Contemporary World." *World Politics* 60, no. 3 (2008): 390–437.

Booth, Anne. "Development: Achievement and Weakness." In *Indonesia Beyond Suharto: Polity, Economy, Society, Transition*, edited by Donald K. Emmerson, 109–35. Armonk, NY: M. E. Sharpe, 1999.

Boquiren, Arturo C. *Advancing Regional Autonomy in the Cordillera: A Source Book*. Baguio City; Pasig, Metro Manila: Cordillera Studies Center University of the Philippines College Baguio; Friedrich Ebert Stiftung Manila Office, 1994.

Bouchard, Gérard. *La Nation Québécoise Au Futur Et Au Passé*. Collection Balises. Montréal: VLB, 1999.

Brancati, Dawn. "Decentralization: Fueling the Fire or Dampening the Flames of Ethnic Conflict and Secessionism." *International Organization* 60, no. 3 (2006): 651–85.

Brubaker, Rogers and David D. Laitin. "Ethnic and Nationalist Violence." *Annual Review of Sociology* 24, no. 1 (1998): 423–52.

Brubaker, Rogers. "Ethnicity, Race, and Nationalism." *Annual Review of Sociology* 35 (2009): 21–42.

Nationalism Reframed: Nationhood and the National Question in the New Europe. Cambridge: Cambridge University Press, 1996.

Bunce, Valerie. "Peaceful Versus Violent State Dismemberment: A Comparison of the Soviet Union, Yugoslavia, and Czechoslovakia." *Politics & Society* 27, no. 2 (1999): 217–37.

Candelaria, Sedfrey. "Comparative Analysis on the ILO Indigenous and Tribal Peoples Convention No. 169, UN Declaration on the Rights of Indigenous Peoples (UNDRIP) and the Indigenous Peoples' Rights Act (IPRA) of the Philippines." International Labour Organization, www.ilo.org/wcmsp5/groups/public/–asia/–ro-bangkok/–ilo-manila/documents/publication/wcms_171406.pdf.

Carling, Joan. "The Cordillera Peoples' Continuing Struggle for Self-Determination." In *International Conference on Indigenous Peoples' Self-determination and the Nation State in Asia*. Baguio, Philippines, 1999.

Carment, David. "Managing Interstate Ethnic Tensions: The Thailand-Malaysia Experience." *Nationalism and Ethnic Politics* 1, no. 4 (1995): 1–22.

Casambre, Athena Lydia. "The Failure of Autonomy in the Cordillera Region, Northern Luzon, Philippines." In *1st National Conference on Cordillera Research*. Baguio City: Cordillera Studies Centre, 2000.

"The Frustrated Discourse on Regional Autonomy in the Cordillera and Notes toward a Productive Discourse." In *6th International Philippines Studies Conference*. Diliman, Quezon City, 2000.

"Interpretation of the Debate on Cordillera Autonomy."1987. (Unpublished manscuript)

Case, William. "Democracy's Quality and Breakdown: New Lessons from Thailand." *Democratization* 14, no. 4 (2007): 622–42.

Populist Threats and Democracy's Fate in Southeast Asia: Thailand, the Philippines, and Indonesia. New York: Routledge, 2017.

"Thai Democracy in 2001: Out of Equilibrium." *Asian Survey* 41, no. 3 (2001): 525–47.

Castro, Nestor T. *Ten Years of the Indigenous Peoples' Rights Act: An Assessment*. Manila: University of the Philippines, Diliman, 2007.

Cederman, Lars-Erik and Manuel Vogt. "Dynamics and Logics of Civil War." *Journal of Conflict Resolution* 61, no. 9 (2017): 1992–2016.

Cederman, Lars-Erik, Andreas Wimmer, and Brian Min. "Why Do Ethnic Groups Rebel? New Data and Analysis." *World Politics* 62, no. 1 (2010): 87–119.

Cederman, Lars-Erik, Kristian Skrede Gleditsch, and Julian Wucherpfennig. "Predicting the Decline of Ethnic Civil War: Was Gurr Right and for the Right Reasons?." *Journal of Peace Research* 54, no. 2 (2017): 262–74.

Cederman, Lars-Erik, Kristian Skrede Gleditsch, and Simon Hug. "Elections and Ethnic Civil War." *Comparative Political Studies* 46, no. 3 (2012): 387–417

Cederman, Lars-Erik, Simon Hug, and Lutz F. Krebs. "Democratization and Civil War: Empirical Evidence." *Journal of Peace Research* 47, no. 4 (2010): 377–94.

Cederman, Lars-Erik, Simon Hug, Andreas Schadel, and Julian Wucherpfennig. "Territorial Autonomy in the Shadow of Conflict: Too Little, Too Late?." *American Political Science Review* 109, no. 2 (2015): 354–70.

Chandra, Kanchan. "What Is Ethnic Identity and Does It Matter?." *Annual Review of Political Science* 9 (2006): 397–424.

Chandra, Kanchan and Steven Wilkinson. "Measuring the Effect of 'Ethnicity'." *Comparative Political Studies* 41, no. 4–5 (2008): 515–63.

Chandra, Siddarth and Douglas Kammen. "Generating Reforms and Reforming Generations: Military Politics in Indonesia's Democratic Transition and Consolidation." *World Politics* 55, no. 1 (2002): 96–136.

Chauvel, Richard. *Constructing Papuan Nationalism: History, Ethnicity, and Adaptation*. Washington, DC: East-West Center, 2005.

Che Man, Kadir. *Muslim Separatism: The Moros of the Southern Philippines and the Malays of Southern Thailand*. Singapore: Oxford University Press, 1990.

Choudhry, Sujit. *Constitutional Design for Divided Societies: Integration or Accommodation?*. Oxford: Oxford University Press, 2008.

"Constitutional Politics and Crisis in Sri Lanka." In *Multination States in Asia: Accommodation or Resistance*, edited by Jacques Bertrand and André Laliberté, 103–35. Cambridge: Cambridge University Press, 2010.

Chua, Amy. "Markets, Democracy, and Ethnicity: Toward a New Paradigm for Law and Development." *The Yale Law Journal* 108, no. 1 (1998): 1–107.

Coakley, John. "'Primordialism' in Nationalism Studies: Theory or Ideology?" *Nations and Nationalism* 24, no. 2 (2018): 327–47.

Cockett, Richard. *Sudan: The Failure and Division of an African State*. New Haven, CT: Yale University Press, 2016.

Colaresi, Michael and Sabine C. Carey. "To Kill or to Protect: Security Forces, Domestic Institutions, and Genocide." *Journal of Conflict Resolution* 52, no. 1 (2008): 39–67.

Colino, César. "Constitutional Change without Constitutional Reform: Spanish Federalism and the Revision of Catalonia's Statute of Autonomy." *Publius: The Journal of Federalism* 39, no. 2 (2009): 262–88.

Collier, Paul. "Rebellion as a Quasi-Criminal Activity." *Journal of Conflict Resolution* 44, no. 6 (2000): 839–53.

Collier, Paul and Anke Hoeffler. "On the Economic Causes of Civil War." *Oxford Economic Papers* 50, no. 4 (1998): 563–73.

"On the Incidence of Civil War in Africa." *The Journal of Conflict Resolution* 46, no. 1 (2002): 13–28.

Collier, Paul and Nicholas Sambanis. *Understanding Civil War: Evidence and Analysis*. Volume 2. Europe, Central Asia, and Other Regions, Washington, DC: World Bank, 2005.

Colomer, Josep M. "The Spanish 'State of Autonomies': Non-Institutional Federalism." *West European Politics* 21, no. 4 (1998): 40–52.

"The Venturous Bid for the Independence of Catalonia." *Nationalities Papers* 45, no. 5 (2017): 950–67.

Community-Based Reintegration in Aceh: Assessing the Impacts of BRA-KDP. Indonesian Social Development Paper No 12, edited by Patrick Barron and the Indonesia World Bank Office. Jakarta: World Bank, 2009.

Congrès Mondial Amazigh. "Amazighs of Morocco: An Indigenous People Despoiled, Presented at UN Committee for Human Rights 118th Session, October 17 to November 4, 2016, Geneva."

Connor, Walker. "Beyond Reason: The Nature of the Ethnonational Bond." *Ethnic and Racial Studies* 16, no. 3 (1993): 373–89.

Connors, Michael Kelly. *Democracy and National Identity in Thailand*. Abingdon, Oxon: Taylor & Francis, 2004.

Cornell, Svante E. "Autonomy as a Source of Conflict: Caucasian Conflicts in Theoretical Perspective." *World Politics* 54, no. 2 (2002): 245–76.

Coyne, Christopher J. and Peter J. Boettke. "The Problem of Credible Commitment in Reconstruction." *Journal of Institutional Economics* 5, no. 1 (2009): 1–23.

Crawford, James. *The Creation of States in International Law*. New York: Oxford University Press, 2006.

Crawhall, Nigel. "Africa and the UN Declaration on the Rights of Indigenous Peoples." *The International Journal of Human Rights* 15, no. 1 (2011): 11–36.

Crisis Management Initiative. *Aceh Peace Process Follow-up Project: Final Report*. Helsinki: Crisis Management Initiative, 2012.

Crispin, Shawn W. "Gearing up for a Fight." *Far Eastern Economic Review* 167, no. 19 (2004): 21–22.

"Love Vs. War." *Far Eastern Economic Review* 167, no. 20 (2004): 17.

"Spotlight: Thai Power Play." *Far Eastern Economic Review* 165, no. 29 (July 25, 2002): 11.

Croissant, Aurel. "Unrest in South Thailand: Contours, Causes, and Consequences since 2001." *Contemporary Southeast Asia* 27, no. 1 (2005): 21–43.

Crouch, Harold A. "The TNI and East Timor Policy." In *Out of the Ashes: Destruction and Reconstruction of East Timor*, edited by James J. Fox and Dionisio Babo Soares, 141–68. Canberra: Australian National University Press, 2003.

Cunningham, David E., Kristian Skrede Gleditsch, and Idean Salehyan. "It Takes Two: A Dyadic Analysis of Civil War Duration and Outcome." *Journal of Conflict Resolution* 53, no. 4 (August 2009): 570–97.

Curaming, Rommel A. "Historical Injustice and Human Insecurity: Conflict and Peacemaking in Muslim Mindanao." In *Human Insecurities in Southeast Asia*, edited by Paul J Carnegie, Victor T King, and Zawawi Ibrahim, 121–40. New York: Springer, 2016.

Daes, Erica-Irene. "Protection of the World's Indigenous Peoples and Human Rights." In *Human Rights: Concept and Standard*, edited by Janusz Symonides. Ashgate: UNESCO Publishing, 2000.

Dahl, Robert. *Democracy and Its Critics*. New Haven, CT: Yale University Press, 1989.

Davenport, Christian. "Multi-Dimensional Threat Perception and State Repression: An Inquiry into Why States Apply Negative Sanctions." *American Journal of Political Science* 39, no. 3 (1995): 683–713.

——— *State Repression and the Domestic Democratic Peace*. Cambridge Studies in Comparative Politics. Cambridge; New York: Cambridge University Press, 2007.

——— "State Repression and the Tyrannical Peace." *Journal of Peace Research* 44, no. 4 (2007): 485–504.

DeNardo, James. *Power in Numbers: Political Strategy of Protest and Rebellion*. Princeton, NJ: Princeton University Press, 1985.

Diamond, Larry Jay. "Toward Democratic Consolidation." *Journal of Democracy* 5, no. 3 (1994): 4–17.

Diamond, Larry and Marc F Plattner, eds. *Nationalism, Ethnic Conflict, and Democracy*. Baltimore: Johns Hopkins University Press, 1994.

Dixon, Jeffrey. "What Causes Civil Wars? Integrating Quantitative Research Findings." *International Studies Review* 11, no. 4 (2009): 707–35.

"Draft Memorandum of Understanding (GRP and MILF, as of February 18, 2008)."

Drooglever, Pieter. *An Act of Free Choice: Decolonisation and the Right to Self-Determination in West Papua*. London, UK: One World Publications, 2009.

Elbadawi, E., and N. Sambanis. "How Much War Will We See?: Explaining the Prevalence of Civil War." *Journal of Conflict Resolution* 46, no. 3 (2002): 307–34.

——— "Why Are There So Many Civil Wars in Africa? Understanding and Preventing Violent Conflict." *Journal of African Economies* 9, no. 3 (2000): 244–69.

Elkins, Zachary and John Sides. "Can Institutions Build Unity in Multiethnic States?." *American Political Science Review* 101, no. 4 (2007): 693–708.

Emmerson, Donald K. "Voting and Violence: Indonesia and East Timor in 1999." In *Indonesia Beyond Suharto*, edited by Donald K. Emmerson, 344–61. Abingdon, Oxon: M. E. Sharpe, 1999.

Encarnación, Omar G. "Beyond Transitions: The Politics of Democratic Consolidation." *Comparative Politics* 32, no. 4 (2000): 479–98.

Fearon, James D. "Commitment Problems and the Spread of Ethnic Conflict." In *The International Spread of Ethnic Conflict: Fear, Diffusion, and Escalation*, edited by David A. Lake and Donald S. Rothchild, 107–26. Princeton, NJ: Princeton University Press, 1998.

Fearon, James D. and David D. Laitin. "Ethnicity, Insurgency, and Civil War." *American Political Science Review* 97, no. 1 (February 2003): 75–90.

Feith, Herbert. *The Decline of Constitutional Democracy in Indonesia*. Ithaca, NY: Cornell University Press, 1962.

Ferrer, Miriam Coronel. "Recycled Autonomy? Enacting the New Organic Act for a Regional Autonomous Government in Southern Philippines." *Kasarinlan* 15, no. 2 (2000): 165–89.

Finin, Gerard A. *The Making of the Igorot: Contours of Cordillera Consciousness*. Quezon City: Ateneo de Manila University Press, 2005.

Florendo, Nela. "The Movement for Regional Autonomy in the Cordillera from a Historical Perspective." In *Advancing Regional Autonomy in the Cordillera: A Source Book*, edited by Arturo C. Boquiren, 30–48. Baguio City; Pasig, Metro Manila: Cordillera Studies Center University of the Philippines, Baguio; Friedrich Ebert Stiftung Manila Office, 1994.

Forsberg, Erika. "Do Ethnic Dominoes Fall? Evaluating Domino Effects of Granting Territorial Concessions to Separatist Groups." *International Studies Quarterly* 57, no. 2 (2013): 329–40.

Fry, Howard Tyrrell. *A History of the Mountain Province*. Quezon City, Philippines, 1983.

Funston, John. "Malaysia and Thailand's Southern Conflict: Reconciling Security and Ethnicity." *Contemporary Southeast Asia* 32, no. 2 (2010): 234–57.

Gereja Kemah Injil Indonesia, Paroki Tiga Raja, and Gereja Kristen Injili di Irian Jaya. *Laporan Pelanggaran Hak Asasi Manusia Dan Bencana Di Bela, Alama, Jila Dan Mapnduma, Irian Jaya*. Timika, Irian Jaya.

Gilquin, Michel. *Les Musulmans De Thailande*. Paris: L'Harmattan, 2002.

Ginsburg, Tom. "Constitutional Afterlife: The Continuing Impact of Thailand's Postpolitical Constitution." *International Journal of Constitutional Law* 7, no. 1 (2009): 83–105.

Gleditsch, Kristian Skrede and Andrea Ruggeri. "Political Opportunity Structures, Democracy, and Civil War." *Journal of Peace Research* 47, no. 3 (2010): 299–310.

Gleditsch, Kristian Skrede and Håvard Hegre. "Regime Type and Political Transition in Civil War." In *Routledge Handbook of Civil Wars*, edited by Karl R. DeRouen and Edward Newman. Abingdon, Oxon; New York: Routledge, 2014.

Gleditsch, Nils Petter, Håvard Hegre, and Håvard Strand. "Democracy and Civil War." In *Handbook of War Studies III: The Intrastate Dimension*, edited by Manus I. Midlarsky, 155–92. Ann Arbor, MI: University of Michigan Press, 2009.

Goodwin, Jeff. *No Other Way Out: States and Revolutionary Movements, 1945–1991*. Cambridge: Cambridge University Press, 2001.

Gowing, Peter G. *Mandate in Moroland: The American Government of Muslim Filipinos 1899–1920*. Quezon: New Day, 1983.

Greenfeld, Liah. *Nationalism: Five Roads to Modernity*. Cambridge, MA: Harvard University Press, 1992.

Guibernau, Montserrat. *Catalan Nationalism: Francoism, Transition, and Democracy.* London; New York: Routledge, 2004.

Gurr, Ted Robert. "Ethnic Warfare on the Wane." *Foreign Affairs* 79, no. 3 (2000): 52–64.

Minorities at Risk: A Global View of Ethnopolitical Conflicts. Washington, DC: United States Institute of Peace Press, 1993.

Peoples Versus States: Minorities at Risk in the New Century. Washington, DC: United States Institute of Peace Press, 2000.

Why Men Rebel. Princeton, NJ: Princeton University Press, 1970.

Gurr, Ted Robert and Will H. Moore. "Ethnopolitical Rebellion: A Cross-Sectional Analysis of the 1980s with Risk Assessments for the 1990s." *American Journal of Political Science* 41, no. 4 (1997): 1079–103.

Hale, Henry E. "Divided We Stand: Institutional Sources of Ethnofederal State Survival and Collapse." *World Politics* 56 (2004): 165–93.

Han, Enze and Christopher Paik. "Ethnic Integration and Development in China." *World Development* 93 (2017): 31–42.

Hangen, Susan I. *The Rise of Ethnic Politics in Nepal: Democracy in the Margins.* Abingdon, Oxon: Routledge, 2010.

Hartzell, Caroline A. and Matthew Hoddie. *Crafting Peace: Power-Sharing Institutions and the Negotiated Settlement of Civil Wars.* University Park, PA: Pennsylvania State University Press, 2007.

Hashim, Ahmed. *When Counterinsurgency Wins: Sri Lanka's Defeat of the Tamil Tigers.* Philadelphia: University of Pennsylvania Press, 2013.

Hawes, Gary. *The Philippine State and the Marcos Regime: The Politics of Export.* Ithaca, NY: Cornell University Press, 1987.

Hechter, M., and D. Okamoto. "Political Consequences of Minority Group Formation." *Annual Review of Political Science* 4, no. 1 (2001): 189–215.

Hechter, Michael. *Containing Nationalism.* Oxford: Oxford University Press, 2000.

Internal Colonialism: The Celtic Fringe in British National Development, 1536–1966. Berkeley: University of California Press, 1975.

Hegre, Håvard and Nicholas Sambanis. "Sensitivity Analysis of Empirical Results on Civil War Onset." *Journal of Conflict Resolution* 50, no. 4 (2006): 508–35.

Hegre, Håvard, Tanja Ellingsen, Scott Gates and Nils Petter Gleditsch. "Toward a Democratic Civil Peace? Democracy, Political Change, and Civil War, 1816–1992." *The American Political Science Review* 95, no. 1 (2001): 33–48.

Heraclides, Alexis. "Secessionist Minorities and External Involvement." *International Organization* 44, no. 3 (1990): 341–78.

Hicken, Allen. *Building Party Systems in Developing Democracies.* Cambridge: Cambridge University Press, 2009.

Hill, Daniel W. and Zachary M. Jones. "An Empirical Evaluation of Explanations for State Repression." *American Political Science Review* 108, no. 3 (2014): 661–87.

Hinsley, Francis Harry. *Sovereignty.* 2nd ed. New York: Cambridge University Press, 1986.

Horowitz, Donald. *Constitutional Change and Democracy in Indonesia.* Problems of International Politics. Cambridge; New York: Cambridge University Press, 2013.

"Democracy in Divided Societies." *Journal of Democracy* 4, no. 4 (1993): 18–38.

Ethnic Groups in Conflict. Berkeley: University of California Press, 1985.

The Deadly Ethnic Riot. Berkeley: University of California Press, 2001.

Human Rights Watch. "Indonesia Alert: Trouble in Irian Jaya." www.hrw.org/news/19 98/07/06/indonesia-alert-trouble-irian-jaya.

Indonesia: Human Rights and Pro-Independence Actions in Papua, 1999–2000. Jakarta: Human Rights Watch, 2000.

Huntington, Samuel. *The Third Wave: Democratization in the Late Twentieth Century*. Norman, OK: University of Oklahoma Press, 1991.

Husain, Farid and Salim Shahab. *To See the Unseen: Scenes Behind the Aceh Peace Treaty*. Jakarta: Health & Hospital Indonesia, 2007.

Hutchcroft, Paul D. and Joel Rocamora. "Strong Demands and Weak Institutions: The Origins and Evolution of the Democratic Deficit in the Philippines." *Journal of East Asian Studies* 3, no. 2 (2003): 259–92.

Hutchinson, John. "Myth against Myth: The Nation as Ethnic Overlay." *Nations and Nationalism* 10, no. 1–2 (2004): 109–23.

Hyndman, David. "Organic Act Rejected in the Cordillera: Dialectics of a Continuing Fourth World Autonomy Movement in the Philippines." *Dialectical Anthropology* 16, no. 2 (1991): 169–84.

Institute for Human Rights Study and Advocacy – Irian Jaya. *Kasus Abepura – 07 December 2000 [the Case of Abepura – 7 December 2000]*. Jayapura: ELS-HAM Irian Jaya, 2000.

Institute for Policy Analysis of Conflict. *Aceh's Surprising Election Results*. Jakarta: Institute for Policy Analysis of Conflict, 30 April 2014.

International Crisis Group. *Papua: The Dangers of Shutting Down Dialogue*. Jakarta: International Crisis Group, 2006.

Philippines Peace Process: Duterte Playing for High Stakes. Brussels: International Crisis Group, 2016.

The Philippines: The Collapse of Peace in Mindanao. Brussels: International Crisis Group, 2008.

Southern Philippines Backgrounder: Terrorism and the Peace Process. Brussels: International Crisis Group, 2004.

Southern Thailand: Dialogue in Doubt. Brussels: International Crisis Group, 2015.

Thailand: The Evolving Conflict in the South. Brussels: International Crisis Group, 2012.

International Foundation for Electoral Systems. "Elections in Aceh: Another Step Forward." www.ifes.org/news/elections-aceh-another-step-forward (accessed October 10, 2018).

Jardine, Matthew. "Power and Principle in East Timor." *Peace Review* 10, no. 2 (1998): 195–202.

Jayapura, Tim SKP. *Memoria Passionis Di Papua*. Jayapura: Sekretariat Keadilan dan Perdamaian, 2005.

Jemadu, Aleksius. "Democratisation, the TNI, and Resolving the Aceh Conflict." In *Verandah of Violence: Background to the Aceh Problem*, edited by Anthony Reid, 272–91. Singapore: Singapore University Press, 2006.

Jitpiromsri, Srisompob. "An Inconvenient Truth About the Deep South Violent Conflict: A Decade of Chaotic, Constrained Realities and Uncertain Resolution." Deep South Watch, https://deepsouthwatch.org/en/node/5904.

Jitpiromsri, Srisompob and Duncan McCargo. "The Southern Thai Conflict Six Years On: Insurgency, Not Just Crime." *Contemporary Southeast Asia* 32, no. 2 (2010): 156–83.

Jones, Gregg R. *Red Revolution: Inside the Philippine Guerrilla Movement.* Boulder, CO: Westview Press, 1989.

Jubair, Salah. *The Long Road to Peace: Inside the GRP-MILF Peace Process.* Cotabato City: Institute of Bangsamoro Studies, 2007.

Kahin, George McTurnan. *Nationalism and Revolution in Indonesia.* Ithaca, NY: Cornell University Press, 1955.

Kalyvas, Stathis N. *The Logic of Civil War.* Cambridge: Cambridge University Press, 2006.

Kalyvas, Stathis N. and Laia Balcells. "International System and Technologies of Rebellion: How the End of the Cold War Shaped Internal Conflict." *The American Political Science Review* 104, no. 3 (August 2010): 415–29.

Kammen, Douglas. "Notes on the Transformation of the East Timor Military Command and Its Implications for Indonesia." *Indonesia* 67 (1999): 61–76.

Keating, Michael. "Rival Nationalisms in a Plurinational State: Spain, Catalonia, and the Basque Country." In *Constitutional Design for Divided Societies: Integration or Accommodation?*, edited by Sujit Choudhry, 316–41. Oxford: Oxford University Press, 2008.

"Stateless Nation-Building: Quebec, Catalonia and Scotland in the Changing State System." *Nations and Nationalism* 3, no. 4 (1997): 689–717.

Keefer, Philip. "Insurgency and Credible Commitment in Autocracies and Democracies." *The World Bank Economic Review* 22, no. 1 (2008): 33–61.

Kell, Tim. *The Roots of Acehnese Rebellion, 1989–1992.* Ithaca, NY: Cornell Modern Indonesia Project, 1995.

King, Dwight Y. and M. Ryaas Rasjid. "The Golkar Landslide in the 1987 Indonesian Elections: The Case of Aceh." *Asian Survey* 9, no. 9 (September 1988): 916–25.

Kirby, James Marshall. "Satisfaction and Dissatisfaction with Political Leaders in Indonesia, Korea, the Philippines, and Thailand." In *Incomplete Democracies in the Asia-Pacific: Evidence from Indonesia, Korea, the Philippines, and Thailand*, edited by Giovanna Maria Dora Dore, Jae H Ku, and Karl D Jackson, 220–55. New York: Palgrave Macmillan, 2014.

Kivimäki, Timo. *Initiating a Peace Process in Papua: Actors, Issues, Process and the Role of the International Community.* Washington, DC: East-West Center, 2006.

Klein, James. *Democracy and Conflict in Southern Thailand: A Survey of the Thai Electorate in Yala, Narathiwas, and Pattani.* Washington, DC: The Asia Foundation, 2010.

Krasner, Stephen D. *Sovereignty: Organized Hypocrisy.* Princeton, NJ: Princeton University Press, 1999.

Kymlicka, Will. *Multicultural Citizenship: A Liberal Theory of Minority Rights.* Cotswold: Clarendon Press, 1995.

Multicultural Odysseys: Navigating the New International Politics of Diversity. Oxford: Oxford University Press, 2007.

Labrador, Mel C. "The Philippines in 2001: High Drama, a New President, and Setting the Stage for Recovery." *Asian Survey* 42, no. 1 (2002): 141–49.

Lacina, Bethany. "Explaining the Severity of Civil Wars." *Journal of Conflict Resolution* 50, no. 2 (2006): 276–89.

Lake, David A. and Donald Rothchild. "Containing Fear." *International Security* 21, no. 2 (1996): 41–75.

Lamcheck, Jayson S. *Human Rights-Compliant Counterterrorism: Myth-Making and Reality in the Philippines and Indonesia*. Cambridge: Cambridge University Press, 2019.

Lebovich, Andrew. "AQIM and Its Allies in Mali." The Washington Institute for Near East Policy, www.washingtoninstitute.org/policy-analysis/view/aqim-and-its-allies-in-mali.

Lecours, André. *Basque Nationalism and the Spanish State*. Basque Series. Reno: University of Nevada Press, 2007.

Levitsky, Steven and Lucan Way. *Competitive Authoritarianism: Hybrid Regimes after the Cold War*. Cambridge: Cambridge University Press, 2010.

Lichbach, Mark Irving. "Deterrence or Escalation?: The Puzzle of Aggregate Studies of Repression and Dissent." *Journal of Conflict Resolution* 31, no. 2 (1987): 266–97.

Liddle, R. William. "Indonesia in 1999: Democracy Restored." *Asian Survey* 40, no. 1 (January–February 2000): 32–42.

Lijphart, Arend. "Consociational Democracy." *World Politics* 21, no. 2 (1969): 207–25.
Democracies: Patterns of Majoritarian and Consensus Government in Twenty-One Countries. Yale University Press, 1984.

Lindemann, Stefan and Andreas Wimmer. "Repression and Refuge: Why Only Some Politically Excluded Ethnic Groups Rebel." *Journal of Peace Research* 55, no. 3 (2018): 305–19.

Linz, Juan J. and Alfred Stepan. "Toward Consolidated Democracies." *Journal of Democracy* 7, no. 2 (1996): 14–33.

Liow, Joseph Chinyong. *Muslim Resistance in Southern Thailand and Southern Philippines: Religion, Ideology, and Politics*. Washington, DC: East-West Center, 2006.
Religion and Nationalism in Southeast Asia. Cambridge: Cambridge University Press, 2016.
"The Security Situation in Southern Thailand: Toward an Understanding of Domestic and International Dimensions." *Studies in Conflict and Terrorism* 27, no. 6 (November 2004): 531–48.

Livermore, Douglas. "The Case for Azawad." *African Security Review* 22, no. 4 (2013): 282–93.

Lumley, Sarah. *Sustainability and Degradation in Less Developed Countries: Immolating the Future?* Farnham: Ashgate, 2002.

MacDonald, Charles. "Indigenous Peoples of the Philippines: Between Segregation and Integration." In *Indigenous Peoples of Asia*, edited by R. H. Barnes, Andrew Gray, and Benedict Kingsbury, 345–56. Ann Arbor, MI: Association for Asian Studies, 1995.

Magdalena, Federico V. "The Peace Process in Mindanao: Problems and Prospects." *Southeast Asian Affairs* (1997): 245–59.

Majul, Cesar A. *Muslims in the Philippines*. Quezon: Asia Center, 1973.

Mansfield, Edward D. and Jack Snyder. "Democratic Transitions, Institutional Strength, and War." *International Organization* 56, no. 2 (2002): 297–337.

Martinez-Herrera, Enric and Thomas Jeffrey Miley. "The Constitution and the Politics of National Identity in Spain." *Nations and Nationalism* 16, no. 1 (2010): 6–30.

May, R. J. "Muslim Mindanao: Four Years after the Peace Agreement." *Southeast Asian Affairs* (2001): 263–75.

"The Philippines under Aquino: A Perspective from Mindanao." *Journal Institute of Muslim Minority Affairs* 8, no. 2 (1987): 345–55.

McCargo, Duncan. "Democracy under Stress in Thaksin's Thailand." *Journal of Democracy* 13, no. 4 (2002): 112–26.

"Network Monarchy and Legitimacy Crises in Thailand." *The Pacific Review* 18, no. 4 (2005): 499–519.

Rethinking Thailand's Southern Violence. Singapore: NUS Press, 2006.

Tearing Apart the Land: Islam and Legitimacy in Southern Thailand. Ithaca, NY: Cornell University Press, 2008.

McCarthy, John and Mayer N. Zald. "Resource Mobilization and Social Movements: A Partial Theory." *American Journal of Sociology* 82, no. 6 (1977): 1212–41.

McGarry, John. "Asymmetry in Federations, Federacies and Unitary States." *Ethnopolitics* 6, no. 1 (2007): 105–16.

McGarry, John and Brendan O'Leary. *The Northern Ireland Conflict: Consociational Engagements*. Oxford; New York: Oxford University Press, 2004.

McGibbon, Rodd. *Secessionist Challenges in Aceh and Papua: Is Special Autonomy the Solution?* Washington, DC: East-West Center Washington, 2004.

McKenna, Thomas M. *Muslim Rulers and Rebels: Everyday Politics and Armed Separatism in the Southern Philippines*. Berkeley: University of California Press, 1998.

Mendelsohn, Matthew. "Measuring National Identity and Patterns of Attachment: Quebec and Nationalist Mobilization." *Nationalism and Ethnic Politics* 8, no. 3 (September 2002): 72–94.

Mendoza, Diana J. and Maria Elissa Jayme Lao. "Corazon Aquino: The Reluctant First Female President of the Philippines." In *Women Presidents and Prime Ministers in Post-Transition Democracies*, edited by Veronica Montecinos, 205–20. London: Palgrave Macmillan, 2017.

Mietzner, Marcus. "Local Elections and Autonomy in Papua and Aceh: Mitigating or Fueling Secessionism?" *Indonesia* 84, (2007): 1–39.

Military Politics, Islam, and the State in Indonesia: From Turbulent Transition to Democratic Consolidation. Singapore: Institute of Southeast Asian Studies, 2009.

Miller, Michelle Ann. "What's Special about Special Autonomy in Aceh?" In *Verandah of Violence: Background to the Aceh Problem*, edited by Anthony Reid, 292–314. Singapore: Singapore University Press, 2006.

Molintas, Rocky. "Advancing Cordillera Autonomy beyond the Local Government Code." In *Advancing Regional Autonomy in the Cordillera: A Source Book*, edited by Arturo C. Boquiren, 134–43. Baguio City; Pasig, Metro Manila: Cordillera Studies Center, University of the Philippines, Baguio; Friedrich Ebert Stiftung Manila Office, 1994.

"The Philippine Indigenous Peoples' Struggle for Land and Life: Challenging Legal Texts." *Arizona Journal of International and Comparative Law* 21, no. 1 (2004): 269–306.

Molloy, Ivan. "The Decline of the Moro National Liberation Front in the Southern Philippines." *Journal of Contemporary Asia* 18, no. 1 (1988): 59–76.

Montinola, Gabriella R. "Parties and Accountability in the Philippines." *Journal of Democracy* 10, no. 1 (1999): 126–40.

Moore, Will H. "Repression and Dissent: Substitution, Context, and Timing." *American Journal of Political Science* 42, no. 3 (1998): 851–73.

"The Repression of Dissent: A Substitution Model of Government Coercion." *Journal of Conflict Resolution* 44, no. 1 (2000): 107–27.

Moreno, Antonio F. "Engaged Citizenship: The Catholic Bishops' Conference of the Philippines (CBCP) in the Post-Authoritarian Philippines." In *Development, Civil Society and Faith-Based Organizations: Bridging the Sacred and the Secular*, edited by Gerard Clarke and Michael Jennings, 117–44. New York: Palgrave Macmillan, 2008.

Moreno, Luis. *The Federalization of Spain*. London: Frank Cass Publishers, 2001.

Morgan, Rhiannon. "Advancing Indigenous Rights at the United Nations: Strategic Framing and Its Impact on the Normative Development of International Law." *Social & Legal Studies* 13, no. 4 (2004): 481–500.

"On Political Institutions and Social Movement Dynamics: The Case of the United Nations and the Global Indigenous Movement." *International Political Science Review* 28, no. 3 (2007): 273–92.

Morris, Eric Eugene. "Islam and Politics in Aceh: A Study of Center-Periphery Relations in Indonesia." Thesis (Ph.D.) – Cornell University, 1983, University Microfilms International, 1984.

Mote, Octavianus. "West Papua's National Awakening." *Tok Blong Pasifik* 55, no. 3 (2001).

Mousseau, Demet Yalcin. "Democratizing with Ethnic Divisions: A Source of Conflict?" *Journal of Peace Research* 38, no. 5 (2001): 547–67.

Muller, Edward N. "Income Inequality, Regime Repressiveness, and Political Violence." *American Sociological Review* 50, no. 1 (1985): 47–61.

Muller, Edward N. and Erich Weede. "Cross-National Variation in Political Violence: A Rational Action Approach." *The Journal of Conflict Resolution* 34, no. 4 (December 1990): 624–51.

"Multi-Stakeholder Review of Post-Conflict Programming in Aceh: Identifying the Foundations for Sustainable Peace and Development in Aceh." Banda Aceh, Indonesia: Multi Stakeholder Review, 2009.

Munck, Gerardo L. "What Is Democracy? A Reconceptualization of the Quality of Democracy." *Democratization* 23, no. 1 (2016): 1–26.

Niezen, Ronald. *The Origins of Indigenism: Human Rights and the Politics of Identity*. Berkeley and Los Angeles: University of California Press, 2003.

NRC Thailand. *Overcoming Violence Through the Power of Reconciliation*. Bangkok: National Reconciliation Commission, 2006.

O'Donnell, Guillermo. "Illusions about Consolidation." *Journal of Democracy* 7, no. 2 (1996): 34–51.

O'Donnell, Guillermo and Philippe C. Schmitter. *Transitions from Authoritarian Rule: Tentative Conclusions about Uncertain Transitions*. Baltmore, MD: Johns Hopkins University Press, 1986.

O'Shaughnessy, Thomas. "How Many Muslims Has the Philippines?" *Philippine Studies* 23 (1975): 375–82.

Ockey, James. "Political Parties, Factions, and Corruption in Thailand." *Modern Asian Studies* 28, no. 2 (1994): 251–77.

Olzak, Susan. *The Dynamics of Ethnic Competition and Conflict*. Palo Alto, CA: Stanford University Press, 1992.

Osborne, Robin. *Indonesia's Secret War: The Guerilla Struggle in Irian Jaya*. Sydney: Allen and Unwin, 1985.

Oxfam America. *Free Prior and Informed Consent in the Philippines: Regulations and Realities*. Boston, MA: Oxfam America, 2013.

Panlipi. "Initial Assessment of the Extent and Impact of the Implementation of IPRA." Panlipi under the auspices of the International Labour Organization 2005.

Paris, Roland. *At War's End: Building Peace after Civil Conflict*. Cambridge; New York: Cambridge University Press, 2004.

Pemberton, John. *On the Subject of Java*. Ithaca: Cornell University Press, 1994.

Peou, Sorpong. "The Limits and Potential of Liberal Democratisation in Southeast Asia." *Journal of Current Southeast Asian Affairs* 33 (2014): 19–47.

Philippine Center for Investigative Journalism. "New Law on Indigenous Peoples Faces Legal Challenge." Manila 1998.

Philippines Indigenous Peoples ICERD Shadow Report. Committee on the Elimination of all forms of Racial Discrimination, 2009.

Philpott, Daniel. *Revolutions in Sovereignty: How Ideas Shaped Modern International Relations*. Princeton, NJ: Princeton University Press, 2001.

Phongpaichit, Pasuk and Christopher John Baker. "'Business Populism' in Thailand." *Journal of Democracy* 16, no. 2 (2005): 58–72.

Pierskalla, Jan Henryk. "Protest, Deterrence, and Escalation: The Strategic Calculus of Government Repression." *Journal of Conflict Resolution* 54, no. 1 (2010): 117–45.

Pitsuwan, Surin. *Islam and Malay Nationalism: A Case Study of the Malay-Muslims of Southern Thailand*. Bangkok: Thai Khadi Research Institute, Thammasat University, 1985.

Power, Timothy J. and Mark J. Gasiorowski. "Institutional Design and Democratic Consolidation in the Third World." *Comparative Political Studies* 30, no. 2 (1997): 123–55.

Prapertchob, Preeda. "Islam and Civil Society in Thailand: The Role of NGOs." In *Islam and Civil Society in Southeast Asia*, edited by Mitsuo Nakamura, Siddique Sharon, and Omar Farouk Bajunid, 104–16. Singapore: Institute of Southeast Asian Studies, 2001.

Prill-Brett, June. "Indigenous Land Rights and Legal Pluralism among Philippine Highlanders." *Law and Society Review* 28, no. 3 (1994): 687–97.

Putzel, James. *A Captive Land: The Politics of Agrarian Reform in the Philippines*. Philippines: Ateneo de Manila University Press, 1992.

"Survival of an Imperfect Democracy in the Philippines." *Democratization* 6, no. 1 (1999): 198–223.

Quimpo, Nathan Gilbert. "Mindanao, Southern Philippines: The Pitfalls of Working for Peace in a Time of Political Decay." In *Autonomy and Ethnic Conflict in South and South-East Asia*, edited by Rajat Ganguly, 114–37. New York: Routledge, 2012.

"Options in the Pursuit of a Just, Comprehensive, and Stable Peace in the Southern Philippines." *Asian Survey* 41, no. 2 (2001): 271–89.

Rasul, Amina. *Broken Peace? Assessing the 1996 GRP-MNLF Final Peace Agreement.* Manila: Philippines Council for Islam and Democracy, in collaboration with the Konrad Adenauer Stiftung, 2007.

Regan, Patrick M. "Substituting Policies during U.S. Interventions in Internal Conflicts: A Little of This, a Little of That." *Journal of Conflict Resolution* 44, no. 1 (2000): 90–106.

Regan, Patrick. M., and David Norton. "Greed, Grievance, and Mobilization in Civil Wars." *Journal of Conflict Resolution* 49, no. 3 (2005): 319–36.

Regan, Patrick M. and Errol A. Henderson. "Democracy, Threats and Political Repression in Developing Countries: Are Democracies Internally Less Violent?" *Third World Quarterly* 23, no. 1 (2002): 119–36.

Reid, Anthony. *The Blood of the People: Revolution and the End of Traditional Rule in Northern Sumatra.* Kuala Lumpur, New York: Oxford University Press, 1979.

Reilly, Benjamin. "Democracy, Ethnic Fragmentation, and Internal Conflict: Confused Theories, Faulty Data, and the 'Crucial Case' of Papua New Guinea." *International Security* 25, no. 3 (2000): 162–85.

"Review of Recent Developments in the Cordillera Provinces: Northern Luzon; Statement to the UN Working Group on Indigenous Populations." Center for World Indigenous Studies, www.hartford-hwp.com/archives/54a/224.html.

Reynal-Querol, Marta. "Ethnicity, Political Systems, and Civil Wars." *Journal of Conflict Resolution* 46, no. 1 (2002): 29–54.

Reynolds, Andrew. *The Architecture of Democracy: Constitutional Design, Conflict Management, and Democracy.* Oxford: Oxford University Press, 2002.

Rico, Ruth Lusterio. "The Dynamics of Policy-Making: The Enactment of the Indigenous Peoples' Rights Act (IPRA)." PhD diss., University of the Philippines, 2006.

Roberts, Sean R. "The Biopolitics of China's 'War on Terror' and the Exclusion of the Uyghurs." *Critical Asian Studies* 50, no. 2 (2018): 232–58.

Robinson, Geoffrey. "'Rawan' Is as 'Rawan' Does: The Origins of Disorder in New Order Aceh." *Indonesia* 66 (1998): 127–56.

Roeder, Philip G. "Ethnofederalism and the Mismanagement of Conflicting Nationalisms." *Regional & Federal Studies* 19, no. 2 (2009): 203–19.

"Soviet Federalism and Ethnic Mobilization." *World Politics* 43, no. 2 (1991): 196–232.

Where Nation-States Come From: Institutional Change in the Age of Nationalism. Princeton, NJ: Princeton University Press, 2007.

Romano, David. "The Long Road toward Kurdish Accommodation in Turkey: The Role of Elections and International Pressures." In *Democratization and Ethnic Minorities: Conflict or Compromise?*, edited by Jacques Bertrand and Oded Haklai, 164–80. New York: Routledge, 2013.

Rood, Steven. "Issues Surrounding Autonomy: Insights from the Work of the University of the Philippines Cordillera Studies Center on Cordillera Autonomy, 1986–1994." In *Advancing Regional Autonomy in the Cordillera: A Source Book*, edited by Arturo C. Boquiren, 6–18. Baguio City; Pasig, Metro Manila: Cordillera Studies Center, University of the Philippines, Baguio; Friedrich Ebert Stiftung Manila Office, 1994.

    Protecting Ancestral Land Rights in the Cordillera. Diliman, Quezon City: University of the Philippines Press, 1994.

Roosa, John. "Finalising the Nation: The Indonesian Military as the Guarantor of National Unity." *Asia Pacific Viewpoint* 48, no. 1 (2007): 99–111.

Ross, Michael L. "How Do Natural Resources Influence Civil War? Evidence from Thirteen Cases." *International Organization* 58, no. 1 (2004): 35–67.

Rothchild, Donald. "Liberalism, Democracy, and Conflict Management: The African Experience." In *Facing Ethnic Conflicts: Toward a New Realism*, edited by Andreas Wimmer, Richard J. Goldstone, Donald L. Horowitz, Ulrike Joras, and Conrad Schetter, 226–44. Lanham, MD: Rowman & Littlefield Publishers, Inc, 2004.

Rothchild, Donald and Caroline A. Hartzell. "Security in Deeply Divided Societies: The Role of Territorial Autonomy." *Nationalism and Ethnic Politics* 5, no. 3–4 (1999): 254–71.

Rustow, Dankwart A. "Transitions to Democracy: Toward a Dynamic Model." *Comparative Politics* 2, no. 3 (1970): 337–83.

Saideman, Stephen M., David J. Lanoue, Michael Campenni, and Samuel Stanton. "Democratization, Political Institutions, and Ethnic Conflict: A Pooled Time-Series Analysis, 1985–1998." *Comparative Political Studies* 35, no. 1 (2002): 103–29.

Saideman, Stephen M. and R. William Ayres. "Determining the Causes of Irredentism: Logit Analyses of Minorities at Risk Data from the 1980s and 1990s." *The Journal of Politics* 62, no. 4 (2000): 1126–44.

Salehyan, Idean. "Transnational Rebels: Neighboring States as Sanctuary for Rebel Groups." *World Politics* 59, no. 2 (January 2007): 217–42.

Salehyan, Idean, Kristian Skrede Gleditsch and David E. Cunningham. "Explaining External Support for Insurgent Groups." *International Organization* 65, no. 4 (2011): 709–44.

Sambanis, Nicholas. "A Review of Recent Advances and Future Directions in the Quantitative Literature on Civil War." *Defence & Peace Economics* 13, no. 3 (2002): 215–43.

    "Do Ethnic and Nonethnic Civil Wars Have the Same Causes?: A Theoretical and Empirical Inquiry (Part 1)." *Journal of Conflict Resolution* 45, no. 3 (2001): 259–82.

    "What Is Civil War? Conceptual and Empirical Complexities of an Operational Definition." *Journal of Conflict Resolution* 48, no. 6 (2004): 814–58.

Samudavanija, Chai-Anan and Parichart Chotiya. "Beyond Transition in Thailand." In *Democracy in East Asia*, edited by Larry Diamond and Marc F. Plattner, 147–67. Baltimore and London: Johns Hopkins University Press, 1998.

Satha-Anand, Chaiwat. "Hijab and Moments of Legitimation: Islamic Resurgence in Thai Society." In *Asian Visions of Authority: Religion and the Modern States of*

East and Southeast Asia, edited by Charles F. Keyes, Laurel Kendall, and Helen Hardacre, 279–300. Honolulu: University of Hawaii Press, 1994.

Schedler, Andreas. "Taking Uncertainty Seriously: The Blurred Boundaries of Democratic Transition and Consolidation." *Democratization* 8, no. 4 (2001): 1–22.

Schiller, A. Arthur. *The Formation of Federal Indonesia, 1945–1949*. The Hague: W. van Hoeve, 1955.

Schmitter, Philippe C. and Terry Lynn Karl. "What Democracy Is . . . And Is Not." *Journal of Democracy* 2, no. 3 (1991): 75–88.

Schneider, Gerald and Nina Wiesehomeier. "Rules That Matter: Political Institutions and the Diversity—Conflict Nexus." *Journal of Peace Research* 45, no. 2 (2008): 183–203.

Scott, William Henry. *The Discovery of the Igorots: Spanish Contacts with the Pagans of Northern Luzon*. Quezon City, Republic of the Philippines: New Day Publishers, 1974.

Sekretariat Kabinet Republic Indonesia. "Transfer Anggaran Ke Daerah Rp 518,9 Triliun, Pemerintah Percepat Pembangunan Di Papua Dan Papua Barat [518.9 Trillion Rupiah Budget Transfer to Regions, Government Speeds up Development in Papua and West Papua]." setkab.go.id/berita-5416-transfer-anggaran-ke-daerah-rp-5189-triliun-pemerintah-percepat-pembangunan-di-papua-dan-papua-barat.html

Sheehan, Deidre. "Erap's Rebound." *Far Eastern Economic Review* 163, no. 31 (August 3, 2000): 22–23.

"Estrada's Mindanao: Troubles Grow Worse." *Far Eastern Economic Review* 163, no. 19 (May 11, 2000): 52.

Sheehan, Deidre and David Plott. "A War Grows." *Far Eastern Economic Review* 164, no. 40 (October 11, 2001): 24.

Singh, Bilveer. *Papua: Geopolitics and the Quest for Nationhood*. New Brunswick: Transaction Publishers, 2008.

Siroky, David. "The Sources of Secessionist War: The Interaction of Local Control and Foreign Forces in Post-Soviet Georgia." *Caucasus Survey* 4, no. 1 (2016): 63–91.

Siroky, David S. and John Cuffe. "Lost Autonomy, Nationalism and Separatism." *Comparative Political Studies* 48, no. 1 (2015): 3–34.

Sjamsuddin, Nazaruddin. *The Republican Revolt: A Study of the Acehnese Rebellion*. Singapore: Institute of Southeast Asian Studies, 1985.

Smith, Anthony. *The Ethnic Origins of Nations*. Oxford: Blackwell, 1986.

Snitwongse, Kusuma. "Thailand in 1994: The Trails of Transition." *Asian Survey* 35, no. 2 (1995): 194–200.

Snyder, Jack. *From Voting to Violence*. New York: W. W. Norton and Company, 2000.

Spruyt, Hendrik. *The Sovereign State and Its Competitors: An Analysis of Systems Change*. Princeton Studies in International History and Politics. Princeton, NJ: Princeton University Press, 1994.

Staniland, Paul. *Networks of Rebellion: Explaining Insurgent Cohesion and Collapse*. Ithaca, NY: Cornell University Press, 2014.

Stedman, Stephen John. "Spoiler Problems in Peace Processes." *International Security* 22, no. 2 (1997): 5–53.

Stein, Eric. *Czecho/Slovakia: Ethnic Conflict, Constitutional Fissure, Negotiated Breakup*. Ann Arbor, MI: University of Michigan Press, 1997.

Suberu, Rotimi T. *Federalism and Ethnic Conflict in Nigeria.* Washington, DC: United States Institute of Peace Press, 2001.

Suhrke, Astri. "Irredentism Contained: The Thai-Muslim Case." *Comparative Politics* 7, no. 2 (1975): 187–203.

Summers, James J. "The Right of Self-Determination and Nationalism in International Law." *International Journal on Minority and Group Rights* 12, no. 4 (2005): 325–54.

Surin, Maisrikrod. *Thailand's Two General Elections in 1992: Democracy Sustained.* Singapore: Institute of Southeast Asian Studies, 1992.

Tambiah, Stanley Jeyaraja. *Leveling Crowds: Ethnonationalist Conflicts and Collective Violence in South Asia.* Berkeley: University of California Press, 1996.

Tan, Andrew. "Armed Muslim Separatist Rebellion in Southeast Asia: Persistence, Prospects, and Implications." *Studies in Conflict and Terrorism* 23, no. 4 (October2000): 267.

Tarrow, Sidney. *Power in Movement: Social Movements and Contentious Politics.* Cambridge: Cambridge University Press, 1998.

Tasker, Rodney. "A More Peaceful South." *Far Eastern Economic Review* 126 (October 11, 1984): 28–30.

Taylor, Brian D. "Force and Federalism: Controlling Coercion in Federal Hybrid Regimes." *Comparative Politics* 39, no. 4 (2007): 421–40.

Thompson, Mark R. "Off the Endangered List: Philippine Democratization in Comparative Perspective." *Comparative Politics* 28, no. 2 (1996): 179–205.

"The Limits of Democratisation in ASEAN." *Third World Quarterly* 14, no. 3 (1993): 469–84.

Timberman, David G. *A Changeless Land: Continuity and Change in Philippine Politics.* New York: M. E. Sharpe, 1991.

Toft, Monica Duffy. "Ending Civil Wars: A Case for Rebel Victory?" *International Security* 34, no. 4 (2010): 7–36.

Securing the Peace: The Durable Settlement of Civil Wars. Princeton, NJ: Princeton University Press, 2010.

The Geography of Ethnic Violence: Identity, Interests, and the Indivisibility of Territory. Princeton, NJ: Princeton University Press, 2003.

Toft, Monica Duffy and Yuri M. Zhukov. "Islamists and Nationalists: Rebel Motivation and Counterinsurgency in Russia's North Caucasus." *American Political Science Review* 109, no. 2 (2015): 222–38.

Tuyor, Josefo B. et al. "Indigenous Peoples Rights Act: Legal and Institutional Frameworks, Implementation and Challenges in the Philippines." *Discussion Papers, East Asia and Pacific Region. Social Development, and Rural Development, Natural Resources and Environment Sectors.* Washington, DC: World Bank, 2007.

Van den Broek, Theo and Alexandra Szalay. "Raising the Morning Star: Six Months in the Developing Independence Movement in West Papua." *The Journal of Pacific History* 36, no. 1 (2001): 77–92.

Varshney, Ashutosh. *Ethnic Conflict and Civic Life: Hindus and Muslims in India.* New Haven, CT: Yale University Press, 2002.

Villegas, Bernardo M. "The Philippines in 1986: Democratic Reconstruction in the Post-Marcos Era." *Asian Survey* 27, no. 2 (1987): 194–205.

Vreeland, J. R. "The Effect of Political Regime on Civil War – Unpacking Anocracy." *Journal of Conflict Resolution* 52, no. 3 (2008): 401–25.

Walter, Barbara F. "Building Reputation: Why Governments Fight Some Separatists but Not Others." *American Journal of Political Science* 50, no. 2 (2006): 313–30.

Weingast, Barry R. "Political Stability and Civil War: Institutions, Commitment, and American Democracy." In *Analytic Narratives*, edited by Robert H. Bates, Avner Greif, Margaret Levi, Jean-Laurent Rosenthal, and Barry R. Weingast, 148–93. Princeton, NJ: Princeton University Press, 1998.

  "The Political Foundations of Democracy and the Rule of Law." *American Political Science Review* 91, no. 2 (1997): 245–63.

Weinstein, Jeremy. "Resources and the Information Problem in Rebel Recruitment." *Journal of Conflict Resolution* 49, no. 4 (2005): 598–624.

White, Lynn T. *Philippine Politics: Possibilities and Problems in a Localist Democracy.* London: Routledge, 2015.

Widjojo, Muridan S. and Sherry Kasman Entus. *Papua Road Map: Negotiating the Past, Improving the Present, and Securing the Future.* Jakarta and Singapore: LIPI, ISEAS, 2009.

Williams, Robin M., Jr. "The Sociology of Ethnic Conflicts: Comparative International Perspectives." *Annual Review of Sociology* 20 (1994): 49–79.

Wimmer, Andreas. *Nationalist Exclusion and Ethnic Conflict: Shadows of Modernity.* Cambridge: Cambridge University Press, 2002.

Winichakul, Thongchai. *Siam Remapped: A History of the Geo-Body of a Nation.* Honolulu: University of Hawaii Press, 1994.

Wurfel, David. *Filipino Politics: Development and Decay.* Ithaca, NY: Cornell University Press, 1988.

Young, Crawford. "The Heart of the African Conflict Zone: Democratization, Ethnicity, Civil Conflict, and the Great Lakes Crisis." *Annual Review of Political Science* 9, no. 1 (2006): 301–28.

Young, Joseph K. "Repression, Dissent, and the Onset of Civil War." *Political Research Quarterly* 66, no. 3 (2013): 516–32.

Yu, Samuel CK. "Political Reforms in the Philippines: Challenges Ahead." *Contemporary Southeast Asia* 27, no. 2 (2005): 217–35.

Index

CPSIA information can be obtained
at www.ICGtesting.com
Printed in the USA
LVHW082023190921
698206LV00003B/272